MARX WITHOUT MYTH

Marx Without Myth

A CHRONOLOGICAL
STUDY OF HIS LIFE AND WORK

Maximilien Rubel
and Margaret Manale

BASIL BLACKWELL·OXFORD·1975

ISBN 0 631 15780 8

Set in Linotype Juliana (text) and Perpetua (display)
Printed in Great Britain by
Northumberland Press Ltd., Gateshead
and bound by Richard Clay
(The Chaucer Press) Ltd., Bungay

Contents

vi *Contents*

INTRODUCTION

Destroyed by silence during his lifetime, Karl Marx has been posthumously victimised by an heroic myth which has harmed his work more than did the conspiracy of silence imposed by his contemporaries. The man who could have boasted of having discovered the law of ideological mystification himself became the target of new efforts at mystification by his own school. While his personality is caricatured in extremes—from lifeless travesty to the awesome image of an intellectual monster—his words are taken to be the sibylline proclamations of an omniscient oracle and used to mask the deeds and misdeeds of modern social leaders seeking to evade personal responsibility. The doctrines Marx intended as intellectual tools for the working class in its struggle for emancipation have been transformed into political ideology to justify material exploitation and moral slavery. His postulate of the dictatorship of the proletariat, in particular, conceived of as the democratic rule of the overwhelming majority in the interests of the overwhelming majority, has been distorted into ideological legitimation for the exploitation and oppression of one social group (or class) by another and invoked as justification for the abolition of basic human rights. Under the label of 'Marxist socialism' the inhuman social relations of feudal and pre-capitalist society have been legitimised for today's world. To cap this process of mystifying Marx while stunting the mental and moral development of the masses he tried to reach with his works and his political activity, the supreme ethical principle of proletarian self-emancipation through class struggle has been resolved into the moral code of a new élite—'Marxist' politicians and 'Marxist' statesmen. With the most modern techniques of human self-destruction at its disposal, this new élite is both partner and rival of the ruling élites in 'imperialist countries', their common goal the maintenance or extention of their supremacy. Modern history is no longer the history of class struggles, as was stated in *The Communist Manifesto*, but of global wars planned and executed in defence of what are proclaimed as 'moral', 'human' or 'religious' values.

In the face of such distortion of his spiritual and theoretical legacy, the present chronology has been conceived to defend the non-legendary Marx. Its principal concern is to counter the universal myth and misunderstandings with a portrait of the man, the revolutionary thinker, the militant. We have been guided by the desire to highlight those steps and events in his career which most clearly bear witness to a life dedicated to one single goal—the emancipation of mankind through the conscious activity of its poorest but, in mind and spirit, potentially richest members. To do justice to Marx's central motivation a certain selectiveness in the choice of material presented was thought appropriate and we were naturally compelled to neglect or condense radically many aspects which are not without significance in other contexts.

Marx sacrificed not only personal success and wealth but also his health, family and friends to the self-appointed life-task of contributing intellectual support to the labouring class for its long and arduous fight against enslaving capital. First and foremost he wanted to participate in the struggle for emancipation, whose outcome would decide the fate of mankind, and did not consider himself called upon to create a new system of thought or a universal social science. But not theory alone characterises Marx's contribution to the working class movement; at every promising occasion he actively associated with proletarian organisations: the international correspondence committees (1846-47); the Communist League (1847-52); the workers' educational societies; and the International Working Men's Association (1864-73) together with the Reform League. He did so because of a compelling belief that the truth of any theory can be affirmed only in human practice, understood here not as party politics but as the socio-political movement of the entire working class. The dialectic relationship between scientific cognition and the practical fulfilment of the proletarian mission did not in his opinion demand a special, highly centralised workers' party but rather a well-developed capitalist system of economy with its ruling bourgeoisie and its antithesis, the disinherited, impoverished, but conscious working class. He saw a correlation between the action of the latter and the inner decay of capitalism and therefore considered his role to be that of a social theorist adding scientific insights to the actual proletarian movement.

Marx often spoke of his 'bourgeois misery' and he had every reason for doing so. His income as a writer was never sufficient to support himself and his family adequately, hence they depended on the financial generosity of his life-long friend Friedrich Engels. He spent most of his adult years in exile, a pariah from the age of 26, experiencing the tragedy of an outsider who threatens society's tenuous equilibrium. Only a small part of his many writing projects were ever brought to fruition; penury, illness, family difficulties, journalistic hackwork made his life a long chain of disappointments and insoluble problems. Yet he turned a deaf ear to generous offers tendered by government agents to collaborate on official publications which would have brought him to the attention of a much wider public and secured his reputation in the scholarly world. He felt nothing but disdain for the prejudices of 'so-called public opinion' and never cared for popularity. His attitude is typified by a quotation from Dante's *Divine Comedy* which closes the Preface to *Capital*, Book I: 'Segui il tuo corso, e lascia dir le genti.'

Long before he had published even the first part of his 'Economics', many of his friends expected him soon to head a new school of thought. His charismatic personality and quick mind fascinated and impressed them profoundly, although few of his contemporaries recognised his genius and obstinately supported him in face of uninterested public opinion and the slanders or polemical attacks of men such as Karl Vogt and Brentano or of the Prussian state police. In a well-meaning effort to compensate for these slanders his loyal friend Engels tried to popularise Marx's writings by reinterpreting them, yet he succeeded only in initiating the transformation of Marx's social theory into a proletarian *Weltanschauung*. Engels's identification of Marx with 'scientific socialism' in *Anti-Dühring*, his graveside eulogy of his friend as the source of proletarian consciousness were unfortunate statements that unwittingly fathered the self-contained ideological system of Marxism. He failed to respect the dialectic unity of revolutionary action by the conscious proletariat, the ethical imperative of Marxian thought, and scientific insight into the socio-economic mechanism of the historic process, replacing this subtle dualism with revolutionary phraseology. Every interpretation of Marx's intellectual achievements which lays claim to the discovery of a new system of thought or philosophy necessarily amounts to a fundamental perversion of his actual intentions.

An impartial examination of Marx's political career shows, however, that he was not always able to reconcile his conduct with his theoretical views, thereby furnishing his political opponents with fuel for their polemical fire. He was accused of vanity, of desiring personal power and despotic control over the working class movement; and whereas it is certain that he did possess traits which sometimes exasperated his friends and made their relations problematic, to expect a 'full-blooded' man like Marx to be free of human weaknesses is unreasonable and dangerous. His favourite maxim, 'Nihil humani a me alienum puto', is conveniently overlooked by those who wish to make him a cult figure, while his detractors too, although assiduous in their criticism, have so radically distorted the dimensions of the man that he is no longer compatible with any reality, past or present.

Marx's own fate reflects in part the disheartening drama of the world's deprived and injured working population. Living under the most uninspiring auspices and with a minimum of recognition for years of solitary study and reflection, he never imagined himself the founder of any system of thought or political movement whatsoever, nor did he presume to have discovered a universally valid or revolutionary theory of social development. Discerning enough not to place himself above those who formed him, he never forgot his debts to his predecessors and teachers. Indeed, any profound appreciation of Marx's achievements is impossible without an awareness of the 19th-century intellectual panorama which produced such thinkers as Saint-Simon, Charles Fourier, Robert Owen, Proudhon, Lorenz von Stein, Alexis de Tocqueville and, of course, Hegel and Feuerbach. The first three in particular saw, before Marx, the actual as well as the impending dangers of technologically advanced society, and they proposed remedies to solve the crisis of modern civilisation. Marx's study of philosophy and history, not of economics, engendered his protest against the prevailing social system and his determination to serve the cause of what Saint-Simon called 'la classe la plus nombreuse et la plus misérable'. He concluded that society's ills could be overcome only through the political and social maturation of this class and then turned to concentrate on political economics in order to support his views with scientific argument. During the course of his extensive studies he absorbed impulses from many different intellectual currents, using them to create an inspiring, albeit somewhat ambiguous, vision of future society. At the centre of his writing was an ethical force: the postulate that human society or social humanity should ultimately result from technological progress, that man's barbaric prehistory would be superseded by an era of human self-realisation. It was not because he fortuitously reread Hegel's *Logic* that Marx predicted the inevitable fall of an economic system based on profit and the simultaneous construction of a classless, stateless and moneyless society, but because he was filled with the hopes and dreams of a Saint-Simon, a Robert Owen, a Fourier. Lenin once stated that *Capital* is incomprehensible for the reader who is ignorant of Hegel's *Logic*; yet there is even more reason to maintain that those who are unacquainted with Shakespeare's humanity or the world of Charles Dickens cannot understand Marx, for the tenor of his real achievements lies far beyond the range of those schools which claim him as their intellectual father.

This chronology is not intended to replace the definitive biography of Marx which has yet to be written but to lay its foundation and at the same time to destroy the legendary image of the author of *Capital*. If in these pages the reader misses the wealth of anecdotal detail normally included in a biography, he should bear in mind that the omission is deliberate and has enabled us to treat more intensively the material selected, especially the works themselves and the correspondence. Marx's life is divided here into six main periods, each introduced with a brief historical resumé of significant world events. His essential contributions to economic theory and social analysis have been outlined by using writings from before 1867 as well as his often very explicit letters to Engels and others, a procedure which allowed us to abstain from quoting passages out of *Capital* itself. Principally, this volume is a forum for Marx's own statements

concerning his troubled and turbulent life, his goals and intentions, his motivation, and should, despite its brevity, com-
municate an understanding of the fundamental human and
scientific premises behind Marx's social theory. Accent has been
placed on the dual character of this theory: theoretical-critical
comprehension of economic relations and, integrally linked to it,
the ethical-practical solution to problems arising from the
incessant, revolutionary social developments in the modern
world.

Even though the revolutionary maturation of the working
class has not kept pace with the continued expansion of the
capitalist system, as Marx had hoped and postulated, the alter-
natives inherent in the decline of this system are becoming
increasingly significant: man must either embrace a rational
social order on a world-wide scale or through gradual self-
destruction sink into a state of barbaric chaos. The responsibility
for this fatal dilemma lies with each of us; only the personal
decision of the majority of individuals can realise the rational
utopia that will end the indignities of man's inhuman past, secure
the survival of all humanity and usher in an era of universal
self-determination.

AUTHORS' NOTE

I. CHRONOLOGICAL SUMMARIES

The present work has been confined in part to an account of general historic and cultural events during the years 1818-1883, the span of Marx's lifetime. Each of the six summaries which introduce distinct periods in his life and writing covers those world happenings which are echoed in some way either in his journalism or in other, more theoretical, texts. The historical summaries are followed by chronological lists of important works published and scientific advances with emphasis on the fields in which Marx was most interested.

These world events did more than simply aid Marx in illustrating his theoretical concepts—an important part of his research actually consisted in historical analysis and he carefully studied the current events which marked the destiny of post-Napoleonic Europe. For those who understand the evolutionary essence of Marx's theoretical views and who acknowledge the presence of a rationally intelligible process recorded in the course of history, the details in our summaries will not seem superfluous.

The most obvious reason for Marx's preoccupation with current events was of course his journalism, pursued out of financial necessity. Yet would it be unjustified to assert that this preoccupation also corresponded with his intellectual needs? His unfulfilled desire for discussion with his contemporaries gave rise to a permanent interest in the daily realities of 19th-century society. His readings for the 'Economics' corroborate the fact that he had no constitution for a steady diet of theory alone but sought concrete evidence of capital's advances in the factory, in parliament, on the battlefields. Marx was no stranger to *belles-lettres* either. In addition to his passion for certain classic authors—Shakespeare and Molière at their head—his favourite contemporary author was undoubtedly Charles Dickens, as may be seen from the chronologies of books which follow. A number of works have been deliberately included which escaped Marx's attention or interest. Certain of these may perhaps account for particular limits or insufficiencies in his general theoretical knowledge. Since he was also profoundly interested in signs of cultural progress and his letters abound in comments on inventions and scientific experiments, we illustrate this progress with a selection of the key discoveries leading to the development of modern industries and with well-known milestones in technological achievement.

Should our readers find the Chronology at times too succinct or too abrupt, we refer them to the glossary of *dramatis personae* and to the list of secondary sources in the bibliography, many of which may be effectively used to supplement the present representation of Marx's era, his life and his thought.

II. ABBREVIATIONS

References to original sources are made only for the literary works; letters and for the most part articles as well have been designated with the date of their composition (for letters) or publication (articles). Volume and pagination are given thus: MEW 2 : 217 = *Marx, Engels Werke*, volume 2, page 217.

IISH   refers to the source of as yet unpublished letters in the Marx-Engels *Nachlaß* at the International Institute of Social History, Amsterdam.

IRSH   *International Review of Social History*, published by the IISH, Assen, The Netherlands.

MEW   *Marx, Engels Werke*. Berlin, Dietz, 1957-72. 39 vols.

MEGA   *Marx, Engels Gesamtausgabe*. Berlin and Moscow, 1927-35. 11 vols.

EB   *Marx, Engels Werke. Ergänzungsband*. 2 vols.

SW   *Marx, Engels Selected Works*. Moscow, 1950. 2 vols.

Documents 1   *The General Council of the First International, 1864-1866. The London Conference, 1865. Minutes.* Moscow, no date (also abbrev.: *Minutes*).

Documents 2-5   *Documents of the First International 1866-1872*. Moscow, no date (also abbrev.: Minutes).

Freymond   *La Première Internationale. Recueil de documents publié sous la direction de Jacques Freymond*. Geneva, 1962. 2 vols.

Oeuvres   Karl Marx Oeuvres. Economie t. 1 & t. 2. Paris, 1965, 1968. Edition établie par M. Rubel. 2 vols.

The names of newspapers and reviews to which Marx frequently contributed have been abbreviated as follows:

RhZ=*Rheinische Zeitung für Politik, Handel und Gewerbe*. Cologne, 1842-43.

NRhZ=*Neue Rheinische Zeitung*. Cologne, 1848-49.

NRhZ-*Revue*=*Neue Rheinische Zeitung. Politische-ökonomische Revue*. Hamburg, 1850.

DBrZ=*Deutsch-Brüsseler Zeitung*. Brussels, 1847-48.

NOZ=*Neue Oder-Zeitung*. Breslau, 1852-53.

NYDT=*New-York Daily Tribune*. New York, 1851-62.

DP=*Die Presse*. Vienna, 1861-62.

I
1818-1843

1818   At the Congress of Aix-la-Chapelle the four powers of the Holy Alliance (Russia, Britain, Prussia and Austria) sign a convention committing themselves to joint action to prevent a revival of Jacobinism in France. During the Congress the British socialist Robert Owen petitions the assembled heads of state to adopt his plan of agricultural-industrial co-operative communities, arguing that growing industrial production is bound to lead to social and economic disaster.

—   The German *Länder* of Baden and Bavaria grant constitutional forms of representation to their populations.

1819   At the Conference of Karlsbad (Austria) the delegates of the German Confederation (*Bund*) ratify a series of measures the purpose of which is to suppress revolutionary turmoil, especially that generated by the patriotic student societies, and to enforce rigid censorship of the press.

—   A peaceable demonstration is held at St Peter's Fields, Manchester, England, in protest against the insufferable conditions of the industrial working class. The unarmed demonstrators are brutally attacked by yeomanry and reserve cavalry. Later in the year the policy thus initiated by these police measures is reconfirmed in the passage of the *Six Acts*, directed against sedition and radicalism.

1820   A military insurgency in Southern Italy, supported by the secret society of revolutionary conspirators known as the *Carbonari*, achieves its goal in forcing the king, Ferdinand I, to promulgate a national constitution. This provokes the powers of the Holy Alliance to call

1821   the Congress of Leibach, where it is agreed that Austria should invade Italy in order to provide a pretext for restoring the earlier absolutist government. Austria occupies Naples for three years, while the king takes vengeance by imprisoning or sentencing to death hundreds of liberals and *Carbonari*.

1822   At the Congress of Verona another scheme is produced by the Russian Czar, Austria's Prince Metternich and the French diplomat Chateaubriand, whereby France is charged with waging war against Spain should there be no retraction of Spain's liberal constitution of 1812. This congress marks the separation of Britain from the

1823   other partners in the Alliance. France then invades Spain, abolishes the constitution and restores the absolutist king Ferdinand VII to the throne. The king revives the Inquisition and orders the prosecution of all connected with the liberal constitution.

1824   Trade unions are legalised in Great Britain and laws are passed permitting both coalitions and strikes.

1828   Protestant dissenters in England are granted civil liberties.

1829   The Catholic Emancipation Act is passed, permitting Catholics to hold a seat in the British Parliament.

1830   Catholic Belgium is declared independent of Protestant Holland.

—   The July Revolution in France results from a collision between the monarch and the ever growing number of liberal elements. In a show of power to quieten the opposition King Charles X conducts a victorious war of conquest against Algeria. Then, counting on his military success to produce the necessary support, he dissolves the Chamber of Deputies and issues 'Five Ordinances', which would make the electoral law a privilege of the richest landowners and abolish the freedom of the press. Republican Paris revolts, declares the king deposed and proclaims the Republic. Parliament offers the crown of constitutional monarch to the Duke of Orléans, who becomes the 'citizen king' Louis-Philippe I.

1831　　Joseph Mazzini, a participant in the Carbonarist uprisings, founds the 'Young Italy' movement in order to arouse popular support for national unity in the struggle against the Papacy and Austria. He advocates the expulsion of Austria through a mass insurgency, the abolition of Papal influence in temporal affairs and the establishment of a democratic Italian republic.

1832　　The British Parliament approves the Reform Bill, which makes representation more 'democratic' and extends the franchise in the boroughs to households with a minimum income of ten pounds.

—　　In Germany a revolutionary appeal to arms is made by students and intellectuals gathered at the Castle of Hambach for a festival. The Prussian government answers this provocation with renewed political reprisals.

1832-33　A cholera epidemic, brought in from Asia, breaks out and causes many thousands of deaths in England, France and Germany. In 1833 all of Bohemia is touched by the ravages of this disease.

1833　　A tariff union (*Zollverein*) is established among the German *Länder*.

—　　The government of Louis-Philippe in France passes an Education Act which is intended to establish state-aided primary schools in every community.

—　　Civil war erupts in Spain and Portugal over the question of a liberal constitution. Unrest lasts until 1840 and causes Spain to lose her colonies and all overseas resources except Cuba and the Philippines.

—　　The British Parliament passes a Factory Act regulating conditions for the employment of young people in textile factories and instituting inspectors to enforce the law.

—　　Robert Owen launches in England a plan for communist production to be realised through the Grand National Consolidated Trade Union. About a half a million working men and women join this organisation which, however, soon dies away for lack of a clear programme and financial means.

1833   Britain sets an example to the Western world by passing a law prohibiting slave trade and slavery in its territories.

1834   Mazzini founds the 'Young Europe' movement in Germany, Poland and Switzerland.

—   The Whig Poor Law in England reforms the system of relief aid and reorganises the work houses.

—   After the French government passes a law restricting the rights of association, Mazzini succeeds in inciting the working men of Lyon to revolt and the uprising spreads throughout the country. The Massacre of the rue Transnonain illustrates the brutality of the government troops who suppress these outbreaks. In protest against such reprisals new secret societies are organised. Auguste Blanqui founds the *Société des familles*, whose immediate purpose is military action, later reconstituting it as the *Société des saisons* (1847). German refugees in Paris found the League of the Banished, which is renamed League of the Just in 1836 and is a forerunner of the Communist League.

1838   General discontent with the 1832 Reform Bill and with the present system of trade-unionism in England manifests itself in the Chartist movement. William Lovett and Francis Place draw up a six-point 'People's Charter' which serves as the movement's political platform. The Chartists demand (1) adult male suffrage; (2) secret balloting; (3) abolition of property qualifications for members of parliament and (4) payment for their terms in office; (5) annual general elections and (6) equal electoral districts.

1839   Agitation also begins in England for the repeal of the restrictive corn laws. Richard Cobden establishes the Anti-Corn Law League and there are popular demonstrations in support of its free trade policy.

1840   After expulsion from France for participation in a Blanquist conspiracy German emigrants in London found a Workers' Educational Society.

1842   The British Parliament passes a bill limiting the labour of women and children in the mines, but rejects the

Chartist petition. Between 1842-45 Prime Minister Sir Robert Peel passes a series of liberal budgets which reintroduce income tax and establish a sliding scale of duties on corn.

1843   The Irish demonstrate for the repeal of the Act of Union. Home rule becomes the cry of Catholic Ireland, and of her representative in Parliament—Daniel O'Connor.

—   In Spain a military junta assumes power in Barcelona, proclaiming Isabella queen and ending the military regency of General Espartero.

EASTERN EUROPE AND THE MIDDLE EAST

1821-29 The Greek War of Independence develops out of popular resistance to Turkish hegemony and to the repressive

1822   treatment of Christians by the Moslems. The Turks massacre over 20,000 Greeks on the Island of Chios. However, the Holy Alliance denies any official international aid to the threatened people, who are considered to be insurgents.

1825   Russia's childless Czar Alexander I dies and his succession becomes a matter of prolonged dispute. With the support of the secret societies, the Russian army stages a revolt, hoping to call a national assembly and establish a constitution. This mutiny—the Decembrist Uprising—is rapidly quelled and the throne assumed by Nicolaus I. The new Czar now

1827   sends aid to the Greek Christians; eventually France and England follow suit. The London Treaty guaranteeing protection for the Greeks is signed jointly by all three countries, who subsequently send military and naval forces to Turkey. At Navarino Bay the

1829   Turkish fleet is destroyed by allied sea powers. Hostilities end with the conclusion of the Treaty of Adrianople which recognises the independence of Greece. Russia receives the territory south of the Caucasus in Asia and the islands of the Danube delta and is proclaimed protector of the Sultan's Christian subjects. The Straits of Constantinople and the Dardanelles are opened to free merchant shipping.

1830   Republican sentiment begins to threaten the hegemony
        of the Russian Czar in Poland, where an uprising leads
1831   to his dethronement by proclamation of the Polish
        parliament. Russian troops invade the country and
        force the patriotic troops to retreat. Government and
        parliament flee, while the Czar revokes the constitution
        of 1815 and proceeds to govern Poland henceforth as
        a Russian province.

1833   With the secret Treaty of Unkiar-Skelessi between
        Russia and Turkey the latter agrees to close the
        Dardanelles to all ships except the Russian in case of
        war, thus rendering the Straits a Russian stronghold.
        Russia in turn promises to support the Porte in case of
        a conflict with Egypt.

1839   Hostilities break out between the Turkish sultan and
        his Egyptian vassal. Anglo-French intervention pre-
        vents Russia from exploiting the dispute.

1840   A quadripartite alliance of England, Russia, Austria
        and Prussia, excluding France who supported the
        Egyptian cause, negotiates a settlement which repre-
        sents a diplomatic defeat for the French. To offset
        this France demands the return of the Western Rhine
        provinces from Germany. The matter is ultimately
1841   settled by a five-nation conference held in London,
        where the Dardanelles Treaty is concluded. Henceforth
        the slave trade is prohibited and the Borporus and
        Dardanelles are closed to all ships of war.

THE FAR EAST

1839   The First Opium War begins after the Chinese
        authorities vainly protest against the British opium
        trade by destroying the stocks of opium in Canton.
1841   A British naval victory permits the colonialists to
        declare Hong Kong a British possession. Hostilities
        continue until the superior forces of the British compell
1842   the Chinese to agree to the terms of peace stipulated
        in the Treaty of Nanking. Britain is accorded the right
        to trade in opium at four ports in addition to Canton
        and paid an indemnity of 21 million dollars.

1841-42   The first Anglo-Afghan War begins when the British attempt to take possession of Afghanistan, buffer territory between India and Russia. The British resident is slain and thousands on both sides lose their lives
1843   before the colonial power emerges victorious. At the same time British troops subdue the rulers of Sinde and annex this strategic passage-way to India.

SCIENTIFIC AND TECHNOLOGICAL PROGRESS

1820   André Ampère presents a new theory of magnetism as electricity in motion, thus founding the science of electrodynamics.

1826   Nicéphore Niepce produces the first true photograph, a heliogravure.

1830   The first railway line is opened between Manchester and Liverpool.

—   Barthélemy Thimonnier takes out a patent in France for the invention of the sewing machine.

1831   Michael Faraday discovers the generation of electric currents by means of magnets. This phenomenon comes to be called electromagnetic induction.

1832   The American Joseph Henry, working independently on electromagnetic phenomena, discovers self-induction.

1833   Carl Friedrich Gauss and Wilhelm Weber in Germany use electromagnetism to effect the first long-distance telegraphic communication.

1834   Cyrus McCormick patents the first horse-drawn mechanical reaping machine in the USA.

1838   Faraday formulates a coherent précis of his theory of electricity.

1839   Louis Daguerre, an associate of Niepce, carries on and perfects the latter's work with the construction of the first photographic apparatus known as the 'daguerreotype'.

—   The German baron Justus von Liebig marks the founding of the science of agro-chemistry with the publication of his book on chemistry applied to agriculture.

IMPORTANT WORKS PUBLISHED

* read by Marx
† presumably read

1819   David Ricardo: *Principles of Political Economy.**
—   L. S. de Sismondi: *Principes d'économie politique.**
—   Arthur Schopenhauer: *Die Welt als Wille und Vorstellung.*
1821   G. F. W. Hegel: *Grundlinien der Philosophie des Rechts.**
—   Claude Henri de Saint-Simon: *Du Système industriel.**
1825   Claude Henri de Saint-Simon: *Le Nouveau Christianisme.**
1828   Ludwig Gall: *Philanthropische Blätter.*
—   Philippe Buonarotti: *La Conspiration pour l'égalité, dite de Babeuf.**
1829   François Guizot: *Histoire générale de la civilisation en Europe.**
—   Charles Fourier: *Le Nouveau Monde industriel et sociétaire.**
1830-45 Georg von Gülich: *Geschichtliche Darstellung des Handels, des Gewerbes und des Ackerbaus.**
1830-42 Auguste Comte: *Cours de philosophie positive.*
1831   L. J. A. de Potter: *De la Révolution à faire.**
1833   Heinrich Heine: *Französische Zustände.**
—   Thomas Hamilton: *Men and Manners in America.**
1834   Georg Büchner: *Der hessische Bote.*
—   Félicité de Lamennais: *Paroles d'un croyant.*†
1835   D. F. Strauss: *Das Leben Jesu.*†
1835-40 Alexis de Tocqueville: *De la Démocratie en Amérique.**
1836   Charles Fourier: *La Fausse Industrie morcelée.**
—   Malthus, Thomas Robert: *An Inquiry into the Nature and Progress of Rent* (2nd ed.).
1836-38 Victor Considerant: *Destinée sociale.*
1836-44 Robert Owen: *The Book of the New Moral World.**
1837   H. C. Carey: *Principes d'économie politique.**
—   L. S. de Sismondi: *Etudes sur l'économie politique.**
—   G. F. W. Hegel: *Vorlesungen über die Geschichte der Philosophie.**
1837-39 Charles Dickens: *Oliver Twist.**

1838	Wilhelm Weitling: *Die Menschheit wie sie ist und wie sie sein sollte.**
—	Louis Blanc: *Organisation du travail.**
—	J. F. Bray: *Labours Wrongs and Labours Remedies.**
—·	August Cieszkowski: *Prolegomena zur Historiosophie.*†
1840	Pierre Leroux: *De l'Humanité, de son principe et de son avenir.**
—	Etienne Cabet: *Voyage en Icarie.*†
—	Eugène Buret: *De la Misère des classes laborieuses en Angleterre et en France.**
—	P.-J. Proudhon: *Qu'est-ce que la propriété?**
1841	Friedrich List: *Das nationale System der politischen Ökonomie.**
—	Moses Hess: *Die europäische Triarchie.**
—	Ludwig Feuerbach: *Das Wesen des Christentums.**
—	Théodore Dezamy: *M. Lamennais réfuté par lui-même.**
1841-44	Louis Blanc: *Révolution française. Histoire de dix ans.**
1842	W. Weitling: *Garantien der Harmonie und der Freiheit.**
—	Lorenz Stein: *Sozialismus und Communismus des heutigen Frankreichs.**
—	Théodore Dezamy: *Code de la communauté.*†
—	Constantin Pecqueur: *Théorie nouvelle d'économie sociale et politique.**
1843	Flora Tristan: *L'Union ouvrière.**
—	Wilhelm Schulz: *Die Bewegung der Produktion.**
—	Bruno Bauer: *Das entdeckte Christentum.**
—	B. Bauer: *Die Judenfrage.**
—	Marquis de Custine: *La Russie en 1839.**
—	Søren Kierkegaard: *Enter-Eller* (Either/Or).
—	George Sand: *Jean Ziska. Episode de la guerra des Hussites.**
—	George Sand: *Jean Ziska. Episode de la guerre des*
—	Victor Considerant: *Principes du socialisme. Manifeste de la démocratie au XIXe siècle.* (2nd ed. 1847) †

KARL MARX
1818-1843

1818-1834 Born in Trier in the Prussian Rhineland on May 5, 1818, Karl Marx was the third of nine children. Two of his brothers and three sisters died at early ages of tuberculosis. Their parents were the lawyer Heinrich Marx (1782-1838) and his wife Henriette, née Pressburg (1787-1863), both descended from long lines of rabbinical families. Heinrich Marx, a patriotic Prussian citizen, moderate liberal and deist in the tradition of Voltaire, Newton and Locke, converted to the Protestant faith in 1816-17, thus sparing himself and his family the disadvantages to which Jews were exposed in the Rhineland after Napoleon's fall and the annexation of this region to Prussia. The Marx children were baptised in 1824, the mother in 1825. In 1830 Karl entered the Trier secondary school, the Friedrich-Wilhelm Gymnasium, and he was confirmed in the Evangelical Church of his town four years later. It evidently left a certain impression on Karl that his father had broken with the faith of their ancestors and converted the whole family to Protestantism, religion of a minority in the Catholic Rhineland. The day was to come when the young man would turn his attention to religious matters as well—and pronounce against all forms of religious alienation.

1835-1804 In August and September of 1835 Marx passed his school leaving examinations, for which he wrote a series of seven compositions. His German essay, 'Reflections of a Young Man on the Choice of a Profession', reflects the influence of the moral training he had enjoyed and to which he was perhaps particularly inclined:

... dignity can be gained only in a profession which does not reduce us to servile tools, one which permits us to create independently within our own realm ... it is not always possible for us to assume the station in life for which we believe we have the calling; our social relations have, to a certain extent, already begun forming before we are able to determine them ... However, the decisive motive guiding us in our choice of profession must be the welfare of mankind, our own perfection ... man's nature is such that he can only attain his own perfection when working towards the perfection, for the general welfare of his world (MEGA 1,2: 166f.).

In his composition on religion he remarked that:

The striving for knowledge supplants an inferior striving for earthly goods ... when we reflect upon human nature, we always see indeed a Divine spark in man's breast, an enthusiasm for the Good, a striving for knowledge, a longing for truth ... (MEGA 1,2: 171f.).

Marx matriculated in the autumn at the University of Bonn as a student of law. The first year he attended lectures on classical mythology and poetry, art history and the courses in the history of Greek and Roman law and legal institutions as required of law students. Apart from his studies, Marx was active in student affairs and joined a circle of youths interested in poetry.

An intimate correspondence sprung up between Marx and his father; all but one of the younger man's letters have been lost. From an early letter written by Heinrich Marx we glean a notion of the father-son relationship and especially of the father's respect for Karl's intellectual talents:

I wish to see in you what I might have become, had I first seen the light of day under more favourable auspices ... it may be unjust and ill-advised as well to put one's greatest hopes in a single person and thus perhaps undermine one's own equanimity (Nov. 18-29, 1835).

In Bonn Marx rapidly accumulated a number of large debts which his father was forced to liquidate for him. The expenses of student life, books and amusements as well, kept the young man continually writing for money. Finally, in June, his excesses led to arrest on charges of drunken rowdiness. He served a one-night sentence for this on June 16, 1836.

During the summer of 1836 he withdrew from Bonn with the intention of changing universities and became secretly engaged to his childhood sweetheart Jenny von Westphalen

(1814-1881). Daughter of Prussian privy councillor Johann Ludwig von Westphalen (1770-1842) and his (second) wife Caroline, née Heubel (1779-1856), Jenny was descended on her father's side from the highest ranks of Scottish nobility, the Argyle and Campbel families. Her half-brother Ferdinand von Westphalen (1799-1876), of conservative Christian-monarchical leanings, was the well-known Prussian minister of internal affairs during the period 1850-58. Jenny's brother Edgar was a Trier classmate of Marx's and entertained a close friendship with the young couple during their stay in Brussels in 1846.

In October Marx enrolled at the University of Berlin to continue his law studies. He attended lectures on Pandecta held by F. K. Savigny, penal law by Eduard Gans (a converted Jew who later became a Hegelian) and anthropology. He began writing verse and made other poetic efforts, filling with lyrics three notebooks which he presented to his fiancée. Although these romantic essays have been lost, a number of poems and ballads remain from the year 1837 along with a comic novel *Scorpion and Felix* and a dramatic fantasy *Oulanem*, both in fragmentary form. Marx himself characterised his poetic writings as pure idealism, as:

onslaughts on the present, broad and shapeless expressions of feeling, unnatural, constructed out of the blue, the perfect opposite of what is actually there and what ought to be, rhetorical reflection instead of poetic thoughts, yet perhaps a certain warmth of sentiment and a struggle for dynamism as well ... (to his father, Nov. 10, 1837).

Among the extant poems are four short and critical epigrams on Hegel. In Marx's poetic interpretation the great philosopher speaks as follows:

> Words I teach, confused in demonic chaos
> So that each may thus think what pleases him
> And in any case none is ever constrained by bridling limits.
> For, just as the poet conceives the words and thoughts of
>   his beloved
> Out of a roaring torrent, tumbling from a lofty cliff,
> And what senses, acknowledges, conceiving in thought
>   what he feels,
> So may each man sip the delightsome nectar of wisdom,
> Indeed, I am telling you everything, having told you a
>   Nothing (MEGA 1,2: 42).

Marx *père's* reaction to his offspring's poetic inclinations and to his varied university activities was rather less than enthusiastic:

It is now high time that you cure yourself of this restlessness which destroys mind and body ... You have assumed serious responsibilities ... You cannot imagine—with all the exaggerations and exaltations of love in a poetic spirit—that it is possible to establish the equanimity of that person to whom you have given yourself with body and soul ... I have spoken with Jenny ... she is making a priceless sacrifice for you. Only sober reason can appreciate the self-denial which she shows.

May God protect you, should you ever in your life be able to forget this! (Dec. 28, 1836)

It is not surprising that Heinrich Marx was reluctant to sanction his son's early engagement, fearing his 'demonic and Faust-like nature' might put Karl in an unseemly position in face of his fiancée's family and damage her reputation:

I am not pretending to be an angel and I know that man does not live by bread alone, but any secondary intentions must be quelled when it is a question of fulfilling a sacred duty. And I repeat: a man has no more sacred duty than that which he assumes in the interest of the weaker sex. Thus I am asking you to be as open to me in this respect as in all others, as you would be towards a friend (Nov. 9, 1836).

In the summer semester of 1837 Marx attended lectures in philosophy and history along with jurisprudence. He became involved in a group known as the *Doktorklub*, students, recent graduates and aspiring writers distinguished by their pronounced Hegelian leanings. Here Marx made friends with Bruno and Edgar Bauer, Carl Friedrich Köppen, Adolf Rutenberg and others.

Marx presented to his father a hand-written volume with a selection of his literary efforts for his birthday in March 1837. Heinrich Marx came to acknowledge this aspect of his son's talents and frequently referred to his desire for a literary career, suggesting how he might realise it without abandoning his plans for law. He felt, however, that this gifted young man was best suited for another career:

I applauded your decision to make the teaching profession your goal, whether this be in jurisprudence or philosophy, and in the final analysis I thought the latter would be the most fitting for you (Sept. 16, 1837).

Overshadowing these varied plans and aspirations, however, is a premonition of the difficult course which Marx's life was to take; Heinrich Marx wrote:

I cannot and will not hide my weakness for you. From time to time my heart swells up with thoughts of you and your future. And then sometimes I cannot rid myself of sad, portentous and frightening feelings at moments when the thought strikes me like a bolt of lightening: is your heart equal to your head and your talents? ... What brings me on to this train of thought? ... Something strange occurs to me when I regard Jenny. She, entirely devoted to you with her pure, childlike heart, at times shows involuntarily against her own will, a sort of fear, fear pregnant with premonitions, a fear that does not escape me but which I know not how to explain. What can this mean? I cannot explain it, yet unfortunately my experience keeps me from being easily led astray (March 2, 1837).

Despite—or perhaps because of—his affection for his son, Heinrich Marx did not let himself be blinded to Karl's weaknesses: the father's letters always remained candid, straightforward and strict in their criticism. Marx could not well ignore his father's questions and reproaches and from his only extant letter we have a detailed account of his studies in Berlin, his extra-curricular activities, his personal aspirations. Here he first mentions his life-long habit of 'scribbling down reflections' while making resumés or excerpts of books he read. He also recounted having composed a 'new basic system of metaphysics':

A curtain had fallen, my most holy of holies was torn asunder and new gods had to be installed. Turning from the idealism which I had, incidentally, nourished and compared with that of Kant and Fichte, I came to seek the idea in reality itself ... I had read fragments of Hegel's philosophy, but its grotesque and rocky melody I found displeasing (Nov. 10, 1837).

He began writing a philosophical-dialectical analysis of the concept of the *Gottheit* [divinity] manifested as religion, nature and history. His ambition was to construct a new system of logic uniting art and knowledge, which Marx considered were set at variance in contemporary speculation But when he completed his system, 'this my most cherished offspring, nurtured by moon-light, delivers me into the arms of the enemy like a treacherous siren'. This enemy was Hegel, whom Marx studied 'from begin-ning to end together with most of his disciples' during a period of prolonged illness earlier that year.

On May 10, 1838, Marx's father died in Trier. His last letters reflect the concern and discontentment which preoccupied the ailing man as he learned of his son's intellectual crisis and irresponsible behaviour:

Scarcely had the wild abandon in Bonn come to an end, your debts but recently paid—and these existed in numerous connections—when to further disconcertus the love sorrows began … we have never had the consolation of a reasonable correspondence … we have never received an answer to our writings; your letters never continued on from the previous ones nor from our answers … The last letter contained only a few badly written lines and an excerpt from your diary entitled 'A Visitor', whom I would much prefer to turn out of the house than to receive as company, a mad hack-job, which simply announces how you are wasting your talents and staying up for nights on end in order to bring such monsters into the world … (Dec. 9, 1837).

Henriette Marx, also concerned about her son's physical and mental well-being, procured him a medical certificate which she sent with the remark:

Enclosed you will find your certificate. Use every means possible to avoid your year of military service. You have every right to do so. Don't ignore your eye trouble, you will save yourself much annoy-ance and much money … (Feb. 15-16, 1838).

His mother's thoughtfulness and devotion to her family were traits which Marx appreciated highly at the time, as is indicated in the following letter from Heinrich Marx to his son:

You yourself have described in such beautiful terms the life of your fine mother, you felt so deeply how it has been a continual sacrifice of love and devotion and in fact your words were not exaggerated (Aug. 12-14, 1837).

In any event, Marx was exempted from his military service by the Trier Commission for the Recruitment of Military Personnel because of his health. The certificate read:

> 1838, (Karl Marx) is admitted to voluntary military service in Berlin for one year, but at the present time is declared unfit for duty by the departmental physician in Berlin due to thoractic weakness and periodic coughing up of blood. The same for 1839 (Schiel, *Die Umwelt des jungen Karl Marx,* ..., p. 23).

1839-1841 Marx began research in the philosophy of Epicurus in 1839 in preparation for a doctrinal thesis. During the summer semester in Berlin he attended only one lecture course, 'Jesaias' given by Bruno Bauer. Marx frequently visited the Bauer home in Charlottenburg and his friend encouraged him to write his thesis quickly and finish with the 'farce' of an examination. Both young men felt that there was much to be done in Prussia, where the general problems were more diverse than elsewhere and complicated by political apathy. Bauer insisted that Marx prepare himself for the tasks ahead with the least possible delay.

From the outset Marx's work on the dissertation took a most un-Hegelian turn through the simple choice of Epicurus, a moral philosopher whose practical wisdom aimed at achieving peace of mind as the highest good. The preliminary notes and remarks for this paper are contained in seven notebooks, all entitled 'Epicurean philosophy'. Included are excerpts from Epicurus, comments from Diogenes Laertius, Sextus Empiricus, Plutarch, Gassendi and Lucretius, as well as commentaries on Plato, Aristotle and Hegel and a schema of the Hegelian philosophy of nature. The themes thus touched upon—deformation of Hegelian philosophy by his followers, relation between Platonism and Christianity, the tasks of the philosophical historian, the Stoic ideal of the wise man—far surpass the central orientation of the thesis itself. These notes reveal how Marx gained distance from Hegelian thinking. The state, for Hegel, was the incorporation of universal reason at its highest level; thanks to the state as the realisation of liberty in concrete form, human freedom becomes possible. Marx began his notes on Epicurus with passages on the Epicurean notion of the state, based in sharp contrast to that of Hegel, on contract and serving the principle of utility for its members. Neither deification of civil institutions nor attachment to any sort of alien god is to be found in Epicurus, who holds that 'the sole good which man has in relation to the world is the negative moment of being free from it'. To use the words of Epicurus's celebrated disciple Lucretius, 'For my song is first concerned with higher things. I seek to liberate the spirit further from the bonds of religion.' From these extracts it seems that Marx's attention is drawn to Epicurus by his naturalness, his manifestation of intellectual and sensual freedom, a freedom from gods and from doctrines which concedes to chance an equally great, if not greater, role in human life as to necessity. Individual will is asserted; an understanding of contingency becomes central to the wisdom of life. Man free himself here from superstition and fear and becomes capable of forging his own happiness:

Further, Epicurus speaks out against simply staring at the heavenly bodies in rigid stupefaction as something limiting, generating fear: he asserts the value of absolute freedom of the mind (MEW, EB 1 : 49).

Man, conscious of his own self and accepting the world as he finds it, gains control over his relations to this world and is able to attain the highest good to which human life may aspire: tranquillity of mind. Science is clearly inessential for such a life, since natural phenomena only affect us as regards their subjective perception. Take the meteor, for example:

It is all the same to [the consciousness] how the meteor is explained and it maintains that not one explanation, but that several, i.e. that any explanation suffices; thus it confesses its own action as active fiction ... for in matters of specialised natural research one must not hold to empty generalities and rules, but should accommodate himself to the demands of the appearances themselves ... so that we may live in peace and security (EB 1 : 53).

Marx underlines Epicurus's naturalness in contrast with the Philistinism of Plutarch, his hero-worship and traditional moralism. Plutarch 'babbles trivialities, he reasons like a craftsman's apprentice', while Epicurus constructs a logical system of values and carries it to necessary, practical conclusions. 'Plutarch's syncretic, mindless treatment cannot hold a candle to this', Marx commented and extended his criticism to all of philosophy:

Ordinary thought always has abstract predicates at hand which it separates from the subject. All philosophers have made the predicates themselves into subjects (EB 1 : 127).

This Feuerbach-inspired remark is evidently meant for Hegel as well, but Marx nevertheless tried to save the Hegelian system by seeing in it his own ideal of a critical orientation towards the existing world order:

... but just as Prometheus, having stolen fire from heaven, began to build houses and to settle on the earth, so philosophy, having expanded to a world, turns against the visible world it finds. Thus Hegelian philosophy today (EB : 215).

Marx's constant admiration for the early philosophers, which is linked with implied criticism of contemporary speculation, is frankly acknowledged at the close of the sixth excerpt notebook:

The Greeks will always remain our teachers because of the grandiose objective naivity which permits each object, though its rays be dim, to shine forth without drapings in the pure light of its own nature. Our time particularly has brought forth sinful phenomena even in philosophy, phenomena tainted with the greatest sin, that against the mind and against truth, whereby a concealed intention is lodged behind the perception and a concealed perception behind the thing itself (EB 1 : 235).

When working on his thesis, Marx conceived of a plan to write against certain academic authors who envisaged a recon-ciliation between philosophy and religion. He wanted to elaborate some of his thoughts in a farce to be entitled 'Fischer Vapulans', but the project never reached fruition. Having read and excerpted from Aristotle in an edition by Adolf Trendelenburg, Marx also planned to write a critique of Trendelenburg's *Logische Untersuchungen*, but again nothing came of this.

In the autumn of 1839 Bruno Bauer departed from Berlin to take up a teaching post at Bonn University. Marx then became close friends with C. F. Köppen, who was ten years his senior. Through the force of his unusual personality Marx seems to have made such a striking impression on his friends that Köppen, for example, a man who was already established in the teaching profession, dedicated his pamphlet 'Friedrich the Great and His Antagonists' to the 22-year-old student. Köppen's writing was an apology for the royal philosopher and a passionate assertion of faith in reason and progress. Köppen claimed that Friedrich II's greatness as a thinker lay in his successful reconciliation of Epicureanism, Stoicism and scepticism.

Marx succeeded in publishing for the first time in 1841. Two of his highly romantic poems, entitled *Wilde Lieder* (Wild Songs), appeared in the magazine *Athenäum* which had been founded by members of the former *Doktorklub*. In March Marx withdrew from Berlin and received the following academic report:

Regarding his behaviour at the University there is nothing particularly unfavourable to be noted from the disciplinary point of view, and as for his financial affairs, we have only to report that he was brought to court several times for non-payment of debts. The aforementioned student has not been charged with participation in any illegal student society at this university up to the present date (MEGA 1,2: 248).

Marx still had to submit his dissertation to a competent faculty in order to get his degree. Bauer encouraged him to do so, for:

It would be nonsense for you to devote yourself to a practical career. At present theory is the most effective practice and we cannot yet predict in how wide a sense it will become practical (MEGA 1,2: 250).

So in April Marx sent his finished thesis to the philosophical faculty of the University of Jena. His reasons for choosing Jena were the ease and lower financial outlay involved in procuring a doctoral degree from a smaller, little known German university. Without a public examination, as was required in both Bonn and Berlin, Marx was granted his diploma a week after submitting the thesis (April 15, 1841), which he had dedicated to Jenny's father, Ludwig von Westphalen.

'Not ideology nor vain hypotheses do we need for our life, but to live without confusion.' Marx might well have made this quotation from Epicurus the motto of his dissertation, so accurately does it reflect the substance of the paper. Although the breadth of the material treated in the actual thesis is much more restricted than in the preliminary writings, it nevertheless does justice to the intentions stated in the Preface:

Hegel had, to be sure, correctly determined the general characteristics of the systems mentioned ... yet, for one, it was still impossible to delve into details; for another, this grandiose thinker was hindered by his view of what he termed 'speculative' *par excellence* from recognising the deep purpose of these systems in the history of Greek philosophy and for the Greek mind in general ... I hope to have solved one problem in the history of Greek philosophy which has been left unexplained up till now (MEW, EB 1 : 261f.).

In this paper a clear contrast is made between two conceptions of philosophy—what it is and the ends it serves—as expressed in the writings of Epicurus and Democritus. The dissertation was formally entitled 'The Difference between the Philosophies of Nature in Democritus and Epicurus'. Democritus conceived of philosophy as empirical knowledge : 'Unsatisfied in philosophy, he throws himself into the arms of positive knowledge', Marx wrote. Although there is evidently a difference between philosophy as wisdom of life and science as empirical life experience, Democritus attempted to fuse the two : philosophy becomes science. The result is that 'The knowledge he holds to be true is meaningless for his own life, while the knowledge which gives him substance is without truth and so he rejects it' (MEW, EB 1 : 273). Epicurus, by contrast, rejects the positive sciences as worthless for the attainment of true human perfection. For Marx the efficacity of each thinker's philosophy is evidenced in his satisfaction with the life he has led :

While Democritus, finally despairing of knowledge, puts out his eyes at last, Epicurus, as he feels the hour of death approaching, climbs into a warm bath, desires pure wine and recommends to his friends that they be faithful to philosophy (EB 1 : 273f.).

The subjectivity of each thinker's concept of philosophy is evident. In the general relationship which he established between the world and abstract thought, the philosopher is simply objectifying the way in which his particular consciousness relates to the real world. Necessity is in Democritus the principle of his rigid determinism. However, for Epicurus, who does not hold science to be the goal of human effort but rather man's own perfection,

Necessity is an evil, but there is no necessity to live under the control of necessity. Everywhere the paths to freedom are open, are many, short and simple (EB 1 : 275).

Epicurus derives his knowledge *ex principio interno*; he is there-
for the sovereign of his life, complete within himself, an entire
being and not one who leans upon something outside himself,
as Democritus leans upon his teachers. In short, Marx brought
out the distinctions between philosophy as wisdom of life and
philosophy as the totality of the empirical sciences according
to Democritus, whereby Marx's own bias for the former thinker
is not difficult to discern.

In one of the notes appended to the dissertation Marx briefly
considered the question of the relationship between philosophy
and *praxis*, presenting the two as inseparable:

Philosophical *praxis* is itself theoretical. It is the criticism which
measures the individual existence against the essence and particular
reality against the idea. Yet this *immediate* realisation of philosophy
is burdened with contradictions in its innermost essence, while this
essence manifests itself in appearance, leaving its mark thereupon
(EB 1 : 327f.).

Marx, now a fresh university graduate, was full of plans and
inspiration, but as yet had no actual professional occupation. In
a letter to the novelist Berthold Auerbach, Moses Hess characterised his 23-year-old friend Marx as:

... the greatest, perhaps the only real philosopher living today ...
Dr Marx ... is still a very young man and is going to give the death
blow to medieval religion and politics. He combines the sharpest wit
with the most profound philosophic gravity; imagine Rousseau,
Voltaire, Holbach, Lessing, Heine and Hegel united in one person—
and I mean united, not thrown together—there you have Dr Marx
(Sept. 2, 1841).

At the beginning of July 1841 Marx moved to Bonn from
Trier, where he had spent the intervening months since receiving
his degree in April. In Bonn he continued to see much of Bruno
Bauer and planned with Bauer and Ludwig Feuerbach to bring
out a periodical entitled *Archiv des Atheismus*, which they were
determined to make even more radically left-wing than Arnold
Ruge's *Deutsche Jahrbücher*. Georg Jung, at the time involved
in preparations for founding a newspaper to be called the
Rheinische Zeitung, reported in a letter to Ruge that:

Dr Marx, Dr Bauer and L. Feuerbach are getting together to make up a theological-philosophical journal and when so, may all the angels gather around old God the Father and may he have mercy on himself, for these three are certain to throw him out of his heaven and chase him with a legal suit to boot. Marx, for one, calls the Christian religion one of the most immoral, and he is, by the way, albeit a most despairing revolutionary, one of the cleverest heads I know (Oct. 18, 1841).

Bauer was suspended from his lecturing post in Bonn for the winter semester 1841-42 and in May 1842 his dismissal was made permanent. This was a punishment for proposing a toast in the spirit of the left-Hegelians. Marx too saw his hopes for a university career sink radically. In November 1841 Bauer published an anonymous pamphlet on which Marx was assumed to have collaborated. Entitled *The Trumpet of the Last Judgment on Hegel the Atheist and Antichrist. An Utimatum*, this tract presented, under the pretext of attacking Hegel's atheism, a philosophy of universal consciousness which had little in common with Hegel's *Weltgeist*.

1842-1843 In January 1842 Marx again returned to Trier, to the bedside of the ailing Ludwig von Westphalen. He remained at the Westphalen home until the older man's death on March 3, helping the family and devoting but little time to his own affairs. He wrote, nevertheless, one article which he intended to publish in Ruge's *Deutsche Jahrbücher* entitled 'Remarks on the Latest Prussian Censorship Instruction'. Appropriately enough, the Saxonian censor prohibited its appearance in Ruge's Dresden journal and thus it was not published until the following year in a volume called *Anekdota*. Also edited by Ruge, the latter journal was used to bring out those articles and other writings rejected by the Prussian censors. Marx's contribution, signed simply 'by a Rhenish citizen', closed with the following quotation from Tacitus:

Rare is the good fortune of those times in which one may think what one wishes and say what one thinks (MEW 1 : 25).

It is interesting to note that the last chapter of Spinoza's *Tractatus* has a title derived from the above quotation. Marx's excerpt notebooks show that he had actually been reading Spinoza during the earlier part of 1841. His knowledge of

Judaism, later criticised in his essay on 'The Jewish Question', probably stemmed from Spinoza's *Tractatus*, apart from which Marx made two notebooks of extracts from Spinoza's correspondence. Spinoza states in his *Tractatus* that democracy is 'of all forms of government the most natural and the most consonant with individual liberty'. Marx's article on Prussian censorship presents the democratic state as the ethical state, which '... presupposes a "sense of state" [*Staatsgesinnung*] in its members, even when they should oppose an organ of the state' (MEW 1:15). But a government which presumed alone to incorporate reason and morality,

such a government invents tendentious laws, laws of revenge ... based on the lack of character and on an unethical and materialist view of the state (MEW 1:15).

Following his stay in Trier, Marx announced to Ruge his newest writing projects and promised to send as soon as possible two articles, one on Christian art, the second a critique of Hegel's *Philosophy of Right*, the core of which

is the struggle against the constitutional monarchy as a hybrid thing, which is thoroughly self-contradictory and occasions its own dissolution. There is no German translation for *res publica* (March 5, 1842).

In a subsequent letter Marx reported that he had expanded the article on Christian art to a study entitled 'Religion and Art with Special Emphasis on Christian Art' and was thus delayed in delivering it. A few days later he wrote that he was nearly finished and promised Ruge four articles: 1. on religious art, 2. on the romantics, 3. a critique of the historical school of law and 4. on the 'positive' philosophers. Of these only the third essay ever appeared in published form. In preparing his articles Marx read and excerpted numerous passages from Christoph Meiner's *Allgemeine kritische Geschichte der Religionen* (1806), Jean Barbeyrac's *Traité de la morale des Pères de l'Eglise* (1728), Charles Debrosses's *Über den Dienst der Fetischgötter* (1785), Karl August Böttinger's *Ideen zur Kunst-Mythologie* (1826-36), Johann Jakob Grund's *Die Malerei der Griechen* (1810), Karl Friedrich von Rumohr's *Italienische Forschungen* (1827) and Lorenz Stein's book *Der Sozialismus und*

Communismus des heutigen Frankreichs (1842).

In April 1842 Marx moved to Bonn where he began writing for the *Rheinische Zeitung*. His first contributions were a series of essays on the proceedings of the 6th Rhenish Parliament, which had met in Düsseldorf from May to June of the preceding year. The first essay, 'Debates on the Freedom of the Press and the Publication of the Parliamentary Proceedings', appeared in six instalments in May; the second, concerning the religious dispute in Cologne, was struck out by the censor; the third, 'Debates on the Law Punishing Wood-Theft', appeared in five issues of the paper during October and November. Later, in 1859, Marx remarked that these articles, together with a series on the misery of the wine-growers in the Moselle valley, first gave him an opportunity to delve into economic questions. In this connection, Marx's first direct confrontation with the ideas of Saint-Simon and other French socialists seems to have come from the *RhZ* articles published by Moses Hess and Gustav Mevissen and probably as well from Lorenz Stein's book *Socialism and Communism in Contemporary France*, which appeared this same year and was reviewed in the columns of the *RhZ*. However, it was unlikely that Marx read Stein before leaving Germany in October 1843. At the outset he was distrustful of this 'faint philosophic echo' of French socialism echoed in the *RhZ*, especially when produced by the pen of the Berlin *Freien*, a radical group of individualists with anarchistic leanings which also published in the *RhZ*. In a letter to Ruge Marx detailed his objections to their writings:

... I held that it was unsuitable and indeed immoral to smuggle communist and socialist dogmas, i.e. a new world-view, into incidental theatre reviews, etc., and I desired quite a different and more profound discussion of communism, if it were to be discussed at all (Nov. 30, 1842).

In these early newspaper articles Marx directed his attention towards the problem of freedom; his approach is strongly philosophical:

Freedom is so essentially a part of human nature that even its opponents help to realise it in combatting its reality; they want to appropriate for themselves this precious jewel which they deny is a jewel of human nature.... The danger which threatens the life of every being is that of losing itself; the mortal danger therefore for every human being is that of losing his freedom. (MEW 1:51,60)

The press of a nation constitutes according to Marx the 'intellectual mirror' in which a people observes itself, and, since 'observation of self is the first prerequisite of wisdom', repressive censorship laws which prevent the people from attaining wisdom must be vehemently condemned:

In order to fight against freedom of the press, one must defend the standpoint that the human race is incapable of reaching maturity ... If man's immaturity is the mystic reason which speaks against freedom of the press, then censorship is in any event a most highly reasonable measure to assure that men never mature. (MEW 1:48-49)

In May and June Marx was temporarily in Trier due to a death in the family. Personal problems developed and Marx wrote to Ruge:

My family has caused me difficulties which expose me for the moment to the most depressing financial circumstances despite their being well-off. It would not be right for me to burden you with the tale of these private infamies. It is truly fortunate that public infamies make it impossible for any man of character to let himself be irritated by the private ones. (July 7, 1842)

Of the four articles promised Ruge for his Zürich publication *Anekdota* only the one on the historical school of law appeared in print—in the *RhZ*, however, not in *Anekdota*. The article was unsigned and a chapter on marriage was cut out by the censor. Marx's standpoint here is a rejection of the theoretical view which sees present life as the corruption of a once perfect and absolute state of nature. He maintains instead that 'as every century has its own particular nature, so does it engender its own particular natural man' (MEW 1:79).

On October 15 Marx, now settled in Cologne, began work as editor-in-chief of the *RhZ*. In the early editorial he repudiated an attack by the *Augsburger Allgemeine Zeitung* accusing the *RhZ* of communist tendencies. For the first time Marx mentioned the names Fourier, Leroux, Considerant and Proudhon and termed the work of the latter 'insightful'. The *RhZ*, Marx announced, was going to submit socialist ideas to rigorous criticism, for

... ideas which have won over our minds and conquered our way of thinking, ideas forged to our conscience by reason are chains we cannot break out of without breaking our hearts; they are demons which we can overcome only by acquiescing to them (MEW 1 : 108).

As editor of the *RhZ* Marx found himself caught in a dual conflict: on the one side, he faced the paper's shareholders, intent on moderating the editors' political tendency; on the other, he was challenged by the *Freien*, whose superficial articles on communism and atheism Marx rejected. About November 24 he received a letter from Eduard Meyen, written in the name of the Berlin radicals, demanding that he justify his editorial policy. In the midst of this conflict Friedrich Engels paid his first visit to Marx in Cologne on the way to England, where he conducted business for his father's spinning mills in Manchester. Since Engels stood close to the Berlin *Freien* at that time, it is not surprising that Marx received him rather coolly. Towards the end of November the situation finally ripened to an open break between the editor-in-chief and his Berlin contributors, while Engels, tending more and more towards a communist viewpoint, published in the *RhZ* his first articles on the condition of the working class in England.

In November-December the *RhZ* published three articles on the increasingly critical situation of the wine-growing peasants in the Moselle valley. The first president of the Rhineland province, von Schaper, issued an official denial of the alleged conditions and accused the *RhZ* of false reporting, of calumny and of stirring up dissatisfaction among the populace. Marx came to the defence of the correspondent's reports in two articles published in January 1843.

Marx also devoted a three part article to a critique of the Prussian constitution, which was based on the existence of fixed classes or 'estates' [*Stände*]. In this article, published in December, Marx attacked the particularism of parliamentary representation according to such a constitution:

The *Landtage* are, because of their unique composition, nothing more than a society of special interests privileged with the opportunity of making valid their *particular limits* to state encroachment, in other words, they are justified self-constituted anti-state elements within the state. They are therefore by nature inimical to the state since in its isolated activity any special element is always an enemy to the whole. It is precisely this whole which conveys to the particular a feeling of its nothingness by giving it an awareness of its limits (EB 1 : 419).

Staff and shareholders were informed at the beginning of 1843 that a government edict had been issued, forbidding further publication of the RhZ after April 1. This measure was taken on the demand of the Russian Czar Nicolas I after an outspoken article against Russian absolutism appeared in the paper on January 4, 1843. Marx was relieved that he would soon be free of the shackling censorship regulations. He wrote to Ruge :

I cannot begin anything anew in Germany; here one is forced to corrupt oneself ... To me the suppression of the *Rheinische Zeitung* represents progress in political consciousness ... It is a bad state of affairs when one has to perform menial tasks even for freedom and to fight with pins instead of clubs. I tired of this hypocrisy, stupidity, brute authority and of our having to give in, to conform, to turn our backs to things and to split hairs. (Jan. 25, 1843)

Disappointed in the shareholders for their timidity in defending the paper's staff, Marx resigned his position before the actual end of publication (March 17, 1843). His final comments on the government edict are incorporated in a protest address directed to the Prussian government by the shareholders. Marx declared (Feb. 12, 1843) that the policies of the RhZ had always been aimed at serving the true interests of the state. The government officials thought otherwise, however. In a remark noted on the margin of a letter from the censor Wilhelm Saint-Paul, a certain Councillor Bitter pointed out that Marx's ultra-democratic inclinations were the antithesis of the principles upon which the Prussian state was founded.

In a letter to Ruge some weeks before his displacement Marx had already broached the topic of founding a new journal. He suggested that they should publish this new 'people's periodical', as he envisaged the future radical organ, in Zürich with the co-operation of the poet Georg Herwegh. Once the contract was concluded, Marx was determined to go to Kreuznach, where Jenny, his fiancée of seven years, was awaiting him. He confessed to Ruge :

Without any romanticism whatsoever I can assure you that I am head over heels in love and my love is as serious as can be. I have been engaged for over seven years now and my bride-to-be has fought the hardest of battles for me, very nearly ruining her health in the doing (March 13, 1843).

Whatever their fate should be, Marx was set on marrying before leaving Germany, although his financial situation was not very promising. Having broken with his family Marx was unable to touch his paternal inheritance as long as his mother was alive. Towards the end of March Marx made a trip to Holland, presumably to discuss the matter of his inheritance with his mother's Dutch relatives.

While still in Cologne Marx read Feuerbach's *Preliminary Thesis on the Reformation of Philosophy* (1842) which he commented on to Ruge:

I take exception to Feuerbach's aphorisms only in one connection: he refers to nature too often and neglects politics. Yet the only way to transform contemporary philosophy into reality is through an alliance with politics (March 13, 1843).

Marx was on the move again in May: this time to Dresden where he conferred with Ruge on the subject of their joint literary enterprise. Their intention was now to publish *Deutsch-Französische Jahrbücher* (Franco-German Annals) either in Paris or in Strasbourg. Finally at the end of the month Marx moved to Kreuznach, where Jenny and her mother were living. The marriage ceremonies, civil and religious, took place on June 19 in Kreuznach. Shortly thereafter Marx received an offer, which he immediately rejected, to enter the Prussian civil service as editor-in-chief of the *Preussische Staatszeitung*. During his sojourn in Kreuznach he devoted himself to a study of the revolutions in France, England and America. A number of his readings helped him arrive at a view of communism as the inevitable outcome of democracy. He also undertook a 'critical revision' of Hegel's political philosophy. This critique, the bulk of which was most probably written in Kreuznach, marks his open and definitive break with Hegel's idea of the state and acknowledges democracy as the 'solution to the enigma of all constitutions':

Man does not exist for the benefit of the law, the law exists for the benefit of man; law is human existence, whereas in all other political forms man has only juridical existence. This is the main distinction of democracy (MEW 1:213).

Marx's conception of democracy goes as far as to question the existence of the state as a political body in democracy, and he suggests that in some way the state is to be overcome:

Recent French thinkers have understood this as meaning that the political state disappears in a true democracy. This is correct in so far as the state *qua* political state, *qua* political constitution is no longer valid for the whole (MEW 1:232).

Marx renounced altogether the idea of the state as a rational institution and with it Hegel's system which culminated in the state as the highest embodiment of reason. While pretending to a spiritualism of the highest order, Hegel's justification of the existing monarch is, according to Marx, nothing better than the crassest materialism. Reading Hegel one discovers that:

At all the highest points in the political state it is the contingency of birth which makes certain individuals into the embodiments of the highest political tasks. The highest activities in the state are attributed to individuals according to birth, just as the situation of an animal, its nature, way of life, etc., is given immediately at its birth. The state in its highest functions is endowed with an animal-like reality (MEW 1:310).

Within this structure the bureaucracy develops; what is actually the form of the state constitutes and perpetuates itself as its content. The bureaucratic mind is engendered, 'a Jesuitical, theological mind through and through':

The aims of the state transform themselves into the aims of bureaux or the aims of bureaux into those of the state. The bureaucracy is a circle from which no one can escape. Its hierarchy is a hierarchy of knowledge (MEW 1:249).

Control over this knowledge in the Hegelian state means that the subjects are deprived of participation in political life. They are virtually forced to live outside the state and their sole access to it is by examination, which admits them to the echelons of the bureaucracy:

... the *examination* is nothing other than the *bureaucratic baptism* of knowledge, the official recognition of the trans-substantiation of profane knowledge into sacred (it goes without saying that for every examination the examinator knows all). We do not hear about Greek or Roman statesmen ever taking examinations. But what then is a Roman statesman in comparison with a member of the Prussian government! (MEW 1 : 253).

Hegel's superstitious deification of the state, Marx explained, originated in his particular mode of thought which reversed subject and object. Whereas in reality man experiences his existence as both political and social, Hegel in his fantastic abstractions separates the political aspect of man, an attribute, from man and examines it as an abstract entity embodied in the state:

He made into a product, a predicate of the idea, what is actually its subject. He does not develop his thought from the object, but rather he develops the object according to thought which is complete in itself and in the abstract sphere of logic. It is not a task of developing the particular idea of the political constitution, but of relating the political constitution to the abstract idea, of giving it a place in the life-story of the idea, what evidently amounts to mystification (MEW 1 : 231).

The studies pursued during this period contributed fundamentally to Marx's subsequent formulation of a 'materialist' view of history. He excerpted fifty pages of notes from the German translation of a book entitled Men and Manners in America (1833) by Thomas Hamilton. The Scotsman Hamilton had observed in the United States certain inequalities in class relations which he held to be incompatible with true democracy. In Hamilton Marx found what de Tocqueville had failed to notice: the revolutionary implications of American democracy. Hamilton derived the historical necessity of a rupture in American society from the social discrepancies, the class barriers founded on and reinforced by an unequal educational system 'incompatible with the true democratic principle of absolute equality'. From this he concluded that:

... if the question be conceded that democracy necessarily leads to anarchy and spoliation, it does not seem that the mere length of road to be travelled is a point of much importance. In the United States, with the great advantages they possess, it may continue a generation or two longer, but the termination is the same. The doubt regards time, not destination (Hamilton, op. cit., p. 166).

Other works read by Marx at this time included Rousseau's *du Contrat social* (1762), Montesquieu's *L'Esprit des lois* (1748), Machiavelli's *Il Principe* in German translation, de Tocqueville's *de la Démocratie en Amérique* (1835-40) and Gustav Auguste Beaumont de La Bonninière's *Marie ou de l'esclavage aux Etats-Unis* (1835). Still planning to collaborate on the *Deutsch-Französische Jahrbücher*, now intended for publication in Paris, Marx corresponded with Ruge, and defined his concept of the new journal's policy: it must be unwavering in its criticism of the existing order in the name of humanity; it should support the political fight for a democratic system which should encompass more than the machinery of a political state; it would strive to reform the individual's consciousness not by means of communist or socialist dogmas, but through analysis of confusion, be it of religious or political nature, in the human consciousness (Sept. 1843). Among the writings completed during the Kreuznach period was the essay *On the Jewish Question*, composed at a time when Marx was severing his last ties with the idealist Hegelian notion of the state and bureaucracy and at a time when the conflict with his Jewish relations in money matters was particularly acute. This essay has overtones which recall a 'prophetic' diatribe against money and the state. Published in 1844 in the *Deutsch-Französische Jahrbücher*, this essay and the *Critique of the Hegelian Philosophy of Right* (probably written in Paris at the end of 1843) constitute the first draft of a communist manifesto which was to be given its final form in the text of 1848.

Marx and his wife left Germany for Paris on October 11. There they lodged in an apartment in rue Vaneau, situated in the area of Faubourg St Germain, where their neighbours were other German immigrants including Herwegh and Ruge. Heinrich Heine became a regular visitor to the Marx's beginning in December and the two men saw much of one another during the coming months.

II
1844-1849

1844   The economic distress of the cotton weavers in the Silesian Riesengebirge in Germany is aggravated by the competition of foreign products as well as by the mechanisation of the German weaving industry. Out of misery and frustration the weavers damage local cotton mills and destroy equipment. The revolt is ruthlessly crushed by Prussian military intervention.

In Rochdale, England, two dozen Chartists and Owenite workers open a co-operative store called the 'Equitable Pioneers'. They operate on the principle of selling goods at current market prices and distributing the returns among members according to their purchases.

1845   A bad harvest and potato blight in Ireland create massive famine. There is violent opposition to the Corn Laws which prohibit importation of food to the starving population. Between the years 1841 and 1847 Ireland's population is reduced by half by famine and emigration.

1846   After a decade of widespread agitation the Corn Laws are finally repealed.

1846   Nobles and intellectuals in Galician Poland revolt against the domination of the feudal lords. By simultaneously inciting a peasant revolt against the landowners, the Habsburgs of Austria are able to exploit the general turmoil and assert their hegemony.

The formerly independent city of Cracow is annexed to Austria.

1846-47 A new wave of anti-Austrian sentiment is manifested in Italy as Prince Metternich attempts to occupy the Papal city of Ferrara. The Austrians are ultimately forced to withdraw.

1847 A law is passed fixing the 10-hour maximum working day for women and children in Great Britain.

— Prussia's king Friedrich Wilhelm IV calls a united provincial Diet (*Landtag*) at Berlin, the first representative body to assemble in Germany for the purpose of advising the king.

— In France political reform banquets are held in Lille, Strasbourg and Rouen. The banquet scheduled for Paris is postponed by Prime Minister Guizot until the following year.

— Daniel O'Connell takes leave from the House of Commons and remarks in his farewell address: 'I am afraid that the English people are not sufficiently impressed with the horrors of the situation in Ireland ... It has been estimated ... that one-fourth of the whole population must perish unless something is done.'

— Europe experiences its worst economic depression, as a bad harvest coincides with a slump in business after a very active period of construction, especially in the railroad industry.

THE REVOLUTIONS OF 1848-1849

1848 In Italy a separatist revolt of the Sicilians against the domination of the king of Naples provides the spark which ignites a general insurrection. The kings of Naples and Tuscanny hastily agree to liberal constitutions in an effort to ward off revolution and save the monarchy. A counter-revolution is undertaken by the Austrians under Radetzki in the summer and defeats the popular forces of Northern Italy. The king of Naples suspends the constitution and reverts to earlier methods of rule. The republicans, led by Mazzini in

Rome, Daniele Manin in Venice and Giuseppe Garibaldi, continue to fight for a united Italian nation.

1848   In France after the liberals' reform banquet is banned
once again the people of Paris take to the streets to
demonstrate against repressive misrule. Barricades are
thrown up and the Hôtel de Ville captured. Louis-
Philippe abdicates and liberal members of parliament
establish a new provisional government. They proclaim
measures of social and political reform : national workshops, abolition of press restrictions and the extension
of suffrage rights to all male citizens over 21 years of
age. The conservative royalists and moderate republicans nevertheless triumph at the polls. The radicals
and socialists, led by Louis Blanc, Armand Barbès,
Auguste Blanqui, stage an unsuccessful *coup d'état*
which is quickly quelled and plays into the hands of
the conservatives, who now pass a series of repressive
measures. The decision to close the national workshops
precipitates a popular uprising, referred to as the 'June
Days', but it too is put down by the national military
forces. New censorship laws are passed and the right
of assembly is suspended. Napoleon's nephew Louis
Napoleon is elected president, a sign that full-scale
military dictatorship is in the offing.

—   In Germany general revolution is avoided through
Friedrich Wilhelm's clever tactic of ceding to liberal
pressure for a German *Reich* which would replace the
loose confederation of states (the *Bund*). He permits
a central representative assembly to be convoked at
Frankfurt-am-Main in May; but, since it bypasses
existing governments and is composed of non-official
representatives this organisation lacks executive force.
What is more, the members are divided on the question
of leadership : should the future German *Reich* be
constituted so as to include Catholic Austria (the
Großdeutsch plan) or should the boundaries be more
narrowly drawn, giving hegemony to Protestant
Prussia (the *Kleindeutsch* plan)? The Frankfurt parliament is caught in a stalemate.

—   At Vienna, in the Austro-Hungarian Empire, news of
the uprisings in Paris encourage demonstrators to take

to the streets and demand the resignation of Prince Metternich. Both he and Emperor Ferdinand give in to liberal pressure and the Diet is convoked to discuss the question of a new constitution. The 'March Laws' are passed, realising the demands for a separate Hungarian parliament and ministerial responsibility as put forth by their leader Louis Kossuth. However, the trilateral rivalries between the chief racial groups—Germans, Slavs and Magyars—within the Empire prohibit a harmonious functioning of the democratic apparatus; each group wishing for national unity at the expense of the others. Moreover, the internal conflicts between the various Slav groups—Czechs, Slovaks, Serbs, Croatians, Poles and Ruthenians—add to the dissension and hostility. Civil war erupts in Hungary but is forcibly repressed by the greater strength of the Austrian army under the Czech general Windischgrätz. A second mass uprising occurs in Vienna in October, but this movement for separate Austrian and Hungarian nations is also crushed by Windischgrätz and his troops. Two representatives of the Frankfurt assembly sent to Vienna with messages of sympathy are arrested and one, Robert Blum, is executed in November.

1849   The Italian republicans manage to take Rome, where they proclaim the republic and call a national constituent assembly. However, a four-nation attack on Rome, led by Austria, defeats this last stronghold of republicanism in August.

—   Her strength now reconfirmed by military successes, Austria decides to withdraw from the Frankfurt parliament and declares herself in favour of reviving the old *Bund* which had previously operated to Austria's advantage by maintaining the particularism of the numerous German *Länder*. The parliament offers the crown of the German *Reich* to Friedrich Wilhelm of Prussia who refuses, certain that there will be no popular revolution to fear. When Prussia's representatives walk out of parliament as well, the project of a united Germany is killed.

—   Kossuth continues the struggle for Magyar national

unity in Hungary. In April the Hungarian parliament declares the country's independence, Kossuth enters Budapest and proclaims himself dictator. As in Italy, the insurgents are defeated with the aid of a foreign monarch, this time Czar Nicolaus of Russia, who sends an army to aid the Habsburgs. The Austrians under the leadership of Windischgrätz and Joseph Jellachich, a second Czech general, invade the country and re-establish the old order. Kossuth flees the country.

THE AMERICAS

1845   Under pressure from the pro-slavery states which need more land for agriculture, the US Congress annexes the independent region of Texas, thereby provoking Mexico to declare war.

1848   After three years of hostilities a peace settlement is negotiated granting the USA full rights to the territories of Arizona, New Mexico and California along with Texas in return for payment of an indemnity to Mexico.

—   Colonel Sutter discovers gold in the Sacramento River in California; a 'gold rush' to the West quickly populates the new US territory with fortune-hunters.

THE FAR EAST

1845   Concessions are won from the Chinese emperor which permit Christian missionaries to enter all five treaty ports. This agreement stirs up virulent hatred for the foreigners among the Chinese masses.

1845-46   The first war against the Sikhs, a religious sect living in the Punjab region of India, is brought to a successful close for the British colonialist power. The British Empire is extended to the banks of the Navi river. War

1848-49   erupts again two years later when the Sikhs revolt against the foreign presence. The British succeed this time in subjugating the whole of the Punjab (Northern India). India is now entirely a British colony.

SCIENTIFIC AND TECHNOLOGICAL PROGRESS

1844   Samuel F. B. Morse sets up the first working telegraphic communication between Baltimore, Maryland, and Washington, D.C.
1845   The first clipper ship is constructed.
1847   The German physicist Hermann von Helmholtz formulates the principle of the conservation of energy.

IMPORTANT WORKS PUBLISHED

1844   Heinrich Heine: *Deutschland, ein Wintermärchen.**
1845   Max Stirner: *Der Einzige und sein Eigentum.**
1846   P.-J. Proudhon: *Système des contradictions économiques, ou Philosophie de la misère.**
1847-53   Jules Michelet: *Histoire de la Révolution française.**
1848   John Stuart Mill: *Principles of Political Economy* (2 vols.).*
1849   Adolphe Quételet: *Du Système social et des lois qui le régissent.**
—   Henry David Thoreau: *On the Duty of Civil Disobedience.*
1849-50   Charles Dickens: *David Copperfield.**

KARL MARX
1844-1849

These years were the last of Marx's engagement on the European continent, years in which he elaborated the so-called materialist theory of history and was confronted with the reality of the 1848 revolutions as a test of its analytic strength. During his sojourn in Paris (1843-Feb.1845) Marx began studying political economy in earnest. Circumstances permitting, he deepened his knowledge with the intense devotion to his subject matter that characterises the alert and conscientious scholar. What is more, he combined theoretical research with educational activity, helping to found the Communist League as an international centre for socialist propaganda.

1844 In February the first and unique issue of the *Deutsch-Französische Jahrbücher* appeared in Paris. Personal and financial reasons destined it to a brief existence: 800 copies were confiscated by the police while being smuggled across the border into Germany from Switzerland: Ruge and Marx, the two editors, were soon at odds, as Ruge felt himself rebuked by Marx's radical political views and his authority.

Marx made three important contributions to the *Jahrbücher*, the most polemic of which was a two-part article 'On the Jewish Question', a reply to two articles by Bruno Bauer on Judaism and Christianity published in 1843. In the first section of his article Marx pleaded for the political emancipation of the Jews in order to solve, within the limits of the existing political order and contrary to the view of Bauer, the 'Jewish problem'. However, this possibility offered by democracy was not the ultimate solution to the problem, as Marx saw it. Rather:

The *political* emancipation of the Jew, the Christian, of religious man in general, is the emancipation of the state from Judaism, from Christianity, from religion in any form (MEW 1 : 353).

For the individual 'political' emancipation means emancipation via a detour 'through a medium, although this be a necessary medium' (*ibid.*) and represents progress towards true human emancipation although still a form of emancipation '*within* the world order as it has existed up till the present' (MEW 1 : 356). Marx then developed his views on the real, the 'human emancipation of the Jews' in the second part of the essay. This solution to the Jewish problem entails the conscious emancipation of the individual being from the shackles of a religion which tolerated one person's becoming rich at the expense of another and condoned wealth as a means towards social liberty. Yet to condemn such a religion would be meaningless, Marx held, for every religion is a product of inhuman society, Christianity—the perfection of Judaism—included. Yet Marx saw the Jews as well, through their suffering, as the emancipators of the Christians and of all humanity in so far as they work consciously towards changing society.

A social organisation which would eliminate the conditions favourable to fraudulent dealings would make the existence of the Jew impossible as well (MEW 1 : 372).

The Jew must recognise his 'practical being' as something to be overcome, as self-alienation, which can only be superseded in a new form of society. The rights which he gains through political emancipation are the limited rights of egoistic man in civil society, where the individual is 'isolated from the community [*Gemeinwesen*], retires into himself, his private interests and his own personal initiative' (MEW 1 : 366). Once society has abolished the conflict between the individual, sensuous existence and the existence of the species as a whole, the basis which permits the Jew to exist as 'money-changer' and cunning trader will be destroyed: The social emancipation of the Jew means therefore that the society must be emancipated from the negative elements which compose 'Judaism' as 'practical self-interest' (MEW 1 : 372).

The theme of this essay recurs in *The Holy Family* where Marx formulated its central argument, saying that:

It was proved that the task of abolishing the essence of Judaism is in truth the task of abolishing Judaism *in civil society*, abolishing the inhumanity of today's practice of life, which culminates in the *money system* (MEW 2 : 116).

Marx's second contribution to the *Jahrbücher* was an Introduction to the critique of Hegel's political philosophy, which he had begun to work out the preceding year, but had left unfinished and unpublished. This Introduction was politically far more developed and far more radical than the critique itself and represents, in a sense, the germ of the future *Communist Manifesto*. For the first time Marx speaks here of the proletarian 'class' and of the 'formation' of an industrial working class which is to act as a social emancipatory force. Outlined as well in this essay is Marx's 'sociological', to use a more recent term, analysis of religion, the state and law as elements of the social superstructure. Religion is the point of departure and man the orientation for this discourse. It is man who creates religion, Marx began, and not vice-versa : religion is man's theory of the world and his fantastic self-realisation because he lives under conditions which prohibit him from realising himself in the real world :

Religious misery is both *expression* of and *protest* against real misery. Religion is the sigh of the oppressed creature, the heart of a heartless world and the meaning of spiritless circumstances. It is the *opium* of the people (MEW 1 : 378).

The task of one who proposed to criticise religion is therefore to analyse the real world conditions which require the 'illusory' happiness and fulfilment of religion, i.e. 'The critique of religion is thus in essence the critique of the valley of sorrows whose halo is religion' (MEW 1 : 379). This is the stand-point which prompted Marx to undertake a critical analysis of Hegel's philosophy of the state and right as the most complete expression of German political philosophy and of the modern state in its ideal form.

The conditions in Germany were, in Marx's view, 'anachronistic' for the present age; Germany had by-passed the revolutions which had advanced the other peoples politically and participated only in the restoration movements of the reaction.

Philosophy for the Germans was the form in which they relived their past, just as the ancient peoples had had the imaginative form of mythology for their history. However, the only aspect of German history which stood 'on equal footing with the official modern present' was the philosophy of law and the state and being 'illusory history' was the direct negation of real conditions (MEW 1 : 383). To negate this philosophy, in turn, would finally be to realise it in *praxis*, to overcome it by abolishing the conditions which generate illusory thinking. The root of this radical negation is man himself, who as his own supreme being must resolve the 'categorical imperative to overthrow all conditions in which man is a debased, enslaved, neglected, contemptible being' (MEW 1 : 385). The German emancipation from philosophy is hence a revolution which realises the material needs of the people: 'It is not enough that the idea strive to become reality; reality must itself feel the need for the idea' (MEW 1 : 386).

A human and radical revolution will take place in Germany when, thanks to the progress of industrialisation, a particular class has developed, concentrating in itself all the evils of the present social order 'so that the emancipation of this social sphere appears as the self-emancipation of the generality' (MEW 1 : 388). To regain its humanity this class must redeem all humanity, in the process of which it will overthrow the social order and raise its own principle of the negation of private property to the general principle of society:

The only *practically* feasible emancipation of Germany is based on the *particular* theory which declares man to be the supreme being for man (MEW 1 : 391).

The 'head' of the German emancipation is therefore philosophy, its heart the proletariat and 'the emancipation of Germany is the emancipation of mankind'. When the conditions are ripe for this step, 'the day of German resurrection will be proclaimed by the crowing of the Gallic cock' (*ibid.*).

Marx's third contribution to the *Jahrbücher* was a series of three letters he had written to Ruge in 1843 on the present situation in Germany. Engels contributed as well to this publication with an essay entitled 'Outline for a Critique of Political Economy', which Marx later termed 'genial' (1859). This work and probably Proudhon's first and second *Mémoire sur la propriété* (1840-41) as well provided Marx with the theme for his life-work. Inspired by the subject of political economy, Marx began a systematic study in April, reading, in French translations, the British economists Adam Smith, David Ricardo, James Mill and John Ramsay MacCulloch, the Frenchmen Jean-Baptiste Say, J. C. L. Simonde de Sismondi, Constantin Pecqueur (*Théorie nouvelle d'économie sociale et politique*, 1842), Antoine Eugène Buret (*De la Misère des classes laborieuses en Angleterre et en France*, 1840) and the German economist Wilhelm Schulz (*Die Bewegung der Produktion*, 1843). Marx's excerpts and notes on his readings reveal more than just his theoretical interests: they are a key to his own moral predisposition. The attitudes indicated here towards money and religion clarify certain concepts (i.e. the integral or all-sided man, money fetishism, alienation) which come up in later works, especially the *Grundrisse* (1857-58) and *Capital*, although in less philosophic and less Feuerbachian language. Here Marx has given as well his vision of a future society, of man freed from money and religion, the mediators of his present social existence. Here we find, further, the same quotations on money from Shakespeare and Goethe found in later works. Viewed in retrospect, Marx's excerpt notebooks show the permanence of his basic orientation: he was never to deviate in his life-work from the standpoint defined here. A social system which valuated men in terms of money and made morality a function of financial creditability was unworthy of the human being. In such a system, moreover,

The only comprehensible language which we can speak with one another is that of our objects in terms of their mutual relations. We cannot understand human language, and as such language would be ineffective ... we are so far removed from human nature that to us the direct human language seems to be a violation of human dignity, while, contrarily, the alienated language of object values appears worthy of man, justified, confident and conscious of itself (EB 1 : 461).

Ruge, whose friendship with Marx came to a definitive break about March 26, nevertheless had a certain respect for his scholarly and intellectual qualities, although he considered him unsuited for journalism. In a letter to Feuerbach Ruge wrote:

He reads a great deal, works with unusual intensity and possesses a critical ability which sometimes degenerates into arrogant dialectics; but he does not finish anything, continually breaks off with what he is working on and plunges time and again into an endless sea of books (May 15).

To his mother Ruge described Marx as a 'most extraordinary fellow and an insolent Jew' (October 6) and to Julius Froebel he wrote that 'Marx professes communism, but he is the true believer in egoism ... with his teeth bared in a grin Marx would be capable of cutting down any and all who come across his path' (Dec. 16, quoted in P. Nerrlich, ed., *Arnold Ruges Briefwechsel und Tagebuchblätter aus den Jahren 1825-1880*. Vol. 1, Berlin, 1886, p. 381).

In the spring of 1844 Marx took an interest in the work and activities of the 'League of the Just' and until the end of his Paris stay he frequented meetings of workers and artisans. Writing to Feuerbach, he commented on these gatherings and noted particularly 'the virgin freshness, the *noblesse* of these working men. The English proletariat is making enormous progress as well, but he lacks the cultivation characteristic of the French ... the German artisan is still too much of a craftsman'. The letter continues with an account of the activities in the German immigrant groups: '... the communists among them ... have been attending lectures twice weekly on your *Essence of Christianity* and have shown themselves remarkably receptive' (August 11).

After some months of studies in economics Marx attempted in summer to put on paper his ethical and anthropological thoughts on man's fate as a member of bourgeois society. As a social being, through his productive activity, man confirms his individuality and his products are means of self-realisation. Man's need is therefore to 'objectify' himself in his work but not to 'dispossess' [*entäussern*] or 'alienate' [*entfremden*] himself in the production process as is the case under bourgeois social conditions, where reduction of the human self appears as the realisation of labour, 'objectification as the loss of the object and subjection to its domination, while appropriation appears as alienation, as dispossession of the self' (EB 1 : 512). The products of labour, through which man naturally fulfills himself, no longer belong to the producer in the present system of private ownership. Man is not able to give free expression to his physical and mental energies. He is consequently dissatisfied with his labour and finds contentment only during his leisure time: Labour is thus for him not a pleasure, not a completion and expression of himself, but compulsion. Rooted in the institution of private property, the present production system renders impossible the development of the 'integral' or 'all-sided' man who realises himself as an individual through his social participation, through his productive activity.

Four fragmentary or incompleted manuscripts remain from this early critique of political economy, commonly referred to as the 'Paris Manuscripts'. Three of them treat specific economic themes such as land-rent, wages, profit, human needs, etc., and depart from a critique of the classic political economists. The fourth was intended as an analysis of the Hegelian dialectic but developed into a general critique of all philosophy. Here Marx applied dialectic reasoning to actual human existence, inducing a 'materialist' ethic for the transformation of society. Marx envisaged these manuscripts as part of a larger work divided into discussions of law, ethics, politics, etc., and to be concluded with a critical summary of the whole. The task which he set himself was to understand the social reality through a critical examination of its elements, the institutions of bourgeois society. He began, as we have noted, with political economy.

The passages devoted to labour recur in Marx's mature work on political economy, albeit in a more scientific form. The social relations of our world are governed by the values established in the productive sector and based on private property:

The world of men decreases in value in direct proportion to the increase in value attributed to the world of objects. Labour produces not only commodities, it produces itself and the labouring man as commodities in the same proportion that it produces commodities in general (EB 1:511).

The fundamental relation of man to woman, in particular, is altered by social circumstances in which money is the mediator between man and labour, man and man, man and society. Money is, Marx wrote, paraphrasing and quoting Shakespeare, 'the visible godhead, the transformation of all human and natural qualities into their opposites ... it is the universal whore, the universal procurer of men and of peoples' (EB 1:565). Marx stressed the relation of man to woman as a criterion of man's humanity, of his level of cultural development. In this relation-ship is revealed 'the extent to which the other person as a human being has become a need for him ... In man's behaviour towards woman, prey of and servant to the communal lasciviousness, is expressed the infinite degradation of man towards himself' (EB 1 : 535).

Marx undertook to examine nature through man; his analyses are therefore a kind of naturalist anthropology. Hegel, by con-trast, had incorporated his 'philosophy of nature' into a discourse on logic. Marx pointed out that neither Feuerbach nor Hegel had understood the importance of labour in the development of the human personality and as a creative expression of life. However, Marx, in the manuscript on Hegelian dialectic, gave credit to both of these thinkers for their contributions to a new understanding of human history: To Feuerbach he owed a *serious, critical* approach to Hegelian dialectics', while Hegel's merit lay in his description of man's self-realisation as a *process* and therefore as the product of his own labour, although he failed to grasp the material aspect of labour and conceived of it as simply an intellectual or spiritual process. Marx in turn empha-sized the sensuous nature of man and denied what Hegel postulated as the 'ultimate reality':

A being which is not objective is not real, cannot be sensed and is merely a product of the imagination (i.e. a fantastic being) and of abstraction. To be sensuous, i.e. to be real, is to be an object of the senses, of sensuous objects ... To be sensuous is to suffer (EB 1 : 579).

Hegel sublimates each of the social institutions to a higher level. The family, for example, is sublimated as civil society, 'sublimated' private law is morality, etc. Yet in all these move-ments reality has remained unchanged, untouched: they are simply 'moments' in a theoretical process of realising Hegel's *Weltgeist*. These philosophical acrobatics are possible because Hegel established social institutions as abstract concepts void of their real-world content. Marx criticised this dialectical play on concepts: 'It is to be avoided,' he wrote, 'that "society" again be established as an abstract, apart from the individual. The *individual* is a *social being*' (EB 1 : 538).

The task of resolving the evident gap between existing social conditions and the requirements of a *human* existence was for Marx more than theoretical, as the philosophers imagined. He sought, however, a profound theoretic understanding of the discrepancies between the real economic situation and his ideal of the truly human society. He rejected at once the most obvious proposals to alleviate economic inequalities, such as rises in wages and salaries, which would serve only to make working men 'better-paid slaves' and 'would win neither for the labourer nor for his labour their human destiny and their human dignity' (EB 1 : 520f.). Even Proudhon's suggestion of equal wages would be futile, would only extend to all producers the alienation which the working man now experienced as regards his labour. When, however, the capitalists' private ownership of the means of production and therefore of the products themselves has been abolished, the individual labourer may once again appropriate the results of his social activity, i.e. the products, which are his own human nature. Self-alienation in the production process is overcome through the suppression of private property. Marx terms this 'the conscious return of man to himself as a *social*, i.e. as a human person, which is accomplished in virtue of the entire wealth of prior development' (EB 1 : 536). Thus Marx understands communism as 'fully developed naturalism= humanism' and, moreover:

as fully developed humanism=naturalism. It is the *genuine* resolution of man's conflict with man and with nature, of the conflicts between existence and being, objectification and self-affirmation, freedom and necessity and between the individual and the species (EB 1 : 536).

This was the positive form of communism which Marx differentiated sharply from a more primitive form which generalises private property by raising it to its highest level as 'universal private property'. This form of communism destroys everything which cannot be generalised, ignores real differences in human abilities and talents, negates human personality and individuality. He compared it to the 'community of wives' in which 'woman becomes the common and debased property of all':

One might say that the notion of the community of wives is the open and confessed secret of this still very primitive and thoughtless communism (EB 1 : 537).

Where the state as a political institution has not yet been abolished entirely, communism necessarily remains tainted with alienation. Communism must do more than overcome private property: it must grasp the 'positive nature' of this institution on a higher level at which the 'human nature' of needs is recognised. While 'communism is the necessary form and dynamic principle of the immediate future, communism is, how-ever, as such not the goal of human development. This goal is human society made real' (EB 1 : 546).

While engaged in writing and studying in Paris, Marx was unable to secure his family's support—in May their first child Jenny was born—through any regular source of income. Aware of their financial situation, Claessen announced that he was opening a national subscription on Marx's behalf for the sacrifices he was assuming in order to promote the common cause and as a tribute to his 'talent and effectiveness'. He wrote to Marx that: 'Momentarily we are not in any position to do more than day-labourers. It is up to you to score for all of us' (March 13, IISH).

Meanwhile Marx was making new acquaintances: with Proudhon, who became his debating partner in long nightly discussions on Hegelian dialectics; with Bakunin, who later joined these discussions which ended with Marx's departure from Paris in early 1845; with the editors of the Paris journal Vorwärts!. On June 26 Georg Jung in Cologne wrote to Marx about the recent revolts of the Silesian weavers, maintaining that they were:

a brilliant confirmation of the truth of your analysis of the present and future situation in Germany, outlined in the Introduction to the Philosophy of Right ... (June 26, IISH).

Shortly thereafter, on August 7 and 10, Marx published in Vorwärts! an article entitled 'Critical Remarks on "The King of Prussia and Social Reform"'. Replying to an article published by Ruge in the same journal, Marx energetically refuted the argument that Germany lacked the 'political soul' needed to cure the social evils such as those responsible for the uprising of the Silesian weavers. Ruge confounded social solutions and political ones and thus failed to realise that to overthrow the present conditions a social solution, namely revolution, was necessary in order to overcome the state which was the real source of social abuses: 'The existence of the state and the existence of slavery are inseparable' (MEW 1:401f.). Germany, moreover, has a '*classical* calling' for social revolution, even though it has always been unable to use effectively, in behalf of social progress, the political means at its disposition within the existing order. Only Germany's proletariat possesses the necessary *social* consciousness to reverse the existing order—this was shown most clearly by the Silesian revolt:

The Silesian uprising *begins* precisely where the French and British labour revolts end, with the consciousness of the nature of the proletariat. The action itself bears this *superior* character (MEW 1 : 404).

Although these revolts were restricted to one sector of the proletariat and were ultimately suppressed, they provided evidence of social consciousness:

A social revolution ... is a protest of man against dehumanised life, even if it occurs in only *one* factory district ... because the individual is reacting against his separation from a community of men (MEW 1 : 408).

At the end of July Marx received from Jung several recent issues of Bruno Bauer's literary monthly, the *Allgemeine Literatur-Zeitung*, containing among other articles a review of Eugène Sue's popular novel *Les Mystères de Paris* (1842-43). Jung encouraged Marx to develop his critical ideas on Bauer and his circle into an essay for publication. Marx did in fact decide to compose a pamphlet of his writings on economics and philosophy and to add an introduction in which he would openly attack Bauer's standpoint while defending Feuerbach. On August 11 Marx wrote directly to Feuerbach, sending him his introductory essay to the 'Critique of the Hegelian Philosophy of Right' and expressing his great respect for Feuerbach's achievements. It was he, Marx wrote, who had given socialism a philosophical foundation, and his writing was more important than all the rest of contemporary German literature.

Between August and October *Vorwärts!* published two essays on the British constitution and the situation in England during the 18th century. The author of these articles, Friedrich Engels, was at the time engaged in writing a larger work on England, published in 1845 as *The Condition of the Working Class in England*. On his return to Germany from Manchester at the end of August, Engels paid a ten-day visit to Marx in Paris, during which time the two men discovered many similarities in their thinking. Marx suggested that they collaborate on a pamphlet against Bauer. Engels consented and prepared his brief contribution before leaving Paris. Marx, however, found it impossible to concentrate his ideas into the space agreed upon for a pamphlet and ended by producing a book-length manuscript. The two contributions were sent to the publisher Zacharias Löwenthal in Frankfurt at the end of November and Marx received the author's fee of 1000 francs.

From Barmen, where he divided his time between his father's commercial enterprise and writing his book on England, Engels wrote to Marx, suggesting that he use the material he had been accumulating for a book on economics (Oct.). Engels later reported that he had read Max Stirner's recent book *Der Einzige und sein Eigentum*. Taking up Stirner's theme of human egoism, Engels remarked that, taken to its extreme, 'his egoistic men must necessarily, out of pure egoism, become communists'. They could appropriate for their own cause the element of truth in Stirner's principle and make egoism serve their ends:

> ... we are ... even apart from material hopes, communists out of egoism, we want to be men out of egoistic motivation and not just individuals ... Just as the corporeal individual is the true basis, the true point of departure for our 'human being', so egoism—not Stirner's egoism of reason alone, but the *egoism of the heart* as well —follows as the natural basis of our human love, otherwise it hangs in the air (Nov. 19).

Marx read Stirner's book shortly thereafter and planned to write a critique of it for *Vorwärts!*.

1845 Engels continued to encourage Marx to prepare a work on economics with the least possible delay, even if this meant leaving his research in an unfinished state. He urged Marx to 'forge the iron while it is hot' for interest was high and people would welcome such a work. 'Do as I do,' he counselled, 'set yourself a date by which you definitely want to be finished and try to get it published as quickly as possible' (Jan. 20). It was his position as the son of a well-to-do factory owner which caused Engels difficulty: the double role he was forced to play, communist by conviction and capitalist by profession, caused him considerable heart-searching. To Marx he wrote that:

... it is possible to be a communist and *outwardly* a dirty bourgeois trademonger, if you don't write. But to make communist propaganda on a large scale and to be involved at the same time in trademongering and industry, that won't do at all (Jan. 20).

Marx's Paris activities were abruptly interrupted in January. Pressured by the Prussian government which had been anxiously surveying its citizens who had migrated to France, Minister of the Interior Guizot ordered the expulsion of the collaborators on the radical German-language periodical *Vorwärts!*. After negotiations it was agreed to suppress the journal on condition that the expulsion order be revoked. The editor-in-chief of the journal, Ferdinand Cölestin Bernays, nevertheless spent a year-and-a-half in prison, while Marx chose to leave the country. Shortly before his departure for Brussels, Marx was visited by the German publisher Hermann Leske who offered him a contract for a two-volume work on economics to be entitled 'A critique of Politics and Political Economy'. An agreement was signed on February 1. Of all he was leaving behind in Paris, Marx wrote to Heine: 'the most saddening for me is to part with the person of Heine. I wish I could pack you up along with us' (Jan. 12).

As soon as he learned of Marx's move to Belgium, Engels made an effort to collect funds from friends and associates in order to 'redistribute the extra cost thus entailed in a communist manner', and thus save the Marxes from financial distress. 'But,' Engels added, 'I am afraid that even in Belgium they will molest you sooner or later and that your final resort will therefore have to be England' (Feb. 22). Marx's stay in Brussels lasted three years: from February 1845 to March 1848. Although he would have preferred to return to Germany, the way was barred, for the Prussian government had issued a warrant for his arrest. For the time being he was in less danger in Belguim, where nevertheless the government had obliged him to sign a paper agreeing to refrain from writing on current political affairs. Having done so, Marx and his family were assured of political asylum and he was able to continue his studies in economics.

Engels soon followed Marx to Brussels in April and they began to collaborate intensely. One of their projects was to publish a collection of writings by the foremost socialist writers from France and England in German translation, beginning with Fourier, Owen and the Saint-Simonians. Among Marx's readings of this period was an *Essay on the Origin of Political Economy* (1825) by the British economist John Ramsay MacCulloch. For the history of technology and technical development he read Andrew Ure; for commercial history Thomas Tooke, William Cobbett and Gustav von Gülich. He became acquainted with the problems of population growth through readings from William Petty, while Quesnay's economic table and his work on *Natural Law* also drew his attention. He also continued his inquiries into English socialism with works, read in French translation as with all English authors at this time, by Robert Owen and John Bray.

Shortly after Marx had settled in Brussels, *The Holy Family or Critique of Critical Critique* by Friedrich Engels and Karl Marx—this was the order of the authors' names on the title page—was published by J. Rütten in Frankfurt—a.M. Engels, whose actual contribution amounted to some twelve pages, found his friend's work 'very fine. Your discussion of the Jewish question, of materialism and the *Mystères* is magnificent and it will certainly achieve an excellent effect' (letter to Marx, March 17).

In *The Holy Family*, while attacking the left-Hegelian group around Bauer, Marx developed his own basic ideas of socialism as inspired by French materialism and English sensualism. To a certain extent he continued his discourse on various topics broached in the unpublished manuscripts of 1844 and in earlier articles and essays, without reaching more than a limited circle of readers. Taking up the important theme of alienation from the 'Paris Manuscripts', Marx showed that in civil society all sectors are alienated, the propertied classes as well as the class which lives from its labour alone, whose condition of life is the 'outright, decisive and comprehensive negation of his human nature' (MEW 2 : 37). The propertied classes have, however, a 'semblance of human existence', seeing in their alienation power and self-confirmation. Man believes *himself* free when observing the free movement of the objects of his alienated life: property, industry, religion, etc., 'while in reality this is the perfection of his slavery and his inhumanity.' (MEW 2 : 113). Yet the proletariat, the deprived class in a social order founded on private property, becomes conscious of its physical and moral state of deprivation. Here lies the germ of the social revolution which will abolish the proletariat as a class and with it all classes of the present inhuman system of economic relations:

It follows that the proletariat can and must free itself, yet it cannot do so without abolishing the conditions of its own life. It cannot abolish the conditions of its own life without abolishing all the inhuman conditions of life in today's society as they are epitomised in his own situation (MEW 2 : 38).

Marx saw that an element of historical necessity could be deduced from the proletarian condition: its very being would compel it to follow a particular course of action which would emancipate it together with all the rest of society.

Marx's attack on Bauer was above all a critique of Geist, of mind and spirit, as the solution to the problems of modern industrial society. The left-Hegelians believed they could intellectualise these problems and solve them on the level of abstractions. But, while they reasoned away the evils of capitalist production,

The masses of common working men toiling in the ateliers of Manchester and Lyon do not think themselves capable of reasoning away their industrial masters through pure thought (MEW 2 : 55).

The reality of the conditions under which the industrial proletariat lived and worked must be changed 'so that man may become man not only in thought, in consciousness, but in his existence as a member of the mass, in his actual life' (MEW 2 : 56).

According to the Hegelian construction it was history, manifestation of the Weltgeist [universal spirit], which brought progress into the world. Marx termed this concept of history as 'the speculative expression of the Germano-Christian dogma which opposes spirit and matter, God and the world' (MEW 2 : 89). Not history, however, but man would be the agent of social change which promised to overcome the alienation and misery of industrial society: 'History is nothing but the activity of man pursuing his aims' (MEW 2 : 98). Marx underlined the simple truth that:

Ideas can never lead beyond an old world system but only beyond the ideas of that system. Ideas cannot carry out anything at all. To carry out ideas men are needed who dispose of a certain practical force (MEW 2 : 126).

Marx found these men in the masses of the oppressed industrial proletariat, which he had come to know personally in the Paris working men's groups:

One must have first discovered how well-instructed the French and English workers are, how strong is their craving for knowledge, their moral energy and their urge for self-development, in order to imagine the *human* nobleness of this movement (MEW 2:89).

Based on his understanding of man's productive activity, his social needs, Marx developed a 'materialist' view of a free society governed by the principle that each man must be given social scope for the vital manifestation of his being:

If man is shaped by his surroundings, his surroundings must be made human. If man is social by nature, he will develop his true nature only in society ... (MEW 2:138).

One chapter of *The Holy Family*, related thematically to the discussion on alienation, dealt with the article which had appeared in the *Allgemeine Literatur-Zeitung* on Sue's *Mystères de Paris*. The central figure in this novel was a young prostitute, Fleur de Marie, who possessed, according to Marx, a 'human nobleness of soul' that enabled her in spite of her inhuman environment to develop positive traits of character. She lived according to the Epicurean principle of 'free and strong nature' and for her goodness was not a function of a Perfect, Godly Being but a measure of the humanness between fellow beings, a sign therefore that:

the bourgeois system has only grazed her surface which is simply her bad fortune and that she is neither good nor bad, but *human* (MEW 2:180).

Marie was eventually persuaded to adopt a religious attitude towards life; her human values were destroyed so that she might receive a system of religiously-orientated values. God became the mediator of her relations with other human beings; happiness was no longer part of her human nature but came to her through the grace of God; her appreciation and love of nature became the expressions of religious fascination for the metaphysical essence behind real objects. Marie became, in short, self-conscious and lost her original human virtue, became an object to be manipulated henceforth by religious dogma. Marx contrasted this religious 'emancipation' of the young Marie from the world of vice and with Fourier's 'masterly' thoughts on woman's emancipation:

The humiliation of the female sex is an essential feature of civilisation as well as of barbarism. The only difference is that the civilised system raises to a compound, equivocal, ambiguous, hypocritical mode of existence every vice that barbarity practises in the simple form ... Nobody is punished more for keeping woman a slave than man himself (MEW 2:208).

An appreciation of *The Holy Family* came from Georg Jung towards the end of the year. Jung added that he and his friends were enthusiastically looking forward to Marx's next volume on political economy, which was both essential and urgent. The struggle against religion was now finished and a new one could begin with Marx at its fore:

What you are now for all your friends you must become for all of Germany. With your exceptionally sharp style of writing and the great clarity of your argumentation you will and must achieve your goal and become a guiding light of the first magnitude (Nov. 24, IISH).

Sometime early in 1845 Marx began working on a critical analysis of Friedrich List's *Das nationale System der politischen Ökonomie* (1841) and drafted four fragmentary chapters which were never developed or incorporated in any finished or published work. This writing contains an important discussion of Marx's own views on labour, exchange value, productive forces, industry, bourgeois nationalism, etc. He denies List's theoretical system as a 'camouflage in idealist phrases of the industrial materialism represented by honest economy' (BZG, p. 425), and reproaches him for criticising only the theoretical expression of this society and not the actual social conditions themselves:

It may never occur to Herr List that the real organisation of society is a spiritless materialism, individual spiritualism, individualism. It can never occur to him that the political economsts have expressed theoretically only this social condition. Otherwise he would have to oppose, not the political economists, but the present *organisation of society* (BZG, p. 433).

Engels's book *Die Lage der arbeitenden Klasse in England*
[*The Condition of the Working Class in England*], published
in Leipzig in May, contained a wealth of information on the
actual material circumstances of the English factory workers and
their families. Moreover, the author analysed the symptoms of
crisis observed in the cities with high unemployment, concluding
that an upheaval was near, one which could lead to open war
between the classes:

The war of the poor against the rich will be the most bloodthirsty
the world has seen ... Were it possible to turn all the English
workers into Communists before the outbreak of the revolution,
then the revolution itself would be a peaceable one. But that is not
possible. It is too late (p. 334f.).

During the summer Marx and Engels worked together on
topics of an economic nature. Engels moved into a house close
to Marx in a Brussels suburb. Sometime in the first half of the
year Marx made a private attempt to summarise his critique of
Feuerbach and Hegel in view of his insights into philosophy
and speculative thinking in general. He jotted down his thoughts
in a series of 'theses', which were found in one of his notebooks
after his death and published by Engels in an appendix to his
own work on Ludwig Feuerbach (1888). These eleven short
points, popularly known as the 'Theses on Feuerbach', leave no
doubt about Marx's critical orientation towards speculative
philosophy. The human 'essence' which philosophers sought to
define was no abstraction to be studied apart from actual human
existence, from practical life. To study man, philosophy should
turn to the ensemble of social relationships in which man lives
and works. The sole value philosophy might have for man
would therefore be of an ethical nature, i.e. in aiding man to
orientate his activities according to the goal of a *human* life
in a *human* society:

[8.] All mysteries which lead theory to mysticism find their rational
solution in human practice and in the comprehension of this practice

Marx stressed 'practical' human activity combined with critical
thought, 'practical-critical' activity, which could be realised only
in 'revolutionary practice':

[11.] The philosophers have only *interpreted* the world in different ways; the point is to *change* it.

In July Marx and Engels travelled together to England in connection with their studies, also using the occasion to meet Wilhelm Weitling and other members of the London League of the Just. They spent some time in Manchester for the purpose of reading and making extracts from the most important British economists. His notebooks from this period reveal that Marx had devoted particular attention to the work by the socialist William Thompson entitled *An Inquiry into the Principles of the Distribution of Wealth* (1824) and read as well works by William Petty, G. Browning and William Cobbett.

After their return to Brussels at the end of August, Marx and Engels came upon the most recent issue of *Wigands Viertel-jahresschrift* (vol. 3, 1845) in which they discovered philosophical articles by Bauer and Stirner. Speculative philosophy was not yet vanquished, they concluded and decided therefore to launch a polemical attack against these and other speculative thinkers in an article to be entitled 'The Leipzig Council'. Their writing for this project continued into January of 1846.

Jenny Marx, who had paid a first visit to her mother in Trier during the summer, returned to Brussels in August bringing with her the 26-year-old Helene Demuth (1820-1890), who had been the maid-servant of the Westphalen family since 1837. Leni or Lenchen, as she came to be called, became virtually a member of the Marx family, sharing their fate and their disappointments during all the long years in exile. In September a second daughter Laura was born to Karl and Jenny. Shortly thereafter, Marx submitted to the civil authorities in Trier a request to be released from his duties as a Prussian citizen in order to emigrate to America. The responsible officials in Berlin seemed to have been only too happy to divest themselves of this heretic Marx who was, in the words of the Prussian functionary Rudolf von Auerswald, 'guilty of attempted high treason and of insults to the person of His Royal Majesty'. The request was granted and Marx, who feared renewed reprisals should he prolong his stay in Belgium, announced the family's forthcoming departure in the local newspapers (Nov. 23). It is not known why this plan never materialised.

1846 Although Leske, the publisher with whom Marx had signed
       for the 'Economics', had already advanced 1500 francs on
the promised manuscript, Marx now put aside his writing on
political economy in order to devote himself temporarily to the
'last battle' against purely speculative thought and criticism.
He and Engels decided to expand the polemic against Bauer and
Stirner into a much more comprehensive work containing a
critical analysis not only of the left-Hegelians but also of Feuerbach and the 'true socialists'. With such a work to prepare the
German public the foundation would be laid for Marx's radical
analysis of society—for economics rather than metaphysics.

Apart from this attack on the chief representatives of German
ideology, Marx and Engels launched a practical project to create
a chain of international correspondence committees whose purpose was to give the industrial proletariat through contacts with
similar emancipation movements in other countries the means
for self-education and to acquaint the working men with socialist
efforts and proposals on an international scale. Engels later
formulated the committees' goals as '(1) to realise the interests
of the proletariat as opposed to those of the bourgeoisie; (2) to
achieve this end by abolishing private property and replacing
it with collective property; (3) to recognise no other means for
achieving these goals than that of a violent democratic revolution' (letter addressed to the Brussels Correspondence Committee, Oct. 23). Marx and Engels solicited the support of
prominent socialists and labour leaders in establishing these
committees and preparing international reports and exchanges
of information. Marx addressed a letter to Pierre-Joseph Proudhon, inviting him to join their organisation. Their primary
purpose, he wrote, was to air differences in opinion and to
exchange criticism of and information on the progress being
made by socialist movements in the various countries:

This is a step which the social movement must take in its *literary*
form of expression, if it is to rid itself of *national* limitations. And
at the moment of action everyone will certainly benefit from being
well-instructed on the state of affairs abroad as well as at home
(May 5).

Proudhon replied that he found the organisation's goal 'most
useful' and agreed to lend his support. However, what disturbed
him in Marx's letter was the talk about revolution. Although

he had once espoused such means as well, Proudhon maintained that his more recent studies had brought him to regard revolutionary action as unnecessary for social reform. What was needed, instead, was a suitable economic 'combination', 'what you other German socialists term "commune" '. Professing himself a 'nearly absolute economic anti-dogmatist', Proudhon seconded Marx's efforts to discover the laws of society and analyse the modes of social progress, but warned that 'for God's sake, after demolishing all dogmatisms *a priori*, let us not in turn entertain the notion of indoctrinating the people'. More than that, he continued:

Let us offer the world an example of wise and prudent tolerance; let us not, because we are at the head of a movement, be the masters of a new intolerance; let us not pretend to be the apostles of a new religion, be it the religion of logic or of reason (May 17).

The proletariat, with its profound thirst for knowledge and understanding, desired more to quench that thirst than blood. Proudhon added that he was presently engaged in writing a book which would explain his reform plans in detail and would, while awaiting his turn to reply, graciously submit to Marx's 'ferule'. At a meeting of the Correspondence Committee organised by Marx and Engels in Brussels, the question of political propaganda in Germany was put to the members for discussion (March 30). Marx used the opportunity to make a vehement attack against the 'sectarianism' of Weitling's 'artisan communism' which tended to negate the political struggle and against the 'true socialists' with their 'philanthropic communism'. According to a letter from Weitling to Hess (March 31) Marx demanded that the group be purged of certain elements, that contact be sought with financially solid parties and that they begin secret propaganda-making. Weitling quoted Marx as having said: 'As yet there can be no talk of realising communism; the bourgeoisie must first assume the helm' (Quoted in: Moses Hess, *Briefwechsel*. ed. E. Silberner. The Hague, 1955, p. 151). Paul Annenkov, however, recounted that Marx had branded as deceit all attempts to rouse the popular masses to action without first giving them a constructive basis for their protest. To do otherwise 'was equivalent to vain dishonest play at preaching which assumes an inspired prophet on the one hand

and only gaping asses on the other' (*Reminiscences* ..., p. 271).

On May 11 the Brussels Committee passed a resolution on Hermann Kriege, German emigrant in America and editor of the New York newspaper *Volkstribun*. The resolution protested against the paper's orientation as incompatible with its professed communism. In the name of the committee Marx and Engels composed a circular attacking the 'prophet' Kriege's 'sentimental communism' which was distributed to the correspondence committees in Germany.

Leske, meanwhile, fearing that Marx's economics would prove to be revolutionary rather than scientific, decided to annul the contract on the grounds that the book would probably be censored in Germany (March 31). Four months later Leske wrote again, demanding that Marx return the money advanced or deliver the completed manuscript at once. On August 1 Marx replied, promising to have the first of the two volumes promised ready by the end of November.

It was about this time that Marx and Engels decided to abandon the manuscript of their work on *The German Ideology* to the 'gnawing critique of the mice' (MEW 13 : 10), after their efforts to find a publisher failed. Marx explained to Leske why he had felt it important to write this book:

I thought it important to *precede* my *positive* development with a polemic writing against German philosophy and recent German socialism. This is needed in order to prepare the public for the viewpoint of my economics which is diametrically opposed to German science hitherto (August 1).

The German Ideology, abandoned with several of its chapters in an unfinished state, is divided into two volumes each containing several sections; there are numerous digressions inspired by but not pertinent to the stated themes. The first chapter entitled 'Feuerbach' is known to be the last written and is the most theoretical, containing the premises which are essential to an understanding of the relationship between Marx's early philosophical investigations and the forthcoming work on economics. This part as well as all other theoretical passages may be ascribed with near certainty to Marx. Engels, by his own later admission, was at this time a listener to and disciple of Marx and hardly capable of formulating and applying the theoretical views which Marx had just recently shared with him. The theoretical material

falls into three categories: first, a presentation of the methodological procedure which distinguishes the Marxian analysis from
other methods of historiography; the application of this method
in analysing bourgeois society and its development; finally, the
postulates based on a valuation of the results of this analysis
and intended as incentives to a certain future course of social
action and development.

[I.] History had always been written by scholars and philosophers who each sought to explain the course of human
existence by recourse to particular intellectual categories or
constructions. Marx sought, however, to use as his reference
point not an abstract category but practical human life. To this
end he established five premises for the analysis of human
development:

1. Men must be able to live in order to make history and must
therefore first satisfy their material needs. The primary historical
act is necessarily the production of the material means to satisfy
these needs.

2. Once the prime needs are satisfied, new needs arise: the chain
of material production is consequently infinite.

3. After satisfying their own material needs and reproducing
their material existence, men begin to reproduce their own kind
as well.

4. The way in which needs are satisfied corresponds to a certain
form of co-operation and organisation among men, i.e. to their
level of social development. The productive forces available
determine, moreover, the type of organisation which they may
establish. Therefore 'the "history of mankind" must always be
studied in connection with the history of industry and commerce'
(MEW 3:30).

5. The necessity of interacting with other human beings has
led man to develop language as an instrument of social, productive exchange. Language and the consciousness from which it is
inseparable are at the same time social products and social
instruments, intimately bound to the existing level of social
production.

This then was Marx's formulation of the views which he used
to orientate himself in studying 'real, active men' along with
their 'ideological reflexes and echoes' which are the 'necessary
sub-limitations' of the life process (MEW 3:26).

[II.] As Marx saw it, the mode of production was a determing factor not only for the material existence of the individual but also for the manner in which he expressed his life: 'As individuals express their life, so are they. What they are thus coincides with their production, both with *what* they produce and *how* they produce as well' (MEW 3:21). As a result: 'It is not consciousness which determines life, but life which determines consciousness' (MEW 3:27).

Marx perceived that in contemporary society the productive forces and their products did not necessarily belong to those whose task it was to work the productive forces. He examined therefore the relation between these productive forces and their ownership, i.e. property relations. Marx found that private ownership of the means of production was necessary at certain industrial levels. Not until industry is very highly developed on a broad scale does a conflict arise between the property relations and the instruments of production (cf. MEW 3:66).

For the optimal functioning of the highly developed system of industrial production, 'division of labour' is essential. The labour force necessarily becomes specialised and one-sided. The individual can maintain his life, i.e. enter into the production system, only by performing a specialised activity and thus deforming his nature which is manifold:

For such an individual the few remaining desires, rooted in the constitution of the human body rather than in his mundane inter-action, are expressed only by *reaction*, i.e. they take on in their restricted development the same one-sided and brutal nature as his thinking ... and express themselves violently, passionately, and with the most brutal repression of ordinary and natural desires, leading thus to further domination of the thought processes (MEW 3:246f.).

This division of labour leads, moreover, to the separation of mental or intellectual activity from material or physical. Thus, an attempt is made to separate 'thought' and 'action' into two different and independent spheres, whereas in reality 'the production of ideas, of mental images and of the consciousness is directly interwoven in the material activity and material exchange of men, the language of real life' (MEW 3:26).

Basing themselves on this pretended separation, the left-Hegelians and other philosophical schools had attributed an independent existence to ideas, concepts and other products of the mind and maintained that ideas were the chains hindering

man from progress and development. Marx attacked with particular sharpness the Hegelian philosophy, last of the scholarly
tradition in Germany 'whose centre of interest is not real, not
even political, but pure thought' (MEW 3:39). All ideological
and religious systems, Marx continued, had their roots in the
material world; the ruling thoughts were the thoughts of the
ruling class: 'i.e. the class which represents the ruling *material*
power in society is at the same time its dominating *intellectual*
power' (MEW 3:46). The state as well represents 'the will of
the class in control of the means of production. If it loses its
sovereignty, it is not just the will which has changed but the
material existence and life of the individuals and their will is
simply a result of the foregoing elements' (MEW 3:312).

[III.] Marx held that social theory as developed up to this
point was meaningful and worthwhile only if it provided the
motivation for the revolutionary practice which would change
the inhuman conditions exposed by the social analysis. His
transformation of scientific theory into a weapon in the struggle
for social, human emancipation may be summarised as follows:
1. At a certain stage in technological development of the productive forces which secure man's material existence, these forces
are turned into means of destruction.
2. One class arises under such conditions, which lacks all means
for self-expression, having only the most inhuman relation to
its labour and the products of its labour. Only this class is
capable of the all-encompassing effort to regain its humanity by
appropriating the *ensemble* of the instruments of production in
the name of all humanity. This class therefore possesses a communist consciousness, which may be shared by members of other
classes who are aware of and understand the situation of the
dispossessed class.
3. The conditions of technological development are dictated by
the dominating class using an idealised state for support and
enforcement of its will. The proletariat, finding itself in direct
opposition to the existing collective form of individual self-
expression, i.e. to the state, must overthrow the state 'in order to
realise its personality' (MEW 3:77).
4. The conflict arising through a situation in which the conditions of everyone are dictated by the dominating class leads to a
revolutionary struggle.
5. In contrast to all previous revolutions which were political

and led merely to the construction of new political institutions, the communist revolution can be brought about only by opposing the entire system of production based on private property and culminating in the apparatus of the state.

6. Revolution is the driving force in history. When the productive forces, composed of both the technological means of production and the labour force, are hindered in their development by the form of social organisation, by the property relations and therefore by the concentration of ownership in the hands of one particular class, this conflict will erupt in revolution. The exploited, dispossessed class will cease to tolerate its circumstances: a change in its behaviour will revolutionise the whole production process which depends on the submission of this class for its effective operation.

7. Such a revolution is the basis for founding a new society, where the expression of the individual's life corresponds to the creation of his material life, enables him to develop as an all-round human being and rise above his primitive nature:

The Communist society is the only society in which the creative and free development of the individual is no empty phrase. It is rendered possible by the solidarity of the individuals, a solidarity which is produced in part by the economic preconditions, partly by the necessary solidarity for the free development of all, and finally in the universal mode of activity of the individual on the basis of the existing productive forces (MEW 3 : 425).

Society will be an association of individuals who realise that their personal freedom and development can be attained only in a community where division of labour has been abolished, where property relations no longer prohibit their universal expression of self:

The exclusive concentration of artistic talent in particular individuals and its repression in the broad masses is a result of the division of labour . . . In a communist society there are no artists, but, rather, men who among other things paint as well (MEW 3 : 379).

In September Marx again resumed his reading in economics, excerpting from works by Owen, Quesnay and Bray. Through Engels he learned of Proudhon's forthcoming book *Système des contradictions économiques ou Philosophie de la misère* which was still in the press. Engels sent him a detailed outline of the Proudhonian economic solution to the *misère* of the working class, a plan 'to make money out of nothing and bring heaven closer to the workers', and he remarked:

Just imagine: proletarians are to *save up* to buy small shares of stock! ... What these people have in mind is nothing less than *to buy up all of France* ... and later perhaps the whole world by dint of proletarian savings ... Blokes who cannot manage to keep six sous in their pockets for drinks want to buy up *toute la belle France* out of their savings (Sept. 18).

Marx's first opportunity to acquaint himself with Proudhon's book came in December. Immediately thereafter he wrote a lengthy critique of it in a letter to Annenkov, which may be considered as a sort of preamble to his rejoinder of 1847 in *Misère de la Philosophie*. Since the manuscript of *The German Ideology* had been abandoned 'to the mice', the Russian Annenkov was the first person apart from Engels whom Marx instructed on his materialist theory of history and social change. While criticising Proudhon's book, which he found 'very bad indeed', Marx summarised certain essential points developed at length in *The German Ideology*. The history of human society, Marx pointed out, 'is nothing other than the history of the development of individuals' and not the history of ideas, as the German thinkers would have us believe. Proudhon failed to understand that ideas and abstract categories rest on the material basis of human productive activity as well and are as historical and transitory as the social relations they reflect. Since Proudhon therefore took abstractions to be 'the primordial cause', he was unable to recognise that economic categories represent the laws of a particular epoch of social development and are not eternal. His own bourgeois mentality hindered him from imagining a social order in which the laws of bourgeois production had been surpassed. He 'must justify in theory what he is in practice', and Marx characterised him therefore as 'the scientific interpreter of the French petit-bourgeoisie' (Dec. 28).

By the end of the year the Correspondence Committee in Brussels had succeeded in establishing numerous contacts with groups in England and on the Continent. George Harney and the German immigrant group under Karl Schapper in London declared their solidarity with the Brussels organisation. Contacts were established, moreover, in Wuppertal, Kiel and in Silesia in Germany. In France rivalry existed within the three sections of the League of the Just, whose members were divided into supporters of Proudhon and his German translator Karl Grün and the followers of Wilhelm Weitling. In August Engels had been sent to Paris to win support for the revolutionary Marxian concept of working men's organisations and to aid these artisans' and workmen's groups in establishing themselves as an association. By October it was clear that Engels's efforts had not been in vain: he met regularly with groups of tanners, joiners and tailors to discuss historical problems and explain current economic questions. 'What they come to learn at these weekly meetings is drummed into the heads of their listeners at the Sunday meetings,' Engels wrote to the Brussels Committee (Sept. 16).

In December Edgar Marx, first son of Jenny and Karl, was born. He was named after Jenny's brother who was at the time one of their most intimate friends and a member of the Brussels Committee.

1847 The publisher Leske formally annulled the contract for Marx's 'Economics' in February, threatening to take drastic measures should he fail to repay the advance immediately. Marx, however, was preoccupied with writing a critical reply to Proudhon's recent book and with the affairs of the Brussels Correspondence Committee.

Without consulting the Brussels Correspondence Committee —with whom they enjoyed close but unofficial relations—the London Committee of the League of the Just decided to call an international communist congress for May of 1847, a step which of course caused the Brussels group to feel it had been slighted. Thus, in an effort to re-establish an atmosphere of harmonious co-operation, the League sent Joseph Moll as its ambassador to Brussels in February. Moll was charged with inviting Marx, Engels and other Committee members to join the League and to assist them in reorganising their association and in redefining its goals. The offer was accepted in view of the considerable influence which the League enjoyed in London, where it directed two large workers' educational societies with 500 other members of different nationalities. The First International Congress was held from June 2 to 9 in London. The Brussels Committee was represented by Wilhelm Wolff and the Paris Committee by Engels, while Marx was prevented from attending by financial difficulties. Although this congress did not resolve all the members' differences, they agreed to the founding of a new organisation to be called the Communist League [*Kommunisten-bund*] and drafted a credo, which was distributed to all the committees for discussion. This paper, written in Engels's hand, was prefaced with the slogan 'Working Men of All Countries, Unite!' which replaced the League's old motto of universal brotherhood.

In July Marx's critique of Proudhon, entitled *The Poverty of Philosophy. An Answer to the 'Philosophy of Poverty' by M. Proudhon*, was issued in French by the Brussels publisher C. G. Vogler. The first of Marx's writings on economics to appear in print, this work not only treated the 'poverty' of philosophy as a means for comprehending and solving the problems posed by modern industrial society, it also analysed the immediate situation of the European working classes, its causes and, in Marx's view, its inevitable outcome.

All progress had resulted from class antagonisms and society had been industrialised thanks to a system of individual exchange, free production and wage-labour. Social relations, founded on the needs of the production process, had required the exploitation of one class by another and the misery and suffering of the greatest part of mankind. The wages paid to the working man correspond to their needs as part of the productive force and not to their needs as human beings: what they received sufficed to reproduce and maintain their kind. Commercial exchange coloured every aspect of social existence, whether moral or material; everything is valued in terms of money, is alienated, becomes part of the market trade:

... all the things which men had previously regarded as inalienable became the objects of exchange ... virtue, love, conviction, know-ledge, conscience, etc. ... in a word, everything became part of trade (*Oeuvres* 1 : 12).

Marx, who saw in the proletariat the complete negation of bourgeois society and the debasement of human nature, applied to this situation the Hegelian dialectic and concluded that in this negation was the force to overcome the two antagonistic elements and establish mankind at a higher level of social development. The proletarian emancipation would not be the result of socialist theorising or utopian-system-building, but of the present contradiction between the social organisation and the instruments of production, the most powerful of which is the proletariat, the 'revolutionary class' itself. At the point when the productive forces have developed sufficiently to create acute class struggles, the proletarians 'no longer need to search in their minds for a science, they need only take note of what is happening before their eyes and make themselves the organ of this change' (*Oeuvres* 1:93).

Proudhon desired to eliminate social antagonisms by replacing wages with a value system based on hours of labour, or 'constituted value', and exchangeable for gold or silver. Marx remarked that this was essentially a reform in wage-distribution which merely gave money a new form. He pointed out that 'Every commodity whose value is constituted on the basis of labour time will always be exchangeable, always be money ... Money is not a thing but a social relation' (*Oeuvres* 1:53). Only when the social structure itself is changed can money be eliminated. Labour time, moreover, is under the capitalist system of production the measure of value and therefore the 'formula for the modern slavery of the working man' (*Oeuvres* 1:27).

The upheaval of the proletariat, in contrast to all previous revolutions, will eliminate 'what is commonly called political power, for political power is exactly equal to an official compendium of the antagonisms in civil society' (*Oeuvres* 1:136). The revolution is prepared through the organisation of the working class in permanent coalition or trade-unions whose dual purpose is to put a stop to competition among the workers themselves and to rival the bourgeoisie for political power. While destroying the traditional social forms, the revolution will conserve 'the fruits of civilisation, the acquired productive forces' (MEW 4:410) in order to establish a higher social order. Time in this new society will no longer be the criterion determining production and value, but the usefulness of an object for human needs and self-expression:

What is produced today through the interaction of capital and competitive labour will be accomplished through an agreement relating the sum-total of the production forces to the sum-total of existing needs, after the present relation between capital and labour has been abolished (*Oeuvres* 1 : 50).

In September the monthly *Westphälisches Dampfboot* published a chapter taken from the unpublished *German Ideology* and devoted to Karl Grün's book, *Die soziale Bewegung in Frankreich und Belgien* (1845). Marx criticised Grün for plagiarising Hess and other socialist thinkers and for, consciously or unconsciously, falsifying the authors he presumed to explain in his book. Marx depicted Grün as vain and boastful, priding himself on being Proudhon's teacher and critical of Cabet's narrowmindedness. In fact Grün had 'read as little of the Saint-Simonians as of Saint-Simon himself', namely nothing, and was most inaccurate when copying from the works he did read on Saint-Simon and his followers (MEW 3 : 492f.). Marx had little esteem for Grün for employing the 'empty ideological phrases of German philosophy', while imagining himself superior to the 'superficial French' socialists who examined the real circumstances of man's material existence (MEW 4 : 492f.).

In an article against the communism of the *Rheinischer Beobachter*, published anonymously in the *DBrZ* on September 12, Marx exposed the fraud of a government socialism propagated by Prussia in the interests of the proletariat, and of income tax as a measure which would necessarily lead to communism. He ridiculed the *Beobachter's* proposal to offer the people 'panem et religionem' in place of 'panem et circenses', ignoring the fact 'that the proletariat expects no one's help but its own' (MEW 4 : 194). The people, and especially the communists among them, are aware that 'the liberal bourgeoisie is only pursuing its own interest, that one cannot rely on its sympathy for the masses' (MEW 4 : 193). The proletariat nevertheless, supported, the bourgeois struggle for liberalism in political representation, knowing that bourgeois freedoms would help it in turn to gain recognition and strength as a political party. Religion, by contrast, had never served the interests of the proletariat. Christianity, in particular, preached the necessity of class domination and appeased the oppressed masses with promises of heavenly recompense and with clarity. It justified worldly crime instead of looking for the roots of crime and misery in actual social circumstances. While Christianity taught him to be cowardly, humble, meek, 'the proletarian who refuses to be treated like

scum needs his courage, his self-respect, his pride and his sense
of independence even more than he needs his bread' (MEW
4:200).

In October and November the *DBrZ* published in instalments
an article by Marx entitled 'The Moralising Critique and the
Criticising Moralism. A Contribution to German Cultural
History. Against Carl Heinzen.' Again, Marx espoused the cause
of the proletariat, in its struggle to wrest political power from the
bourgeoisie. The first need of the proletariat was unification. To
this end the liberal bourgeoisie granted a number of concessions
which facilitated the political organisation of the proletariat as
a class. While the proletarians were willing to support the cause
of the bourgeois revolution as a precondition for their own revolution 'not for an instant can they consider it to be their final
goal' (MEW 4:352). In preparing its social upheaval, the working
class 'must first produce the material conditions of a new
society' (MEW 4:338) and neither good will nor purely intellectual effort can spare it this task.

At the beginning of August the Correspondence Committee
in Brussels was reorganised into a branch of the newly founded
Communist League. This group, which also assumed the League's
regional directorate in Belgium, elected Marx president of the
local organisation and member of the directorate. Later in the
month Marx founded with Engels the Brussels German Working
Men's Society, an open and public organisation under the control
of the secret Communist League, which served as its recruiting
organ. Marx participated—as a liberal democrat—in a Free Trade
Congress held in Brussels September 16-18. Although he had
prepared a speech on protective tariffs, free trade and the working
class, he was refused the opportunity to speak. He consequently
later elaborated the speech into an article published in the
Brussels newspaper *Atelier démocratique* (Sept. 29) and translated into English for publication in *The Northern Star* (Oct. 9).
Marx declared himself in favour of free trade in the interests of
the working class which wanted a betterment of its condition
and not a continuation of the *status quo*. Free trade would
expand the territory where the laws of capitalist production
produced their inevitable conflicts and antagonisms:

from the uniting of all these contradictions into a single group, where
they stand face to face, will result the struggle which will itself

eventuate in the emancipation of the proletarians (MEGA 6:431).

Marx was obliged to leave Brussels for a short time at the end of September. He travelled to Holland where he again engaged in discussion with his mother's relatives on the matter of his paternal inheritance. In his absence the *Association démocratique* was founded in an effort to turn the 'miserable little working men's union' into an association which would rival the Fraternal Democrats in scale and size. Engels was elected vice-president pending Marx's return, for the group held Marx to be the only person able to represent the German democrats in Brussels.

Engels, who returned to Paris in mid-October, was invited by the directorate of the local League organisation to prepare a 'catechism' containing the basic tenets of the communist programme. He composed thereupon a series of 25 questions and answers which he entitled 'Principles of Communism', explaining to Marx that he thought of it more as a manifesto than a catechism 'since it has to deal more or less with history, the old form is not at all suitable' (Nov. 23-24). The 'Principles' treated the history of the industrial working class, differentiated this class from all others, present and past, and recounted how the development of social antagonisms between classes leads to crises which will eventually erupt in revolution. This revolution 'will take place in all civilised countries at the same time, i.e. at least in England, America, France and Germany, and will develop according to the degree of the given country's industrial advancement, its wealth and productive forces' (MEW 4:374). He insisted, further, on the evolutionary nature of this revolution which would have nothing in common with conspiracies which are 'not only useless, but also harmful'. Revolutions cannot be made arbitrarily, Engels stated, 'but they have always been, everywhere and at every time, the necessary consequence of circumstances thoroughly independent of the will and leadership of individuals and entire classes' (MEW 4:372).

Marx, now vice-president of the *Association démocratique*, was enthusiastic about the activity developing in Brussels. In little Belgium, he wrote to Georg Herwegh, 'there is more to be done in the way of immediate propaganda than in France.' Although the country was small, public activity proved to be 'an endlessly refreshing stimulus for everyone' (Oct. 26-27,

IISH). Marx was commissioned to represent the Brussels section of the League at the 2nd Congress in London (Nov. 29-Dec. 10), while Engels attended as the delegate of the Paris group. During the Congress the League's statutes were adopted and Engels and Marx appointed to compose a manifesto. The working of the new statutes attests to the influence which the two friends exercised over the other delegates: whereas the League's purpose had previously been conceived of as 'the diffusion and the most rapid realisation of the theory of communal property', the statutes now read:

The purpose of the League is to bring about the fall of the bourgeoisie and the rule of the proletariat, to abolish the old society based on class differences and to found a new society without classes and without private property (MEW 4:596).

In London Marx attended a banquet held by the Fraternal Democrats in memory of the Polish rebellion of 1830 (Nov. 29). In the name of the *Association démocratique* he invited those present to participate in an international democratic congress for the coming year. In his address Marx exhorted the triumph of the working class as the basis for real unity between the peoples of Poland, England, Germany and France. England, as the most developed industrial country and the most fraught with crises, was destined to be the battlefield where the decisive triumph of the proletariat would be achieved:

Thus it is not in Poland that Poland will be liberated but rather in England. And you, Chartists, it is not your task to pronounce pious wishes for the liberation of nations. Destroy the enemies within your own country and you may then enjoy the glory of having destroyed all of previous society (MEW 4:417).

Before leaving England, Marx also spoke privately with the Chartist leaders Harney and Ernest Jones. Harney subsequently informed Marx that the Chartists and the German Working Men's Association had accepted the invitation to participate in an international democratic congress.

At the end of the year Marx held a series of lectures for the members of the German Working Men's Society in Brussels on 'Wages'. He later developed the thoughts expounded there into an article published in instalments in the NRhZ beginning in

April 1849. Among Marx's posthumous manuscripts a paper
was found which is assumed to be a preparatory draft for one
of these lectures. Here Marx exposes the fundamental relation
between capital and labour which has both a negative and
a positive aspect. On the one hand, capital engenders the
misery of the working class; on the other, it brings material
progress, developing the productive forces to a point at which
rebellion against the existing property relations will be inevitable.
Capital demands a maximum available labour force in order to
keep wages down. Overpopulation is therefore favourable to
the development of capital. At the same time the proletariat in
its misery can hardly avoid excessive reproduction, 'for its
situation makes the sexual instinct its principal source of pleasure
and favourises the one-sided development of this instinct' (MEW
4:553). The bourgeoisie, which sees this excessive population
growth as a 'natural phenomenon', is able to ignore its own role
in creating the misery of the proletariat and 'can observe the
proletariat reduced by famine just as it observes other natural
phenomena, without being moved, and considers the misery of
the proletariat as its own doing, to be punished as such' (ibid.).
Marx reduced his investigations on capital to the general
statements that: 'As the productive forces grow, that part of
productive capital which is transformed into machines and raw
materials, i.e. into capital as such, grows in infinitely greater
proportion than the part allocated to wage-labour' (MEW
4:551). The growing number of working men consequently has
to share a proportionately smaller part of the capital available
to the whole working class for its sustenance and reproduction.
The purpose of the working men's organisations is to prevent
the bitter competition which would naturally result from such
circumstances and, moreover, to organise the proletariat in the
struggle to overthrow the rule of capital: Marx described the
revolutionary activity of these working men's groups:

... the best-paid workers form the most coalitions and spend all they
can spare from their wages in order to establish political associations
in industry and cover the costs of this movement ... from their
revolutionary activity they derive a maximum of delight in life
(MEW 4:555).

1848 On January 9 Marx spoke to the *Association démocratique*
on the question of free trade. His speech, published by the
Association in February as a separate pamphlet, was reported
in the *DBrZ* to have made that meeting one of the most interesting held. Marx defined free trade as 'the freedom for capital to
crush the working man' (MEGA 6 : 446). Protectionism, however,
was no better. While furthering the development of particular
industries in one country and promoting free competition,
protectionism still left the country dependent on universal trade
and therefore on the free exchange system. For capital to grow
and produce the class conflicts which would lead ultimately to
social revolution, there must be free exchange on the widest
possible basis: 'If capital remains stationary, industry will not
simply remain at a standstill, it will decline and its first victim
in this case will be the working man' (MEGA 6 : 441). As it
grows capital becomes more and more concentrated, creating a
greater usage of machines and division of labour. The worker's
craftsmanship and special qualifications become superfluous and
he is left performing a simple task which requires a minimum of
training. The worker exists therefore only in his function as
a primitive productive force, and he may be easily replaced.
Marx showed that, unless conventional economic policies be
renounced entirely, the working class will ultimately be hit at
full force by the economic laws governing the prevailing free
exchange system. The results of such a collision must necessarily
be the destruction of wage-labour and capital.

On March 4, the London *Northern Star* published a résumé of
a February meeting held by the *Association démocratique*, at
which members unanimously adopted the proposal for an international democratic congress in Brussels during September. The
Star noted that the association was creating considerable interest
among the working men of Ghent, Belgium's chief manufacturing city, and in the provinces as well.

In memory of the Cracow uprising of 1846, a meeting was held
in Brussels on February 22, at which Marx and Engels were
invited to speak. Marx underlined the social nature of the
questions which led to open rebellion in Poland. The special
significance of the Cracow uprising was that it 'identified the
national cause with the cause of democracy and the emancipation
of the oppressed class' (MEW 4 : 521). Because Poland had taken
the initiative in fighting for this triple cause, its emancipation

was 'the point of honour for all European democrats' (MEW 4:522).

After Engels's return to Paris towards the end of 1847, Marx continued to work on the manifesto commissioned by the London Central Committee of the Communist League, which sent him a reminder on January 24 demanding delivery of the manuscript by February 1. The text was finished in the first days of February and was published the same month in London by the Working Men's Educational Association. Although Engels's assistance is indisputable, the final version was the work of Marx alone. In expressing his scientific arguments and moral postulates for the revolutionary action of the working class, Marx achieved in this pamphlet a terseness of language which is unique in his writing. Despite the sharp observations on the state of modern industrial society, the *Manifesto* is by no means a dispassionate scientific discourse. In every line of this call of action can be read Marx's passionate adherence to the cause of the oppressed classes. As in *The German Ideology*, we find here the same elements of empirical sociological study mingled with his views of the future conduct of society. A slight echo of the League's old 'catechism' is heard here in the use of the question-and-answer form to expose the communist standpoint on the essential issues.

Marx defined the bourgeois, propertied class in industrial society, as being itself 'revolutionary' in the sense that it 'can not exist without continually revolutionising the instruments of production, consequently the production relations and finally all social relations whatsoever' (MEW 4:456). Its advent signaled a more sober view of life and of human relations; men came to realise the material-pecuniary basis of their existence:

The bourgeoisie has profaned every occupation hitherto honoured and respected with reverend awe. It has converted the physician, the lawyer, the priest, the poet and the scientist into wage labourers (MEW 4:465).

Henceforth human relations are calculated in terms of blatant self-interest and financial gain. The family is affected as well: the bourgeois sees in his wife a 'mere instrument of production' and in his children potential wage-earners (MEW 4:478).

By contrast, the proletarian has nothing in common with the ruling class—neither property, nor social power, nor national identity, and 'for him law, religion, morality are just so many

bourgeois prejudices hiding bourgeois interests behind them'
(MEW 4:472). The proletarian lives at a mechanistic level of
existence, since the work demanded of him requires only the
simplest and most monotonous of efforts. Deprived of the
opportunity of expressing himself as a human being in his
entirety, the working man is deprived of his individuality.

The revolutionary aspect of the proletarian situation lies in
the fact that the uniformity of their tasks and their remuneration
makes the oppression and the interests of working men everywhere the same. Moreover, the bourgeoisie, which is dependent
on the masses for support in the struggle against the vestiges of
feudalism, or against rival ruling classes in other nations, grants
it certain political freedoms and a general education, important
aids for its struggle against the bourgeoisie.

The industrial development process leads inevitably to crises
of overproduction, which the bourgeoisie overcomes only by
recourse to the opening of new markets or the destruction of
productive forces. The final crisis will come, however, when
markets can no longer be extended and new territories discovered.
It will then be the proletariat which takes into its hands the
reorganisation of society: 'What the bourgeoisie therefore produces above all else, is its own gravediggers' (MEW 4:474).

Basing himself on Engels's 'Principles of Communism', Marx
enumerated ten measures which the proletariat would employ
during the transitory period of reorganising social and property
relations with the ultimate goal of eliminating class distinctions,
the first step towards a communist society:

In place of the old bourgeois society with its classes and class
antagonisms we shall have an association in which the free development of each individual is the condition for the free development
of all (MEW 4:482).

The measures which Marx set down included: expropriation of
landed property and abolition of inheritance rights; state monopoly of credit, means of transport, and communication; heavy
progressive income tax; equal obligation to work for all and the
combination of education with industrial production; cultivation
of wastelands and the abolition of the distinctions between town
and country. The fundamental issue in the actual proletarian
struggle is one of property understood as bourgeois property, i.e.
of capital.

When capital therefore is converted into common property, into the property of all the members of society, this does not mean that personal property is transformed into social property. It is merely the social nature of property that is changed. It loses its class character (MEW 4 : 476).

The agent of this revolutionary change will be the entire proletariat, not the communists for or in the name of the proletariat. The communists are distinguished by their international orientation in contrast to the individual proletarian who fights a national battle against a particular bourgeoisie. The communist, moreover, possesses theoretical understanding of the historical development and of the ultimate course of the movement (cf. MEW 4 : 474). The ranks of the communists contain defectors from other classes, persons who have come to espouse the proletarian cause, knowing that their interests will also be furthered by a radical social transformation. The theoretical tenets of communism are not inventions of ideologists or of utopian reformers. Rather,

They simply express in general terms the real relationships of the existing class struggle. Property is the key to the social and production reform which the proletariat wishes to accomplish. The key to the future communist society will be labour, not labour as a means of increasing accumulated labour, which is capital, but accumulated labour as a means of expanding, enriching and advancing the life process of working men (MEW 4 : 476).

A fortnight before the *Manifesto* appeared in London, Marx collaborated on a reply of the *Association* to the Fraternal Democrats, congratulating the English Chartists 'for the steps taken ... to arrive at last at a close alliance between the Irish people and that of Great Britain', an important advance of the democratic cause (Feb. 13; MEGA 6 : 652f.).

At the end of February preparations were under way in Brussels to stage an armed republican uprising. The immigrants added moral and material assistance to the movement and Marx, who had recently come into part of his paternal inheritance, was able to help financially. The *Association*, enthused by the revolutionary events in France, addressed a letter to George Harney of the *Northern Star* and to the Fraternal Democrats, declaring that in Belgium efforts were being made for 'peaceful but energetic agitation in order to obtain through the channels *proper* to the political institutions of Belgium the advantages which the French people have just conquered' (MEGA 6:655). On the same day (Feb. 28) they also sent an address to the newly installed provisional government in Paris with congratulations for the unexpected progress made, in the name of all humanity, towards true democracy.

At the beginning of March Marx received an invitation, signed by Ferdinand Flocon of the provisional French government, to return to live in Paris:

Stout-hearted, loyal Marx! The soil of the French Republic is a refuge for all friends of freedom. The power of tyrants sent you into exile; free France opens her gates to you. To you and to all who are fighting for the sacred cause of brotherhood among all peoples (MEW 14:676).

When news came of the revolution on the Continent, the Central Office of the Communist League in London transferred its authority to Brussels. The Belgian police, however, began hunting down political refugees and activists and on March 3 Marx received a command signed by the royal powers to leave the country within 24 hours. The Brussels section of the League was dissolved and Marx empowered to reconstitute the group in Paris. During the night of March 3-4, while preparing to flee to France, Marx was taken into custody for questioning, held for several hours and then expelled over the Belgian frontier into France. He arrived in Paris on March 5. Jenny Marx was arrested the same night upon presenting herself at police headquarters in search of her husband. After several hours in a cell with three prostitutes, she was led before a judge for questioning and finally released in the early afternoon.

In Paris Marx immediately set to work reestablishing the Central Office of the Communist League and was elected to its presidency on March 10. The League decided to found a German Working Men's Club whose task would be to educate and prepare the exiled Germans for the return to the homeland. The 300-400 Germans whom the club attracted were 'armed' for their return with propaganda material on the communist movement, taking with them the *Manifesto* and a fly-sheet entitled 'Requisitions of the Communist Party in Germany', which was restricted to that country's specific and immediate problems. The list of requisitions was headed by the most compelling need of the

39 German *Länder*: unity. For the rest it followed the points set down in the *Manifesto* as regards state appropriation of privately-owned farm lands, of the means of transport and credit institutions, while omitting industrial property (Grünberg, p. 91). At Mainz on the Rhine local members of the League founded a Workers' Educational Society in order to co-ordinate the functioning of a larger number of clubs whose founding they anticipated after the return of the numerous refugees abroad. Early in April Marx also left Paris, returning to Cologne via Mainz where he conferred with his associates of the League on immediate organisational questions.

In Cologne plans were already afoot to publish a new daily newspaper, the *Neue Rheinische Zeitung*. Support was volunteered by both communists and democrats, who turned the organisation over to Marx immediately after his arrival and appointed him editor-in-chief (April 10-11). Engels joined Marx in Cologne on May 21 with the intention of settling there and collaborating on the paper. In its first issue, dated June 1, the NRhZ published a sharp critique by Engels of the Frankfurt National Assembly which caused a great number of the paper's democratic shareholders to withdraw their financial support. Marx continued the critique of the Frankfurt liberals with a leading article on June 7, opposing both the liberal programme and the manifesto of the radical democrats. Marx held that Germany could not achieve unification simply by issuing decrees or proclamations but that 'German unity and the German constitution as well can result only from a movement whose decisive elements will be, in equal measure, the internal conflicts and the war with the East' (MEW 5 : 4).

The war with the East—Russia being understood as the 'East' —became one of the pet topics of the NRhZ along with the liberalism of the Frankfurt parliamentarians and the conservative fears of the German bourgeoisie. Marx viewed the March Revolution as 'only a semi-revolution', the beginning of a long revolutionary movement (June 14). However, he recognised the value of the democratic freedoms, such as that of the press, which had been won and had made the clandestine activities of the League superfluous. The League was therefore disbanded in June.

For the most part Marx's 1848 articles in the NRhZ were written on topics related to the recent revolutionary insurgencies and to the currents of democratic endeavours everywhere in Europe. Marx was particularly aggressive in attacking the German bourgeoisie, as, for instance, in the article 'The Prague Uprising' (June 18). Here he took the Germans to task for allowing themselves to be used as an instrument for oppressing other nations and peoples, for their indecisiveness, their cowardice and lack of unity.

In a brief editorial note on the June Revolution in Paris, Marx announced that events in France had 'developed into the greatest revolution that has ever taken place, the revolution of the proletariat against the bourgeoisie' (June 27). The following day an article appeared by Marx which compared the battle of the Parisians with that of the Roman slaves against their masters and with the 1834 insurrection in Lyon. This standpoint again aroused the displeasure of a large segment of the paper's financial backers, who quickly withdrew their support. In an article, written jointly with Engels and entitled 'Arrests', the Frankfurt liberals were exhorted to act energetically and decisively on the problem of German unity and democracy (July 5), and on July 12 Marx urged them to make use of extra-parliamentary measures, i.e. a revolutionary war against Russia, in order to 'cleanse itself of the sins of the past'. In an article on August 1 Marx defined the source of conflict between the bourgeoisie and the other social classes as the 'monopoly of capital' : 'It is precisely this monopoly which is *specifically modern* and produces modern class antagonisms; and it is the specific task of the 19th century to find a solution to these antagonisms'.

At a general meeting of the Democratic Society on July 21 Wilhelm Weitling spoke in favour of separating the political movement for democracy from the social. He also advocated a personal dictatorship, within the movement, of the 'most insightful' members. Marx was given the opportunity to reply to Weitling's suggestions at the next meeting on August 4. Defending the founding principles of the society, Marx underlined the importance of a political struggle led by the masses and explained that the intermingling of the political with the social aspects would facilitate victory. Marx wished to see at the head of the movement, not Weitling's corps of élite, but 'heterogenous elements whose task it would be to elaborate a line of efficient direction through the exchange of ideas' (quoted according to H. Meyer, 'Karl Marx und die Revolution von

1848', *Historische Zeitschrift*, Munich, Dec. 1951, p. 524.

Having been without nationality since he renounced his Prussian citizenship in 1845, Marx applied for the citizenship of the city of Cologne. The request was immediately granted by the city council (April), but vetoed by the Royal Prussian Government in Berlin. Marx wrote a letter of protest to the Minister of the Interior on August 12 without, however, effecting a change in the government's decision. A commentary on this affair was published in the NRhZ on September 5.

August and September were months of major political crisis in Germany due first to the ministerial affair in Prussia and to popular uprising against the Malmö Armistice at Frankfurt-am-Main. During this period Marx travelled to Vienna and to Berlin on a double mission (Aug. 23-Sept. 12). While establishing contacts among left-wing German democrats and the Vienna working men's organisations, he also made efforts to raise financial support for the NRhZ. In Berlin he spoke with Karl Ludwig d'Ester, Gustav Julius and Jung, met with his friend of university days C. F. Köppen and with Bakunin. In Vienna he conversed privately with leading radicals of the revolutionary movement and addressed the working men's organisations and democratic societies. He lectured on 'Wage Labour and Capital' to the First Vienna Working Men's Club on September 2.

Following his return to Cologne Marx wrote in the NRhZ that in Prussia a potentially revolutionary crisis was building which would lead to the 'unavoidable war with Russia' (Sept. 14). When news of the street battles in Frankfurt reached Cologne, the paper published a proclamation in favour of the rebels and solicited subscriptions to support them and their families. (Sept. 20). Fear of similar battles led the authorities in Cologne to declare the city in a state of siege on September 27; all democratic institutions and organs were suspended indefinitely, including the NRhZ; and other measures were taken by the military in order to repress popular democratic sentiment. Four of the paper's editors, among them Engels, fled Cologne in face of threatened police prosecution and sought asylum either in Switzerland or Paris. The state of siege persisted until October 3, but financial difficulties kept the NRhZ from reappearing before the 12th.

The paper continued its energetic support of revolutionary activity. On November 1 it published a call for volunteers to constitute a corps which would be sent to aid the revolution in Vienna. Marx followed closely in his articles the events in the Austrian capital and, when defeat was imminent, concluded that the German bourgeoisie was incapable of emancipating itself from feudal-aristocratic domination and that democracy would triumph only in a struggle against the bourgeoisie. He saw but one way left to achieve a social revolution:

There is but one means for shortening, simplifying, concentrating the murderous death pangs of the old society and the bloody labour pains of the new, *only one means*: *revolutionary terrorism* (Nov. 7).

As a gesture of opposition to the despotic measures taken by the Brandenburg ministry Marx proposed that the Prussian citizens refuse payment of taxes. On November 15 the Berlin National Assembly actually issued a proclamation to withhold all further payment. The NRhZ urged its readers to support this measure and to form local militias paid for by the communities or by donations. In 'The Bourgeoisie and the Counter-revolution', which appeared during December, Marx reviewed the stages of the revolutionary movement in Prussia. Again he stigmatised the cowardice and indecision of the German bourgeoisie which had caused it to betray both its own revolution and its allies in the other classes who were all struggling to overthrow feudal rule. The choice was now clear: either a feudal-absolutist counter-revolution or the social-republican revolution. There could be no reckoning with a 'purely bourgeois revolution'. For the coming year Marx predicted: 'revolutionary insurgency of the French working class, world war' (Jan. 1).

1849 Under Marx's editorship, the NRhZ continued its sharp attacks on the bourgeoisie, denouncing in particular the latest measure of the local authorities to control the employees on municipal projects in Cologne through the introduction of 'work passports'. Marx termed this a 'historical document of the cynicism of the German bourgeoisie', evidence that the Germans were in no way inferior to the British in their 'brazen mistreatment of the working class' (Jan. 5). Seized by an irrational fear of the revolution which it had itself prepared through industrial development, the bourgeoisie now permitted a constitution to be passed which ignored the demands of democracy entirely and drove 'the entire nation back into medieval barbarism' (Jan. 22).

The March Revolution had produced, in Marx's view, only counter-revolution, 'the most extensive, most decisive, the bloodiest and the most violent' of all history (Jan. 28). However, it was soon to produce a reaction as well: 'a new universal and victorious counter-blow' to be struck by the 'three most radical and most democratic classes', the petit-bourgeoisie, the peasantry and 'the specifically *red* class', the proletariat, in concert (Feb. 1). While Marx was assailing the German bourgeoisie, Engels wrote an article against the 'slavic barbarians', in which he sanctioned the use of 'red terror' to avenge the oppression of the Magyars by the Slavs (Jan. 13).

On January 15 at the committee meeting of the Working Men's Club, Marx attempted to persuade the members to participate in the coming parliamentary elections. From a practical standpoint, he argued, it was important that members of the democratic opposition should win seats in parliament in order to carry on the political fight against feudalism, 'to prevent the victory of our common enemy, the absolute monarch' (Jan. 21).

The NRhZ went to court twice in February. As one of the accused parties, Marx spoke for the defence on February 7 against charges of libelling a public servant and the following day against charges of inciting to open rebellion. In the first speech Marx pointed out that freedom of the press in Prussia was in grave danger if the government could prevent news organs from openly and accurately reporting events which might in some way detract from its self-image. He closed his speech with an analysis of the abortive March Revolution which had failed because:

It merely reformed the highest political echelons and left untouched the lower strata supporting them ... The first duty of the press, therefore, is to *undermine the entire foundation of the existing political structure* (NRhZ, Feb. 14).

The charges of inciting to rebellion were based on the paper's appeal, dated Nov. 18, 1848, urging the citizenry to refuse to pay taxes and to offer armed resistance to the government. Marx took the stand that it was the state and not the people which had broken the laws; the people were being called upon to defend the laws. Moreover, the people possessed the right of resisting certain laws which maintained the social interests of an era that was now past and of classes that were in decline:

Law must be based on society; it must be the expression of common interests and needs which arise from the particular means of production and must therefore be opposed to the particular will of each individual (NRhZ, Feb. 25).

As soon as law ceases to reflect the existing social relations, it loses its validity: 'it is no more than a wad of paper'. The accused were cleared of charges in both instances.

Provoked by the apologetics of the *Kölnische Zeitung* in defence of Germany's liberal bourgeoisie, Marx wrote an article in which he categorically rejected the notion that any revolution, present or future, would be based on the struggle between bourgeoisie and feudal-absolutist monarchy. The bourgeoisie was clearly not on the side of democracy and therefore the revolutionary combat would result from the opposition of republicans and absolutists (Feb. 11).

During February a two-part article by Engels, entitled 'The Democratic Panslavism', was published anonymously in the *NRhZ*. Engels pilloried Bakunin's sentimental, romantic plan for an alliance of independent Slav nations and remarked that only the Russians, the Poles and perhaps the Turks could expect to have a future as independent nations. The remainder of the Slav peoples lacked an independent history and the viability needed to achieve self-sufficiency. Moreover, since political centralisation would be necessary for the growth and stability of the larger nations, the smaller Slav groups would have to be subjected to their domination. Hatred of the Slav peoples, the Russians, Czechs and Croats had always been and still was the '*first revolutionary passion* of the Germans', Engels added. Revolution must therefore be carried out by the Germans together with the Poles and the Magyars using the 'most decisive terrorism' against the Slavs: 'We know now where the enemies of the revolution are concentrated: in Russia and in the Slav lands of Austria' he concluded (Feb. 16).

In February Marx and about ten other communists in Cologne met with Joseph Moll, emissary of the German refugee communists in London, to discuss the possibility of reorganising the League. Marx rejected the statutes proposed by Moll on the grounds that the League's purpose as stated there—creation of a 'unified, indivisible social republic'—was not communist and that moreover the statutes had a rather conspiratorial slant. The leftist journal *Freiheit, Arbeit*, organ of the Cologne Working

Men's Club, accused Marx on February 25 of working contrary to the interests of the revolutionary, proletarian party and of 'not being seriously concerned with the liberation of the oppressed'.

On March 18 the *NRhZ* announced that this year it would celebrate not the anniversary of the March Revolution but that of the bloody and unsuccessful June uprising in Paris. Marx's orientation now shifted from the radical elements of the bourgeoisie to the proletarian groups, whose revolutionary movement he began to support in practice to the exclusion of all others. Recognising that the presence of many heterogenous elements within the various democratic groups hindered their practical action, Marx resigned from the Rhenish district council of democratic organisations but retained his membership in the Working Men's Club.

The *NRhZ* published from April 5-11 Marx's study on 'Wage-Labour and Capital', based on his lectures for the Brussels Working Men's Association. As Marx remarked in the 'Introduction', these pages were intended for the workers themselves, for those who were ignorant of the jargon and concepts of bourgeois political economy. In contrast to the latter, Marx presented the economic relations of present society not as absolute, eternal and immutable phenomena but as relations founded at a specific level of industrial development and presupposing a class which possesses nothing but its own labour power. He explained for bourgeois society the relation between capital and wages, which are the price paid for a certain number of hours of labour power. The working man who sells this labour power to the owner of the means of production uses the time and energy which would otherwise be devoted to his self-realisation through labour to the production of mere wages. He earns in so doing the means of subsistence for a life which begins effectively after his labour has ceased and which is thus reduced to his hours of sleep, eating and recreation:

Twelve hours' labour does not have meaning for him as weaving, spinning, drilling, etc., but as *earnings* which bring him to the table, to the public house, into bed. If the silkworm were to spin in order to be able to continue its existence as a caterpillar, it would be a perfect wage-earner (MEW 6:400).

Capital is accumulated through the consumption of living labour and grows only when its power increases in relation to the wages paid the worker. While bourgeois economists maintain that the interests of capital and those of the wage-earner are identical, Marx revealed that the very opposite is true. Any increase in the absolute value of wages in periods of rapid capital expansion is only a semblance of progress and of amelioration in the situation of the working class. In reality the only change is that the working class labours under more favourable conditions at its task of enriching the capitalist class and therefore seems 'content with forging for itself the golden chains by which the bourgeoisie drags it in its tow' (MEW 6:416).

On April 14 Marx set out on a propaganda trip through Westphalia and Northern Germany to solicit funds for the NRhZ. This provided him with the opportunity to gather information on the revolution planned by petit-bourgeois democratic elements for early May and to visit members of the old Communist League. Once again in Cologne, Marx wrote an article for the NRhZ which treated the history of the powerful Hohenzollern family of Prussia. Its success, Marx showed, and pre-eminence in political affairs was achieved through the use of violence, breach of treaties, inheritance swindles, treachery and its servile obedience to Russian despotism (May 10).

On May 16 Marx received a royal order demanding his expulsion from Prussian territory on the grounds that he had abused the government's hospitality with articles inciting to open rebellion against the existing state (NRhZ, May 19). The last issue of the NRhZ appeared on May 18 and was printed entirely in red. The editors appealed to the working class of Cologne to resist any attempted *putsch* under present militarist conditions and warned them against the perfidy of the bourgeoisie. In his lead editorial Marx recounted the principles which had guided the paper since its founding. The NRhZ had worked towards undermining the foundations of the existing order; it had spoken out for the social-republican revolution and for the use of revolutionary terrorism as a means for achieving a new social-republican order. The spirit of the NRhZ had been the spirit of the June Revolution. In closing Marx recalled the motto of the paper on January 1, 1849: Revolutionary war against Russia and creation of the 'Red Republic' in France (NRhZ, May 19).

Their editorial duties at an end, Marx and Engels left Cologne on May 19, accompanying Marx's family to Frankfurt, where they were received by the Weydemeyer family. From there the two men journeyed throughout the Rhineland, conferring with left-wing members of parliament. Their plan was to gather support for an insurrection at Frankfurt and to have the militias of Baden and the Palatinate come to protect the Assembly, but they failed to arouse sufficient interest among the hesitant and indecisive democrats of Karlsruhe, Mannheim, Speyer, etc.

About June 1 Marx obtained a mandate from the Palatinate which enabled him to leave the Rhineland for France. Engels remained in Bingen on the Rhine where he joined in the revolutionary campaign of the Baden army. Marx arrived in Paris about June 3 and immediately contacted his former associates of the League, members of the secret working men's societies and his friend Heine. After the defeat of a Montagnard uprising, supported by the secret societies, repressive measures were taken by the French government which affected Marx as well. On June 19 he was notified that, should he wish to remain in France, he would be required to take up residence in the department of Morbihan. At this moment Marx was 'sans le sou', as he wrote Weydemeyer (July 13). His wife, who had sold all their household furnishings before leaving Germany to avoid having them confiscated, was now forced to pawn all her jewellery. To the family's great relief Ferdinand Lassalle was able to collect a larger sum for them among his Rhenish friends and associates. With this aid Marx left Paris on August 24 for London; his wife and three children followed on September 15. In a letter to Engels shortly before his departure, Marx predicted that revolutionary agitation would soon reach a climax in England, thanks to the Chartist-bourgeois coalition. With this prospect and the promise of financial support to found a new German review, Marx urged Engels to come to London as well (cf. August 17 and 23).

Upon arrival in London his first major task was to begin preparations for the aforementioned journal. He joined the Central Committee of the reconstituted Communist League and their front organisation the German Working Men's Association, both in a state of near stagnation. The Central Committee had lost contact with most of the associated groups and consequently lacked an organisation. Together with several

other German communists Marx organised an action for aid to
German refugees beginning in mid-September. Jenny Marx
arrived about this time in London. Six weeks later their second
son Guido was born.

Theodor Hagen in Hamburg, a member of the local Communist
League, informed Marx about November 21 that his efforts to
find a printer and a publisher for the new review had been
successful. Marx thereupon began soliciting contributions for
the *Neue Rheinische Zeitung. Politisch-ökonomische Revue* as it
was to be called, and sought aid in publicising its forthcoming
appearance. Reporting on his recent activities to Weydemeyer in
Frankfurt, Marx wrote that he believed a violent crisis in
industry, agriculture and commerce was approaching. Should a
revolution occur on the Continent before the outbreak of this
crisis, it would be an ill-timed misfortune, for the masses,
momentarily content with the rising trend in trade and commerce, were not in a revolutionary mood (Dec. 19).

At the close of the year Marx and Engels attended a banquet
given by the Fraternal Democrats and presided over by George
Harney.

III
1850-1856

1850   Restoration of the empire proves to be the goal of Louis Napoleon who now begins to consolidate his power, first by limiting the freedom of the press; then, under pretext of saving the Republic, he carries out

1851   *a coup d'état* with the aid of the military and dissolves both the council of state and the national assembly. He orders the arrest of all leading republicans and liberal members of parliament. After holding a so-called popular plebiscite, he assumes a ten-year mandate as president, fortified with quasi-monarchical powers.

1852   Early in the year he promulgates a new constitution. On the anniversary of the first *coup* he stages a second and thereupon assumes the throne of France as Napoleon III.

—   In France the brothers Isaac and Jacob-Emile Péreire establish the joint-stock companies *Crédit mobilier* and *Crédit foncier*.

—   A tariff union is set up between the German *Länder* and Russia.

—   Throughout Germany a postal and telegraph union is instituted. Austria agrees to participate in the German tariff union for a period of 12 years.

1850-52   Reactionism also makes itself felt in Germany as Prussia is forced to abandon the Erfurt Union, a nationalist endeavour established together with the smaller German states, and to rejoin the old *Bund* under Austria's domination. The Habsburgs are able to profit from two diplomatic humiliations suffered by

Prussia. The first, known as the 'Humiliation of Olmütz', is provoked by a popular uprising in Prussia's neighbour state of Hesse against despotic rule. Prussia intervenes on behalf of the Hessians, but Austria moves to check this aid. After an armed encounter with the Austrians, Prussia is forced to retreat. The Treaty of Olmütz obliges her to withdraw her troops from Hesse and annul the existing conventions with the smaller German states in view of a new German union. Furthermore, Prussia agrees to renounce all claims to Schleswig-Holstein, a territory which the Danes also wish to annex, and suffers a second humiliation as Austria decides to give this land to Denmark. The *Bund* is convened with all its old participants. Appearing for Prussia is Otto von Bismarck.

1852   In London a treaty is signed—the London Protocol—by the five great powers, and Sweden and Denmark, fixing the territorial limits of the Danish state and the order of royal succession.

—   Metternich reappears in Austria's internal politics. He suspends ministerial responsibility and abolishes the right to trial by jury.

1853   Reactionism now manifests itself in Italy, where popular liberalism is suppressed. Mazzini incites an unsuccessful rebellion in Milan; in Rome a revolutionary plot is unearthed and 150 conspirators are arrested.

THE CRIMEAN WAR

—   Under the pretext of protecting the Sultan's Orthodox Christian subjects Czar Nicolaus I attempts to realise Russia's traditional plans of conquest in the Balkans. He threatens Turkey, demanding the protectorate over all Greek Christians in the Turkish empire. English and Austrian attempts at mediation fail; Russia occupies the Danube principalities of Moldavia and Wallachia and destroys a Turkish squadron of 11 ships at Sinope.

1854   After a new Whig ministry under Lord Palmerston takes office in England, both England and France declare war on Russia and send troops to the Crimea. Austria, supported by Prussia, demands the evacuation of the Danube principalities. French and English forces defeat the Russians at the Battle of Alma (Sept.) and then at Inkerman (Nov.), while the outcome of their siege of Sebastopol, the Russian naval base on the Crimea, remains undecided. Diplomatic considerations induce Austria to sign a defensive alliance with France and England (Dec.) and to call a peace conference at Vienna. However, no consensus is reached on the 'Four Points' proposed for discussion, the most important of which concerns the limiting of Russia's influence in the Black Sea.

1855   Joined by Sardinia and Piedmont, the allied troops now renew the attack on Sebastopol. The son of Nicolaus I, Alexander II, assumes the Russian throne and continues to pursue his father's policy in the Crimea. Despite large losses caused by cholera and privation, the besiegers finally take Sebastopol in September and thus decide the outcome of the war in their favour. An English stronghold at Kars is subsequently captured by the Russians (Nov.).

1856   Peace negotiations are held in Paris. According to the provisions of the Treaty of Paris Sebastopol is returned to the Russians, Kars to the Sultan; the Danube and the Black Sea are opened to world commerce; Russia is denied a special protectorate over Greek Christians in Turkey; and certain moot points in international law are settled. This diplomatic event marks Austria's decline as a dominant European power and reveals for the first time the rising stars of diplomacy: Prussia's Bismarck and Sardinia's Count Camillo di Cavour.

THE AMERICAS

1850   The Compromise Act settles the question of whether California should be admitted to the Union as a slave— or a free state. A majority is gained for the admission of California as a free state and the Fugitive Slave Bill is passed. Henceforth Southern slave-owners have the right to demand the return of slaves escaped to the North and prosecute those aiding them in their flight.

1854   The slavery question in the as-yet-unopened territories of the Middle West is decided by the Kansas-Nebraska Bill which permits the residents of each area to vote on the issue.

THE FAR EAST

1850   The *Taiping Rebellion* begins in the South of China. A group of peasants, the Taipings, opposed to opium and in favour of land redistribution, equality of the sexes and the return to 'old virtues', revolt against the rich landlords and the presence of Christian missionaries.

1851   Hoping to extend their commercial influence in Burma, British merchants call for protection from the Royal Navy against presumed aggression on the part of the

1852   natives. The capital of Rangoon is captured and the whole of the Province of Pegu annexed.

—   The Taipings gain territory and attack the provinces of Central China. With the seizure of Nanking, which becomes their capital, they represent a formidable op-

1854   position to the imperial Manchu dynasty. Their march is stopped by the Emperor's troops, but they nevertheless succeed in extending control over a wide territory along the Yangtse river.

1856   The Persians attempt to seize the principality of Herat, the object of dispute between Afghanistan and Persia. The British use this move as a pretext for intervention and the Anglo-Persian War erupts.

—   After suffering severe losses, Persia renounces her claims to Herat and the territory is returned to Afghanistan (Mar. 1857).

—   The second Opium War breaks out over the issue of a small Chinese-owned and -manned vessel the lorcha, 'Arrow', which harboured two sea pirates. British demands about the settlement of the affair are refused by the Cantonese, whereupon the former take reprisals against Canton and against Chinese junks on the waterways.

SCIENTIFIC AND TECHNOLOGICAL PROGRESS

1850   The first transatlantic underwater electric cable is laid from Calais to Dover.

1854   Marcelin Berthelot establishes the principles of thermochemistry.

1856   The Englishman Sir Henry Bessemer invents a new method of preparing steel.

—   Fossils are found in the Neanderthal, a valley in Germany, which are identified as the bones of a Paleolithic or early Stone Age man.

IMPORTANT WORKS PUBLISHED

1850   Robert Owen: *The Revolution in the Mind and Practice of the Human Race.**

—   William H. Prescott: *History of the Conquest of Mexico.**

—   Wilhelm Wachsmuth: *Allgemeine Kulturgeschichte.**

—   Frédéric Bastiat: *Harmonies économiques.**

1851   Harriet Beecher-Stowe: *Uncle Tom's Cabin.*

1851-54   Auguste Comte: *Système de politique positive.*

—   P.-J. Proudhon: *Idée générale de la révolution au XIXe siècle.**

1852   George Campbell: *Modern India.**

1852-57   Herbert Spencer: *Principles of Psychology.*

1854   Georg Maurer: *Einleitung zur Geschichte der Mark-, Hof-, Dorf- und Stadtverfassung.**

1856   Ludwig Lange: *Römische Altertümer.**

—   Ludwik Mierosławski: *Histoire de la commune polonaise du Xe au XVIIIe siècle.**

KARL MARX
1850-1856

1850 The first issue of the NRhZ-*Revue* appeared in Hamburg at the beginning of March. It included a historical essay by Marx on the 'Defeat of June 1848', in which he attempted an economic explanation of the reasons for this unsuccessful revolution. He intended to show that the defeats of 1848-49 were valuable lessons for the insurgent party and helped them mature to a 'truly revolutionary party'. The second part of the essay, entitled 'June 13, 1849', appeared in the next issue of the NRhZ-*Revue* and continued the analysis of the French class struggles up to June 13. The third number of the *Revue*, published in mid-April, contained the conclusion of Marx's analysis entitled 'The Consequences of June 13, 1849'. The essence of revolutionary socialism, Marx stated, is the declaration of 'revolution in permanence' and the dictatorship of the proletariat is a necessary stage leading to the abolition of class differences, a precondition for the 'overthrow of all ideas which arise from the existing social relations'. This issue included as well a review of current events which the authors Marx and Engels predicted—for August at the latest—a new British trade crisis and social revolution.

From the end of February throughout the month of March Marx gave a number of lectures on political economy in his home for his friends. At this time the Communist League, which was under Marx's leadership, decided to begin reorganising. Together, Marx and Engels composed a circular entitled 'A Warplan against Democracy' which was distributed to the League's local groups, primarily in Germany. This pamphlet analysed summarily the unsuccessful 1848-49 revolutions and gave detailed directives for the coming struggle of the proletariat, whose task was far vaster than the struggle of the liberal bourgeoisie against feudal and reactionary elements. To achieve its own proper goals, the proletariat should work hand-in-hand with the bourgeoisie only until the latter had assumed political predominance. As soon as the bourgeoisie was in power, the working class should constitute itself as an independent political body and establish 'revolutionary workers' governments' parallel to the official government organs. This revolutionary government might be established in the form of city councils, clubs or armed workers' committees which would undermine the popular support of official institutions and set up rival candidates for the representative national assembly. The proletariat should demand the radicalisation of bourgeois reform measures. Instead of the appropriation of factories and railways, expropriation and confiscation; not proportional taxation, but progressive and heavy taxation of capital. Conditions permitting, the proletarian political organisation should be open to public and should maintain a watchful and distrustful attitude towards the bourgeoisie. Marx and Engels characterised the democratic party as 'far more dangerous than the earlier liberal party' (MEW 7 : 246). It would continue to be powerful even among the rural proletariat as long as the proletariat in the industrialised cities had not yet developed an independent political position. The tactics of the bourgeoisie consisted of bribing the working men with higher wages, attempting to destroy the revolutionary strength of the proletariat by making their present situation more tolerable. The proletariat must always remain on its guard against the ruses of the bourgeoisie: 'Their battle cry must be: the revolution in permanence' (MEW 7 : 553).

In mid-April Engels, Marx and August Willich, representing the League, Adam and Jules Vidil for the Blanquists and Harney for the revolutionary faction of the Chartists met to discuss the founding of a *Société universelle des communistes révolutionnaires* [World Society of Revolutionary Communists]. The society's statutes were established and its purpose formulated as 'the overthrow of all privileged classes, their subjection to the dictatorship of the proletariat under which the revolution shall be maintained *sine die* until the communists society, the final organisational form of the human family, has been realised' (MEW 7 : 553).

At a summer gathering of the German Working Men's Society

Marx made the acquaintance of the German socialist Wilhelm Liebknecht, recently arrived in London after release from a Swiss prison (May). At about this time he also contacted for the first time two representatives of the 'determined revolutionary party' of Hungary, Stephan Türr and Johann Bangya.

The fourth issue of the NRhZ-Revue came out about May 20 with a number of book reviews and a monthly review of events, composed by Marx and Engels jointly. Commenting on the memoirs of the professional conspirator Adolphe Chenu and those of the police spy Lucien de la Hodde, Marx gave a historical analysis of the function served by secret societies in France. The revolutionary proletarian party, Marx stressed, would find conspiratorial methods ill-suited for promoting its cause; rather, the party must rely exclusively on the broad masses of working men in carrying out the modern social revolution.

A second subject which Marx wrote upon in this Revue was suggested by Emile de Girardin's book Le Socialisme et l'impôt [Socialism and Taxation]. Here he explained the communist notion of 'abolition of the state' as meaningful only when classes had first been abolished and therefore a state apparatus was no longer needed to enforce the domination of one class over the others (cf. MEW 7:286). In the 'Revue' for the months of March and April a crisis was predicted for the immediate future in British trade and commerce and in America, accompanied by revolution of a socialist nature on the Continent, where the effects of the commercial crisis would be particularly serious.

In the Marx household during these months there were also visible signs of crisis. In March they had been evicted from their flat for failing to pay the rent, had pawned the last of their furniture and moved into a German hotel in the centre of London. Jenny Marx shared her distress with their friend Joseph Weydemeyer:

My husband has nearly been crushed to death here with all the pettiest worries of bourgeois life and in such an offensive way, what is more, that he has needed all his energy, all his calm and level-headed self-assurance to keep his courage up during these hourly and daily struggles ... I am asking you to send please as soon as possible any money that has been or will be received from the sale of the Revue. We need it very, very much (May 20).

The proceeds from the Revue enabled Marx to move his family

into a two-room flat in Dean Street, Soho, in May. Here Marx was able to continue throughout the summer months the lecture series on political economy which he had begun in February. In June Marx's request for admittance to the reading room of the British Museum Library was granted and there he began an intensive study of the past decade of economic history. Of particular help to him was the London journal *The Economist*.

A second bulletin of the League's Central Committee went out to the member groups in June. It reported on the present status of the organisation on the Continent and in England and warned the members to be wary of the secret refugee organisations under the leadership of petit-bourgeois elements. The authorship of this circular is uncertain.

In a letter to the Frankfurt *Neue Deutsche Zeitung* Marx replied to a critique of the *NRhZ-Revue*, explaining that the *Revue* advocated not only 'the rule and dictatorship of the proletariat' but also the 'abolition of all class differences whatsoever' (MEW 7:323).

Conflicts within the Central Committee finally led to an open split between the Willich faction and the supporters of Marx and Engels on September 15. The League's ties with the German Working Men's Society were dissolved and the seat of the Central Committee transferred to Cologne. The two dissident factions were established as independent communist groups within the League. Marx and the other members of his faction soon withdrew from the Working Men's Society and the Refugee Committee.

In autumn Marx resumed work on the volume of political economy while reading on money and finance at the British Museum. He also continued reading and taking notes on recent economic history. Towards the end of the year he corresponded with Hermann Becker in Cologne, who was interested in publishing his 'Collected Essays'. A first section of the text was set during December.

In November George Harney's *Red Republican* published the first English translation, by Helen Macfarlane of *The Communist Manifesto*. Marx and Engels were named as the authors.

Plagued by debts and gravely worried about his family's immediate future, Marx requested Weydemeyer in Frankfurt to redeem his wife's silver from a local pawnbroker and to sell them in order to surmount the crisis (Oct. 29). On November 19

Marx's younger son Guido died suddenly of a convulsive fit. At this time Engels left London for Manchester to assume the position in his father's spinning mill which he was to retain until 1869.

The final issue of the NRhZ-Revue appeared on November 29. It included Engels's 'The Peasant War in Germany' and a lengthy review of the monthly events from May to October, written by the two friends in collaboration. There was also a detailed analysis of the past decade of economic history and a prognosis of social developments, based on Marx's recent study of economic trends. The review concluded that a genuine revolution was impossible in times of prosperity and would be provoked only by a new economic crisis. Crisis and then revolution—both were seen to be inevitable (cf. MEW 7 : 440).

1851 Apart from attendance at meetings of the London Council of the Communist League, Marx devoted himself intensively to his studies in economic history and theory at the British Museum. During the year he filled about 14 notebooks with excerpts from the authors he read. In the following the subjects are broken down by month:

Jan.: *Ground rent.* In a letter to Engels Marx gave a detailed critique of Ricardo's rent theory (Jan. 7), emphasising how modern technology had changed land fertility and made obsolete Malthus's theory of the declining rentability of land. He noted that the so-called 'laws' governing land rent are merely laws of bourgeois competition, based on the interplay of prices on the capitalist market. Money and currency circulation (Bailey, Carey and Jacob). The results of Marx's investigations are summarised in a letter to Engels on February 3, where he denied the validity of the classic theory that the flux of precious metals determines the trade balance and exchange rates on the world money market.

Feb.—March: *Money and currency* (Gray, Smith, Bosanquet, Torrens, Hume and Locke).

April—May: *Money* (Torrens, Serra).

General economic theory (Ricardo).

Land Fertility. Marx became interested in the problem of fertility in agriculture after reading an article in the *Economist* which reported the successful use of electricity

for increasing land productivity. Marx discussed the problem
in his correspondence with Engels and Roland Daniels.

May: Wages (Carey).

Population problems (Malthus).

June: Theory of value and wealth (Torrens, Carey, Malthus).

July: Labour problems, the factory system and agriculture.
Marx read the English socialists Owen, Hodgskin, Fielden,
Hopkins on the labour situation in Britain, reread Malthus
on population and took up several authors on agriculture
and agrochemistry.

Aug.: Population and Agriculture (Thornton, Johnston).

Colonisation and Slavery (Prescott, Howitt).
Marx also read Proudhon's recent publication *Idée générale
de la révolution au XIXe siècle*, whose contents he recounted
in a letter to Engels. Both men agreed that the book was
considerably better than Proudhon's earlier writings but
criticised his reform proposals as too limited. 'The more I
get into this stuff, the more I am convinced that agricultural
reform, and therefore the dirty property business which is
based on it, will be the essence of the coming revolution,'
he wrote to Engels (Aug. 14).

Political Economy of the Ancient Romans (2 vols. by Dureau
de la Malle).

Sept.: Sketches of the Coming War by Gustav Adolph Techow.
Marx discovered this political manifesto through a book
review in the *New Yorker Staatszeitung*. Techow presented
his reflections on the unsuccessful revolutions of 1848-49
and predicted that the coming revolution would be waged
in Germany and Italy as a European war, staged by the
military, and would be neither a class struggle nor the
result of a civil war, as Marx predicted.

Sept.—Oct.: Banking, agronomy and technological history.

Nov.: Gratuité du crédit by Proudhon. To Engels: 'This
surpasses in charlatanry, blustering, bragging and deficiency
all the fellow's previous achievements' (Nov. 24).

In this year we see Engels assume what was to become his
perennial role as financial and moral supporter of the Marx
family and as the goad stimulating his friend to 'finish with the
"Economics"'. On January 8 he sent Marx £1 to pay the overdue rent.

Towards the end of February a serious dispute arose within

the ranks of the London emigrants because of George Harney's relations with the Willich-Schapper faction, now estranged from the group around Marx and Engels. Harney had been helping promote among the Chartists and other liberal organisations an international banquet planned by the Willich-Schapper group in commemoration of the February Revolution. While Marx and his friends officially boycotted the banquet, they nevertheless sent two of their number as unofficial observers. Recognised as members of the rival group, the two were beaten up and thrown out of the hall, while Harney, who also recognised them as friends of his own, remained silent. Following this episode the relations between Harney and Marx and Engels cooled considerably and Engels withdrew his manuscripts submitted for publication in Harney's *The Friend of the People*.

In a letter to Engels on April 1 Marx estimated that in about five weeks he would be able to start writing his 'Economics', which he now planned to publish in three volumes. He wrote to several friends in Germany, asking for their aid in finding a publisher.

Desperate for money, Marx drew a bill on his mother in Trier during March, causing a heated dispute with her over the Marxes' financial situation. In the midst of this trouble, Franziska Marx was born on March 28. Shortly thereafter, Engels sent his friend an amount sufficient to cover their most urgent expenses. Up to his ears in 'petit-bourgeois muck', Marx also wrote to Engels about a certain 'mystère' in which the latter was to play a role as well and promised to explain this affair in a subsequent letter (March 31). On April 2, however, Marx informed his friend that he had decided to make the trip to Manchester at the end of the month to explain this 'mystère' tête-à-tête. Marx was in Manchester from April 20-26.

Ferdinand Lassalle, who had been recently released from prison after serving a sentence for his political activities, made several vain attempts to regain the confidence of the Cologne communists and be admitted to their ranks. Daniels wrote to warn Marx of Lassalle's pose of friendship (April 12) and characterised Lassalle as a 'superficial joker and a genuine democratic charlatan' (April 24). On May 12 Lassalle wrote to Marx personally, announcing that he had recommenced his studies of economics and was burning with interest and impatience to read Marx's political economy, 'the three-volume monster of Ricardo turned socialist and Hegel turned economist'.

At the end of April Marx was informed that the first (and only) instalment of his *Collected Essays*, published by Becker, had appeared in Cologne. This pamphlet of five printer's sheets (16 pages to a sheet) contained a selection of articles he had written as a liberal journalist in Germany. Becker had issued a prospectus announcing that Marx's *Essays* would be published in two volumes of 25 printer's sheets. However, a series of arrests in Germany put an abrupt end to this project. On May 10 a member of the Cologne League was arrested in Leipzig, and this was followed by the arrest of Becker and Peter Röser in Cologne and Heinrich Bürgers in Dresden. Marx asked Lassalle to help him find a new publisher in Düsseldorf. Lassalle reported on June 26 that his efforts had proved unsuccessful.

On May 18 Marx attended a lecture held by Robert Owen on the occasion of his 80th birthday. During the course of the evening he was drawn into an unavoidable conversation with George Harney, the first since the episode in February.

An event occurred on June 23 in the Marx residence which has been interpreted as the solution to the 'mystère' mentioned in March and April. Helene Demuth gave birth to a son, Frederick Lewis Demuth, whose paternity was not recorded on the birth certificate. The baby was not retained by its mother but quickly removed from the household in Dean Street. Expenses for its lodging and later schooling were assumed by Engels. Letters and documents, first published in 1962, reveal that the child's father was Marx and that Engels had confessed this fact to Eleanor Marx, the youngest of Marx's children, in 1895, shortly before his death (cf. Blumenberg, p. 115f. and Tsuzuki, p. 263f.). Following this event, the Marx family seems to have been in quite some uproar. Marx described this state of affairs to Engels in a letter of July 31 :

For about the past fortnight now I have written absolutely nothing, for when I am not at the library I am hunted like a dog and therefore, despite the best of intentions, I am constantly interrupted in my work ... at home disruptions and disturbances are too much for me. Everything is constantly in a state of siege and the streams of tears for nights on end try my nerves and drive me mad. Naturally I cannot do much. I feel sorry for my wife. She has the heaviest load to bear and *au fond* she is right. Industry ought to be more productive than marriage.

Documents found on the person of the arrested members of the League were published in a number of German newspapers at the end of June. They included the League's statutes and the 1850 address written by Marx and Engels which, being 'au fond nothing other than a war plan against democracy' not only brought a certain notoriety to Marx's ideas but also damaged the case of the arrested communists (Marx to Engels, July 13).

Marx, who was now deeply in debt and without a source of income, was forced to accept the generous support of his friends in order to feed and lodge his family and himself. On August 5, however, he received an offer from the New York publisher Charles Dana inviting his contributions to the *New-York Daily Tribune*. The first articles which Dana published under Marx's name were actually written by Engels in English. Eighteen in all, these articles appeared from October 1851 to October 1852 under the title 'Revolution and Counter-Revolution in Germany'.

Upon the recommendation of Ferdinand Freiligrath Marx sent Hermann Ebner in Frankfurt a plan of his 'Economics', hoping that he would be able to find a publisher for it. At this time Ebner was actually a secret agent of the Austrian police. Marx also sought a publisher for a pamphlet against Proudhon's *Idée générale* and wrote to the Hoffmann and Campe in Hamburg (August 20). Their reply was negative. Freiligrath also reported, on September 25, that his efforts to find a publisher through Ebner had failed. Wilhelm Pieper in Cologne announced that he too had only disappointing news to report. Lassalle then came up with a plan to form a publishing house on a joint-stock basis which would bring out Marx's 'Economics'. Marx turned this plan down, fearing that financial backing would not be forthcoming from the bourgeoisie because of the political situation and that, were his present financial state to become public, his position would be compromised.

Members of the Willich-Schapper faction were arrested in Paris in September. Documents found in their possession were falsely attributed to Marx, as the German press began a vicious campaign against him. Marx disavowed authorship of the documents in question in declarations which appeared in October in two German papers.

In November Marx spent ten days in Manchester with Engels. The major topic of their discussions was the plan for Marx's 'Economics'. The three volumes were to contain: (1) a critique of political economy, (2) a critique of the socialists and (3) the history of political economy (cf. letter to Engels, Nov. 27).

On September 29 Joseph Weydemeyer, one of Marx's and Engels's closest friends and former editor of the *Neue Deutsche Zeitung*, left Frankfurt to settle in America, where he planned to publish a news weekly entitled *Die Revolution*. Marx's first contribution to this journal was to be a historical-critical study with the provocative title *The Eighteenth Brumaire of Louis Bonaparte*. In mid-December Marx set to work on this sardonic critique of Napoleon III, proposing to Weydemeyer at the same time a second article on Proudhon's *Idée générale*. His work, however, did not advance as quickly as expected and the *Brumaire* was delayed 'not only through the precipitous course of current events but to an even greater extent through personal circumstances' (Marx to Weydemeyer, Jan. 1, 1852).

1852 Marx had scarcely finished the first instalment of his article for Weydemeyer when illness interrupted his writing for most of the month of January. Jenny Marx, meanwhile, took over her husband's correspondence and sent Weydemeyer the second part of the article on January 8. In Marx's name she also asked Weydemeyer to break the 'conspiracy of silence' in the press against the imprisoned Cologne communists:

These people are languishing in the prisons, are being terribly mistreated and now have to stay there another three months while the great men of the future are pocketing thousands in the name of the revolution and are already distributing among themselves the posts in the government to come.

In early February Marx was visited for the first time by the Hungarian officer János Bangya, who was, unknown to Marx, a secret police agent and emissary of Louis Kossuth. He provided Marx with information on the relations between the various rival revolutionary leaders and national heroes. Attracted by Bangya's offer of £25 sterling in payment, Marx accepted the proposal to write a pamphlet containing character sketches of prominent members of the German immigration in exile. However, before giving his definitive answer on this project, Marx had asked Engels for an opinion (April 30). Engels replied that he had already been putting together files of such material in order to have information at hand 'when things start popping' and advised Marx to accept (May 1).

Marx was indeed sorely in need of the £25, for he again found himself in serious financial difficulty. This man, whom Hermann Ewerbeck characterised as a critical genius of a rank no less than Lessing (cf. H. Ewerbeck, *L'Allemagne et les Allemands*. Paris, 1851, p. 587f.), was now hardly able to concentrate on his writing projects. In February the family's situation was so critical that Marx had pawned his overcoat and was consequently unable to leave the house and had lost his credit at the butcher's. Despite small sums from friends and the proceeds from the first *New-York Daily Tribune* articles, their misery grew until on April 14 the youngest child, Franziska, died of bronchitis. They were forced to borrow money from their French neighbours in order to pay for the little girl's coffin and her burial. Jenny Marx later wrote:

She had no cradle when she came into the world and for a long time was refused a last resting place. With what heavy hearts we saw her carried to her grave! (*Reminiscences of Marx and Engels*, p. 228).

Since Bangya had insisted that the pamphlet was urgent and that payment would be made on delivery, Marx quickly set to work together with Ernst Dronke to draft a text which he intended to revise with Engels's aid. About May 26 he went to Manchester, where he and Engels spent about a month revising the manuscript, which he sent to Bangya at the end of June. The expected payment did not arrive on time, however, nor was there a sign of the published text. Not until the end of the year did Marx learn from Gustav Zerffi that Bangya was a secret agent for the police of several European countries. Zerffi disclosed that Bangya had probably turned Marx's manuscript over to the Prussian police lieutenant Greif with whom he was in regular contact. Marx decided not to expose Bangya until he had had the opportunity to look for a publisher for his pamphlet entitled *Great Men of Exile*. The objects of Marx's critique and biting sarcasm included Gottfried Kinkel, August Willich, Gustav Struve, Arnold Ruge, Karl Heinzen and Harro Haring, whose quarrels and differences gave ample material for a lively picture of the German immigration since 1848.

Meanwhile in New York Weydemeyer was having difficulty financing his journal and wrote to Marx that he was not certain to be able to publish *The Eighteenth Brumaire*. As Marx finished writing the sections of this manuscript, he sent them off to New York. With the March 5 delivery he enclosed a letter which summarised the difference between his approach to economic theory and the theories of the other socialists and the bourgeois economists:

As for me, I cannot claim the honour of having discovered either the existence of classes in modern society or the struggle of these classes among themselves. Long before me, bourgeois historiographers had shown the historical development of this class struggle and bourgeois economists have traced out the economic structure of this very struggle. The novelty of what I have done is to prove simply that the *existence of classes* with *certain historic phases* of the *development of production*, that the class struggle necessarily culminates in the *dictatorship of the proletariat*, and that this dictatorship is itself only a transitional form leading to the *abolition of all classes* and a classless society (Mar. 5).

The final instalment of *The Eighteenth Brumaire* was sent off on March 25. Not until two months later did the work appear as the first issue of Weydemeyer's new revue *Die Revolution*, thanks to the financial assistance received from a German immigrant in America. A mixture of history, sociology and political pamphleteering, *The Eighteenth Brumaire* retraced the chain of events from 1848 to the *coup d'état* of 1851 as France regressed from a bourgeois republic to a praetorian regime dominated by the histrionic autocrat Louis Napoleon. Frightened by the prospect of social revolution, the propertied classes had preferred to abandon their political power to a man who seemed capable of turning back the clock of history and helping them retain their dominant social position. For Marx, this relapse into an earlier form of state power showed that the social republic in France was still a utopia and that there was not yet any real participation by the proletariat in the governing process. The real social revolution to come

cannot draw its poetry from the past but only from the future. It cannot begin with itself before it has shed all superstitious belief in the past. Earlier revolutions needed reminiscences of history in order to deceive themselves as to their own significance. The revolution of the 19th century must let the dead bury the dead if it wants to arrive at its own proper destiny (MEW 8:117).

Marx found that the authoritarian regime of Louis Napoleon was most popular among the small-holding peasants [*Parzellen-bauern*], who, as he remarked in passing, actually formed no real social class at all. Each being self-sufficient and independent of his neighbours, these peasants had 'no sense of community, no national ties and no political organisation among themselves' (MEW 8:198). However, Bonaparte's state organisation was preparing its own inevitable demise through the growing state centralisation which turned the governing apparatus into a nearly autonomous force, existing side-by-side with the social classes. The task of the coming proletarian revolution, which would make allies of the small-holding peasants and the industrial proletariat, would thus be to destroy the state machinery while conserving the advantages of centralisation:

Bureaucracy is only the vulgar and brutal form of centralisation still afflicted with its opposite, with feudalism. When he loses faith in the Napoleonic Restoration, the French peasant will abandon faith in his own small holding and the proletarian revolution will then obtain its chorus, for want of which its solo song becomes a swan song in all peasant nations (MEW 8:204).

Although Marx did not return to his readings on economics until July, he had made numerous efforts in the meantime to find a publisher for his projected work. The publisher Wigand in Leipzig turned down the offer 'on account of the risks to which one would be exposed in view of the state' should he venture to publish Marx (*see* Wigand to Marx, March 20). Ebner in Frankfurt also reported negative results in the search for a publisher (Ebner to Engels, July 19). In July and August Marx then began his studies afresh with works on cultural history, the history of woman (Wachsmuth), of feudalism and literature in general. He was also interested in a number of works by and about Giordano Bruno.

During the summer Marx began writing his own articles for the *New-York Daily Tribune* with Engels providing the translations into English. The first, entitled 'The Elections: Tories and Whigs', appeared on August 26 and was followed by six others

on the Chartists, British political institutions and electoral corruption, all translated by Engels and published between August
and November. For one article on the 'Movements of Mazzini
and Kossuth. League with Louis Napoleon' (Oct. 19) Marx
used information furnished by Bangya on the secret ambition of
Kossuth and his accomplice Mazzini to win the tyrant Napoleon
for an alliance with revolutionary Hungary—a goal which could
only discredit the revolutionaries in the eyes of their people.
One of Marx's articles, on the Disraeli budget, was translated
by Pieper and appeared in the *New-York Daily Tribune* on
December 28.

Constantly penniless, increasingly indebted to the landlord
and the neighbourhood shopkeepers, Marx tried to find new
sources of income through translations of earlier publications
and contracts for articles. He proposed to the publisher Brockhaus an article, to be based on his readings at the British
Museum, dealing with 'Modern Literature on Political Economy
in England, 1830-1852' for the Brockhaus periodical *Die Gegen-
wart*. Here Marx intended to treat (1) general works on political
economy, (2) writing on specialised topics such as population
problems, colonisation, banking, protective tariffs, free trade, etc.
The proposal was declined on August 27. Efforts to bring out an
English edition of *The Eighteenth Brumaire* or to publish it in
Germany were likewise fruitless. As Stephan Naut wrote to
Marx (Sept. 14): 'The name alone [Marx] suffices to bring a
mass of unpleasantries down on one's head.' In September, with
three members of the family ill, Marx lacked money to pay the
doctor or to buy the English dailies which he used in writing
correspondent's reports for the *Daily Tribune*. Engels and Freiligrath helped him over this crisis.

After numerous delays the trial of the Cologne communists
began on October 4. Marx sent a detailed letter for the defence
of the accused to their attorney Karl Schneider in Cologne (Oct.
14). Determined to bring this trial to the attention of the public,
Marx wrote a pamphlet and called upon Engels to help find the
funds for its publication. This pamphlet, he wrote Engels, 'is
not a vindication of principles, but a denunciation of the Russian government, based on a presentation of facts and the
course of events' (Oct. 27). Judgment in the case was delivered
on November 12: seven of the accused were sentenced, four
acquitted. Marx finished his pamphlet on December 2 and sent

it off to Schnabelitz in Basle and to Adolph Cluss in Washington, who had both agreed to publish it.

At a meeting of the League on November 17 Marx moved that the group be disbanded and declared that since the arrests in Cologne its existence was no longer in keeping with the times. The motion was passed (cf. Marx to Engels, Nov. 19).

Through Cluss in America Marx received a letter from someone claiming to be Kossuth's secretary in reply to Marx's two *Daily Tribune* articles on the Hungarian leader. Marx wrote to Kossuth personally and learned that in fact he had no American secretary and was furthermore grateful to Marx for the warnings about Louis Napoleon. Kossuth's statement appeared in the *Daily Tribune* on January 4, 1853.

On December 30 Szemere, another of the Hungarian immigrants wrote to Marx to warn him about the informant Zerffi who was reputed to be 'good at best as a source of information about the enemy's camp'.

1853 The 'sleepless night in exile' had begun for the Marx family in London. In the previous three years the family's situation, both financial and social, had grown even more precarious than on the Continent and Marx's reputation as a writer, scholar and activist had, if anything, diminished. While the interest in his writings and studies remained limited to a small circle of loyal adherents, following the trial in Cologne he was branded as the head of an international conspiratorial organisation, the 'Marx party', whose goal was said to be the overthrow of the Prussian monarchy. The worst fears of the German publishers who had not dared accept his writings for publication were realised.

Although he had expected to be far enough advanced in his studies to begin writing the 'Economics' in the spring of 1851, Marx did not resume his reading until this year. Yet instead of starting to put his own thoughts on paper, he continued making extracts from the authors he was reading, as if his research were still far from being finished. He began with works by Opdyke, Banfield and Herbert Spencer on social and industrial organisation but was soon forced to abandon his reading again. Because of illness and the need to support his family by writing articles for the *Daily Tribune*, Marx did not take up his private studies again until 1856.

It was not long before he began writing his *Daily Tribune* articles directly in English, choosing topics of current economic or political interest which provided him with material for brief social or historical critiques. The documentation thus furnished a vivid illustration of his theoretical viewpoint. In discerning the profit-drive, the hunger for power within the dominant classes of Victorian England and continental Europe, Marx exposed the hidden forces behind the contemporary course of events.

Along with several articles on the recent British elections the *Daily Tribune* published a contribution by Marx on 'The Duchess of Sutherland and Slavery' which reported on a protest address sent by a group of aristocratic Englishwomen to their American sisters. The president of the protesting group was none other than the Duchess of Sutherland, whose family had made its fortune by driving Scottish peasants from their lands and appropriating them as grazing pastures for Sutherland sheep. Marx concluded, therefore, that:

The enemy of British wages slavery has the right to condemn Negro slavery; a Duchess of Sutherland, however, a duke of Athol, a Manchester cotton lord—never ! (Feb. 9).

Marx wrote his first article in English on the subject of 'Capital Punishment' in reply to another article in the London *Times*. He condemned this 'hangman's apotheosis' praised by the *Times* and showed that the argument of its deterrent effect was untenable from both a moral and an empirical standpoint:

... it would be very difficult, if not altogether impossible, to establish any principle upon which the justice or expediency of capital punishment could be founded in a Society glorying in its civilization (Feb. 9).

Hegel had once given a systematic theory of punishment, Marx noted, and had maintained that 'Punishment is the *right* of the criminal. It is an act of his own will'—that the criminal's negation of right is negated to give an ultimate confirmation of right. For Marx, however, Hegel's dialectic game was 'only a metaphysic expression for the old "jus talionis" ', in other words, the law of vengeance.

Other important topics which Marx dealt with in the first part of the year included the Milan uprising, 'symbol of the approaching revolutionary crisis on the entire European Continent' (March 8), as well as the Turkish question.

It had been arranged that the *Neu-England Zeitung* in Boston was to publish Marx's *Revelations on the Communist Trial in Cologne* in instalments (March-April), while Schnabelitz in Basle would print it in pamphlet form for subsequent distribution in Germany (Jan.). In the *Revelations* Marx narrated the 'repugnant comedy of lackeys and police agents' staged by the Prussian government using its own secret agents and aided by the French police together with other corruptible elements. Mounted in order to put the Cologne communist who entertained relations with Marx behind bars, this spectacle depicted the latter as the head of an international organisation of conspirators, plotting to overthrow the Prussian government. Since the documents found in the possession of the accused, such as *The Communist Manifesto*, did not provide adequate proof that the accused had actually established a programme of revolutionary action, the Prussian government, assisted by its agents and 'hired hands' in France and England, resorted to the manufacture of the missing pieces, to forgery and to perjury so that the 'facts' would coincide with the indictment. The infamy did not stop there, however; they had even attempted to buy a false witness. With this magnificent production the Prussian government had risked its own international reputation, imagining itself forced to abuse all the laws of the criminal code in order to defeat this small but treacherous party of conspirators. The issue at stake was not therefore the guilt or innocence of the accused, but their guilt or the guilt of the Prussian government. The verdict of guilty was duly pronounced against the seven members of the League.

In recapitulating the complicated story of this piece of Prussian justice, Marx had intended to enlighten the German public about the numerous scenes of the drama which had been played, as it were, in the wings. Publication of the document did not, however, assure that it would actually reach its audience. Schnabelitz's stock of 2000 copies was seized by the police while being smuggled across the Swiss border into Germany (March 7). As Jenny Marx wrote to Cluss:

At the moment the pamphlet would have had the most colossal effect. It would have struck like a thunderbolt amidst the trembling, shaking police people ... You can imagine what an effect this news has had on my husband's health, etc. (March 10).

Marx's first bout with hepatitis dated from this episode. Apart from the anger and frustrations related to the trial and the publication of his pamphlet, he was again without income or other means of support for his family. While he tried vainly to find a publisher for the manuscript of *Great Men of Exile*, Jenny wrote to all their friends and relatives, 'terrible letters' in which she was obliged to beg for aid for her 'hungry family' (cf. Jenny Marx to Engels, April 27).

For the April issues of the *Daily Tribune* Marx reported on Mazzini, O'Connor and the affairs of the British government. He also wrote three articles for Jones's *People's Paper* based on his *Daily Tribune* reports and dealing with Gladstone's fiscal policies. In May he began investigating the question of British influence and hegemony in the East in preparation for his articles on British rule in India and China. He made numerous excerpts from authors such as Thomas Raffles, Washington Wilks, George Campbell, R. P. Patton and David Urquhart, and examined numerous documents on British diplomatic relations with India, in particular the publications of the India Reform Association and Urquhart's *Portfolio*. Between June and October eleven articles by Marx on India, British rule in the East, and the East India Company appeared in the *Daily Tribune*. On June 14 Marx's article on 'Revolution in China and Europe' was published as well. Here he recapitulated the recent history of Western, and especially British, trade with the East, calling attention to the social changes wrought by the influx of foreign commercial goods: the patriarchal authority of the Chinese emperor was being undermined; the population unsettled through the abundance of inexpensive British textiles and the growing use of opium; Eastern isolation was brought to an end as industrialisation drove the West to seek new and unexplored markets:

Now, England having brought about the revolution of China, the question is how that revolution will in time rest on England and through England on Europe ... it may safely be augured that the Chinese revolution will throw the spark into the overloaded mine of the present industrial system and cause the explosion of the long-prepared general crisis, which, spreading abroad, will be closely followed by political revolutions on the Continent (June 14).

His studies on the developmental history of Eastern society led Marx to conclude that '... Bernier rightly considered the basis of all phenomena in the East—he refers to Turkey, Persia, Hindustan—to be the *absence of any private property whatsoever in land*. This is the real key, even to the Oriental heaven ...' (letter to Engels, June 2). As for India, Marx maintained that the incursion of the British bourgeoisie had, as such, no effect of a social-revolutionary nature and explained the 'stationary character' of the East as due to:

1. the public works which are the affair of the central government.
2. Besides this, the whole empire except for the few larger cities is divided up into *villages*, each having an entirely distinct organisation and forming a little world in itself (June 14).

From June to September Marx continued his correspondent's reports on the growing conflict between Russia and Turkey, the Irish question, parliamentary affairs in Britain and the crisis symptoms, war, strikes, price increases, etc. In an article on the 'Russian Question' (Aug. 12) Marx reviewed Russia's historical role as aggressor in Central Europe, noting the consistency of the goals pursued by the Czars. He attributed this aggression to Russia's geographical circumstances and the need for access to seaports in order to maintain her influence in Europe, as well as to her traditions: 'If the success of her hereditary policy proves the weakness of the Western powers, the stereotyped mannerism of that policy proves the intrinsic barbarism of Russia herself.' While the cunning of Russian politics succeeded in impressing the courts of Europe, Marx believed that Russia would prove herself 'utterly powerless with the revolutionised peoples'. The approaching social revolution which will over-throw the domination of the Christian Rome of the West will also prove to be the 'real antagonist' of Russian tyranny and put an end to the demonaic influence of Constantinople, the Eastern Rome at stake in the present conflict between Russia and the West. In another article from June 14 Marx had also warned about the Russian tactics of expansion in Europe using religious pretexts and summed up the account of its territorial gains as protector of Orthodox Christianity: 'The total acquisitions of Russia during the last sixty years are equal in extent and importance to the whole empire she had possessed in Europe before that time'.

British aggression in the East, on the other hand, achieved a double purpose—first, in destroying the old primitive society and, secondly, in constructing a modern, industrialised Indian nation. With the introduction of the railway system in the East the British paved the way for modern industry and the development of the country's productive power. Moreover, this step put an end to the isolated craftsmen's enterprises and dissolved the 'hereditary divisions of labour upon which rest the Indian castes, those decisive impediments to Indian progress and Indian power' (August 8). In India as elsewhere the bourgeoisie of industrialised Europe was fulfilling its historic task of developing the material basis upon which a new social order might be founded: 'Bourgeois industry and commerce create these material conditions in the same way as geological revolutions have created the surface of the earth.'

In the London *Morning Advertiser* the Russian immigrants Ivan Golovin and Alexander Herzen attacked Marx for having supposedly written a defamatory article against their countryman Bakunin on August 23 in the same journal. Marx's reply, published on September 2, refuted this assumption and declared his solidarity with Bakunin's activity in past revolutionary efforts.

Although he continued his regular contributions to the *Daily Tribune*, Marx still found himself in financial distress and was aided by occasional one-pound or five-pound notes from Engels. From time to time he contributed as well to the *People's Paper*, yet, as he confessed to Cluss:

This continual journalistic hack-work is getting on my nerves. It takes up a lot of time, destroys any continuity in my efforts and in the final analysis really amounts to nothing at all. You can be as independent as you please, nevertheless you are tied down to the paper and to the readers, especially when you are paid in cash as I am. Purely scientific endeavours are something totally different (Sept. 5).

Marx continued to follow the events of the Turkish conflict until the end of the year with about 16 articles published beginning in September. He also treated British economic and political affairs—Peel's Bank Act of 1844, strikes, the misery of Britain's industrial workers—and wrote a series of six articles on Lord Palmerston, published in full in the *People's Paper* and in abridged form in the *Daily Tribune*. The London publisher E. Tucker brought out one of these articles on 'Palmerston and Russia' as a fly-sheet in a printing of 15,000 copies. This publication soon proved to be Marx's greatest literary success. Although the first edition was out of print within a few weeks, Marx himself realised no financial gain from the enterprise. The articles on Lord Palmerston were written in the same satirical tone which characterised his polemics against Bruno Bauer and his followers. Marx attacked both the personality and the politics of the renowned British statesman, whom he depicted as a man of neither profound ideas nor high objectives, but rather as one who 'exults in show conflicts, show battles, show enemies, ... in violent parliamentary debates, which are sure to prepare him an ephemeral success, the constant and the only object of all his exertions' (Marx, Engels, *On Britain*, p. 394). Submissive to foreign influence in deed if not in word, Lord Palmerston helped Europe's tyrants to consolidate their power, while declaring himself the champion of constitutional freedom and democracy. In Marx's eyes, his greatest shortcoming was to be extremely credulous in his dealings with the Russians, thereby helping them to achieve dominance over the Danube shipping routes.

There is no such word in the Russian vocabulary as 'honour'. As to the thing itself, it is considered to be a French delusion ... For the inventions of Russian honour the world is exclusively indebted to my Lord Palmerston, who, during a quarter of a century, used at every critical moment to pledge himself in the most emphatic manner, for the 'honour' of the Czar (Hutchinson, p. 209).

Thus the vaunted merits and services of Palmerston to the world and to his people were in fact but the pose of an aristocratic 'agent' of Russian absolutism.

Marx's *Revelations*, which had appeared in America only, provoked an attack by August Willich, also conducted in the German-American press. Cluss in Washington sent Marx copies of Willich's articles, published during October and November in the *Belletristisches Journal und New-Yorker Criminal-Zeitung*. Willich had inspired earlier in the year (April) a series of articles against Marx by Wilhelm Hirsch, who revealed Marx's relations with the spy Bangya in an attempt to discredit him among the revolutionary and proletarian groups. Marx decided to prepare a rejoinder to Willich's remarks and wrote during November a pamphlet ironically entitled *The Knight of the Noble Consciousness*, which he sent to Cluss on the 29th for publication in America.

1845 Willich's attack on Marx had been motivated by the feeling that Marx had wrongfully insulted and betrayed both him and his faction in the Communist League with his 'revelations'. He accused Marx of having falsified and distorted the evidence presented in defence of the Cologne communists. In *The Knight of the Noble Consciousness* Marx denied that he had used unseemly tactics or committed indiscretions against his fellow communists. He underlined the essential difference between the Working Men's Educational Association and the Communist League, contrasting the 'public, exoteric' functioning of the first with the secret nature of the League, and explained in detail the issues which had led to a split between the group around Marx and Engels and the sectarian 'party of adventurers' under the leadership of Willich and Schapper. This 16-page pamphlet appeared in New York in mid-January.

Marx continued his bi-weekly contributions to the *Daily Tribune*, for which he received one pound per article in payment. He was at variance with the *Tribune's* editors who allowed 'only rubbish' to appear under his name, while the best of his articles were used as leaders without any mention of his authorship (*see* letter to Engels, April 22). In the course of the year Marx and Dana reached an agreement whereby Marx's articles were to appear henceforth as the anonymous contributions 'from our London correspondent'. The chief preoccupation of the year's *Tribune* reports was the war between Russia and Turkey and its repercussions in the West. Marx hoped for a massive proletarian uprising to be ignited by the European war on the Eastern problem and foresaw this revolution as the 'sixth and greatest European power' which would intimidate the other five (Feb. 2). He criticized the European statesmen and politicians for their failure to provide an effective policy to check the Russian advances. He pilloried, for example, a liberal member of the British Parliament, Richard Cobden, for sympathising with the Czar's foreign policy (Feb. 16). Cobden was the author of numerous pamphlets in support of Czarism. The French commander-in-chief of the Crimean troops, A. Leroy de Saint-Arnaud, also provoked Marx to a sharp critique which presented the French officer as an unscrupulous adventurer and the prototype of Louis Bonaparte's party of power-mongers (June 24). Similarly, Marx attacked the war policies of the Prussians and the Austrians, terming Austria a tool in the hands of the Russian monarch and his English allies, while Prussia was characterised as 'greedy, vacillating and pusillanimous', ready to support whatever party offered it the greatest advantages, regardless of its principles (Feb. 2). Two articles in the *Daily Tribune* were devoted to the secret diplomatic correspondence between Britain and the other great powers for a division of conquered Turkey. Apart from this war, in the first half of the year Marx also treated British finances, electoral laws and the general politico-economic situation as well as the insurrection in Greece and the Allied occupation.

In early February E. Tucker prepared, with Marx's aid, a revised edition of the first political fly-sheet under the new title *Palmerston and Poland*. At the same time Tucker brought out a second Palmerston fly-sheet entitled *Palmerston, what has he done?* or *Palmerston and the Treaty of Unkiar Skelessi* and containing two more of the six *People's Paper* articles. Noting that there was 'a pretty brisk demand' for these two publications, Tucker suggested to Marx a third (cf. Marx to Engels, July 27).

In February the first meeting took place between Marx and the 'thorough-going monomaniac' Russophobe David Urquhart in London. The latter paid Marx the high compliment of saying that his anti-Palmerston articles left the same impression 'as if a Turk had written them'. Marx retorted that his orientation was rather more revolutionary than Turkophile (Marx to Engels, Feb. 9).

The predominant topic of discussion in Marx's correspondence with Ferdinand Lassalle was also the Crimean War. Lassalle, who had access to the highest official sources of information on the war, in Prussia, furnished Marx with material for a *Tribune* article on 'The Mission of Count Orloff' (Feb. 20-21). The two men differed on the question of Palmerston and his true intentions and on a definition of the nature of this war. Lassalle maintained that England had no plan for waging a 'phoney war', but that, on the contrary, the British ministry feared the war would become 'gruesomely serious' (March 7). Lassalle attempted to correct Marx's image of Palmerston who, whatever might be the results of his politics, was not deliberately acting in the interests of the Czar. Marx replied that for him nothing was more certain than the conclusion that 'Palmerston is a *Russian agent*' (April 6). They did agree, however, that 'the present apathy cannot be overcome by theory' but only through the heat of an open conflict (Lassalle to Marx, Feb. 10) and that a German revolution would result from an all-out war against Russia.

In March the Chartists called together a 'Labour Parliament' and invited Marx to attend as an honorary delegate. Marx declined the invitation but sent a message of congratulations to the assembly, which was published subsequently in the *People's Paper* (March 18). 'The mere assembling of such a Parliament marks a new epoch in the history of the world' and was certain to arouse the hopes of the working class in Europe and America that it would soon be possible to free their productive powers from the 'infamous shackles of monopoly' and subject them to the joint control of their producers. Having conquered nature, the working classes now had the task of conquering man and the most effective step towards this goal, Marx concluded, would be a national organisation of their forces modelled on the Labour Parliament (Marx, Engels, *On Britain*, p. 403).

Wilhelm Weitling's German newspaper *Die Republik der Arbeiter*, published in New York, brought out a series of articles on 'The Fundamental Trends of the Times', among them a critique of Marx's economic thought which Marx referred to as a 'furious onslaught on our "corrupt ideas" and unprincipled "frivolity"' (Letter to Engels, May 6). The author, E. Wiss, compared Marx and his adherents to the Neptunists who maintain that the earth was formed by the striking of the waters with the difference that the former steadfastly persist in their belief that the 'development of class contradictions' and the effects thereof, alternating periods of crisis and prosperity, are the moving factors. 'They calculate that a new society will be constituted when the revolution with its primary impulses is at work among the peoples, when vulcanic man finally rises up on this vulcanic earth to break through the petrified products of his past, to melt down and destroy its tyrannic insolence and oppressive strata of class contradictions with subterranean fire' (*Die Republik der Arbeiter*, Apr. 1).

The Marx family's financial circumstances continued to be dismal; they were frequently ill, yet lacked the money for medicine and doctor's fees. In May the children came down with measles, while Marx was suffering from a facial ulcer which hindered his work. In June Jenny Marx was pregnant and, when she became seriously ill, Marx was unable to call the doctor to whom he owed a total of £26. He wrote to Engels for assistance and remarked: 'Beatus ille who has no family' (June 21).

Marx's reading for the year was orientated around the themes he treated for the *Tribune*. In March he took up a history of the Ottoman Empire by Joseph Hammer-Purgstall. He began learning Spanish with the intention of studying the current events and history of Spain, and before long was reading *Don Quixote* in the original, Calderón, etc. A work which he found most interesting was Augustin Thierry's *Essai sur l'histoire de la formation et des progrès du tiers état* (1853). 'Father of the class struggle' in French historical writing, Thierry expressed in his Preface a certain indignation with writers who tried to discover class antagonisms between proletariat and bourgeoisie and to find the roots of this conflict in the history of the *tiers-état* before 1789. 'If M. Thierry had read us,' Marx wrote to Engels, 'he would have known that the decisive antagonism between bourgeoisie and *peuple* does not arise of course until the former has ceased its opposition to the *clergé* and the *noblesse* as the *tiers-état*' (July 27). Characteristic of France, Marx noted in reading Thierry, was that the bourgeoisie had traditionally gained strength through parliamentary representation and the bureaucracy and not, as in England, exclusively through commerce and industry.

After doing intensive research in Spanish history with works by Carlos Luis Federico de Bransen, H. Wood, Chateaubriand and Manuel de Marliani, Marx wrote nine articles for the *Tribune* which were published under the heading 'Revolutionary Spain' from September to December. At the same time he continued to send the *Tribune* regular reports of the actual course of the 1854 revolution which began in summer. Thus, taken together, Marx's series of articles on Spain provide at once a historical analysis of the circumstances which made that country ripe for revolution and a descriptive account of the most recent outbreak.

In the first article on 'Revolutionary Spain' (Sept. 25) Marx explained the unique character of Spain's feudal monarchy, which he compared to Asiatic forms of government. Although headed by an absolutist sovereign, the 'agglomeration of mismanaged republics' called Spain did not become centralised and the local independence nourished popular civil liberties (Marx, Engels, *Revolution in Spain*, p. 26). This 'oriental' system of despotism tolerated self-government and since Labour was not repartitioned on a national scale nor was there extensive internal exchange of goods, the transition to centralisation was checked.

Marx devoted the third article to an analysis of the 1808 war for Spanish independence against the Napoleonic forces (Oct. 20). This great popular movement was both nationalist—in opposing the French aggressors—and dynastic, reactionary, superstitious and fanatical, 'regeneration mixed up with reaction' (*ibid.*, p. 31). For the defenders of Spanish sovereignty the past offered a powerful source of resistance against French encroachments and the country's 'oriental' peculiarities prevented the invaders from localising their attacks: '... the center of Spanish resistance was nowhere and everywhere' (*ibid.*, p. 36). In the provinces juntas were successfully established, but the weak central junta failed in its revolutionary mission and permitted the old monarchic order to be restored. The people, however, retained their eagerness for regional insurrection and came to support the military in 1820, when the 1812 constitution was reintroduced under Riego.

In the current revolutionary endeavour the military again played the role of the *avant-garde*, supported by a broad popular movement. However, this was no social revolution which Spain was experiencing, Marx pointed out, for 'the social question in the modern sense of the word has no foundation in a country with its resources yet undeveloped, and with such a scanty population as Spain ...' (*ibid.*, p. 126). The country's sole national institution was its army which therefore symbolised for the people the 'state'. Consequently, 'the movable part of the nation has been accustomed to regard the army as the natural instrument of every national rising' (*ibid.*, p. 96).

Just at the point when the revolution seemed likely to succeed, the vivid Spanish imagination made of the General Espartero a great national hero, whose reputed greatness, however, had no logical connections with the facts. With his return to power the counter-revolution began. Marx observed:

It is one of the peculiarities of revolutions that just as a people seem about to take a great start and to open a new era, they suffer themselves to be ruled by the delusions of the past and surrender all the power and influence they have so dearly won into the hands of men who represent, or are supposed to represent, the popular movement of a by-gone epoch (ibid., p. 102f.—Aug. 19).

In October, in connection with his studies on Spain, Marx read Chateaubriand's *Congrès de Verona* (1838) which was written in a style he described as a most repulsive mixture of 'elegant scepticism and Voltarianism of the 18th century and fashionable 19th-century sentimentalism and romanticism' (letter to Engels, Oct. 26). The 'conceited dandy' Chateaubriand openly admitted in his book to having been personally responsible for the French aggression against Spain in 1822.

As the fighting in the East continued, Marx reviewed the issues, covert and professed, which motivated this prolonged struggle. Under the guise of religious protectionism, rival bourgeois and aristocratic powers were exploiting nationalist movements for their own expansionist aims. Under the pretext of sacredness, the Crimean conflict was as much racial as national and represented a 'democratic revolt against ecclesiastical authority', which authority still retained a strong hold over state and population in Czarist Russia. 'Russia has claimed for its war of might against right a religious sanction as a war of the viceregent of God against the infidel Turks' (Blackstock and Hoselitz, p. 152). Nonetheless, this revolt marked a trend whose ultimate development was undeniably 'towards abrogating absolute authority and establishing the independence of the individual judgment and conscience in the religious as well as the political sphere of life' (ibid., p. 153).

The proletarian revolution, however, which Marx had hoped for at the outset of this conflict, failed to take place and, related to this failure, Europe proved incapable of conducting a real war, 'a decent, hardy, hard-fought war', as Marx imagined it, which would bring the Eastern Question to a decisive climax (August 17).

Reading Roswell Ripley's history of *The War with Mexico* (1849), Marx was particularly struck by the figure of General

Scott, reputedly America's first general, but according to Ripley a most 'vulgar, petty, untalented, whining, jealous bastard and a humbug, who, while conscious of owing everything to the bravery of his soldiers and the skill of his divisions, plays low-down tricks in order to assure himself of glory' (letter to Engels, Dec. 2).

Lassalle invited Marx to become a London correspondent for the Breslau *Neue Oder-Zeitung*, whose ownership had just been assumed by Lassalle's cousin. On December 20 Marx accepted this offer in a letter to the editor Moritz Elsner.

1855 With the new year Marx began his work for the NOZ, which published roughly a hundred of his reports during the next twelve months along with a substantial number by Engels. Marx's contributions to the *Daily Tribune* numbered only ten and it was Engels who wrote more frequently for New York this year.

Marx reported for the NOZ on international issues as well as on British politics and current events. His first article was a retrospective on recent world political affairs. He remarked that the British declaration of war against Russia was evidence of the weight of the popular masses on Parliament's decisions and signaled the end of bourgeois political domination (Jan. 2). In January Marx wrote several articles on the latest developments in the Crimean War, in particular on the 'Four Points'; and also commented on British trade and the present commercial crisis.

On January 16 Eleanor Marx was born—into bleak London weather and equally dismal material circumstances. Marx feared the worst for their youngest 'bonafide traveller', he wrote Engels (Feb. 13), for she soon became seriously ill.

Rereading his excerpt notebooks on 'Economics'—he wanted to 'master' their contents and have the essential ready for the moment when he would actually begin writing (letter to Engels, Feb. 13)—Marx overstrained his eyes and caught an inflammation. Thanks to his wealth of notes and excerpts Marx was able to provide Engels with a detailed account of the parliamentary proceedings under the Aberdeen government from 1852-55 and of the machinations between government and business for the same period. Engels's article, entitled 'The Last British

Government' appeared as a leader in the *Daily Tribune* on February 23.

Marx also furnished Lassalle with figures on the importation of grain to England since the repeal of the Corn Laws in 1846. He hazarded the conclusion that, while the price relations of industrial products had not been effected by the change in importation laws, the relative value of wages in agriculture had dropped in respect to the landowner's profit. This was a necessary consequence of the development of capital, as Marx had elaborated in his 1847 pamphlet on the free trade problem. He promised Lassalle statistical material from his notebooks in support of this hypothesis, adding that other works on this topic would undoubtedly appear soon since 'The period of crisis in England is simultaneously that of theoretical investigations' (Jan. 23).

Apart from research necessary for his current journalism, Marx did little reading of a personal nature. In a letter to Engels on March 8 he recounted having studied Roman history at the beginning of the year and drew the following conclusion from his investigations:

The internal history [of Rome] may plainly be resolved into the struggle between small and large landowners, modified naturally by the circumstances specific to slavery. The relations caused by debts, which from the start of Roman history played such an important role, figure now only in a family sense for small property holdings.

Marx declined an invitation of the International Emigrant Committee to attend a banquet on the anniversary of the February Revolution and to become an active member of their organisation. His reasons, he explained to Engels, were threefold: first of all, he considered such gatherings to be pointless; he did not want to attract the attention of the British police unnecessarily; and finally he wished to avoid meeting Alexander Herzen, having no desire 'to see old Europe renewed with Russian blood', an opinion he later repeated in the first edition of *Capital* (Feb. 13).

Marx reported in February and March for the NOZ chiefly on British affairs: on the parliamentary situation and Lord Palmerston, on the military—using information supplied by Engels—on Ireland's misery and growing unrest. He also wrote two articles on the reaction of the British press to the death of the Russian Czar. Typical of Marx's invectives against the British upper class were his remarks on Lord Palmerston, a man who 'with unconscionable adroitness ... has duped and cheated both friend and foe' (NOZ, March 3). He also exposed the corruption in governmental and military affairs, where nepotism and bribery had become 'the two factors that count', just as in the Church. Corruption was facilitated, Marx wrote, by the British Constitution, a document which he analysed in the *Tribune* on March 24. This constitution amounted to no more than a 'superannuated compromise, by which the general governing power is abandoned to some sections of the middle class, on condition that the whole of the real Government ... is secured to the landed aristocracy' (Marx, Engels, *On Britain*, p. 410). Through the war, however, and the commercial crisis which came in its wake the bankruptcy and helplessness of the old system had become evident. Marx predicted that the climax would soon be reached and then 'will the mask be torn off which has hitherto hid the real political features of Great Britain'; the crass antagonisms between proletariat and bourgeoisie would be openly recognised and England 'compelled to share in the general social evolutions of European society' (*ibid.*, p. 412).

Early in March, Marx's eight-year-old son Edgar, 'Musch', was taken ill with a dangerous gastric fever. Marx was himself suffering from frequent coughing spells and the doctor recommended that the family leave the unhealthy district of Soho where they were living. This was of course not financially feasible for the Marxes, who could scarcely make ends meet even with Engels's occasional contributions to their budget. Marx tended his son through weeks of critical illness, yet his condition worsened. The concerned father wrote to his friend Engels:

My wife has been ill for a week now as never before because of mental agitation. My own heart is bleeding and my head is on fire although of course I must maintain my composure. Not for a moment during this illness has the child betrayed his usual nature, at once original, good-natured and self-reliant (March 30).

On April 6 little Musch, 'animating spirit' of the Marx household, died in his father's arms. For Marx and his wife the house seemed suddenly deserted and desolated; both were completely 'down broken'. Only one thought consoled him, Marx wrote to his friend:

Amidst all the terrible moments of anguish which I have gone through in these past days, the thought of you and your friendship has kept me going and the hope that together we still have an intelligent task to accomplish in this world (April 12).

On April 18 Marx and his wife travelled to Manchester where they spent two weeks with Engels. Jenny continued to suffer physically and mentally from her bereavement and Marx, too, admitted to Lassalle how much he felt the loss of their son:

Bacon said that really important men have so many relations to the world and to nature, so many objects of interest that they can easily get over every loss. I do not belong to their number; My child's death has deeply affected me, both mentally and emotionally and I still feel the loss as acutely as on the first day. My poor wife is completely downbroken as well (July 28).

Upon Marx's recommendation Engels undertook to write two articles on the Panslavic movement, which were published subsequently in both the NOZ and the *Daily Tribune* (April-May). Marx transmitted them to Elsner of the NOZ, remarking that they were intended as part of a series and stressing the importance of informing Germany 'of the danger which is threatening' (April 17). The *Daily Tribune* made certain changes in Engels's text which distorted his views in conformity with the Panslavism of one of the editors. Engels's own attitude was most decidedly anti-Panslavic. He described this movement as the drive to liberate the Slav peoples under foreign domination combined with a political action whose aim was the destruction of Western culture: 'It leaves Europe with only one alternative: submission to the Slavic yoke or destruction forever of its offensive strength—Russia' (Blackstock and Hoselitz, p. 85; April 21). Although it had its origins in Austria as the offspring of the Slavic philologists who attempted to extract from linguistic similarities a doctrine of Slavic unity, Panslavism had not found its driving force until it was espoused by Russia, which turned it into a threat for all Europe.

From May to July Marx's articles in the NOZ centred principally around political and economic affairs in England. He wrote on the debates in Parliament, where the bureaucracy created 'an inexhaustible arsenal of parliamentary chicanery, hair-splitting and tactic manoeuvering'; on the association for administrative reform; on the Chartists, who opposed both the war in the East and the reform proposals. Marx reviewed the various Chartist demands, beginning with the universal suffrage, which would assure the popular masses of political power 'as a means towards the realisation of their social needs' (NOZ, June 8).

The Chartists and thousands of other protesting British citizens assembled in Hyde Park on June 24 and July 1 to demonstrate against the passage of a Beer Bill and a Sunday Trading Bill, measures which prohibited small shopkeepers from staying open on Sundays and closed the public amusement centres for the greater part of the day. Marx, who also attended and reported on these demonstrations for the NOZ, saw these laws as attempts by the Church to re-establish and consolidate its power over the masses with compulsory measures that, in fact, fostered the interests of the beer magnates and large commercial enterprises. The arbitrariness of these measures prompted Marx to compare England with medieval France:

In the 15th century the French aristocracy said: Voltaire for us, the mass and tithes for the people. In the 19th century the English aristocracy says: pious phrases for us, Christian practice for the people (June 28).

The scenes he witnessed in Hyde Park provided Marx with ample evidence that the struggle against clericalism had assumed the proportions of a battle between rich and poor and convinced him moreover, 'that *yesterday in Hyde Park the English revolution began*' (ibid.).

In May E. Tucker published in book form three of Marx's Palmerston articles, mentioning the author by name in his Preface. Marx feared that political repercussions might follow which would endanger his precarious situation as an alien in England.

The 'incomprehensible war' against Russia continued and Marx furnished the NOZ with numerous reports, dealing in particular with the military affairs of British and French. In the NOZ on August 31 he drew attention to the frequent desertions from the British army stationed outside Sebastopol. The reason for these desertions was to be found in the traditional

British method of keeping discipline within the ranks, namely, flogging. While the other European armies had begun to abolish corporal punishment, in England 'the cat-o'-nine-tails has been conserved in all its efficiency as an instrument of torture equal in rank to the Russian harrow'. In reality flogging destroyed discipline instead of maintaining it by breaking the soldier's morale and his *point d'honneur*. Translated in social terms, this military practice was but another means of retaining the aristocratic nature of British institutions.

Earlier in the year Lord John Russell, colonial minister and president of the Privy Council, resigned his office in face of the growing crisis in the Crimea. Marx commented on the parliamentary happenings and devoted a special series of six articles to Russell and his parliamentary and ministerial career. The articles were published in the *NOZ* from July 28-August 15 and in the *Daily Tribune* on August 28. A 'classic representative of modern Whiggism', Russell was incapable of transforming his opinions and views into deeds. Whatever the issue might be, Jewish emancipation, anti-clericalism, law reform, free trade or the Irish emancipation, Russell failed each time to realise the standpoint he had taken. His true genius, Marx noted, lay in his ability to reduce these generous political measures to trivial parliamentary bills or to dissolve them magically before they became law. His career and his reputation were built on false pretences, began under the pretence of tolerance and liberalism and ended on a note of bigotry:

Placed by birth, connections and social accident on a colossal pedestal, he always remained the same *homunculus*—a malignant and distorted dwarf on the top of a pyramid. The history of the world exhibits, perhaps, no other man so great in littleness (*NYDT*, Aug. 28).

In a letter to Elsner on September 11 Marx declared that in view of the present financial crisis of the *NOZ* he would be willing to continue his reports even without payment. He valued highly the fact that 'the *NOZ* publishes the extreme limit of what can possibly be published under the present press circumstances' in Germany (to Elsner, Nov. 8). Although this offer might suggest otherwise, Marx's financial circumstances had not improved. On the contrary, he was obliged to hide out with Engels in Manchester from September 12 to December 4 to avoid a legal action for non-payment of medical bills. In October, having mistakenly assumed that Elsner had abandoned the paper to a group of Breslau liberals, Marx interrupted his bi-weekly reports. In November he resumed reporting for the *Daily Tribune* as well and came to an agreement with Dana, whereby he would be paid ten dollars per article for bi-weekly contributions. All of his *Tribune* articles now appeared anonymously. The year's last pieces of journalism dealt with the Crimean War, speculation on the European markets and British politics.

1856 During the winter 1855-56 Marx had several visits with his estranged friend Bruno Bauer, who was spending some time in England. Marx described Bauer as a light-hearted old gentleman, a confirmed bachelor as always, and hazarded the guess that Bauer wanted to introduce 'scientific theology', now dead in Germany, in England. In his letters to Engels Marx recounted the conversations he had with Bauer who held class struggles to be illusory and told Marx that the proletariat had no hatred for the other classes. A few pennies more in wages and everything would be in order (*see* letters to Engels, Jan. 18 and Feb. 12).

This year Marx contributed roughly two dozen articles to the *Daily Tribune* and seven to the Chartist's *People's Paper*. The London *Free Press* reprinted between November 1855 and February of this year the 1853 series on Lord Palmerston. British affairs were the chief topic of Marx's writing for the *Daily Tribune* along with the Crimean War. However, as he wrote to Engels on February 12, 'This newspaper writing is getting to be most bothersome now, since *nothing* at all is going on in England and the change in the economic situation is not very clear yet. At the moment the decisive factor is the swindling on the stock markets, but for this the necessary material is lacking.' Early in February Marx began investigating a number of documents on British diplomatic relations which he had discovered accidentally in the British Museum Library. He then decided to use his findings for a detailed study of the secret collaboration between St Petersburg and London which helped Russia to its place as a world power. Marx was particularly interested in finding a publisher for his 'curiosa' which would expose Britain's complicity with Russia and the conscious submission of British statesmen to the will of the Eastern despots.

In one of his first articles for the *Daily Tribune* this year,

Marx anticipated the viewpoint sketched above. Reporting on 'Traditional English Policy', Marx stated that historical evidence did not corroborate Britain's professed opposition to Russian expansionism but that, on the contrary, British diplomats had always behaved as Russia's lackeys. Marx recounted the example of the statesman Sir James Harris, who, during the American War of Independence, convinced his government of the 'necessity of nourishing the Russian appetite, if her aid against the American colonies was to be secured'. Marx queried the logic behind such an act: 'Was Russia less barbarous then than she is pictured now? Was she less then that hideous depotism which modern Whigs in such terrible colour portray her?' (NYDT, Jan. 12). Marx could only denounce the course chosen by the British as a betrayal of their own interests in Europe.

Marx reported on the approaching conclusion to the long war in the Crimea in an article entitled 'The Results of the War' (Feb. 16). Despite its costs in terms of men and materials, this war had shaken neither the political nor the social state of Europe: 'The squandering of these immense resources and the sacrifice of torrents of blood have gained nothing for the people'. Marx's commentary on the Treaty of Paris, dated March 30, appeared in the *Daily Tribune* on April 14. He attached far greater significance to this treaty than to the treaty of 1840-41 in so far as it signalled the end of the Holy Alliance and pointed to new 'affinities and attractions' between countries, notably France and Russia. The war itself Marx termed 'exclusively diplomatic', and like most other European wars it had been conducted 'by princes for their individual aims and interests; of course the various classes of peoples and nations have not been contemplated and received no real satisfaction' from the struggle.

During the first part of the year Marx began an intensive study of Slavic history, literature and culture. Again he inspired Engels to write a series of articles on Panslavism for the *Daily Tribune*. In corresponding with Engels, Marx provided him with an abundance of bibliographical material and much critical commentary on the works in question. Marx sent the finished manuscripts to Charles Dana, who returned them, however, in September unpublished. Marx later learned that Dana had been influenced by a member of the *Tribune*'s editorial staff who was in the service of the Russian government. Although the articles never appeared in print, 'we have the honour', Marx wrote to

Engels, 'of having, or rather of *having had*, our articles inspected and censured by the Russian legation' (Oct. 30).

For the *Daily Tribune* and both the *People's Paper* and the *Free Press* in London Marx prepared a critique of the British defeat at Kars when this Turkish city fell into the hands of the Russians on November 28, 1855. Supporting his argumentation with official documents and statements of the participants in the struggle, Marx claimed that the British Government deliberately foiled the military defence of Kars by falsifying communiqués and suppressing important papers. A 'phoney war' had been fought; a 'phoney peace' was concluded and the heroes of the British army and diplomacy could collect their rewards:

History exhibits, perhaps, no parallel more bitterly ludicrous than that between the British Government making England the laughing-stock of Europe by its adventures in the Crimea, the Baltic, and the Pacific, and the rewards lavished on the tools of its miscarriages ... (*People's Paper*, April 26).

A series of four articles on 'The Fall of Kars' appeared in *The People's Paper* (April), one in the *Tribune* (April 18) and one entitled 'Kars Papers Curiosities' in the *Free Press* (May 3).

Marx was the only member of the London emigration to be invited to a celebration on April 14 for the fourth anniversary of *The People's Paper*. He delivered a short address in which he spoke of the social revolution which had been foreshadowed by the revolutions of 1848-49. Characterising the 19th century as a time in which 'everything seems pregnant with its contrary', Marx summed up the antagonism between modern industry and scientific progress on the one hand and social relations on the other: 'At the same pace that mankind masters nature, man seems to become enslaved to other men or to his own infamy.' Amidst the signs of dissolution and progress, 'signs that bewilder the middle class, the aristocracy and the poor prophets of regression', Marx saw an element of potential social upheaval in the 'new-fangled men' of modern industrial society. These pioneers, with the English working class at their fore, would aid 'our brave friend, Robin Goodfellow, the old mole that can work in the earth so fast, that worthy pioneer—the Revolution' to emancipate the world from the domination of capital and wages slavery (Marx, Engels, *On Britain*, pp. 446f.). Occasional articles were devoted in this year to the developments in Prussia or

Italy. A new upsurge of constitutionalism in Italy provided the motive for an article on the House of Savoy, ruler of Sardinia and of Piedmont (May). Bourgeoisie and peasant and proletarian masses had begun co-operating in Italy in order to check the power of what Marx referred to as the 'Piedmontese nightmare'. By contrast, Prussia did not seem to be making progress towards constitutional democracy and Marx could only discern signs of dissention and disaccord among all elements of society (NYDT, May 5).

In May Engels, while travelling throughout Ireland, observed the people and their living conditions. He wrote to Marx about the tangible reality of Ireland: famine and devastation. Ireland was indeed England's 'first colony':

How often have the Irish set out to achieve something, and every time they have been crushed down, politically and industrially! Through consistent oppression they have been artificially made into a racked and ruined nation ... (May 23).

Marx's well-documented study of the 18th-century diplomatic affairs between Russia and England which he had been preparing since the beginning of the year was published in abridged form in the *Sheffield Free Press* (June-Aug.). After Marx had objected to unauthorised changes, the full text of *The Revelations of the Diplomatic History of the 18th Century* was later printed in the London *Free Press* (Aug. 1856-April 1857).

The seven documents which Marx revealed in his secret diplomatic history exposed the expansionist plans of the Russian Czar and the deliberate, intentional aid which the British diplomats granted him, while damaging their own national interests, both political and financial. In the secret despatches which Marx discovered and published the British statesmen are found conversing about 'Russia and her rulers in a tone of awful reserve, abject servility, and cynical submission' (*Secret Diplomatic History* ... , p. 91). Despite many warnings at home about the Russian plans for world domination, the British diplomats persisted in fawning for 'a strong glow of friendship' from the Russian Empress Ann without, for their part, receiving even the slightest promise of material advantage. Claims that British trade had expanded during the reign of Peter the Great, who was supported by London, were greatly exaggerated. Neither navigation nor commerce in general profited from the opening of trade relations with Russia, at the expense of the trade with Sweden. Thus 'there devolved on the Cabinet, at least, the *onus* of inventing *mercantile pretexts*, however futile, for the measures of foreign policy' (*ibid.*, p. 91).

Beginning in the 14th century an immense empire emerged in the 'historical arena' under the reigns of Ivan I, Kalita (1328-40) and of Ivan III, surnamed the Great (1440-1505). Ivan Kalita, Marx recounted, overthrew the Tartar yoke with 'the Machiavellianism of the usurping slave. His own weakness—his slavery —he turned into the mainspring of his strength' (*ibid.*, p. 184). His policies endured under his successors and, as Marx stated in a section of the history which was omitted in the first printing, 'A simple substitution of names and dates will prove to evidence that between the policy of Ivan III, and that of modern Russia, there exists not similarity but sameness' (*ibid.*, p. 120).

Peter the Great in the 17th and 18th centuries merited recognition for his successful transformation of the traditional Muscovite methods of local expansion into methods worthy of a country aspiring to unlimited power. He took hold of the Baltic provinces and made Petersburg 'the *eccentric centre* of the Empire' and his own 'abode of cosmopolitan intrigue' (*ibid.*, p. 124). From here was able to win from Europe the necessary elements of culture, military cunning, bureaucrats and teachers 'who were to drill Russians into that varnish of civilisation that adapts them to the technical appliances of the Western peoples, without imbuing them with their ideas' (*ibid.*, p. 125). Czar Peter thus succeeded in coupling 'the political craft of the Mongol slave with the proud aspiration of the Mongol master, to whom Genghis Khan had, by will, bequeathed his conquest of the earth' (*ibid.*, 121).

Marx's commentaries, published in the summer of the year, on the Spanish Revolution and the founding of the French bank *Crédit mobilier* are of particular interest as historical analyses which surpass the scope of ordinary reporting. In Marx's words, the recent Spanish insurrection illustrated anew 'the character of most of the European struggles of 1848-49, and of those thereafter to take place on the Western portion of that continent' (Marx, Engels, *On Spain*, p. 147). The struggle began typically with the battle lines drawn between the middle classes, supported by industry, and the powers of the military and the royal court.

The alignment of forces broke down, however, as soon as the working class joined the rebellious bourgeoisie against the despotic rulers. As in the earlier revolutions, the middle class, frightened by the prospect of social upheaval, sought the protection of the detested military. This, Marx maintained, was the 'secret of the standing armies of Europe, which otherwise will be incomprehensible to the future historian' (ibid., p. 147). The bourgeoisie was thus forced to choose between renouncing all political power to the despots or renouncing its own monopoly on social power to the advantage of the working class (Aug. 8).

In June Marx embarked on a long and detailed analysis of the crisis of speculation which had gripped Europe. He began with three articles in the Daily Tribune on the French joint-stock bank Crédit mobilier. This project began in 1852, when Louis Bonaparte discovered a means to convert 'all the property and all the industry of France into a personal obligation towards Louis Bonaparte'. He was aided in this enterprise by the ex-followers of Saint-Simon, whose belief was that class differences would disappear 'before the creation of universal wealth by some new-fangled scheme of public wealth' (June 24). Bonaparte had the luck to find two such former Saint-Simonians, the brothers Pereire, 'who with their practical experience had the boldness to suspect stockjobbing behind Socialism, law behind Saint-Simon', and became the initiators of 'Bonapartist Socialism' and founders of Crédit mobilier. These banks engaged in activities similar to modern holding companies and realised their greatest revenues by speculating on the stock market. Marx foresaw the onbreak of a new era in political economy thanks to such companies, for they

revealed the productive powers of association not suspected before, and called into life industrial creations on a scale unattainable by the efforts of individual capitalists; on the other hand it must not be forgotten, that in joint-stock companies it is not the individuals that are associated, but the capital ... The concentration of capital has been accelerated and, as a natural corollary, the downfall of the small middle class (July 11).

In a related article published in October and devoted to the 'Monetary Crisis in Europe', Marx endeavoured to trace the significance of socio-economic developments since the 1848 uprisings. This period had been one of respite which permitted capitalist society 'a last, condensed display of all its tendencies. In politics, adoration of the sword; in morals, general corruption and hypocritical return to *explained* superstitions; in political economy, the mania of getting rich without the pains of producing' (NYDT, Oct. 15).

Aided by inheritances from Jenny Marx's deceased relatives, the family was able to move into more spacious living quarters in the healthier district of London near Maitland Park (Sept.). At this time Marx again took up his excerpt notebooks in connection with his *NYDT* articles on economic problems and prepared a collection of quotations on monetary theory. He also studied Polish history, in particular, the divisions of Poland since 1789. He read, in French, a book by Mierosławski on *The History of the Polish Commune from the Tenth to the Eighteenth Centuries*. He became a decided partisan of Poland, noting the historic fact 'that the intensity and vitality of all revolutions since 1789 are to be measured with near certainty in direct relation to their attitude towards Poland' (Marx to Engels, Dec. 2). Poland, in other words, was their 'external thermometer'.

The current conflict between Prussia and Switzerland over the small principality of Neufchâtel inspired Marx to study Prussian history and the rise of the House of the Hohenzollern. He learned that this great Northern power had won its empire through 'small-penny thievery, bribery, outright buys, manipulation with inheritances, etc.', that all its activities were characterised by mediocrity and held upright with 'punctual accounting, avoidance of extremes, exactness in military drill, a certain pedestrian vulgarity and "church regulations"', Marx wrote to Engels. 'It's disgusting!' (Dec. 2).

IV
1857-1863

1857-58   From America, where economic difficulties have fol-
          lowed an excessively rapid development of the railroad
          industry in scarcely populated regions, a financial crisis
          extends to Europe. It is in part responsible for renewed
          agitation for political unity and the consolidation of
          economic interests on the Continent.

—   Friedrich Wilhelm IV, now known to be mentally ill,
          has to abandon the Prussian throne. The regency is
          assumed by his brother Wilhelm.

1858   An Italian refugee in France, Félix Orsini, unsuccess-
          fully tries to assassinate Napoleon III. Following his
          arrest and execution the same year, the diplomats of
          both countries, Italy and France, are stimulated to
          negotiate for closer understanding. Cavour and
          Napoleon meet at Plombières-les-Bains for a secret dis-
          cussion of their interests and conclude an agreement
          which stipulates that France will support Italy in a
          war against Austria. Once the Austrians are expelled
          from Venetia and Lombardy, France is to gain in the
          settlement the territories of Nice and Savoy.

1859   Cavour's plan bears fruit: Austria is provoked to an
          attack and is defeated by united Franco-Sardinian
          troops. A rapidly concluded peace at Villafranca pro-
          viding for the establishment of an Italian confederation
          under Papal rule fails to satisfy Cavour and the
          republicans. Under the leadership of Garibaldi the

1860 fighting continues. Plebiscites are held in a number of Italian provinces and constituent assemblies convened. Nice and Savoy declare in favour of annexation to France, while Lombardy opts for union with the kingdom of Piedmont and Sardinia. Modena and Tuscany soon vote to join united Italy as well. Garibaldi, meanwhile, overthrows the despotic monarch of Sicily and, with the support of Sardinian forces, triumphantly

1861 enters Naples. Naples and Sicily vote for inclusion in the Sardinian kingdom. At the first meeting of the Italian Parliament all the provinces are represented except the Papal state and Venetia. Sardinia's Victor Emmanuel II is elected king of Italy.

1860 The first liberal commercial treaty between Britain and France is signed. According to the provisions of 'Cobden's Treaty', tariffs on goods commonly exchanged between the two countries are radically reduced.

1861 An ukase issued by Czar Alexander II of Russia puts an end to serfdom in that country. Approximately 47 million peasants are affected by this act, which although granting them legal freedom does not provide the economic freedom necessary for their independent well-being. For the most part, they now establish themselves as shareholders in the collective property of the *mir*—the village community—which has to pay redemption money to the former landowners. The individual peasant is not free to leave the collective without permission from the *mir*. The aristocracy profits enormously from the new economic arrangement.

— Wilhelm I is ordained King of Prussia after the death of his brother in January. He immediately reorganises and strengthens the army and then attempts to bend

1862 parliament to his will as well. Confronted by a parliamentary majority in opposition he appoints Bismarck to head his ministry. The liberal opposition unites to found the *Fortschrittspartei* (Progressive Party), which despite a more democratic programme nevertheless fails to defend the popular demands for electoral rights.

1863 Another new party is thus called into life by Ferdinand

Lassalle under the name *Allgemeiner Deutscher Arbeitverein* (ADAV—General Union of German Working Men), its declared first aim the achievement of universal suffrage.

1863   Upon the death of the Danish king Frederick VII the throne passes to Christian IX in accordance with the London Protocol of 1852. His first official act is to confirm a constitutional act annexing Schleswig to Denmark. Although officially bound by the provisions of the London agreement, Prussia and Austria nevertheless declare their opposition to this incorporation and the separation of Schleswig from Holstein. Prussian troops occupy Holstein and Lauenburg.

—   Congress Poland revolts against the domination of the Czar and sets up a provisional national government, which declares the country's independence and proclaims land reforms. The liberals meet with overwhelming opposition from conservative landowners and the bourgeoisie, who prevent the masses from assuming the initiative and extending the revolution to other regions of the country. Despite intervention from England, France and Austria, the national movement is crushed and Russia reasserts its hegemony.

THE AMERICAS

1857   The Dred Scott Decision: The US Supreme Court declares that negroes are not to be considered citizens according to the constitution and therefore do not enjoy the rights and privileges established therein.

1858   In Mexico the establishment of a reactionary government which repeals the liberal measures of its predecessor and suspends payment on foreign debts incites both internal and external opposition.

1859   Self-appointed liberator of the Southern slaves, the abolitionist John Brown invades the South with a party of armed followers and seizes the US arsenal at Harper's Ferry, Virginia. His call to insurrection is not heeded by the slaves, however, and eventually the Southern general Robert E. Lee attacks the fort and captures the Brown party. The affair ends with Brown's conviction on a charge of attempting to incite a slave rebellion and his execution by hanging.

1860   With the election of Abraham Lincoln to the US presidency the slave state of South Carolina secedes

1861   from the Union. Other Southern states soon follow suit and together establish the Confederate Union. They declare negro slavery essential to the cultivation of their sugar, tobacco and cotton crops. War is declared by the North on the grounds that the Union must be preserved. France and England, although officially neutral, show signs of hostility towards the North for blockading the coastline and thereby cutting off European exports to and imports from the South. The 'cotton famine' deprives some two million factory workers in England of their usual employment. The Trent Affair illustrates the diplomacy with which relations between England and the North are managed: The British Prime Minister demands that the North release two Confederate representatives captured on board an English ship, but the Queen, in an effort to avoid an open dispute, countermands his order.

1862   Meanwhile, Napoleon III plans to profit from the Civil War in North America by invading Mexico. Allied with Spain and England he sends troops to force President Juarez to fulfill the financial obligations neglected since 1858. Although a treaty is concluded at Veracruz, France has no desire to abandon her attack and thus breaks with her allies in order to continue singlehanded a war of conquest against

1863   Mexico. The plan succeeds and French troops triumphantly enter Mexico City. They establish a provisional government, which declares itself in favour of a European monarch, suppress the Mexican press and expropriate those who fought against France.

—   In the midst of hostilities, President Lincoln issues an Emancipation Proclamation, freeing the slaves in those states which have repudiated the Union.

THE FAR EAST

1857   With the signing of the Treaty of Karagawa between Japan and the USA, Japan is opened to foreign commerce.

—   In India, a religious incident—the native army is given for use in its weapons cartridges greased with animal fat, a substance forbidden to both Mohammedans and Hindus—provokes the mutiny of native soldiers employed in the British military service and known as 'Sepoys'. The Sepoy rebellion spreads throughout the region of Delhi; British-occupied Cawnpore is attacked and men, women and children hostages are ruthlessly massacred. The turning point comes when British troops receive reinforcements which enable them to recapture Delhi. They exact vengeance for the massacres with equally brutal measures against the natives.

—   Sustained by French military assistance, the British are able to continue the Second Opium War against

1858   China. They occupy Canton, present peace demands to Peking and insist that the treaty be ratified in the Chinese capital. The emperor refuses to comply and so, despite the conclusion of the Treaty of Tien-Tsin which guarantees the British the right to import opium on payment of 50 dollars duty per chest, the fighting

1860   continues. The imperialists ultimately bring about the Treaty of Peking which ratifies and extends the earlier treaty. England is to receive a higher indemnity covering the costs of the war, new ports are opened to foreign trade and the first foreign legations are allowed in Peking.

SCIENTIFIC AND TECHNOLOGICAL PROGRESS

1859   The first accumulator for the storage of electrical energy and its re-conversion into current is constructed by Gaston Planté in France.

1860   Two German chemists, Robert Bunsen and Gustav

Kirchhoff, demonstrate that infinitesimal quantities of metals can be readily detected with the spectroscope. Their discovery marks the beginning of the science of spectral analysis.

— Marcelin Berthelot introduces synthetic organic chemistry with the publication of his book *Chimie organique fondée sur la synthèse.*

— Etienne Lenoir markets an early engine operating on illuminating gas, producing pressure from combustion rather than vacuum. The 'illuminant' was a gas of an unsaturated carbon mixture like benzene, propylene and ethylene.

1863   Charles Tellier invents a process of conservation through refrigeration.

IMPORTANT BOOKS PUBLISHED

1857   P.-J. Proudhon: *Manuel du spéculateur à la bourse.**
1857-59 Carl Friedrich Köppen: *Die Religion des Buddha und ihre Entstehung.**
1858   P.-J. Proudhon: *La Justice dans la Révolution et l'Eglise.*
— James Mill: *A History of British India.**
1859   Charles Darwin: *Origin of Species by Means of Natural Selection.**
— John Stuart Mill: *On Liberty.*
1861   P.-J. Proudhon: *Théorie de l'impôt.*†
— George Eliot: *Silas Marner.*
1862   Herbert Spencer: *First Principles.*
— Victor Hugo: *Les Misérables.*
1863   Charles Lyell: *The Geological Evidences of the Antiquity of Man.**
— P.-J. Proudhon: *Du Principe fédératif.**

KARL MARX
1857-1863

1857 While continuing to act as regular correspondent for the
    Daily Tribune, Marx resumed his work in economics, after
reading recent contributions in that field by his former antagonist
Proudhon (*Manuel du spéculateur à la bourse*, 1857) and Proudhon's disciple Alfred Darimon (*De la Réforme des banques*,
1856). During the first part of the year Marx read and took
notes on Thomas Tooke's *History of Prices* (vols. V and VI, 1857).

When in January and February the *Tribune* temporarily
stopped publishing Marx's contributions, the family found itself
in dismal financial straights, for Jenny's inheritances had been
consumed by the move from Soho Square to Maitland Park.
Marx was obliged to accept Charles Dana's offer of guaranteed
payment for one article per week, whether one be printed or
not, with additional payment only for those articles actually
used. Marx saw himself 'in a more desperate situation than five
years ago', he wrote to Engels, 'I thought I had already swallowed
the quintessence of misery. Mais non. And the worst of the
matter is that this crisis is not temporary. I do not see how I am
going to work my way out of it' (Jan. 20).

Among the topics of international significance which Marx
treated for the *Daily Tribune* the most persistent was British
aggression in the East—Persia, China and India. He also dealt
frequently with financial questions and with political and social
problems in England.

The issue of the lorcha 'Arrow' became a topic of parliamentary debate in England and resulted in the dissolution of
Parliament, as the country's naval forces launched an offensive
against Canton and other Chinese ports. Marx denounced 'this

mode of invading a peaceful country, without previous declaration of war' under the pretence of an insult to the British flag. But while the press was full of outcries against the Chinese wrongs, no word was said about the British crimes: opium trade, corrupting native civil servants, fraud, Chinese slave trade and 'bullying' (Jan. 23). The outbreak of hostilities in India delayed the prosecution of the second opium war until the end of the year. Marx then interrupted his reporting on China until the second half of 1858. The Sepoy rebellion was for Marx a symptom of the general discontent with the British hegemony in the Asiatic world. However infamous the conduct of the natives, it was only a 'reflection' in concentrated form of Britain's own conduct in India during the whole of its rule.

In January Marx began writing a pamphlet in reply to the pro-Russian articles published by Bruno Bauer in 1853-54 and sent to Marx at the beginning of this year by Edgar Bauer. He studied material on Russian history and on the political views of Russia's Scandinavian neighbours and composed a table of events for the 10th-17th centuries in Russian history. The manuscript for this pamphlet was abandoned unfinished.

Upon the request of its editor David Urquart, Marx provided the *Free Press* with pertinent information on the treacherous role played by the spy Bangya in Circassia and his relations with Constantinople. Articles based on this information appeared in the *Free Press* in April and May.

Charles Dana solicited Marx's collaboration in April on a new popular encyclopedia which he was planning to publish together with George Ripley. Engels advised Marx to accept the offer, thinking that this would be an 'enormous lift' for his friend, and suggested that he accept as many articles as possible. Marx agreed to write the articles on economics for *The New American Cyclopedia*, Engels those on military personages. Marx began with a one-page article on 'aesthetics' which he never finished. He did, however, compose a number of biographical entries, notably one on Simon Bolivar (about Oct.). When assembling material for these short biographical sketches, Marx employed various encyclopedias in different languages. The German lexica he characterised as 'written for children under eight', the French as 'partisan but at least mundane. The English cyclopedias candidly copy the French and the German' (letter to Engels, Sept. 25).

The Marx family's financial situation did not improve, especially since they were frequently ill and required medical attention. In July Jenny Marx was delivered of a child that died shortly after birth; in the spring Marx suffered a recurrence of his liver ailment which seriously impeded his work on the 'Economics'. Engels's aid came at two crucial moments, in July— to pay the overdue rent—and in December—for the long overdue taxes.

After eighteen months of silence Lassalle and Marx resumed their correspondence in April. Lassalle reported on his recent voyages, his life in Düsseldorf and the advancement of his 'half-philosophical, half-philological' work on Heraclitus, which he had now taken up again for the first time in ten years. While finishing this theoretical work, Lassalle was also labouring on a more 'concrete, political-economic product' and promised Marx copies of both as a sign of his 'unchanged respect and friendship' (Apr. 26).

Marx, meanwhile, was also making progress on his 'Economics'. In August he drafted a general introduction which, for the first time, elaborated in great detail the plan and procedure he intended to follow in constructing his work. He explained that his method would be to proceed from the abstract to the concrete, since the abstract categories of our thought are the actual starting point of observation and conception, not, however, the source which generates the concrete. He distanced himself with this method from Hegel who:

fell into the error of considering the real as the result of self-coordinating, self-absorbed and spontaneously operating thought, while the method of advancing from the abstract to the concrete is but the way of thinking by which the concrete is grasped and reproduced in our minds as concrete (*Grundrisse*, p. 22).

For Marx, therefore, the simplest abstract category exists only as the one side of a given concrete subject in its relation to man. His plan moved, in accordance with this concept of method, from the most highly abstract categories of political economy, applicable to all forms of society, to their concrete forms, as found in existing society, and used the Hegelian scheme, elaborated in his *Logic*, of following the 'generality' with the concept's 'particularity and its 'singularity'. The plan for Marx's book I of the

'Economics' was sketched out in the second of seven notebooks that contained what was later entitled the *Grundrisse zur Kritik der politischen Ökonomie* [Outlines for a Critique of Political Economy]. Like the overall plan for the 'Economics', it was divided into 6 parts:

I. 1. The general concept of capital.
  2. The particularity of capital: circulating capital, fixed capital. (Capital as a means of subsistence, raw material, instrument of labour.)
  3. Capital as money.
II. 1. The quantity of capital. Accumulation.
  2. Capital as a measure of itself. Profit. Interest. Value of capital: capital as differentiated from itself in interest and profit.
  3. The circulation of capital.
    a. The exchange of capital for capital. Exchange of capital for revenue. Capital and prices.
    b. The competition between capitals.
    c. The concentration of capital.
III. Capital as credit.
IV. Capital as share-capital.
 V. Capital as the money market.
VI. Capital as source of wealth. The capitalist (*Grundrisse*, p. 175).

After finishing with 'capital' Marx intended to embark on part 2, an investigation of bourgeois society as a universal organisation manifested in capital, wage-labour, landed property, social classes, etc. Part 3 was to be devoted to an analysis of bourgeois society as a state apparatus with its institutions such as taxation, public debts, credit; part 4 to the international organisation of production and part 5 to the world market.

Of the abstract categories which Marx undertook to examine, the most fundamental, as far as political economy is concerned, is the concept of value. Value's most concrete expression—money—provided the theme for Marx's second chapter. In the introduction he examined as well the concepts of labour and production, generalising the common elements of the two at all levels of economic development, yet he remarked that alone these concepts were nothing but abstractions which were never at any stage part of the productive process. Production always means a certain mode of production at a certain stage of social development and is inexorably bound to the social circumstances. To imagine that production might exist outside society 'is as great an absurdity as the idea of the development of language without individuals being together' (ibid., p. 6). Marx goes even further, stating that:

Man is in the most literal sense of the word a *zoon politikon*, not only a social animal, but an animal which can develop as a separate individual only in society (ibid., p. 6).

Social, and therefore economic, activity is traditionally divided into four departments: production, consumption, distribution and exchange. Marx's approach to these departments can be distinguished from that of his predecessors in so far as he distinguished for each the historical from the universal qualities, i.e. those qualities which remain true under all social conditions and those which are subject to change. Further, Marx pointed out the social nature of distribution as the two-fold mediator between production and consumption. The means of production are distributed among the members of society and determine accordingly their share in the total social product; secondly, the means of production are distributed as well among the various branches of economic activity. Marx's method of political economy, therefore, demands that, to understand the socio-historical nature of each economic department or category, the social interactions between these categories be constantly kept in mind.

Productivity, a function of man's social relations and social power, has according to Marx three stages of development. At the first stage it is a function of personal dependency between men, e.g., master to slave. On a higher level, personal dependency is replaced by material dependency; finally at the last stage the means of production have become objects of communal control, permitting henceforth free individual activity and universal development of the individual capacities.

The key to universal development for Marx is 'time'. When society is organised so that production has become community production, time will continue to be an essential determining factor, but will, however, no longer be a measure of exchange value. Given the latter, 'an objective meditation is required', that is money as something distinct from the product. Given communal production, on the other hand, time is the measure of social usefulness:

The less time society requires in order to produce wheat, cattle, etc., the more time it gains for other forms of production, material and intellectual. As with the single individual, the universality of its development, its enjoyment and its activity depend on its saving time (*ibid.* p. 89).

The general indifference as to the particular kind of labour performed in modern society implied for Marx that labour had reached a high level of technical development independent of the individual working man: 'This state of affairs has found its highest development in the most modern bourgeois societies, the United States', where individuals attach no great personal importance to the tasks they carry out, regarding them merely as means for creating wealth (*ibid.*, p. 25). Thus a particular form of production, namely that of bourgeois society, must be studied at its most highly developed level, where the greatest degree of abstraction and generality may be formulated, enabling one to understand the abstract categories and workings of production as common to all levels of production hitherto:

The anatomy of the human being is the key to the anatomy of the ape. But the intimations of a higher animal in the lower ones can be understood only if the animal of the higher order is already known (*ibid.*, p. 26).

Beginning then with an analysis of the concepts essential to an understanding of bourgeois society, Marx examined the phenomenon of capital, chief source of value in this the most highly developed system of production. Where capital has established itself as objectified wealth, as a productive force, the individual's labour, which is his creative power, is consumed not in a process of self-enrichment but in enriching capital. Production serves therefore neither the universal development of man nor of society but the one-sided development of wealth.

Marx later abandoned these introductory pages, which he felt went too far in revealing to the reader the conclusions yet to be proved, replacing them in 1859 with the Preface to the *Critique of Political Economy*. He concluded the general introduction with a lengthy passage on the relations between the

level of production in a given society and its artistic achievements, remarking that the perfection of a work of art is not a
function of the material development of the society in which it is
created. However, this level of material development is responsible
for the unique environment from which the artist draws his
inspiration. For example, 'Greek art could in no event originate
in a society which excludes any mythological explanation of
nature, any mythological attitude towards it, or which requires
of the artist an imagination free from mythology' (*ibid.* p. 31).
The 'charm' and attraction of such a work of art for us today,
Marx concluded, was in no way contradicted by the primitive
order of the artist's society.

Towards the end of the year Marx reported to Engels that he
was working on a summary of his economic studies 'in order to
have at least the outlines clear before the deluge' (Dec. 8) and
to get rid of what had become for him a veritable 'nightmare'.
On December 21 Marx answered Lassalle's letter of April 26,
mentioning that the present economic crisis had spurred him on
to advance the state of his writings on the principles of
economics, but that hours of journalistic writing and illness had
limited both time and energy available for this task. He thanked
Lassalle for the latter's recent publication on *Heraklit der Dunkle*,
a figure who had always inspired him with 'great tenderness' and
who after Aristotle was his favourite among the ancient thinkers.

Marx's last journalistic contributions of this year contained
much information on the uprising in India among the Sepoys
and on the financial crisis which presently beset England and the
Continent. He was especially concerned with the effects of the
crisis in France, where the state was intimately associated with
the security markets. He saw little chance that the Bonaparte
régime would survive the coming year.

1858 'Accompanied by lemonade on the one hand and an
immense amount of tobacco on the other,' Marx continued
working on his economic principles at night until illness and
fatigue forced him to break off his writing in April. His investigations on capital involved much arithmetical calculation, always
anathema for Marx, and he began therefore to study algebra
in hopes of overcoming the difficulties (cf. letters to Engels, Jan.
11 and 16). By mere chance he had come upon Hegel's *Logic*

in 1857 and was inspired to use Hegel's method in treating political economy. He informed Engels of his 'discovery', saying:

If there is ever time for such work again, I should quite like to write two or three printer's sheets which would enable the ordinary mind to understand the rational element in the method discovered, yet at the same mystified, by Hegel (Jan. 16).

As with so many of his plans, however, Marx never realised this intention.

Marx reported regularly to Engels on the progress he was making in elaborating his theoretical viewpoints and mentioned on January 16 having 'jettisoned completely the whole theory of profit as it has existed up till now'. He discovered that the source of profit was 'free labour' performed by the working man who sold his labour power in exchange for the means of subsistence and reproduction. In the voluminous notes Marx made during this period, reference is often simply to 'labour'. As he progressed in his writing, however, he began to differentiate 'labour'—that which is realised in the production process—from 'labour capacity' [*Arbeitsvermögen* or *Arbeitsfähigkeit*], being what the worker exchanges for wages. The exchange value of the individual worker's labour capacity is determined like every other commodity by the actual labour time necessary to produce or reproduce it, i.e. by the amount of time which went into the production of all the things necessary to assure the worker's existence. The owner of the means of production, however, acquires the use of the worker's labour capacity for a certain fixed working day which exceeds in hours the actual time required to pay for the worker's maintenance and reproduction. Therefore 'Wage Labour is always composed of paid and unpaid labour' (*Grundrisse*, p. 468). The labour which the working man furnishes has thus a certain exchange value, represented by the wages he receives, which does not correspond to its use value. Moreover for the worker himself labour has only exchange value and not use value and therefore 'does not exist for him as the productive force of wealth, as the means or activity of enrichment' (*ibid.*, p. 214). Only for capital does the worker's labour have use value, becoming activity which increases wealth. The result of capital's exploitation of labour is 'profit', which Marx classes under the general heading of 'surplus value' [*Mehrwert*].

Because of this unique relation between labour's exchange

value and its use value, the rate of profit of the owner of the means of production varies in direct proportion to the amount of living labour involved in the production of a given commodity. Since capital tends to encourage the replacement of men by machines, production costs fall, more objects may be manufactured and the capitalist thus receives a greater quantity of profit, i.e. a greater *absolute* profit. However, since according to Marx profit is created as surplus value only through human labour, the act of reducing human participation in production actually reduces the *relative* profit rate and this, then, ultimately leads to economic crises.

At this stage it may then be said that living labour power or labour capacity is no longer the principle source of wealth; labour time has ceased to be the measure of value and 'the surplus labour of the masses has ceased to be a condition for the development of wealth in general' (*ibid.*, p. 593). The measure of wealth is now the 'disposable time' for society as a whole and for each individual to develop freely, realising his own capacities:

With that the production based on exchange value collapses ... individuals are then in a position to develop freely. Necessary labour time is not reduced in order to create surplus labour, but the necessary labour of society in general is reduced to a minimum. Correspondingly, the individual members of society have at their disposal the time and the means to pursue their artistic, scientific, etc., development (*ibid.*, p. 593).

Marx made several references to the plan of his 'Economics' in corresponding with both Engels and Lassalle. On February 22 he revealed to Lassalle the plan worked out in his notebooks in the chapter on 'Capital':

The whole thing is divided into 6 books: (1) Capital (contains introductory chapters). (2) Landed property. (3) Wage labour. (4) The State. (5) International Trade. (6) The World Market.

The work was to be a 'critical presentation of the system of bourgeois economy', i.e. his descriptive analysis of the present system was to be based on a critical orientation to this system. Marx mentioned his interest in writing two additional works, a critique and history of political economy and socialism along with a historical sketch of economic categories and relations. But for the moment he lacked the 'time, the quiet and the means' to elaborate this first work and condense it to the terse form which he would like to achieve before turning it over to a publisher.

Lassalle proved useful to Marx in finding a publisher for the forthcoming work, one who would be willing to print it in a series of consecutive booklets. Marx wrote Lassalle that he would even be willing to renounce payment on the first booklet, if only a publisher would accept his work (cf. letter of March 11). The publisher of Lassalle's own book on *Heraclitus* declared himself willing to accept Marx's venture and even to pay him a substantial fee.

The first pamphlet, or booklet, was intended as a theoretical foundation for the whole 'Economics' and would encompass value, money and capital in general. The first three booklets together would cover the economic principles, the last three the basic trends of his critique of bourgeois society. He estimated that all six booklets would make up 30-40 printer's sheets (500-600 pages) and that he could have the first instalment ready by the end of May (to Lassalle, March 11).

Shortly thereafter, Marx described in detail the break-down of the first of the six parts which he referred to as 'books'. Book one was to consist of four sections: (1) capital in general; (2) competition; (3) credit; (4) share capital 'as the most perfect form (providing the transition to communism)' (April 2). The first pamphlet was to treat section 1 alone. He began explaining to Engels the transition from capital to landed property, from landed property to wage labour, which is the final, universal product of modern property relations. Marx's account of the contents of this first pamphlet was abruptly interrupted as a sudden attack of hepatitis put an end to his writing. His health worsened in the course of April, and Jenny Marx assumed her husband's correspondence. Writing to Lassalle, she revealed the psychological aspect of this illness:

Mental unrest and turbulence due to his inability to complete his work quickly and without interruptions naturally worsen his physical condition; the same applies to the onerous tasks necessary to earn his 'daily bread' and they, of course, cannot be pushed aside (April 9).

Engels came to Marx's aid in May, giving him the opportunity to come to Manchester, where he could ride on horseback, engage in various sports and recover from the weeks of illness and pressures of family life under such adverse conditions. As he remarked in an earlier letter to his friend:

There is no greater folly whatsoever for people with aspirations of universal dimensions than to marry and thus betray themselves to the *petites misères de la vie domestique et privée* (Feb. 22).

Upon his return from Manchester the task foremost in his mind was to prepare the first instalment of the 'Economics' out of the hundreds of pages he had written in the preceding ten months. 'The hell of it is', he wrote to Engels, 'that in this manuscript (which if printed would make a thick volume) everything is topsy-turvy, and it contains much that is intended for later sections.' (letter of May 31). But once again, illness in the family and financial worries kept Marx from taking up the manuscript again until August. Relentlessly pursued by his creditors, he finally saw no alternative but to make a clean breast of his affairs to Engels and ask his advice on finding a loan. He sent his friend a detailed list of receipts and expenditures. From £24 recently paid him by the *Daily Tribune*, for instance, Marx immediately settled the following outstanding debts and was consequently left with nothing for current expenses:

school for the quarter February, March, April	£8	
amount paid back to Schapper for four weeks' daily expenses	£3	
linen redeemed from pawnbrokers'	£2	
wages [for household aid—eds.]	£1	
tallyman	£1	4 0
butcher	£2	
grocer	£2	
greengrocer	£1	
blouses and dresses, etc., for the children	£2	
baker	£2	

His income scarcely sufficed to pay for their lodging, the children's schooling and enough interest on their debts to keep the bailiff from the door. At wit's end he confided to Engels:

I wouldn't wish it to my worst enemy to have to wade through the quagmire in which I have found myself for the past eight weeks, caught at the same time in the greatest fury because my intellect is being ruined and my capacity to work broken down (July 15).

In vain Marx tried to persuade his mother to pay out his part of the paternal inheritance. Finally aid came from Freiligrath who procured him a loan of £40 at 20% interest. Jenny Marx, whose nervous condition made the doctor fear cerebral meningitis, could then be sent off to the seaside for treatment.

In August Marx did some reading for the 'Economics' on currency, but put off his own writing until September. However, once back into the subject he expected to progress rapidly.

On September 21 he wrote to Engels that he would have the first two instalments for Duncker ready within a fortnight. While elaborating the final draft, Marx noticed that what had been intended for a single booklet now took up two. He had expanded the section on capital in general, hoping to make it more comprehensible for the ordinary reader. When Lassalle wrote to inquire about what had happened to the promised manuscript, Marx replied that illness, his journalistic writing and finally difficulties with the form of the 'Economics' had prevented him from finishing sooner. 'I could smell my liver trouble in the style of everything I wrote', he told Lassalle. The result of fifteen years of research, this project was to present for the first time 'in a scientific manner an important view of social relations' and, therefore, Marx did not want it to be spoiled by a sick liver (Nov. 12).

With Jenny's aid he copied out the first manuscript for publication between November and January 1859. Instead of the planned 5-6 printer's sheets the first section made up 12 sheets in all and contained only the first two chapters on commodities and money. The third chapter, the core of the theory on capital, was deferred till later. Not until 1867, however, did this 'chapter' appear—as volume 1 of *Capital*.

While Marx was engaged in his 'Economics' and with journalism, Engels was busy writing articles for the *New American Cyclopaedia*, chiefly on military subjects. He sent Marx to the British Museum Library to gather information on 'catapult', 'castrum', 'camp', etc. In July Engels asked for Hegel's *Naturphilosophie* which he wished to study in connection with his investigations in comparative anatomy and physiology. In Hegel Engels saw an anticipation of modern science:

Everything is cell. The cell is the Hegelian 'Being-in-itself' and passes through the Hegelian process as it develops, until at the end the Idea, the particular completed organism, results (July 14).

In the sixty-odd articles he wrote for the *Daily Tribune* Marx dealt principally with British affairs at home and abroad: foreign trade, government finances, the fall of the East India Company, the repeal of the 1844 Bank Act. He also devoted numerous articles to the wars in China and India and was particularly critical of British methods for assuring hegemony in the East and of the opium trade. He summarised British foreign policy as 'compulsory opium cultivation in India and armed opium propaganda in China' (Sept. 25). While defending free trade in opium for themselves, the 'Christianity-canting and civilization-mongering British government' used all possible tricks to maintain its own monopoly on production. He was especially caustic in attacking the morality of opium trade, which was based on the worst egoism and the brutalist methods of compulsion against the semi-barbarians who resisted the encroachment of British merchants. In the opium war 'the representatives of the antiquated world appear prompted by ethical motives, while the representatives of overwhelming modern society fights for the privilege of buying in the cheapest and selling in the dearest markets' (Sept. 25). Marx repeatedly mentioned the brutality of British methods used to suppress insurgency and the hypocrisy and deceit of the colonial agents and officials bent on personal enrichment. In Marx's estimation the British army was the most brutal in the Western world, despite the fact that the country as a whole frequently indulged in self-praise for its high moral standards (Oct. 5).

At home in England evils were rampant in the poor houses, which were often used for the mentally ill. Examining statistics on mental illness and poverty, Marx found a direct relationship between the proportion of mentally ill and indigent and the level of British exports and wealth. The misery in these institutions was so great that, Marx wrote, horse stalls in this country would seem like boudoirs in comparison to the mental wards in the poor houses and that horses undoubtedly received better treatment than these British citizens (Aug. 20).

Marx was equally critical of the politics of Napoleon III who was at the time in a precarious financial situation because of the involvement of the French government in stock market speculation. He branded Napoleon as 'the patron of slavery in all its forms', responsible for keeping the slave trade alive among the British. The slave issue, Marx noted, was soon to be the 'battle-cry between Imperialist and Republican camps' (July 2).

In Russia the serfs had already been emancipated and Marx devoted an article to this topic in the *Daily Tribune* on October 19. In his earlier correspondence with Engels Marx had noted that the peasant emancipation in Russia marked the beginning of an internal crisis which might thwart the country's traditional foreign policy (April 29). News of the convocation of 'notables', i.e. the aristocracy and the clergy, at St Petersburg to discuss the matter of emancipation for the enslaved classes was for Marx a consoling sign that 'the Revolution' had at least begun in Russia (letter to Engels, Oct. 8).

With the publication of his work on 'Economics', Marx wrote Lassalle, he hoped that 'a number of better heads' would be induced to take up the study of political economy as well (Nov. 12).

1859 By January 20 Marx had finished the manuscript for the first booklet of the 'Economics' but lacked even the funds to pay for its postage from London to Berlin. 'Iron necessity' forced him to ask Engels for help again and he wrote:

I don't think that anyone has even written about 'money' under such conditions of financial destitution. Most of the authors on the subject were in utmost harmony with the topic of their research (Jan. 21).

Not until February 9 did Marx, sick with worry, receive notification of the receipt of his manuscript. The story of the 'Economics' continued to be marked with delays and the first instalment did not appear until mid-June. While awaiting its appearance, Marx solicited Weydemeyer's aid in arousing interest in America for the forthcoming publication, which, he claimed, 'destroyed at its basis the Proudhonian socialism now fashionable in France' and would help their party to a scientific victory (Feb. 1). Marx also inquired of Charles Dana about the possibility of finding a publisher for an English translation of the 'Economics'. Dana's reply (March 15) was negative.

Marx continued reporting regularly for the *Daily Tribune* which published about 40 articles from him during this year. The central themes of his reports were the Italian war of independence from Austria, British aggression in India and economic and political affairs in England itself. One of the first articles to appear in this year was the third in a series which analysed the emancipation of the Russian serfs, an event which Marx predicted would 'find a great echo in the world and be of greater significance than the papal liberalism of 1846'. Although the aristocratic classes would doubtlessly oppose the Czar's ukase, it was equally certain that the people would resist any further oppression. The reign of the Russian people—those 'semi-Asiatic serfs'—would be, when it came, a reign of terror, something unheard of in all previous history and would mark the beginning of true civilisation in Russia (Jan. 17).

For all the European nations the question of Italian unity was of key importance, for, as Marx remarked in an article on January 24, a war which broke out in any one place in Europe would not end there. Following closely the role played by Napo-leon in this affair, Marx was convinced that the French ruler wanted intimidation and not real war, hoping that a diplomatic victory over Austria would replenish the empty state treasuries. In 'The War Prospect in Europe' Marx predicted that the loss of a single battle in Lombardy might mean the fall of the Napoleonic empire (Jan. 31).

Marx continued to criticise sharply Britain's colonial policies. Reporting on an incident concerning the Ionian Islands, he exposed the system of oppression whereby the colonialists pretended to assume responsibility over foreign territories in order to educate them in the principles of liberty. The facts showed that 'to be free at home, John Bull must enslave abroad' (Jan. 6). Marx also dealt with the ruses and tricks which the British factory owners used in order to avoid compliance with the laws on the employment of children and young people (March 24). He also commented on a reform bill which was up before parliament and which in his opinion would only streng-then class monopolies. A certain number of Marx's reports to the *Daily Tribune* were ostensibly sent from a correspondent in Berlin in order to give them greater plausibility. To add 'local colour' he also requested information from Lassalle who was living in Germany (cf. letter to Lassalle, March 28). In June he predicted that the approaching foreign hostilities coupled with the jealous rivalry of the German princes and social misery would lead to a great internal and external upheaval which would profoundly shake the German states (June 10).

The year's voluminous correspondence with Lassalle contains, apart from the interesting notes on Prussian affairs, a lengthy exchange on the Italian war of independence. When questioned by Lassalle as to the seriousness of the impending war, Marx remarked that Victor Emmanuel of Italy and Bonaparte were most definitely ready to collaborate against Austria and gave four reasons why Napoleon would be induced to support the Italian nationalists: (1) He feared 'the Italian daggers' in revenge for the execution of Orsini; (2) French finances were in a disastrous state and the army could no longer be maintained at home; (3) he hoped to restore his prestige; and (4) he was the tool of the Russians who desired war against Austria to break the latter's hold over the Slav peoples (cf. letter to Lassalle, Feb. 4; also NYDT, Feb. 1). Marx disagreed with Lassalle's view that an Hungarian insurgency would break out once Austria and Italy were at war. Kossuth, he remarked, had degenerated to a travelling lecturer, a *colporteur* of the same drivel everywhere in England and Scotland. While the war would have an immediate counter-revolutionary effect, Marx thought that the ultimate result would be revolution in Europe. On the practical side, Lassalle again offered Marx work as a correspondent for his cousin's newspaper, the Vienna *Presse*. The matter was frustrated by the outbreak of war as Marx's letters to the *Presse* remained unanswered.

In the shadow of the approaching conflict Engels completed writing a pamphlet, *Po und Rhein* which Lassalle arranged to have published by Duncker in April. This pamphlet, which in the first printing did not carry Engels's name, was widely acclaimed both by the general public and in military circles. The object of its critique was the traditional military strategy of 'natural frontiers', according to which France declared the Rhine indispensable for the protection of its Northern frontier, while the Germans held the Po and the Mincio to be the natural lines of protection for their Southern frontier. Engels argued that neither France nor Germany needed such 'natural' lines of defence for internal security and that such conflicts among neighbours over boundary lines only aided Russia in expanding her own frontiers to the West. Germany's efforts should be concentrated around the problem of national unity: 'Once we have this unity, the defensive operations can stop' (MEW 13: 268). The future map of Europe would certainly continue to undergo changes, tending in general towards the true natural frontiers of each of the 'great and viable' European nations, as determined according to language and congeniality, while the 'splinter nations', incapable of unity, would be incorporated into the larger ones (*ibid.*, p. 267).

The publication of this pamphlet and of one by Lassalle on the same topic entitled *Der italienische Krieg und die Aufgabe Preussens* (May) delayed the appearance of Marx's 'Economics' until early June. Meanwhile, Lassalle sent Marx copies of his *Franz von Sickingen*, a drama about the tragic end of the knightly revolutionary Sickingen, and of the pamphlet on the Italian war. Marx found fault with Lassalle's portrayal of the peasant movements and the revolutionary elements in the cities, which, Marx held, should have provided the protagonist Sickingen with a meaningful, vivid background: 'Haven't you', he asked Lassalle, 'fallen into the same diplomatic error as your Franz von Sickingen by ranking the Lutherian-knightly opposition above the plebian-Münzerian?' (April 19). Marx most vigorously opposed Lassalle's views as presented in *The War in Italy*, where he defended the cause of Italian unity with Prussian support against the Austrians. He held that this pamphlet entirely failed to recognise the Russian hand pushing Napoleon into supporting the patriotic cause of Italy. Lassalle defended a cause which would lead only to disorganisation among the German armies and benefit the Czar and Napoleon. It also generated Marx's criticism that Lassalle had presumed to speak in the name of the 'party' on this issue, for he felt that party discipline should be maintained in critical times, if the cause was not to be lost. He proposed therefore to Engels that they compose a party manifesto in order to dispel some of the confusion among the divers revolutionary groups (May 18).

Apropos the impending war, Marx read in May a study by Karl Vogt on the present situation in Europe and became convinced of the author's strong Bonapartist leanings. At this time he also attended as a representative of the *Daily Tribune* a public meeting on the Italian war organised by David Urquhart. Approached by Karl Blind, Marx was informed that Karl Vogt received subsidies from the French government in order to carry out pro-Bonaparte propaganda and that Blind was in possession of material proof that Vogt had betrayed his country (May 9).

Meanwhile Marx met with members of the German Working Men's Association in London to discuss participation on the

German-language newspaper *Die Neue Zeit*, an ineffective organ presently under the editorship of Edgar Bauer. The group decided not to collaborate on any paper which they did not edit themselves and would therefore support the rival organ *Das Volk*, which the Association as a whole planned to found in opposition to the Bauer publication. At this meeting Marx declared that Engels and he were self-appointed representatives of the proletarian party and that their appointment was 'countersigned by the hatred, unqualified and universal, which all old-world factions and parties devote to us' (letter to Engels, May 18).

In the second issue of *Das Volk* on May 14 an article appeared which revealed the true nature of Karl Vogt's activities and was written, without Marx's consultation, by Elard Biscamp. Vogt, who attributed the article to Marx, wrote an open letter to the Swiss *Handels-Courier* (June 2), in which he characterised Marx as the head of a 'band of hooligans', intriguers and extortioners and warned the working class to beware of this unscrupulous agitator.

Even before the first booklet of the 'Economics' appeared by Duncker in Berlin, the journal *Das Volk* published a large part of the Preface, which contained interesting biographical notes on Marx's activities and studies prior to his research in political economy. It began with an exposition of the complete plan for the 'Economics' in six parts, or two triads, constructed according to the methodological principles set down in the 1857 Introduction and the *Grundrisse* themselves, whereby the influence of Hegel's *Logic* had been decisive. Apart from the plan, the Preface summarised briefly the theoretical views which he had developed in Paris and Brussels, departing from the standpoint that 'the anatomy of bourgeois society is to be sought in political economy' (MEW 13:8). These views are four:

(1) The social, political and intellectual life process depends in general on the production mode of material life. 'It is not men's consciousness which determines their existence, but the contrary: their social existence determines their consciousness' (MEW 13:8f.).

(2) The productive forces of a given society develop to the point where they come into conflict with the property relations which had hitherto served as the necessary form of their development.

(3) This conflict leads to social revolution and changes the basis of production. No social form ever disappears, however, before

having developed the productive forces to the maximum possible under the given conditions, nor before the material conditions for the existence of new and higher production relations have been created within the framework of the old society.

(4) Roughly speaking, there have been four eras in the economic development of society, consisting of the Asiatic, ancient, feudal and modern bourgeois modes of production. 'The bourgeois production relations are the last antagonistic form of the social production process ... With this social form the pre-history of human society comes to a close' (MEW 13:9).

Marx's 'Economics' appeared in its first instalment under the title *Zur Kritik der politischen Ökonomie* [Contribution to a Critique of Political Economy]. It is divided into two chapters, on commodities and on money, similar to the first section of *Capital*. But unlike *Capital* each of the two theoretical expositions is appended with historical material; by the time Marx was to finish the book on capital, he had accumulated so much historical material that it could not be included with the theoretical sections, and he was obliged to leave it aside for later publication.

The only serious critique of Marx's long-awaited publication was written by Engels and appeared in *Das Volk* on August 4 and 20. However, Engels treated only the Preface before financial difficulties rendered further publication of the journal impossible. In the first article Engels retraced the history of economic thought in Germany, mentioning the theories Marx had developed in earlier works and outlined in the Preface. In Engels's words the 'materialist interpretation of history' (MEW 13:469) was a 'revolutionary discovery' which provided the theoretical basis for their party (MEW 13:471). In the second critique Engels speaks of Marx as the first thinker since Hegel to 'develop a science according to its own proper inner coherence'. Moreover, Marx had applied to history 'the core of the Hegelian *Logic*', or in other words 'the dialectical method stripped of its ideological wrappings' (MEW 13:474). Engels considered the elaboration of the dialectic method to be Marx's second great achievement and no less important than the materialist conception of history. History, Engels recounted, is the history of economic development and the progress of ideas is the 'reflection, in abstract and consistently theoretical form, of the course of history' (MEW 13:475). Engels's glorifying interpretation of

Marx ends with a simplified outline of *Zur Kritik*, reserving discussion for a later article which was never written.

In *Das Volk* from July 23 to the last issue on August 20 Marx published documents of Russian diplomacy dated 1837 which gave proof of the Czar's expansionist plans. The same document appeared in excerpt in the *Daily Tribune* on August 8 under the heading 'The Foreign Policy of Russia. Memoir on Russia, for the instruction of the present Emperor ...'. Before being discontinued *Das Volk* also printed an unfinished series of four articles by Marx entitled 'Quid pro Quo', a critical analysis of Prussian politics during the Italian war. Prussia's neutrality lent tacit support to Bonaparte's foreign policy, which consisted in the conduct of wars abroad in order to divert attention from his country's internal troubles. In his *Tribune* articles Marx also remarked that 'war was the sole condition which kept Bonaparte on the throne, yet the wars which he fought were always senseless, vain, incited under false pretenses, squandering money and blood and bringing no advantages for the French people' (Aug. 12). Marx feared that following the treaty of Villafranca, which ended hostilities in Lombardy, a Napoleonic governorship would be instituted over Italy (Aug. 4), but he did not exclude the possibility of an Italian revolution which would return Mazzini and the republicans to the forefront of a new national movement.

In the last few months of the year Marx treated British trade, electoral corruption and 'Population, Crime and Pauperism' (Sept. 16), remarking that something must be amiss in a social system where wealth increases without reducing poverty and crime rates rise more rapidly than the population. He also found a disproportion in the trade relations with China: the opium trade continually expanded, but in inverse relation to the importation of Western manufactures. The only market the British could conquer in China was the drug market, for the traditions and habits of the population were so deeply ingrained as to make them inaccessible to Western civilisation (Dec. 3). Marx maintained that, in general, British aggression in China aided Russia and was the work of Palmerston who continued to play deliberately into the hands of the Czar, while ostensibly defending a foreign policy which would thwart Russia's designs on Asia (Oct. 1).

Information provided by Bartholomäus Szemere in September served Marx as the basis for an article on 'Kossuth and Louis-

Napoleon' (*NYDT*, Sept. 24). Double-faced and deceitful, Kossuth was lacking in constancy and steadfastness and was capable of passing himself off at the same time as both a martyr and a courtier of Louis Napoleon, as a tool in the hands of a cruel oppressor and the representative of a subject nation.

Marx resumed work on the 'Economics' in October after receiving an inquiry from Lassalle about the now overdue manuscript for the second booklet. He read and made excerpts from works on political economy, money and fiscal problems by the British economists Richard Jones, Samuel Bailey, Jakob Vanderlint, T. R. Malthus and Thomas Hopkins, but was soon interrupted by financial problems, the articles for the *Daily Tribune* and the developing affair with Karl Vogt. In June the London German-language paper *Das Volk* along with the Augsburg *Allgemeine Zeitung* republished the text of an anonymous fly-sheet *Zur Warnung* [A Warning] dealing with the activities of Vogt as a secret paid agent of Napoleon III. Although the information stemmed from Karl Blind, the latter disclaimed the authorship of this fly-sheet, publishing a declaration to that effect in the *Allgemeine Zeitung* in November. Ferdinand Freiligrath, who along with Marx had been informed by Blind about Vogt's activities at the May 8th Urquhart gathering, refused to aid Marx in establishing Blind's authorship and published in the *Allgemeine Zeitung* a statement of neutrality (Nov. 15). In the same journal shortly thereafter Marx reaffirmed the fact that Blind had been the source of the information on Vogt (Nov. 21). In December Vogt then brought out a lampoon entitled *Mein Prozess gegen die 'Allgemeine Zeitung'* [My Case against the *Allgemeine Zeitung*], directly attacking Marx, who did not learn of the pamphlet's existence until 1860. Vogt interspersed a stenographic account of his proceedings against the Augsburg journal with falsified documents and allegations depicting Marx as the head of a gang of terrorists called the *Schwefelbande*. This attack Marx saw as an attempt to destroy the honour of the proletarian party with Vogt exploiting the fact that the German social democrats considered Marx their 'bête noire'. Vogt tried to discredit Marx through statements to the effect that he was a police agent, lived off working men and 'similar stupidities'. Although Marx repeatedly emphasised that Vogt's libel would have to be refuted to vindicate the honour of their party, Lassalle hesitated to assist Marx in this affair (Marx

to Lassalle Nov. 14). Lassalle, on the other hand, had not refrained from speaking out in the name of the party when propagating his own views on the Italian war. Marx cautioned him
henceforth to avoid actions which might provoke internal party
disputes 'for public polemics are in no way advantageous for a
party with such an inconsiderable membership (which I hope,
however, redeems with its energy all that it loses through its
number)' (Nov. 22).

1860 Only in January and February did Marx find a few short
weeks to work again on his 'Economics' before being consumed by the Vogt affair, illness and his journalism. He re-read
several authors, notably Smith, Ricardo and Malthus along with
Engels's *Condition of the Working Class in England* and studied
a number of political classics (Locke, Montesquieu). The recently
published 'Reports of the Inspectors of Factories 1855-59' served
him both for the 'Economics' and for two articles which the
Daily Tribune published in August. At the end of January
Lassalle reminded Marx of his promise to deliver the second
instalment (chapter 3 of the first of six books) by the end of
1859 and claimed to be personally interested in seeing it appear
soon. Lassalle, who had ambitions to write on political economy
as well, wrote frankly: 'Your book is much too important for
me to publish a systematic treatment of the same topic [while
you are] in the middle of it without considerable misgivings'
(about Jan. 27). Marx answered that Lassalle should wait until
the second part had appeared before beginning his own writing,
because this part was to contain the 'quintessence' of the subject
to be elaborated in the five subsequent books (Jan. 30). Engels,
too, was concerned that his friend should finish with the 'Economics' and counselled him not to let the Vogt slanders divert his
attention from the main task. Moreover, he added, 'For once,
do be a little less conscientious in your affairs; in any case it
will be too good for the lousy public. The main thing is *that*
it materialises and is published. The weaknesses you notice those
asses won't find anyway' (Jan. 31). At this time Marx still
thought that: 'If I apply myself to it resolutely, I can have it
ready in six weeks, and *after* the trial it will be a success' (to
Engels, Feb. 3).

Marx had decided to bring legal action against the Berlin
Nationalzeitung for publishing long excerpts from Vogt's pam-

phlet in leading articles (about Jan. 24 and 27). He was temporarily unable to procure it himself, for the first edition of 3000
copies had already been sold out to a curious German public in
search of sensation. As soon as he had the documents in question,
he was determined to establish a case against both Vogt and the
Berlin newspaper. Through the Urquhartites in London Marx
received the name of a Berlin lawyer who could advise him. He
was convinced, however, that it would be necessary to write a
counterattack against Vogt. As he explained to Szemere, 'This
pamphlet contains the most absurd defamations against me that
I see myself compelled to reply to his scandalous lies even though
it is a real shame to have to waste my time on such a wretched
affair' (Jan. 30).

In February Marx began collecting documentary material,
including letters attesting to his activities in the Communist
League and elsewhere, to his friends, etc. He wrote dozens of
letters seeking support from friends and acquaintances and entrusted to Engels the preparation of the documents on the
Communist League and the first years of exile. The London
Daily Telegraph now republished Vogt's accusations under the
headline 'The Journalist Auxiliaries of Austria'. Marx's letter
demanding a retraction received a very evasive reply. On February 13 Marx sent the first batch of documents and attestations
to *Justizrat* Weber in Berlin. On February 24 he wrote Weber
a long and detailed letter on his professional and literary activities, following this with additional documents on March 3. From
February 16 to March 23 Marx was in Manchester with Engels
and Wilhelm Wolff to discuss the plan for a pamphlet against
Vogt. More information went off to Counsellor Weber in March
on Marx's relations with the Communist League, his occupa-
tions and sources of income since leaving Germany. Vogt claimed,
so Marx wrote to Weber, that he was the head of a secret
band known variously as the *Schwefelbande* or the *Bürstenheimer* and scattered throughout Europe following the 1848-49
revolutions. This group, which Marx was said to have reunited
in the London emigration, engaged chiefly in exorting money
from former participants in the 1846 rebellions under threat of
denunciation. Marx was also imagined to have been involved
in a ring of counterfeiters in Switzerland in 1852 and 1859.
Marx replied to these allegations with proof that he had abandoned all agitation in September 1850 and that the Communist

League had itself been disbanded during the trials of 1851-52. As for the *Schwefelbande* and the *Bürstenheimer*, these were actually two very different Geneva societies, utterly unrelated to one another and to Marx and the Communist League. While the first group had nothing to do with politics whatsoever—it was a drinking club—the second was a working men's educational association. As Marx summed up this affair to the Polish emigrant Joachim Lelewel, 'On the one hand, [Vogt] depicts me as an insignificant person and, on the other, imputes the basest motives to me. He is falsifying my entire past' (Feb. 3).

A sharp dispute arose between Marx and his 'old party friend and long-time personal friend' Ferdinand Freiligrath who had ignored Marx's first two letters asking for support in the Vogt case. Writing for the third time, Marx appealed to Freiligrath's sense of personal responsibility, explaining the importance of the legal action as 'decisive for the *historical vindication* of the party and for its later position in Germany'. What Marx did not want, however, was to cause an estrangement between himself and one of his oldest friends because of Vogt:

If we are both conscious of having waved the banner for the 'classe la plus laborieuse et la plus misérable' high over the heads of the philistines during these many years, each in his own way, placing personal interests in the background and with the purest motives, I would consider it a petty sin against history for us to be set at variance over trivialities, which are all reducible to misunderstandings (Feb. 23).

Freiligrath, who was in a position to vindicate both Marx and the party in this affair, replied that he had no desire whatsoever to get involved in Marx's polemics and protested 'out of a feeling for purity' against any further association of his name with the party: 'The party too is a cage,' the poet Freiligrath wrote, 'and the singing is better, even when it is for the party, on the outside than on the inside' (Feb. 26). This interpretation of 'the party', as Freiligrath used the term, Marx held to be totally false: 'party' as a secret political organisation had ceased to exist for Marx in 1852. What Marx was referring to was 'party in the eminent historical sense', which he was serving through his theoretical writings in the belief that they would achieve more in the long run than participation in any of the political groups that had now outlived their effectiveness. Marx reminded

Freiligrath of his own important role in the League, as contrasted to his present occupation in a bank. The League had an 'excellent position' for its 'purity' in 19th-century history. As for trade and commerce, however, there impurity was really 'in its natural place':

The honourable villainy or the villainous honourability of solvent ... morality does not rank a wit above the irrespectable villainy which tainted both the earliest Christian communities and the Jacobin clubs as well as our erstwhile League. It's just that in bourgeois commerce one generally comes to lose one's feeling for respectable villainy or villainous respectability (Feb. 29).

With this, both the issue and the Marx-Freiligrath friendship came to an end.

Lassalle, too, gave Marx reason to doubt the meaning of their friendship as he wrote that he had found 'much truth' in Vogt's pamphlet and gave only timid suggestions for its refutation. In April Lassalle sent Marx a copy of still another of his publications and reported that his economics as well as three other works were already 'outlined' in his mind. As if that were not enough, Lassalle stated that he was pursuing 'four to five sciences' with the intention of being productive in each of them (April 16).

During the Vogt affair Marx wrote only occasionally for the *Daily Tribune*, while Engels contributed numerous reports on military affairs and produced a sequel to the *Po and Rhine* pamphlet entitled *Savoy, Nice and the Rhine*. Marx's main topics for his articles were foreign relations: Franco-English, Franco-Prussian, Austro-Russian, etc.; he also treated the popular uprising in Sicily, commerce, banking and factory conditions in England. In connection with the Vogt affair Charles Dana wrote for Marx a letter attesting to his personal and professional integrity during nine years of collaboration on the New York paper. In Dana's words Marx was

not only one of the most highly valued, but one of the best paid contributors attached to the journal. The only fault I have had to find with you has been that you have occasionally exhibited too German a tone of feeling for an American newspaper. This has been the case with reference both to Russia and to France. In questions relating to both Czarism and Bonapartism, I have sometimes thought that you manifested too much interest and too great anxiety for the unity and independence of Germany (March 18; MEW 14:679).

When writing on British foreign policy, Marx continued to strike at Palmerston who, after being censured by Parliament for arbitrarily declaring the second Chinese war, undertook the third 'in spite of Parliament ... as if to try the strength of ministerial irresponsibility, wielding the rights of Parliament against the Crown, the prerogative of the Crown against Parliament, and the privileges of both against the people' (Feb. 14). The difference between French policy-making and British, Marx wrote, was 'imperialist usurpation' on the one hand and 'ministerial usurpation' on the other.

'From Berlin' Marx reported on the revolutionary feelings at all social levels. With the people now distrustful of the regent for his blindness in foreign policy, Berlin had become 'the most revolutionary city in Europe' with the possible exceptions of Palermo and Vienna (April 28). Faulty policies, in domestic as well as in foreign affairs, had isolated Prussia from its German neighbours and from all of Europe. Had it continued with the institutional and legal reforms brought by the 1848 revolution, Prussia 'would have commanded the sympathies of all Germany, Austrian Germany included. As it is, she had only divided the German Princes without uniting the German people. She has, in fact, opened the door by which to let in the Zouaves' (May 19).

Rumours were circulating that Napoleon III was preparing to attack the Prussian Rhineland. The threat of war over the Rhine frontier was central to Engels's discussion of military questions in the pamphlet *Savoy, Nice and the Rhine* (Feb.), in which he destroyed theoretically the traditional doctrine of the 'natural frontiers'. France, which was desirous of annexing Savoy and Nice, might use the same arguments legitimising the incorporation of these areas to justify the annexation of French Switzerland as well. Should France succeed in gaining these lands, the old doctrine of 'natural frontiers' would be affirmed, thereby justifying France's aggression in the Rhineland. However, behind the scenes of this battling over frontiers and border regions, Engels pointed out, was Russia, pulling the strings so that others would shed blood while she might expand her territory towards Constantinople 'the fixed goal of Russian foreign policy' (MEW

13 : 607). Russia could have found no better man than Louis Napoleon to help execute these expansionist plans and attack Germany, traditional—although often indirect—victim of Russian aggressions, manipulations, hegemony in the affairs of Europe. Engels produced a long list of Russian 'sins' against Germany and emphasised that 'Russia threatens and insults us constantly, and when Germany rises up against this, Russia puts the French gendarme into action by holding out the prospect of the left bank of the Rhine' (MEW 13 : 611). However, Germany's new comrade-in-arms, the Russian serf, was going to create a revolution which would change the whole structure of Russian society, topple the Czar and with him the present system of foreign policy.

In connection with the question of serf emancipation in Russia Marx had commented to Engels in a letter of January 11 that:

In my opinion the greatest that is happening in today's world is, on the one hand, the American slave movement ushered in by Brown's death, on the other, the slave movement in Russia ... Thus the 'social' movement in West and East has begun. This, together with the impending downbreak (sic) in Central Europe, is going to be magnificent.

Answering a letter from Lassalle, Marx explained in detail his relations with and attitude towards David Urquhart and the London Urquhartites. He characterised Urquhart as a man of 'subjective-reactionary' personal views but said that his orientation in foreign policy was 'objective-revolutionary'. Most important of all, Urquhart was a 'power which Russia fears':

He is that sole official man in England who has the courage and the honesty to offer resistance to public opinion. He is the only incorruptible one (either through money or ambition) amongst them (about June 2).

Because the Urquhartites pursued an anti-Russian foreign policy, the revolutionary groups should nurture an alliance with them, without hesitating, nonetheless, to oppose them on matters of domestic policy.

In the summer Marx received notification from Weber in Berlin that his libel suit against the editors of the Berlin *National-*

zeitung had been rejected by the municipal court. An appeal to a higher court was turned down on July 29, and on a final appeal the High Court rejected the suit on October 23.

Despite frequent illness, Marx continued to put together his pamphlet against Vogt, did occasional readings for the 'Economics' (Sismondi, Tucker, Bellers and the physiocrats) and contributed to the *Daily Tribune* until the end of November. In the factory inspectors' reports, used as the basis for two articles on August 6 and 24, Marx discovered that in industries where working hours were prescribed by law, wages had risen, whereas in the absence of health laws and protective labour laws accident rates had risen in other industrial branches. The most interesting part of the reports treated the development and spread of cooperatives in the spinning industry.

Commenting the outbreak of disturbances in Syria (August 11), Marx pointed out that the Czar saw external collisions as a means of creating a certain national unity and averting an internal eruption in his country: 'It is evident that the Autocrat of France and the Autocrat of Russia, labouring both under the same urgent necessity of sounding the war trumpet, act in common court.' In this and other articles Marx echoed Engels's warnings of Russian aggression (*Savoy, Nice and the Rhine*) and appealed to the Germans to resist the Czar's attempt to manipulate European politics. Germany was a 'lamentable spectacle,' he wrote, for it imagined that a treaty with Russia would protect it from French aggression:

Russian foreign policy, as is well known, does not care one straw for principles, in the common meaning of the term. It is neither legitimist nor revolutionary, but improves all opportunities of territorial aggrandizement with the same faculty ... (Oct. 10).

Only an internal revolution in Germany would shatter the Habsburg empire without endangering the territorial integrity and would establish the unity and freedom essential in order to resist further foreign aggression.

On Sicily, too, Marx foresaw a revolution that would arise from a national movement as the product of reflection and action and not of change (Oct. 15). In September and November he reported on the pending agricultural crisis. A bad harvest combined with serious monetary difficulties might well lead to political instability and even revolution, this time in England.

Efforts to find a German publisher for the Vogt pamphlet proved futile and Marx therefore decided to have it issued in German by the London publisher Albert Petsch. He was moved to do so by the lower printing costs—Petsch, Lassalle, Borkheim and Engels were willing to assume a part of the expenses—and the assurance that the consignments to be sent to Germany would not be confiscated, as had happened with the pamphlets on the Cologne communist trial. The next of Marx's 'literary reply' to Vogt left the press on November 30.

In the 'Preface' to *Herr Vogt* Marx explained that the first part of the text dealing with Vogt's personal attacks against himself was included only after the Berlin courts had refused to hear the case against the *Nationalzeitung*. Had there been a public trial, Marx would have had the opportunity to vindicate himself and his career and the reputation of the party whose interests he represented. In refuting Vogt's 'tall stories' Marx tracked down the actual facts about the *Schwefelbande* and the *Bürstenheimer*, documenting his revelations with letters furnished by former members of the two groups. S. L. Borkheim, for instance, described the *Schwefelbande* as a circle of young people in the Swiss emigration whose chief activity was to dispel their gloom in taverns and wine-cellars, drinking on credit. By contrast, Marx depicted the 'December Tenth Gang' around Napoleon III as 'the scum, offal, dregs of all classes' 'a "welfare society"—in so far as all its members and Bonaparte as well felt the need to do something for their own welfare at the expense of the labouring nation' (MEW 14:395).

Marx presented a letter written to him by a well-known Russian writer, N. I. Sasanov, expressing both the writer's indignation at the calumnies spread by Vogt and his high esteem for Marx's thought:

Your success among thinking men is immense and if it pleases you to know what response your doctrines have found in Russia, I should like to tell you that at the beginning of this year Professor I. K. Babst held a public lecture course on political economy in Moscow and the first of these lectures was simply a paraphrasing of your recent publication (May 10; MEW 14:402).

To disprove Vogt's statements about the Communist League, the trial in Cologne and his theoretical writings on communism,

Marx gave a lengthy account of the events of his career in exile. Vogt had asserted—in quoting a letter from Techow who had participated in the 1848 revolution in Berlin—that Marx had concocted a 'proletarian catechism' in *The Communist Manifesto*, made to measure for the proletariat. Marx replied that:

... on the contrary, I repudiated *all* systems—in the 'Manifesto' which was destined for the working class as well—and replaced them with 'the critical understanding of the conditions, the trend and the general results of the social movement'. Such 'understanding' can be neither imitated blindly nor 'made to measure' like a cartridge pouch (MEW 14 : 449).

Marx then recounted the incidents which provoked Vogt's insidious attack on Marx, beginning with the conversation he had had with Blind in May 1859. He undertook to prove the validity of the statement, confirmed by Blind, that Vogt was a paid agent of Napoleon III. His own views on Bonaparte, Marx added, had been elaborated in detail by Engels in the two pamphlets *The Po and the Rhine* and *Savoy, Nice and the Rhine* and differed radically from the pro-Bonaparte propaganda diffused by Vogt. In Bonaparte Vogt saw a 'friend of the people' and held that Russia's sympathy for France was ample evidence of the liberalism of Bonapartist politics (MEW 14 : 496). Moreover, Russia was for Vogt the 'friend of emancipatory endeavours'. These statements contrasted sharply to the actual history of Russian diplomacy and the foreign relations between Russia and Europe, for Russia was actually striving to create a great Slavic empire. According to Vogt, Poland would be merged with Russia 'through free self-determination', while Hungary would have to be subjected to Russian domination. Marx declared, however, that Russia was not only a threat to the Poles and the Hungarians; she threatened the existence of Germany as a nation as well (MEW 14 : 509). Vogt's position on these questions of Polish and Hungarian independence, on German unity and his confidence in Russia reflected his primary allegiance to Bonaparte.

Marx had hardly finished writing the Preface to *Herr Vogt*, when Jenny became seriously ill with smallpox (Nov. 19). The children were taken in by the Liebknecht family while Marx tended his wife, unable to write, unable to read. 'In order to maintain the necessary tranquillity of mind' he began studying mathematics (letter to Engels, Nov. 23). In December, as his wife was recovering, Marx read Darwin's work *On the Origin of Species* (1859) and reported to Engels that 'although elaborated in a crude English manner, this is the book that contains the biological basis of our conceptions' (Dec. 19).

1861   Another year began for Marx beset with illness and financial troubles, symptoms of the bourgeois *misère* which continued to plague the family in exile. Marx's income was seldom above that of a Manchester worker; he was chronically afflicted with hepatitis and his wife was still weak from the smallpox. Because of political developments in the USA, Charles Dana suspended Marx's articles for six weeks and as for the future he would be commissioned to write only one article a week. As he confessed to Engels:

How I am supposed to carry on here I do not know, for taxes, school, house, grocer, butcher, God and the devil don't want to give me any further respite ... I don't know what I should do, but I have seen this crisis approaching for some time now (Jan. 29).

He finally decided to go to Holland to speak about financial matters with his uncle Lion Philips, who managed the affairs of Henriette Marx. Preoccupied with procuring a pass from a friend and scraping up enough money to finance the trip, he was too busy even to read the daily papers. In the evenings, he reported to Engels, he was reading Appian's work on the Roman civil wars in the original Greek and commented on this 'very worthwhile book' which explained the materialist basis of these conflicts:

Spartacus appears as the most splendid fellow that the whole of ancient history has to offer. A great general (no Garibaldi), noble character, real representative of the ancient proletariat (Feb. 27).

In the meantime it gradually became evident that the publication of *Herr Vogt* had aroused little interest in Germany; very little echo was heard in the press, where Marx's writings seemed to have been placed under a 'conspiratorial ban of silence'. Lassalle read it and admitted that he had been too hasty in criticising Marx: 'Your conviction that Vogt has been bribed by

Bonaparte is entirely justified and in order' (letter to Marx, Jan. 19). He did nothing, however, to publicise or promote the sales of the pamphlet, which was later banned in France (Marx to Engels, May 16).

On February 28 Marx went to Zalt-Bommel in Holland, where he visited the Philips family and succeeded in talking his uncle into an advance of £160 on his maternal inheritance. From there he travelled to Berlin to discuss the possibility of founding a new party journal with Lassalle. Since this project would demand Marx's renaturalisation as a Prussian citizen, he gave Lassalle a power-of-attorney to undertake the necessary steps on his behalf but reserved a final decision on the matter until he had conferred with Engels and Wilhelm Wolff. His impressions from this one-month stay with Lassalle in Berlin are recorded in a number of letters to his cousin Nannette Philips and to Engels.

Upon his arrival in the Prussian capital, which he found to have 'a bold and frivolous atmosphere', Marx was introduced to his host's lady-friend, the Countess Sophie Hatzfeldt. She reminded him, Marx wrote to Nannette, 'of some Greek statues which still boast a fine bust but whose heads have been cruelly "beknappered" by the vicissitudes of time. Still, not to be unjust, she is a very distinguished lady ... deeply interested in the revolutionary movements, and of an aristocrat *laissez-aller* very superior to the pedantic grimaces of professional *femmes d'esprit*' (March 24, IRSH I, 1956, part 1, p. 83). Together with Lassalle and the Countess, Marx attended a performance of the Berlin comedy—'altogether a disgusting affair', he wrote Nannette—and a ballet which he found 'deadly-dull'. From the reporters' box Marx also witnessed a session of the second chamber of deputies in Berlin. In a letter to Engels (May 10), he described the scene as 'a curious mixture of an office of bureaucrats and a schoolroom'. Twice during his stay Marx went out to the taverns with his old friend Carl Friedrich Köppen and found these rendezvous 'a real blessing' after Lassalle, 'who would, for example, think he had been victimised if he ever set foot in a pub' (*ibid.*). Köppen presented Marx with a copy of his two-volume work on *The Religion of Buddha and its Genesis.*

From the Countess Hatzfeldt Marx learned that, in the highest military circles of Berlin, Engels's anonymous pamphlet on *The Po and the Rhine* was considered to be the work of an unknown Prussian general. While he found the atmosphere in Berlin 'boding ill for the powers that be', Marx was not attracted by the prospect of returning there to live. He confided to Nannette that:

if I were quite free, and if, besides, I were not bothered by some thing you may call 'political conscience', I should never leave England for Germany, and still less for Prussia, and least of all for that *affreux* Berlin with its 'Sand' and its 'Bildung' and 'seinen überwitzigen Leuten' (April 13, IRSH, op. cit., p. 85).

On his return to London Marx stopped over for a short visit with his mother in Trier (April 19-20). Although unwilling to give him any direct financial aid, she did nonetheless release him from a number of outstanding debts. 'The old woman interested me,' he wrote Lassalle, 'because of her fine spirit and the indestructible sameness of her character' (May 8). He then went on to Holland 'to conduct business' with his uncle and 'to court' his cousin Nannette, arriving finally in London on April 29.

In the early part of the year Engels had contributed two articles to the *Daily Tribune* and subsequently began writing for *The Volunteer Journal from Lancashire and Cheshire* on military affairs. In the *Daily Tribune* on February 12 Engels predicted a European war instigated by Prussia against Denmark for possession of Schleswig-Holstein. Such a war would eventually lead to a revolution and, should Napoleon be defeated, would cause his downfall. A German revolution, moreover, would result in the case of a Prussian defeat, toppling both the Prussian and the Austrian rulers. Engels later provided Marx with essential information on military affairs for subsequent articles in the *Daily Tribune* and the Vienna *Presse*.

In mid-May Marx helped organise a meeting in London to protest against the arrest and brutal treatment of Auguste Blanqui by the French police. He wrote to the Countess Hatzfeldt asking her to help by having information published in the German press. Thanks to these efforts, news of the Blanqui affair was subsequently published in American and Italian as well as German papers. Marx later received an expression of Blanqui's deep gratitude for the sympathy he and the 'German proletarian party' had shown him. To this Marx replied: 'No one could be more interested than I in the fate of a man whom I have always held to be the head and the heart of the proletarian party in France' (letter to Louis Watteau; Nov. 10).

In June Marx recommenced his reading for the 'Economics', but not until August did he begin working on the third chapter and filled a notebook with material on 'the transformation of money into capital'. In September he worked on the two parts of the transformation process, in October on absolute surplus value and in November on relative surplus value, on cooperation and division of labour.

On July 1 Lassalle informed Marx that he had written a letter to the publisher F. A. Brockhaus, assuring him that the 'Economics' would be a success thanks to Marx's 'masterly skill' in political economy. He had recommended that Brockhaus print the coming work not as a continuation of the first booklet but as a separate and complete work. Brockhaus agreed to consider the work when he had the completed manuscript before him. Lassalle urged Marx to finish as soon as possible.

In the same letter Marx was informed that the Prussian Government had turned down his request for renaturalisation on the grounds that Marx had not led a 'reputable life', his disreputableness consisting of a 'way of thinking' that was 'republican or at least not of royalist nature'. In his statement to the Royal Police President on April 6 Marx had demanded reinstatement as a Prussian citizen on the basis that his renunciation in 1845 had been purely formal, provoked by external pressures, and that he had never seriously desired to give up his citizenship.

After receiving Lassalle's latest book, *System der erworbenen Rechte*, Marx carried on a lengthy discussion with the author on the adoption of the institution of the Roman testament in modern legal systems. Marx held that the paradoxical adoption of Roman legal forms in modern society was attributable to the fact that:

the *legal* conception, which the subject of free competition has of himself, corresponds to that of the Roman *person* (and here I do not want to go into the very essential point that the *legal* conception of certain production relations, in as much as this conception does derive from them, still does not correspond to them) [letter to Lassalle, July 22].

The Roman testament was adopted by Western jurists through

misunderstanding. Similarly, the Greek form of drama was adopted in contemporary French theatre and the English constitution in a misunderstood form came to be the form of other modern constitutions. Marx concluded that 'The misunderstood form is precisely the general and at a certain stage of social development the one which is universally applicable' (ibid.).

In September Marx again took up work for the *Daily Tribune* and simultaneously started as a correspondent for the Vienna *Presse*. His chief topic in current events was the American Civil War and its economic repercussions in Europe. He also ex-changed numerous letters with Engels on the war and reported that, as he saw it:

the conflict between North and South—after the latter had degraded itself in the past fifty years with concession after concession—has finally come to a head ... owing to the weight thrown into the balance by the extraordinary development of the North Western states (July 1).

The secessionist movement was, moreover, no popular movement at all, but a 'usurpation' whose goal was to 'strengthen and increase the oligarchic power of 300,000 Southern slavelords against five million whites ...' (ibid.).

In his first article on the war for the *Daily Tribune* Marx sought to define the motives of the opposing parties: the South, he said, was fighting for the liberty to enslave other people, having recognised in slavery 'a thing good in itself, a bulwark of civilisation, and a divine institution'; the North, on the other hand, was fighting to retain the Union and only indirectly for the abolition of the institution which divided the country (Oct. 11).

Although alone the economic law of slavery necessitated its diffusion over an ever growing expanse of territory, the Southern leaders recognised that, to maintain their social system, they would also have to retain their political sway over the United States. In England, meanwhile, the possibility of a Southern defeat was causing great consternation in the British cotton industry, which itself was built on a two-fold system of slavery: 'the indirect slavery of the white man in England and the direct slavery of the black man on the other side of the Atlantic' (*NYDT*, Oct. 14).

For the Vienna *Presse* Marx treated the attitudes on the

American war as expressed in the British press. In Britain the argument was often advanced that the North should not interfere with the South's decision to separate. Marx retorted that the two sections of the country were neither independent lands, nor distinct geographical regions, nor moral unities and that, in short, '"The South" ... is not a country at all, but a battle slogan' (Nov. 7). This was a struggle between social systems and not one of national independence. At all costs, Marx noted, America must avoid open conflict with England, something which Palmerston certainly wished to see, for the only one to profit from such a complication would be Napoleon III (Nov. 6).

When European intervention in Mexico became a major issue in contemporary affairs, Marx wrote on this topic for both the *Daily Tribune* and the *Presse*. He termed this aggression 'a contrivance of the true Palmerston make', distinguished by its 'insanity of purpose' and the 'imbecility of the means employed' (*NYDT*, Nov. 23). An optimal moment for European intervention had been provided by the American war and the three European nations involved were bent on reconstituting their hegemony in the new world and on colonial expansion, while claiming to restore order to Mexico (*ibid.*).

Now that he had resumed his journalism Marx hoped to 'gain solid ground under his feet' in the financial struggle to support himself and his family and also anticipated finishing his book on capital before long (cf. letter to Engels, Oct. 30). These hopes, however, proved premature: to the family's accumulated debts and the loss of income during the first half of this year came costs for printing *Herr Vogt* which had to be repaid to the publisher. Marx was forced to write his friends and relatives for any aid whatever. His mother refused to help; the landlord threatened eviction; he was being sued for payment of the *Herr Vogt* printing costs; his wife was ailing; the *Presse* was printing not even half the articles he sent them. 'My best wishes for the new year,' he wrote to Engels and added: 'If the new is like the old, for my part it can go to the devil' (Dec. 27).

1862 A year of the most disheartening material suffering for the Marx family and yet at the same time one in which Marx made astonishing progress with his 'Economics'. After reducing his contributions to a minimum in the past year, the *Daily*

Tribune in March gave up Marx altogether as their London correspondent in view of the growing dimensions of the civil war. His financial situation was not helped by the fact that the *Presse* scarcely printed an average of one article by him a week although he sent four or five (cf. letter to Engels, March 6).

The year's work on the 'Economics' filled 13 notebooks (nos. V-XVIII) and began with the material on surplus value theory, which belonged according to the plan of 1858-59 in the third chapter of the first 'book'. He then started a section on the history of surplus value theories to be appended to the theoretical material in notebooks I-V (=chapter 3), just as he had done for the first two chapters published in 1859. The material in notebooks I-V, along with XIX-XXXIII written in 1863, constituted the first rough draft of book I of *Capital*, while VI-XV contain a detailed critique of the history of political economy from the standpoint of surplus value and a number of passages on productivity and unproductive labour not elaborated elsewhere in Marx's writings. Notebooks XVI-XVIII deal with capital and profit, profit rates, merchant's capital and money capital. The historical section on the theories of surplus value treat in particular the theories of Steuart, the physiocrats, Adam Smith, Quesnay, Necker, Linguet, Bray, Rodbertus, Ricardo, Malthus, etc., and is 'embellished' with occasional digressions on related topics. There, for example, Marx's theory of ground rent is developed.

The Civil War in America continued to be a central theme in his reports to the *Presse* and, until March, to the *Daily Tribune* as well. He was especially concerned with the political and economic effects of the war for the industrial working class in England, which was most directly and seriously affected by the Southern blockade. Marx confirmed that 'the anti-war movement is expanding and gathering force from day to day'; at public meetings throughout the country the working people were demanding that the Anglo-American conflict over the *Trent* incident be settled by arbitration (*Die Presse*, Jan. 5). Without official parliamentary representation, the English working class nevertheless exerted considerable influence on the government through '*pressure from without*', 'great, extra-parliamentary popular demonstrations'. While the government waited for 'the intervention cry from below', the suffering working men in Britain remained true to the emancipatory struggle in America, the country with the world's only popular government:

This is a new, brilliant proof of the indestructible excellence which is the secret of England's greatness and which, to speak in the hyperbolic language of Mazzini, made the common English soldier seem a demi-god during the Crimean War and the Indian insurrection (*DP*, Feb. 2).

Even apart from political questions the Englishman's character interested Marx, in particular as it was affected by industrialisation. On February 9 he wrote for *Die Presse* on the traditional view of the Englishman as 'original' or 'individualist'. However, the Englishman of the past was not the man of modern-day industrial England, whose national character had resulted from the development of class differences, specialisation in labour and 'the so-called "public opinion", manipulated by the Brahmins of the press'. Out of this a national 'monotony of character' had arisen such that Shakespeare would no longer recognise his countrymen. Character differences, Marx wrote:

are no longer proper to individuals as such, but to their 'profession' and class. Outside the professions, in daily intercourse, one 'respectable' Englishman so closely resembles another that even Leibnitz would scarcely be able to discover a difference between them. (*DP*, Feb. 9).

Following the government's fever for active intervention in the American conflict, Mexico had become the focal point of interventionist hopes. Marx remarked that, without an official declaration of war, England together with Spain and France, set out 'to cow a half-defenceless country into submission' (*DP*, Feb. 12).

Not until the end of February did Marx write to Engels, explaining that his long silence was not ' "from within" but from the misery of circumstances I didn't want to bore and to bother you with' (Feb. 25). Added to the never-ending financial problems with rent, debts to the neighbourhood shopkeepers, legal suits, etc., Marx now had the worry of little Jenny's health: 'Jenny is now so far along that she feels the whole muck and misery of our circumstances and that, I think, is one of the main reasons for her physical suffering,' he wrote to Engels and then added despondently, 'Taken all in all then, it is in fact not worth while to lead such a lousy life' (*ibid.*). Engels reported that he too was forced to reduce his living standard because of the American crisis and that the factory was operating only at half-power. He collaborated with Marx on a two-part article, published in *Die Presse* on March 26 and 27, which pointed up the enormous dimensions of the American conflict, 'a spectacle without parallel in the annals of military history', 'new in the eyes of the European onlooker'.

From the end of March Marx spent nearly a month with Engels in Manchester and, of course, on his return the family's debts for the 'immediate necessities of life', for the rent, the children's piano lessons, etc., had increased still further. He mentioned his predicament in a letter to Lassalle, in order to avoid the possibility of the latter's misunderstanding his protracted silence: 'I am therefore in a total vacuum. But I don't want to chant you any sort of litany; it is a wonder that I haven't gone completely *mad*' (April 28). With all these interruptions and preoccupations of a material nature Marx remarked that he was often unable to write even a line for the 'Economics'. Moreover, 'I have the peculiar habit that when I see a finished manuscript in front of me after four weeks, I find that it is no longer good enough and then I rework it again entirely' (*ibid.*). Lassalle, who was angered about Marx's long silence, promised nonetheless to write a critique of the first instalment of Marx's 'Economics' (June 9), but failed to be true to his word.

Early in June Marx received still another recent work by the prolific Lassalle entitled *Herr Julian Schmidt der Literaturhistoriker* (pub. March 1862). Writing to thank the author, Marx took up the problem of 'sophos', the 'particular character mask' of Greek philosophy and ideal of Epicureans, Stoics and sceptics: 'It is characteristic of modern philosophy that the Greek combination of character and knowledge, contained in *sophos*, was retained in the popular consciousness only by sophists' (June 16). He also discussed at length the two works, by Rodbertus and by Roscher, which Lassalle had lent him in Berlin for his studies in economics. Rodbertus's *Refutation of Ricardo's Doctrine of Ground Rent and the Construction of a New Rent Theory* (1851) won Marx's approval except for the proposed new rent theory which he characterised as 'rather childish, ridiculous', although admitting that it did tend in the right direction. Roscher, on the other hand, was for Marx a 'pompous eclectic' who lacked the intellectual honesty necessary to arrive at self-instruction and therefore continued in the role of the professional 'professorial student'. Were Roscher to admit that contradictions do exist and were he conscientious in view of the tasks at hand, 'he would be useful to his students ... the students would, on the one hand, receive a certain amount of material and, and on the other, they would be inspired to independent study' (*ibid.*).

The World's Fair had begun in London; it was a time of amusements and gay outings, but the Marx family could share in none of this. Clothing redeemed in April from the pawnbroker's was again pledged in June for a few pounds to buy food. Jenny tried to sell a part of her husband's library and, when this plan fell through, Marx confessed to Engels the depths of their present misery:

My wife tells me every day that she would prefer lying with the children in the grave and, indeed, I cannot blame her for feeling so for the humiliations, anguish and fear which must be withstood are truly indescribable (June 18).

Nevertheless, Marx continued to make great progress with the 'Economics', which he was now expanding to a thick manuscript to please the Germans who 'judge the value of books according to their volume'. To Engels he announced that he had cleared up the difficulties with the theory of ground rent and had also discovered Ricardo's error (June 18). Work was then interrupted by the visit of Ferdinand Lassalle and his Countess, who had come to London for the Fair on July 9. Marx's conversations with his guest frequently degenerated into outright disputes and he found that since their meeting in Berlin Lassalle had become a 'megalomaniac', an 'enlightened Bonapartist'. In his letters to Engels Marx referred to Lassalle as a 'jewish nigger', who 'would rather throw his money in the dirt than to lend it to a "friend", even if he were to have a guarantee for the capital and interest' (July 30). Knowing the crisis Marx was in, Lassalle 'had the impertinence' to ask if one of the Marx daughters would not care to be a companion for the Countess Hatzfeldt. 'To keep up appearances in front of this fellow, my wife has had to carry off to the pawnbroker's everything that wasn't nailed down!' Marx added. The situation was so desperate, however, that Marx was nevertheless pleased to receive a loan of £15 from Lassalle along with the promise that he might draw a bill on Lassalle for any amount, provided a third party would guarantee to cover him. This financial affair soon brought about the crucial conflict between the two men, when Lassalle demanded a written promise-to-pay from Engels for a bill Marx had drawn, and intimated that the affair might lead to a disastrous collision in Lassalle's 'bourgeois' life.

During the summer Marx again read Darwin's *Origin of Species* (1859) where he this time noticed Darwin's application of the Malthusian theory to the plant and animal kingdom, whereas Malthus had developed his principle expressly for human society. For Darwin the beasts and plants reflected English society with its 'division of labour competition, the opening of new markets, "inventions" and the Malthusian "struggle for existence". It is Hobbes *bellum omnium contra omnes* and reminds me of Hegel in the "Phenomenology", where bourgeois society figures as an "intellectual animal kingdom", while in Darwin the animal kingdom figures as bourgeois society' (to Engels, June 18).

After Lassalle's departure in August, Marx went to see his uncle in Zalt-Bommel, hoping to procure the funds which would help the family survive its precarious situation. This time his efforts were in vain. In London once again, Marx tried to get work in a railway office, but was turned down because of his illegible handwriting.

The only steady source of income for the family was the one pound a week which the Vienna *Presse* paid for his journalism. As earlier, the articles he wrote for *DP* were principally concerned with the American conflict. He discussed the conduct and probable outcome of the war in corresponding with Engels and entertained the view that the Yankees would have to change their tactics from 'constitutional' to 'revolutionary' if they were to be victorious. A 'constitutional' manner of conducting war, Marx noted, was to be expected of a '*bourgeois* republic' like America 'where swindle has reigned sovereign for so long' (Sept. 10). He expected nonetheless that the North would succeed because of the untenable economic basis of Southern expansionist demands in the border states and the West. Engels, on the contrary, gave greater weight to the superior militarism and the tactical victories of the Southerners, who seemed 'to be heroes in contrast to the sloppy management in the North' (Sept. 9).

For his Austrian readers Marx wrote an interesting article on Abraham Lincoln (DP, Oct. 12), characterising the American president as a plebeian 'without special greatness of character, without exceptional significance', but a man who proved that, given an advanced social and political organisation as was found in the United States, 'average men with good will suffice to do the tasks for which heroes are needed in the old world'.

* He also came to speak of the problems of the British cotton industry which because of the American crisis was forced to turn many working men out on to the streets. While the cotton lords accumulated speculative wealth, the state supported and conserved the most precious part of their wealth—the worker. For capital, Marx noted, was composed essentially of 'the well-disciplined working men's armies of Lancashire and Yorkshire' (Sept. 27). In a further article concerning industrial Britain Marx remarked on the introduction of large-scale factory methods in the baking industry and termed this 'the turning-point in the history of big industry as it storms the refuge of medieval craftsmanship' (Oct. 30).

In November Marx wrote to Lassalle on the matter of the bill which had been drawn on the latter and was due to be presented for payment November 12. He admitted having been overly sensitive to Lassalle's caution in this affair and that his letter of August 20 had contained unwarranted sarcasm and criticism. Yet he did not wish to sacrifice their friendship over a matter of money:

I think that the substantial element of our friendship is strong enough to withstand even such a shock. I must admit to you, *sans phrase*, that sitting as I am on a keg of dynamite I let myself go to an extent that was unfitting for an *animal rationale*. In any event it would not be very generous of you as a jurist and prosecuting attorney to use against me this state of mind in which I would most prefer to shoot a bullet through my head (Nov. 7).

Despite this bill, Marx was unable to make ends meet during the winter; a 'call for aid' went out to Engels on November 14 for a 'little something' to buy coal and food. Engels answered with a five-pound note and 24 bottles of wine, 'about a dozen Bordeaux and two bottles of old 1846 Rhine wine for little

Jenny and the rest filled with 1857 Rhine wine' (Nov. 15).

Towards the end of the year Jenny Marx took a short trip to Paris to confer with M.-A. Massol and Elie Reclus about a French translation of Marx's 'Economics' after its appearance in Germany. She reported that party spirit and cooperation still characterised the Paris socialists. 'Even fellows like Carnot and Goudchaux declare that Blanqui must be their leader when the next movement comes,' Marx later wrote to Engels (Jan. 2, 1863.)

A letter Marx wrote to Dr Kugelmann on December 28 sheds considerable light on the progress of the 'Economics' at this point. The manuscript, Marx announced, was ready to be recopied and prepared for the printer. He summarised its contents as the 'quintessence' of his theories on 'what the English call "the principles of political economy"' with the exception of competition and credit. Once these basic principles had been worked out, the rest could easily be developed by others, Marx thought, 'except perhaps for the relation of the various forms of the state to the different economic structures of society'. While he doubted that the book would gain much recognition in Germany before being 'certified' abroad, it would certainly be more readily understandable than the first part (*Zur Kritik*) because it treated 'concrete circumstances'. However, he noted cautiously, '*Scientific* attempts to revolutionise a science can never be really popular. Yet once the scientific basis has been laid, the popularising is easy'.

1863   Although he had elaborated eighteen notebooks of material for his 'Economics' during the past year and a half, Marx still put off writing the final draft of the manuscript he wished to publish as the book on 'capital'. Instead he continued his investigations on the theory of surplus value, adding in particular considerable information on the production of relative surplus value. In all he filled five new notebooks with explanations of relative and absolute surplus value (notebooks XIX-XX) and on the transformation of surplus value into capital, primitive accumulation, the colonial system and the reproduction process of capital (notebooks XXI-XXIII). While working on relative surplus value, Marx returned to study his old excerpt notebooks on technology and technological history. In January he attended a practical course, especially designed for working men, on technology and the operation of machinery, which was given by Professor Willis of the Geological Institute in London. This was necessary because, as he explained to Engels, 'I find the simplest technical reality—where visual ability is necessary—more difficult than the largest knots' (Jan. 28). He was interested in the differences between machines and tools, a problem which becomes important when it is a question of 'proving the relation between human production relations and the development of these methods of material production' (*ibid.*). When a mechanism is used to produce something which had originally required human labour, Marx termed this 'industrial revolution'. Tools, by contrast, might be developed and perfected as instruments, but never require that the raw material be worked by human hands. His studies revealed that 'the two material bases which provided the foundation in manufacturing for the development that led to the machine industry are the clock and the mill (first the corn, then the water mill), both products of antiquity' (*ibid.*).

Early in the year Marx sketched out a plan for the chapters he intended to incorporate into the first and third 'sections' [*Abschnitte*] of his book on 'Capital', the first of six pre-figured in the 1858-59 plan of the 'Economics'. He was still thinking of including the theories on surplus value at the end of the third section. Material was foreseen for section I on 'productive and unproductive labour' from both theoretical and historical standpoints which was later omitted in the final draft of *Capital*. Section I in this plan corresponds to book I (volume I) of *Capital*, section III to book III (cf. *Theorien über den Mehrwert*, MEW 26.1 : 389-391).

Financially, for the Marx family, the year began at new depths of privation and misery. There was no money for food or coal; Marx was unable to pay the school bills for his three daughters, who in any case were obliged to stay at home since their winter shoes were at the pawnbroker's. Although he expected that their 'sham' of bourgeois respectability would soon be at an end, Marx kept up a front at home to ward off outbursts of despair from the others and played the 'silent Stoic'. He was hardly able to work, for his time, his intellect, his feelings were being steadily consumed by this 'roasting on a low fire'. So great was his own misery, both mental and physical, that he was incapable of finding more than a few perfunctory words of condolence and sympathy for Engels who announced on January 6 the sudden death of Mary Burns, his loyal companion and friend. Engels took momentary offence at this letter, so filled with Marx's own worries and complaints, chiefly financial, and replied that he regretted being unable to help them until February. Marx later wrote excusing himself for this unfortunate letter and explained his seeming callousness as resulting from 'very desperate circumstances': little Jenny was ill in bed; there was not enough food or coal in the house; his wife was reproaching him for presumably hiding the truth about their predicament from Engels. Without his knowledge Jenny had written to Wilhelm Wolff in Manchester for a pound to buy 'immediate necessities' and Wolff had sent her £2. Engels, of course, forgot his anger and disappointment, 'happy not to have lost at the same time as Mary my oldest and best friend' (Jan. 26).

Should his creditors continue to press for payment, Marx was now decided to declare himself bankrupt, find positions for the two older girls as governesses and move into the 'city model lodging house' with his wife and the youngest. To prevent him from taking this irrevocable step Engels arranged for a £100 bill of exchange—and not without considerable risk to his own financial situation since the American crisis had reduced his earnings to £300-£350 in the past half year. Between March and July Marx received another £250 from their friend Dronke as Engels again promised to repay the loan.

Despite the rupture in their personal relations Lassalle continued to send Marx copies of his most recent publications. This year Marx received his *Arbeiterprogramm* [Working Men's Programme] and the *Offenes Antwortschreiben* [An Open Reply], but did not acknowledge either of them to the author. He reasoned that:

Were I to criticise his stuff, I would only be wasting my time. He adopts every word anyway as if it were his own discovery. To rub his nose in his plagiarism would be ridiculous since I have no desire to accept the form in which he has muddled our things. It wouldn't do either to recognise his boasts and his bad taste (June 12).

The *Arbeiterprogramm* was the text of a speech which Lassalle had held in his own defence before the Berlin Criminal Court— in Marx's words 'nothing other than a bad vulgarisation of the "Manifesto" and other things we have preached so often that they have become in a certain sense banalities' (Marx to Engels, Jan. 28). Lassalle had the impertinence, Marx wrote, to term his work 'more than scientific ... in many respects a scientific *act*', 'a condensed philosophy of history, a development of the "inner soul" of European history'. 'The fellow obviously thinks he is going to take over our stock-in-trade,' Marx remarked in conclusion.

A Polish insurrection broke out on January 15. Marx, upon hearing this news, optimistically announced that an 'era of revolution' had been reopened in Europe under more favourable auspices than in 1848. Although the movement seemed to lack new leaders and, what was so essential, the enthusiasm of the masses, Marx thought that its champions and supporters were more soberly, more wisely prepared for the exigencies of a revolutionary situation. 'We know now the role stupidity plays in revolutions and how they are exploited by scoundrels' (letter to Engels, Feb. 13). Marx suggested that together he and Engels should compose a manifesto on the Polish Question and have it published in the name of the German Working Men's Educational Association in London. It was decided that Engels would begin the project with a section on the military aspect of the question and that Marx would complete it with the diplomatic aspect. Engels seems to have been discouraged by the subsequent turn of events in Poland for he evidently did not write the material agreed upon. Marx attempted several times to put his thoughts on paper, but repeated illness kept him from finishing. Between the end of February and May he accumulated 70 notebook pages of excerpt material on the Polish Question and himself wrote about 42 pages of the text which he entitled 'Poland, Prussia and Russia'. The main objective of this writing was an attack on the Prussian state and particularly its 'tiresome House of Hohenzollern' whose life principle was the Russo-Prussian alliance (cf. *Die polnische Frage*, p. 42). In the Prussian state Marx saw 'Russia's jackal on the European stage' (*ibid.* p. 99) whose very existence was the 'outcome of Poland's ruin and the Hohenzollern's betrayal of Poland' (*ibid.*, p. 96). More explicitly:

If Prussia figured in the first division of Poland as Russia's chief diplomatic agent, it became at the second division the Russian *agent provocateur* and advanced with the third division to *Russian executioner* (*ibid.*, p. 20).

The existence of the Prussian state and its capacity for expansion depended therefore on Poland's division and its subjection to Russian domination. The strength and unity of Germany as a nation would never be achieved until the Hohenzollern state had been destroyed, Poland reconstituted and Russian influence over Germany banished for good. In a letter to Engels Marx remarked that 'the Polish Question is merely a new opportunity to prove that it is impossible for German interests to prevail as long as the state-in-ordinary of the House of Hohenzollern continues to exist' (March 24). In May Marx announced to Engels that he had abandoned the writing project on Poland, explaining that 'it would only have cut off my chance of travelling to Prussia without directly serving any purpose' (May 29).

Marx received a letter from Dr Kugelmann in March, encouraging him to continue the work begun in *Zur Kritik*, which although out-of-date provided a 'theoretical appeasement for a few fine souls'. He commented ironically to Engels: 'The question which never occurs to these gentlemen for an instant is what I am supposed to live on in the meanwhile when doing this "out-of-date" work' (March 24). 'That men of genius also have to eat, drink and be lodged and even have to pay for these things is for the philistine Germans too prosaic a thought that they could ever think it,' Engels replied.

Now that his health permitted, Marx did considerable reading during this period. As he reported to Engels: 'What I did was in part to fill up gaps (diplomatic and historic in the Russo-Prussian-Polish matter) and in part to read and make excerpts from all kinds of works on the history of that part of political economy which I have been working on' (May 29). In April he again reread Engels's *The Condition of the Working Class in England*, this time with a feeling of melancholy as he perceived the difference in style between the youthful passion and boldness of the young Engels and the 'grey in grey' of his own age and the dismal future: 'The whole thing gains a certain warmth and spirited humour through the very illusion that tomorrow or the day after the results will also spring into the light of historical day' (to Engels, April 9).

It was not until early June that Marx actually returned to his writing, thinking that if he were able to work without interruptions the manuscript would be quickly finished. He went once again to the British Museum Library and continued with his notes on the theory of surplus value. Presumably in connection with the investigations of the production process, he also began studying differential and integral calculus. He was working ten hours a day on the 'Economics'. On the basis of the *Tableau économique* compiled by Dr Quesnay, Marx worked out an economic table in three categories: consumer goods, machinery and raw materials, the total reproduction process. By August he could report that the text being prepared for the printer's was gradually assuming 'a passable popular form, except for a few unavoidable C[ommodity]-M[oney] and M-Cs' (letter to Engels, Aug. 15). Jenny Marx also wrote to a friend about the enormous progress her husband was making on his book and said that, had he kept with his original plan to write 20-30 printer's sheets, he would have been finished already:

But since the Germans only believe in 'bulky' books and since for those honourable people it is worthless to reduce it to greater conciseness and cut out all the superfluous material, Karl has now added much historical information. It is going to fall like a bomb, a thick volume of 50 printer's sheets, on to German territory (to Bertha Markheim, July 6; *Archiv für Sozialgeschichte* II, 1962, p. 181f.).

In October the German Working Men's Educational Association published a brief address on the Polish Question which Marx had written. Urging the members to support the Polish insurrectionists, Marx inveighed against Prussia's subserviency to Russia and underlined the fact that Germany unity and Polish independence went hand-in-hand. To realise them would mean the end of Russian influence in Europe. In the light of the American anti-slavery movement, Marx called upon the German working class to protest loudly and vehemently against Germany's betrayal of the Polish cause, just as the English workers had thwarted the attempts of their ruling class to interfere in the American war. Under conditions which meant privation for the workers themselves they had continued their opposition to American intervention, winning 'immortal historical honour'. It was now the task of the German working class 'to write on its banner in flaming characters *Poland's re-establishment*' (MEW 15:577). This address was signed by eleven members of the Association, Eccarius and Lessner among them.

On December 2 Marx received a telegram from Trier with

news of his mother's death. Penniless, suffering from skin ulcers and himself 'already with one foot in the grave', Marx had to ask Engels for money to make the trip to the Rhineland. After leaving London on December 7 he spent about ten days in Trier trying to settle the matters of inheritance but left before the formalities had been completed there. He decided to visit his uncle Philips in Zalt-Bommel, executor of his mother's will and custodian of a substantial part of her fortune. From Trier Marx had written to Jenny about the daily pilgrimages he made to the old Westphalen home in the Römerstrasse, a site which reminded him of the 'happiest time of my youth because it sheltered my greatest treasure' (Dec. 15).

Marx's return to London was delayed by a recurrence of his skin ailment, furuncles and carbuncles, which obliged him to remain under medical care at his uncle's home. Dr Anrooy, the husband of his cousin Henriette Philips, took charge of the patient, while his uncle 'a great old boy, applies my plasters and poultices himself, and my charming, witty cousin with the dangerous black eyes looks after me with the greatest of care' (letter to Engels, Dec. 27). Although anxious to return home, Marx ceded to the doctor's authority and did not leave Holland until pronounced fit to travel in February.

V
1864-1872

1864   During a public meeting held at St Martin's Hall in London the International Working Men's Association (IWA) is founded by members of London trade unions, and by English, French, German, Polish, Italian and Swiss working men, among them numerous emigrants.

—   The Czar issues a series of edicts establishing the jury system, public trials and representation for the accused in the Russian empire. Further, a generous system of local autonomy is created through the *Zemstvos*, locally elected councils which are to manage public services and social welfare in the districts and provinces.

—   Austria is conducting war on two fronts: in the North it is engaged in a battle with Denmark over the disputed territory of Schleswig-Holstein; in the South it is resisting the claims of Italian nationalists to the region of Venetia. Together with the Prussians Austria gains control of Schleswig-Holstein; the Peace of Vienna grants the occupied area to the allied powers and the terms of the division are fixed by the Convention of

1865   Gastein: Austria provisionally assumes control over Holstein, Prussia over Lauenburg and Schleswig. However, Bismarck now contrives to align allies in Europe for a war against Austria using the Schleswig-Holstein question as a pretext.

—   After the end of the American Civil War (April 1865) many Irish who had participated in the fighting return to Europe. Their discontent with conditions in Ireland and the status of the Irish in Britain finds expression in the conspiratorial movement known as Fenianism. The principal Fenian leaders are arrested in Ireland in this same year.

1866   After only three weeks of fighting, Prussia, backed by Italy and the smaller German states, defeats her Austrian rivals despite the latter's support from the larger states of Bavaria, Baden, Saxony. Italy, however, has simultaneously suffered a decisive defeat at the hands of Austria. Bismarck nonetheless achieves favourable treaty conditions for Prussia and her ally through diplomatic manoeuvres. The Peace of Prague guarantees Prussia all rights to Holstein, excludes Austria from the German confederation and, through the intercession of Napoleon III, hands Venetia over to Italy.

—   A new wave of protest arises in Italy, nevertheless, demanding the restitution of the coastal lands (Istria, Fruili) and South Tirol. Mazzini issues a manifesto of the 'Irredentists'.

—   The student Karakozov makes an unsuccessful attempt on the life of the Russian Czar Alexander II.

—   Chiefly to protest against the incorporation of Saxony in the North German confederation August Bebel and Wilhelm Liebknecht found the Saxonian *Volkspartei* (People's Party) with a platform known as the 'Chem-

1867   nitz Programme'. The following year both men are elected to the newly constituted *Reichstag*, the parliament of the reformed confederation, along with two other members of their party. Bismarck is elected chancellor of the *Bund*.

—   At the London Conference Bismarck, who is not yet prepared to go to war with France, negotiates a treaty with France to settle the so-called Luxemburg Question. This territory, hitherto in the possession of the Prussians, is to be neutralised and placed under the sovereignty of the Netherlands.

—   Austria restores Hungary's constitution with full ministerial responsibility and a separate Hungarian parliament. A Magyar ministry is formed under the

Austro-Hungarian crown and a general amnesty granted to political offenders.

1867   After two Fenians, the Manchester Martyrs, are hanged for having killed a guard while trying to escape from police custody, the Irish in Manchester stage a mass uprising.

—   A second Reform Bill is passed in the British Parliament, extending suffrage rights to the adult male population of industrial households but not to field labourers or miners. The total electorate now numbers some 2½-3 million persons, approx. 8-10% of the population.

1868-70 Members of the IWA in France are arrested and tried on charges of illegal political activities.

1868   After alienating the people and her own government with arbitrary and aggressive methods of rule, Queen Isabella is deposed by a Spanish Revolution. Regional juntas are established, headed by Marshall Serrano, president of the Senate, and a popular monarchy is declared. The question of the choice of monarch remains temporarily undecided.

1869   The Protestant Episcopal Church is disestablished in Ireland and religious equality officially proclaimed.

—   To compete with the Lassallean party, now under the leadership of J. B. von Schweitzer, for the working class vote, Bebel and Liebknecht now found a *Sozialdemokratische Arbeiterpartei* (SDAP—Social-Democratic Workers' Party) at Eisenach. In contrast to the rather pro-Bismarckian, pro-Prussian orientation of the Lassalleans, who emphasise social reform, the Eisenach party supports the International, opposes Bismarck and conceives its role as both political and social.

1870   The following year the SDAP's principal leaders are arrested on charges of high treason. While serving a prison sentence Bebel is the only social democrat to be re-elected to the *Reichstag*.

—   The Educational Act is passed in England, guaranteeing free primary schooling for all children.

1870   The Spanish throne is offered to Prince Leopold of Hohenzollern-Sigmaringen, a relative of the Prussian king. The French protest loudly against this threat of

Prussia's 'encirclement' and demand that Leopold withdraw his candidacy. The Prince yields to this pressure. By the 'Ems Despatch', transmitted through his ambassador Benedetti in Germany, Napoleon asks King Wilhelm of Prussia for a guarantee that he will never again support Leopold's candidacy. Having heard the news of the Prince's voluntary withdrawal, Wilhelm quietly lets the matter drop and declines to receive the French ambassador. Bismarck, however, desirous of a pretext for inciting the French to aggression, publishes the text of the messages exchanged in a brief account deliberately construed as a challenge to French honour. As expected, France promptly declares war on Prussia. The modernised German army under Moltke quickly overruns Alsace and forces Napoleon and his troops to capitulate within a month. The French king is taken prisoner at Donchery. In Paris a provisional Government of National Defense assumes power in Napoleon's stead. From Lyon Gambetta organises the continued fight of republican troops against the German invaders.

— Russia, in the meanwhile, profiting from the fact that Central Europe is embroiled in internal struggles for power, repudiates the 1856 Treaty of Paris and reasserts her right to construct naval and military bases on the shores of the Black Sea.

1871 The German army advances upon and blockades Paris.
— Thanks to his military successes Bismarck wins the Southern states, Baden, Württemburg and Bavaria, which are not members of the *Bund*, for the cause of national unity. On January 18 at the castle of Versailles the Northern and Southern states join together to proclaim the German *Reich* with Prussia's king Wilhelm I as Emperor. Bismarck now demands from the French a treaty ceding to Germany the provinces of Alsace and Lorraine and guaranteeing an indemnity of 5 billion francs. Gambetta, who cannot accept these terms, resigns in favour of Adolf Thiers.

In March Paris is suffering from a combination of adverse circumstances: after a humiliating defeat, a German blockade; a pro-monarchist government under

Thiers. The people revolt. Thiers's government retreats to Versailles and the Commune of Paris is proclaimed. A governing council is elected by a 70% vote of all registered electors. In other French cities the Commune is quickly suppressed.

1871   On May 10 Thiers signs for France the Treaty of Frankfurt. The Versailles troops advance on Paris shortly thereafter. On May 22nd a week of fighting begins in Paris, known as the 'Semaine sanglante' (the Bloody Week). 50,000 communards are reportedly killed and half that number taken prisoner. The city is put under martial law. Thiers's government is reinstated and many hundreds of the remaining communards flee the country.

—   After brutally murdering the student Ivanov, a member of his conspiratorial band, Sergei Nechayev flees St Petersburg to hide out in Switzerland. 87 of his fellow conspirators are brought to trial for this crime. In 1872 Nechayev is extradited and finally sentenced in Russia.

1872   The Emperors of Austria, Germany and Russia meet at Berlin to negotiate a means of isolating France from the rest of Europe, fearing that she will seek retribution for the recent defeat.

—   Bismarck begins his prolonged struggle against the hegemony of the Roman Catholic Church and the (Catholic) Centre Party, a struggle which comes to be called the Kulturkampf. Sanctions against the clergy in particular are provoked by the Pope's Dogma of Infallibility, issued in 1870. Laws restricting the sojourn of foreign and Prussian Jesuits are passed, whereupon the members of the Order of Jesus voluntarily leave the country.

THE AMERICAS

1865   The US Congress approves the 13th or anti-slavery amendment to the Constitution. General Lee, commander-in-chief of the Southern armies, capitulates shortly thereafter at Appotomax. Peace has hardly been concluded when President Lincoln is assassinated by a Southern fanatic, the actor John Wilkes Booth, and is succeeded in the presidency by Andrew Johnson.

1864 Archduke Maximilian, brother of the Austrian emperor Franz-Joseph, is offered the crown of Mexico by Napoleon III to compensate Austria for the loss of territories in Italy. The new emperor lacks support from the Mexican people and is unable to win international recognition.

1867 US Secretary of State James Seward purchases from Russia, for the sum of 7 million dollars, the Northwest territory of Alaska.

— When Napoleon III, himself threatened by growing Prussian military strength, withdraws his troops from Mexico, the opposition is easily able to defeat the imperialist government. Maximilian, who refuses to flee the country, is shot, together with two of his generals.

SCIENTIFIC AND TECHNOLOGICAL PROGRESS

1864 Henri Martin invents a new type of furnace for the production of steel.

1865 Johann Gregor Mendel formulates his laws on hybridisation and heredity.

— Claude Bernard inaugurates experimental medicine with the publication of *L'Introduction à l'étude de la médecine expérimentale*.

1866 The first transatlantic cable is laid.

1867 Alfred Nobel receives a British patent for the invention of dynamite.

1868 The Belgian Zénobe Gramme constructs the first industrial dynamo.

1869 The Suez Canal is opened.

1870 The American John Welsley Hyatt synthesizes the first plastic material, celluloid.

1871 Heinrich Schliemann begins his archaeological excavations on the site of ancient Troy.

IMPORTANT WORKS PUBLISHED

1864   Theodor Mommsen: Römische Forschungen.*
—   Frédéric Le Play: La Réforme sociale.
1865   Friedrich Albert Lange: Die Arbeiterfrage.*
1865-66 G. L. Maurer: Geschichte der Dorfverfassung in Deutschland.*
1866   Thomas Huxley: Lessons in Elementary Physiology.
—   August von Haxthausen: Die ländliche Verfassung Rußlands.*
—   Fedor M. Dostoevsky: Prestuplenie i naka tanie (Crime and Punishment).
1868   F. I. Firks: Etudes sur l'avenir de la Russie.*
1869   N. Flerovsky: Polozhenie rabotchego klassa v Rossii (The Situation of the Working Class in Russia).*
—   John Mitchel: The History of Ireland.*
—   J. S. Mill: The Subjection of Women.
1870   Paul von Lilienfeld: Land und Freiheit.*
1871   Eugen Dühring: Kritische Geschichte der politischen Ökonomie und des Sozialismus.*
—   Lewis Henry Morgan: Systems of Consanguinity and Affinity of the Human Family.*
—   William Stanley Jevons: The Theory of Political Economy.*
—   Sir Henry S. Maine: Lectures on the Early History of Institutions.*
—   Ernest Renan: La Réforme intellectuelle et morale.

KARL MARX
1864-1872

1864 Marx was laid up in Zalt-Bommel with furuncles and carbuncles until February 19. At times he was able neither to
walk, to stand nor to sit 'and even lying down is getting to be
damned difficult', He wrote to Engels in his discomfort, asking
for news from Manchester:

It cheers me up just to see your handwriting. And don't forget to
enclose your photograph. I promised it to my cousin and how is
she supposed to believe in our Orestes-Pylades friendship if I can't
even get you to send a photo? (Jan. 20).

He finally returned to London on February 24, travelling via
Amsterdam and Rotterdam, where he also visited relatives, and
immediately wrote to thank his uncle Philips for 'one of the
happiest episodes of my life' despite the carbuncles and furuncles
(Feb. 20). His illness gave him little respite until April, however.
Plagued by 'new and unexpected furuncles breaking through at
different parts of the body', he went to Manchester for a fortnight's stay with Engels (letter to Engels, March 11). Sometime
in March he received an inheritance from his deceased mother,
which enabled the family to move into more comfortable
quarters, still in Maitland Park in North-West London. While
convalescing in London, Marx continued to correspond with his
uncle, in particular, on world politics. Despite the open signs
of serious conflict he hoped that peace would continue, 'for
every war puts off the revolution in France. May God strike me
dumb if there be anything more stupid than this political
chessboard!' (March 29). He reported to Philips on his renewed

readings at the British Museum Library—Boethius's *De arith-metica* which dealt with the arithmetical system of the Romans—and spoke of the difficulties of division using the Roman characters. He also commented on the darkness in the universe according to the theory of light, concluding humorously:

The good Epicurus had a very reasonable inspiration to banish the gods into the intermundia (i.e. the *empty* spaces of the world), and in fact here in these cold, unmoved, pitch-black 'immaterial world spaces' is the place for R[oodhuyzen]'s 'perfect beasts' (April 14).

From Manchester Engels reported that their friend Wilhelm Wolff was suffering from increasingly severe headaches, which the doctor diagnosed as 'rheumatic', and from unrelenting insomnia. Engels finally consulted another doctor who discovered 'Lupus's' illness to be meningitis. The patient grew worse and Marx, scarcely recovered from his furunculosis, went to Manchester where he tended his sick friend until his death on May 9. Marx was among those who spoke at Lupus's funeral, a task which 'affected me so much,' he wrote Jenny, 'that I lost my voice a couple of times ... I don't think that anyone in Manchester was as well liked as our poor little guy ... In his letters I found the warmest expressions of sympathy from all sides, from school girls and school boys and especially their mothers' (May 13). In Wolff's will Marx was left the respectable sum of £800, which together with the maternal inheritance helped the Marx family live for the first time without great financial worries and debts. However, Marx's health had already been undermined by the years of privation so that 'Despite everything that people say about my healthy appearance, I still have the continuous feeling that *something* [is] *wrong* and part of this feeling of inadequacy is caused by the great determination which I must summon up in order to work on more difficult topics' (May 26).

Despite his illness Marx recommenced work on the final manuscript of *Capital*. In April he read *Herr Bastiat Schulze ... or Capital and Labour* which he had recently received from its author Lassalle. The ideas expressed there seemed uncannily familiar, even to the wording. Then in early June 'I glanced just by chance into my series of articles on "Wage Labour and Capital" published in the *NRhZ* ... There I found Lassalle's direct source. As a special gesture of friendship I am going to have the whole lot from the *NRhZ appended* in a note to my book, *on false pretences* naturally and without any reference to Lassalle' (June 3). At this time in Berlin Liebknecht entertained close personal contact with Lassalle through his activity in the Lassallean ADAV. In a regular exchange of letters Liebknecht kept Marx and Engels informed on the party in Germany, while Marx advised on tactical proceedings vis-à-vis Lassalle:

I explained to him that while we consider it good politics to let Lassalle go his own way undisturbed for the present, we cannot identify ourselves with him in any way ... [Liebknecht's] uninterrupted stay in Berlin is very important for us (Marx to Engels, June 7).

Towards mid-June Marx's health again deteriorated to the point where he was forced to abandon temporarily his writing on 'Economics'. Instead, he studied anatomy and physiology (Carpenter, Lord, Kölliker, Spurzheim, Schwann, Schleiden), following in the footsteps of Engels, to whom he wrote: 'You know that 1. I am slow in getting on to everything and 2. I always follow in your tracks. Thus it is probable that I shall study a lot of anatomy and physiology in my spare time and also attend lectures (where the stuff is demonstrated and dissected ad oculos)' (July 4).

The Schleswig-Holstein question recurred frequently in the letters between Marx and Engels during this summer. Marx saw Prussia's conflict with Denmark as advantageous for Russia in so far as it diverted Europe's attention from the Russian manoeuvres in Poland and the Caucasus: 'I consider these two affairs, the suppression of the Polish insurrection and the occupation of the Caucasus, as the two most important European events since 1815' (to Engels, June 7).

The two friends also corresponded on the Civil War in America and on the prospects of Lincoln's re-election in November. Marx seconded Engels's view that Lincoln's chances were high, remarked, however, on a note of caution that: 'In the country which is the prototype of democratic humbug the electoral period is full of contingencies which can most unexpectedly contradict the rationale of the events' (Sept. 7).

On September 2 Marx received news that Ferdinand Lassalle had been killed in a duel with a 'pseudo-prince' for the hand of a Bavarian emissary's daughter: 'One of the many tactless deeds he did during his lifetime', Marx remarked to Engels (Sept. 7), for he considered Lassalle to have been too good to die in such a way; he was one of their own, 'an enemy of our enemies' (Marx to Jenny Marx, Sept. 2). Marx wrote a letter of condolence to the Countess Hatzfeldt on September 12, mentioning the rupture in their friendship as due to deeper reasons than Lassalle's protracted silence or his own illness. Lassalle 'was one of the men whom I held a lot of', he told the Countess. She should take courage in the fact that 'He died young, in triumph, like Achilles'. Shortly thereafter Liebknecht informed Marx that he had been proposed as Lassalle's successor in the ADAV. Marx gave Liebknecht to understand that under certain conditions he would possibly be willing to accept the chair.

THE FOUNDING OF THE FIRST INTERNATIONAL

In September a young French immigrant Le Lubez invited Marx to participate as the representative from Germany at an international working men's meeting to be held that month in St Martin's Hall. Marx sent Eccarius in his place but, after receiving a second invitation from the joiner William Cremer, finally decided to attend as a spectator. At this meeting it was decided to found an international association of working men, the goal of which was stated as 'the social equality of working men' (Sept. 28). Marx and Eccarius were designated as members of a provisional committee charged with editing the statutes and preamble for the association. In a letter to Joseph Weydemeyer in America, Marx explained why he had decided to participate:

Its English members consist mostly of the heads of the local trade unions, that is, the actual labour kings of London ... From the French side the members are themselves insignificant, but they are the direct organs of the leading 'ouvriers' in Paris ... Although for years I have systematically declined all participation in any 'organisations', etc., whatsoever, I accepted *this time* because it involved a matter where it is possible to do some important work (Nov. 29).

While the election of Lassalle's successor in the ADAV was still pending, Marx, who had eliminated himself as a candidate through his new loyalty to the International, commented on the two possible nominees, Moses Hess and Bernhard Becker, saying: '... it is all the same which of the two you choose, for at the decisive moment the men who are needed will turn up' (letter to Carl Klings, Oct. 4); neither would in any case be capable of guiding an important movement.

At the first meeting of the Committee on October 5 Marx was among a group of nine selected to a sub-committee with the specific task of drawing up the platform of principles. However, a new attack of furunculosis prevented him from attending either the sub-committee meeting (Oct. 8) or the next meeting of the General Committee on October 12, at which it was voted to adopt the name 'International Working Men's Association'. Eccarius subsequently informed Marx that his absence had been conspicuous and was variously interpreted. 'It is absolutely essential,' Eccarius added, 'that you set the seal of your exact and profound mind on this, the first-born offspring of the European working men's organisation' (Oct. 12). In Marx's absence John Weston had been charged with editing the declaration of principles, Major Wolff with the Rules, and both papers had been referred back to sub-committee for reworking. The sub-committee's secretary, Cremer, wrote to Marx on October 13 that they hoped to be able to see Marx at the next session. On October 18 Marx was present at a meeting of the Committee which now adopted the title 'Central Council' (changed to 'General Council' in November 1866), where the 'substance' of a programme and rules read by Le Lubez was accepted and then referred back to sub-committee again for a final revision. Shortly thereafter, Marx met several members of the Central Council at his home to discuss the documents in question. It was agreed that he should elaborate the texts in a way suitable for final presentation to the Council.

In a later letter to Engels (Nov. 4) Marx explained what happened with the texts he had been given. The preamble, by Le Lubez, was 'badly written, completely immature and full of atrocious phraseology' and so, to gain a free hand and justify his changes, Marx wrote an address—'a sort of review of the adventures of the working classes since 1845'; then, under the pretext of having already incorporated the essential facts into the address, he threw out the Declaration of Principles, written by Weston, and reduced the rules from forty to ten. All in all, 'It was very difficult to keep the thing in a form which made our views acceptable at the present stage of the labour movement. Time is needed before the movement, now revived, will permit the old vigour of language' (Nov. 4). To the extent that politics were touched upon in the address, Marx pointed out, he spoke of countries and not nationalities and denounced Russia and not the 'minores gentium'.

On November 1 both the address and the statutes were read before the Central Council and, with a few insignificant changes in wording, were adopted unanimously. The Council thanked Marx, Le Lubez and Weston for 'their exertions and the production of so admirable an address'. Both it and the statutes appeared in pamphlet form in London on November 24.

The Inaugural Address speaks of the 'social pest called a commercial and industrial crisis', of the ever-growing poverty of the masses in contrast to the wealth and property concentrated in the hands of a few. Progress in technology and trade would never alleviate the evils of the industrial system and the misery of the working masses, but rather 'on the present false base, every fresh development of the productive powers of labour must tend to deepen social contrasts and point up social antagonisms' (Marx, Engels, SW 1 : 346). We are reminded of the victories of the working class in England, the 'compensating features' for the defeat of the 1848 revolutions: The Ten-Hour Bill had been a victory of working class principles as opposed to the interests of the factory owners; the co-operative movement has shown, 'by deed, instead of by argument', that large-scale production is possible without class divisions and monopolies. 'Like slave labour, like serf labour, hired labour is but a transitory and inferior form, destined to disappear before associated labour' (*ibid.*, p. 347). The address proposes that co-operative labour be introduced on a national scale in order to counter effectively the growth of monopolies; it stresses that the potential success of the working class lies in its numbers, 'But numbers weigh only in the balance, if united by combination and led by knowledge' (*ibid.*, 348).

The provisional rules of the Association begin with the basic tenet proclaiming 'That the emancipation of the working classes must be conquered by the working classes themselves; that the struggle for the emancipation of the working classes means not a struggle for class privileges and monopolies, but for equal rights and duties, and the abolition of all class rule' (*Documents* 1 : 288).

Informed at length about the founding of the IWA, Engels commented that it was certainly important for them to have contact with men who represented the working class; yet he was sceptical about the group's future, expecting it to break up 'very soon into its theoretically bourgeois and theoretically proletarian elements just as soon as the issues have been more clearly defined' (Nov. 7).

During these active days of the founding Marx met Michael Bakunin for the first time in sixteen years and was pleased to find that this Russian was one of the rare men who had 'advanced and not regressed' in the long interval (Marx to Engels, Nov. 4). In Germany, meanwhile, Becker had been named president of the ADAV in accordance with Lassalle's will. Liebknecht informed Marx as well that the ADAV was planning to start a new newspaper, the *Social-Demokrat*, with Liebknecht and Hofstetten as editors, and that his and Engels's participation would be welcome (letter to Marx, Nov. 4). Marx accepted this offer for them both and referred in his reply to the principles set down in the paper's prospectus: solidarity of popular interests, a united people's republic of Germany, abolition of the rule of capital.

At a Central Council meeting on November 22 Marx moved that they invited various working men's groups to stand for membership in the IWA. The Council appointed Marx to write an address congratulating Abraham Lincoln on his recent re-election. Marx found this task more difficult than something 'with contents' since the problem here was to make it 'stand off from ordinary democratic phraseology' (to Engels, Dec. 2). This address, which was presented to the CC on November 29 and adopted by a unanimous vote, interpreted Lincoln's re-election as a triumph which meant death to the slavery interests and would introduce a new era of ascendancy for labour:

The working men of Europe feel sure that as the American War of Independence initiated a new era of ascendancy for the middle class, so the American Anti-Slavery War will do for the working classes (*Documents* 1 : 53).

Marx sent copies of the IWA documents—the addresses and statutes—to friends and family in America and Europe: to Ernest Jones, Dr Kugelmann, Miquel, Tolain, Bakunin, and instructed the latter to pass copies on to Garibaldi in Italy. In December the *Social-Demokrat* published its first specimen issues containing a German translation of the IWA Inaugural Address. Marx was interested in seeing the ADAV and other German associations for the working class adhere to the IWA and wrote, therefore, to Carl Siebel about the importance of these ties between Germany and the Central Council in London:

You understand that we only need the adherence of the *Allgemeiner Deutscher Arbeiterverein* for the beginning here in face of our adversaries. Later on, the whole establishment of that organ will have to be demolished because its foundations are wrong (Dec. 22).

Marx also warned Liebknecht about the definite 'Lassalle cult' which the *Social-Demokrat* seemed to follow in its first numbers.

While Marx had been writing the Lincoln address for the Association, the journalist Peter Fox had assumed charge of a similar address in support of the Polish insurgents. Fox, who like many other English democrats, had a 'fanatical "love" for France' according to Marx, closed his address by 'consoling the Poles with the passionate friendship of the English working classes for the French democrats' (Marx to Engels, Dec. 10). In a sub-committee session Marx sharply criticised Fox's Franco-mania and pointed out that France's treason against Poland had a long history. The address in question was adopted on condition that the conclusion was changed in accordance with Marx's remarks. When the address was then presented to the CC on December 13, a lengthy debate ensued and the matter was deferred until the next session. Referring to Fox, Marx remarked in a letter to Engels: 'Easy as it is, however, to accomplish the rational when dealing with the English working men, one must in equal measure be on one's guard as soon as the intellectuals, bourgeois or the bogus-intellectuals participate in the movement' (Dec. 10).

1865 During this year Marx was an active participant in the CC meetings, except for three weeks in July and August when he retired, on the pretext of travel, into his study to work on the manuscript of *Capital*. On January 30 the Hamburg publisher Meissner agreed to publish the 'Economics' and Marx received his contract on March 23, according to which he was obliged to deliver the 800-page text before the end of May.

At the January 3 CC meeting Marx presented the German translations of the Inaugural Address and the statutes, stating that 50,000 copies had been distributed in Germany. The issue of Fox's Poland address was taken up again; Marx 'in a very able historical résumé argued that the traditional foreign policy of France had not been favourable to the restoration and independence of Poland'. The Council voted that the address should be amended 'to accord with the truths of history' (Minutes, Jan. 3). On January 23 an invitation was read to the Council from a group of bourgeois radicals, inviting them to join a mass meeting to be held in support of universal suffrage and electoral reform. Knowing the connections between the IWA and the British trade unions, the group had appealed to the Council for aid in organising this meeting. Marx moved that a delegation be sent strictly in the role of observers and that it be authorised to support the reformers under two conditions: 'if, in the first place, manhood suffrage is directly and openly proclaimed in their programme and, in the second, if people elected by us are placed on the *regular* committee so that they can watch the fellows and can compromise them when they commit a fresh act of treachery, which, as I made clear to all, is bound to occur' (to Engels, Feb. 1). The Council heard on January 31 the answer of the American Ambassador Charles Francis Adams to the IWA's Address to Lincoln. Adams's message, 'the first answer which is more than strictly formal on the part on the old fellow', (Marx to Engels, Feb. 1) declared that:

the United States regard their cause in the present conflict with slavery maintaining insurgents as the cause of human nature and they derive new encouragement to persevere from the testimony of the working men of Europe that the national attitude is favoured with their enlightened approval and earnest sympathies (Minutes, Jan. 31).

On the request of Liebknecht and J. B. von Schweitzer, Marx wrote a memorial tribue to Proudhon in the form of a letter to Schweitzer that appeared in the *Social-Demokrat* on February 1, 3 and 5. This letter contained—in Marx's estimation—'some very bitter blows, apparently meant for Proudhon' but in fact directed against the ADAV's own founder Lassalle. Like the latter, Proudhon had a 'petit-bourgeois point-of-view' and never advanced beyond sophistry in trying to use the dialectic method: 'he never really grasped scientific dialectics' (SW 1 : 360). His best writing, once praised by Marx as a monumental work,

Qu'est-ce que la Propriété? [What is Property?] (1840), was based on a falsely posed question. 'The question of what this is could only be answered by a critical analysis of "political economy", embracing these *property relations* as a whole ... in their real form, that is, as *relations of production*' (ibid., p. 355). Instead, Proudhon had taken economic categories to be 'eternal ideas' and therefore never superseded bourgeois economy nor understood that science, as a solution to the social question, must be derived 'from a critical knowledge of the historical movement, a movement which itself produces the *material conditions of emancipation*' (ibid., p. 357). Yet Proudhon was for Marx 'epoch-making *after* Hegel' for it was he who had made a certain critique of society, emphasising points that 'Christian consciousness' preferred to overlook and that Hegel had 'left in mystic semi-obscurity' (ibid., p. 354). Although Proudhon was frequently compared with Rousseau, Marx judged his talent to approach that of the French historian Nicolas Linguet, whose work Marx termed 'brilliant'. Despite his talent Proudhon remained a 'living contradiction', in morals, in everything and, governed by vanity—here the implicit reference to Lassalle is especially sharp—became a charlatan in science, an accommodator in politics 'and the only question for him, as for all vain people, is the success of the moment, the sensation of the day' (ibid., p. 357).

A letter received from Liebknecht at the end of January confirmed the worst of the suspicions which Marx and Engels had entertained against Lassalle. Working in league with Bismarck, the ADAV founder had wanted to become, in Marx's words, 'the Richelieu of the proletariat' by selling out the working men's party to the Prussian government. As a result Marx resolved 'not to hesitate in intimating *with sufficient clarity* in the Preface to my book that he was nothing but a blind imitator and a plagiarist' (to Engels, Jan. 30). Marx also took the field against the inheritors of the pro-Bismarck policy in the ADAV and its 'Lassalle-cult'. While Liebknecht was agitating among the Berlin compositors for the repeal of anti-coalition laws in Prussia, the ADAV paradoxically took a stand against the coalition movement. Marx thereupon wrote to Schweitzer, pointing out that coalition rights and trade unions were of great importance not only 'for the open organisation of the working class against the bourgeoisie ... but in Prussia, and in Germany in general, the

right of coalition is a means to break police rule and bureaucracy
... a measure, in short, to make the "subjects" come of age'
(Feb. 13). Naturally the Prussian state would not tolerate
coalitions because they interfered too forcibly with 'police rule,
feudal order, *Gesindeordnung* [servants' regulations] and
bureaucratic tutelage of every sort whatsoever'. Contrarily, the
Prussian government was willing to support the co-operative
movement on a small scale in order 'to bribe a part of the working
class and emasculate the movement'. Such measures had been
interpreted by Lassalle as proof of the 'socialist' attitudes and
orientation of Bismarck. Marx closed this letter with the unequi-
vocal challenge: 'The working class is revolutionary or it is
nothing.'

Slanderous attacks in the *Social-Demokrat* which accused
French members of the IWA of supporting Bonaparte and his
cousin 'Plon-Plon' obliged Marx to send the paper a declaration
on February 8 that he hoped would clear the air and 'sweep the
Party clean of the remaining Lassalle stink' (letter to Engels,
Feb. 3). This declaration stated clearly that:

> ... the Paris proletariat opposes Bonapartism in both its forms, that
> of the Tuileries [Napoleon III] and that of the Palais-Royal
> [Plon-Plon], and has never thought for an instant of selling its
> historic right of primogeniture ... as bearer of the revolution for a
> plate of lentils. We recommend this example to the working men
> of Germany (Draft; cf. letter to Engels, Feb. 6).

In a lengthy letter to Dr Kugelmann on February 23 Marx
explained the reasons which had now led to an open break
between the *Social-Demokrat* and himself and Engels, retracing
his relations with Lassalle and with J. B. von Schweitzer. While
Lassalle had always purported to support the party which Marx
represented, he soon recognised the fact that the latter would
never lend himself to Prussian 'state socialism' nor sanction
Lassallean political tactics. He therefore decided to set himself
up as a 'working man's dictator' in opposition to Marx and the
old party, which he betrayed through his commitment to
Bismarck. Lassalle's behaviour was characteristic of a *Realpolitiker* [realist politician] who thought that as the leader of
a proletarian movement he could make compromises with the
Prussian reactionaries such as the bourgeoisie had permitted itself
to make. Seduced by the idea of realising a project for the

benefit of the working class, i.e. universal suffrage, Lassalle thus 'shook hands with Bismarck in the interests of the proletariat, while the proletariat itself, compromised by the *Realpolitik* of the bourgeoisie since 1848, exploded in cheers for this charlatan-redeemer who promised to help them with a leap into the promised land'. As for Schweitzer, Marx did not doubt the sincerity of his intentions, but since he too was a *Realpolitiker*, he was willing to accept the given circumstances and avoided provoking the government. It was therefore inevitable that Marx, who was no *Realpolitiker*, would be obliged to end his collaboration with such men. Moreover, he added,

I prefer a hundred-fold to agitate here through the '*International Association*'. The influence on the *English* proletariat is direct and of the greatest importance. Now we stir the question of universal suffrage which naturally has an entirely different meaning here than in Prussia (Feb. 23).

The IWA was making unexpectedly fine progress both in England and on the Continent, Marx noted, and its only real competition was offered by the Lassalleans in Germany.

On March 3 in the *Social-Demokrat* a notice appeared signed by Marx and Engels which declared their unrelenting opposition to the liberals and to the 'ministry and feudal-absolutist party'. Moreover they announced the impossibility of collaborating with an organ such as the *Social-Demokrat* which formed an alliance with 'Royal Prussian state socialism' (MEW 16:79).

A lengthy article which Engels had intended to publish in the *Social-Demokrat* was put out by Meissner in Hamburg on March 7 under the title *Die preussische Militärfrage und die deutsche Arbeiterpartei*. During its composition Marx had suggested a number of changes, remarking, for example, that the 1848-49 movement had failed not because the citizens were opposed to universal suffrage (as Engels had written), but because they 'preferred at that time tranquillity with servitude as opposed to the mere *prospect* of a fight accompanied by freedom' (Feb. 11). This writing, which Marx had originally encouraged Engels to undertake, attributes the cowardliness of the German bourgeoisie in political affairs to the feudal remnants of a not yet fully industrialised country. In Germany, therefore, the struggles against feudal powers and against bureaucratic reactionism are inseparable and, in turn, the two are intimately linked with the 'fight for the intellectual and political emancipation of the rural proletariat' (MEW 16:74). Engels warned the proletariat to beware of the 'traps' which the government set against the country's progressive elements, and emphasized that the fight of the bourgeoisie for liberal rights concerned them as well: 'For without freedom of the press and the right of association and union no labour movement is possible' (MEW 16:75). The bourgeoisie cannot win its own political supremacy without giving the proletariat the weapons it needs for its own victory. Armed with freedom of the press, 'it will conquer universal suffrage; with direct, universal suffrage, together with the other means of agitation, it will conquer all the rest' (ibid.)

The IWA had in the meantime succeeded in gaining a controlling hand in the newly formed Reform League, whose immediate goal—universal suffrage—was the key to the progress of the working men's movement. On February 25 Marx announced to Engels that the IWA had managed to place its members in the League's executive committee. Marx himself participated actively in the construction of this group and frequently met with the Chartist leader and reformer Ernest Jones. As a leading figure in the IWA Marx now found himself exposed to attack from many sides and was often forced to reply publicly to slanderous accusations. Bernhard Becker, for example, accused Marx of entertaining relations with the spy Bangya and of inciting the Countess Hatzfeldt against the ADAV. Marx's refutation, entitled 'The President of Humanity', appeared in the Berlin journal Reform on April 13.

On March 1 at a commemorative meeting for Poland the IWA proclaimed, in a statement inspired by Marx, that the integrity and independence of Poland was an indispensable condition for a democratic Europe. As long as this condition had not been met, all revolutionary triumphs on the Continent would be ephemeral preludes to long, renewed periods of oppression and counter-revolution.

'In addition to my work on the book,' Marx wrote Engels on March 13, 'the International Association takes up an enormous amount of my time, since in fact I am head of the whole business.' While Marx was absent for three weeks in March and April visiting his Dutch relatives, John Weston proposed to the Council a debate on the following subjects: (1) that the working men's condition would not be improved by higher wages and (2) that trade unions must consequently be considered to have a prejudicial effect on other sections of industry (Minutes, April 4). The debate was delayed until Marx's return and he subsequently decided to prepare a lecture which would explain his ideas more precisely to the whole organisation.

At a CC meeting on April 25 Marx read a letter from Liebknecht in Leipzig, reporting on his agitation among the compositors and the resulting strike for higher wages. In the name of the Berlin Compositors' Union Liebknecht solicited the support of the CC and of the London compositors.

Pleased with the success of the Reform League and the IWA Marx noted in a letter to Engels that the latter had baffled all the bourgeois attempts to lead the Reform League astray and predicted:

If this re-electrification of the political movement of the English working class succeeds, our Association will have achieved more for the European working class, without making any fuss, than possible in any other way (May 1).

Following the assassination of President Lincoln Marx was charged with composing an address to the new head of state Andrew Johnson. In this address, which was presented to and adopted by the CC on May 13, the IWA called upon Johnson to continue Lincoln's work, which had initiated a new era of the emancipation of labour, of political reconstruction and social regeneration, and characterised the 'great and good' Lincoln as 'one of the rare men who succeed in becoming great, without ceasing to be good' (Documents 1 : 295).

While preparing his answer to the Owenite John Weston, Marx announced to Engels his intention to present two main points : (1) that labour wages determine the value of commodities and (2) therefore prices rise proportionately to rises in wages. 'It is not easy to analyse all the economic questions which arise in this connection when dealing with those who know nothing. You can't compress a course in political economy into one hour. But we shall do our best' (May 20).

The two sessions of this short course on 'Wages, Price and Profit' took place in Council on June 20 and 27. In these lectures Marx exposed in summary form his theories on capital, beginning—in the reverse order of their presentation in the books of Capital—with the real determination of wages and prices on the world markets. Refuting Weston's thesis that higher wages only meant higher prices, he explained how the market functions to create an increase in supply in order to cope with the increase in consumer demand, stimulated by higher wages. He pointed out that the interplay of supply and demand regulates only temporary price fluctuations and says nothing about the actual value of the commodities. What these values are and how they are determined are questions which cannot be answered by market analysis but only by enquiring into the value of labour itself. At this point Marx began to explicate the abstract determination of value just as he had presented it in his earlier manuscripts on labour and value (*Grundrisse* and *Zur Kritik*), and would later do in book I of *Capital* as well. Marx remarked that one of the first men to hit upon the true nature of value was the American Benjamin Franklin who, in 1729, perceived that the relative values of commodities are determined by the respective quantities of labour realised in them under certain average production conditions in a given social system. The greater the amount of labour invested in a product, the higher its value; conversely, the higher the productive power of labour—thanks to the aid of machines, etc.—the lower the value of the commodities produced. Labour is therefore the actual determinant of value, whereas 'the market price expresses only the *average amount of social labour* necessary, under the average conditions of production, to supply the market with a certain mass of a certain article' (Marx, Engels, SW 1 : 383). How, then, are profits realised? Goods are sold at their real value, i.e. at the value of the labour invested in them, but part of this labour is unpaid labour or 'surplus' labour invested in the commodities by the working man and realised by the capitalist through the sale. This is possible because the capitalist buys labour power from the worker for a certain fixed period of time, whereby the value of this labour power in turn is also determined by the quantity of labour necessary to maintain and reproduce it. Its use, however, is limited only by the individual's physical capacities. The capitalist, who has paid for the commodity value of the labouring power, has the right to its use value as a productive force. In this exchange it is evidently the capitalist who benefits, for he realises the surplus value contained in the commodities while paying only for the labour power as a commodity.

Following this brief sketch of the mechanisms of the economic system in which they lived, Marx commented to the working men on the present efforts to ameliorate their lot under the obviously prejudicial capitalist organisation of labour. The fight for shorter working hours is not in vain, he said, but, rather, 'a duty to themselves and to their race' (*ibid.*, p. 397f.). They must try to limit the tyranny of capital, which will otherwise reduce them to wretched beasts of burden, will break them in body and in spirit. Measures such as shorter working hours and higher wages are, however, only palliatives and not cures and do not take into account the fact that 'the present social system simultaneously engenders the *material conditions* and the *social forms* necessary for an economic reconstruction of society' (*ibid.*, p. 404). Similarly, trade unions are effective in a limited guerrilla war against the system which they should be trying to change, 'using their organised forces as a lever for the final emancipation of the working class, that is to say, the ultimate abolition of the wages system!' (*ibid.*, p. 404).

In late July Marx was forced to the painful and embarrassing confession that his inheritances had been consumed and the family was now living on pawnbroker's credit. He made a clean breast of affairs to Engels and admitted that the chief reason behind their rather high standard of living was the need to help the girls 'establish relations and contacts which can secure their future ... even just from a commercial point-of-view, a purely proletarian arrangement would be unsuitable here, although it would be perfectly fine if my wife and I were alone or if the girls were boys' (July 31). The thought which kept him going in all this renewed misery, Marx added, 'was that we two are a company enterprise with me giving my time for the theoretical and party aspects of the business.' As for his work on 'Capital', Marx announced that all three 'books' of the theoretical first section were ready, excepting three chapters of book I. Then only the fourth book—the historic section—remained to be written. He was, moreover, determined not to let any of the manuscript out of his hands until the whole thing—and he termed it 'an artistic whole'—was finished, especially since he expected to condense and eliminate parts in order to keep within the maximum of sixty printer's sheets.

After a period of ill health, which Marx used to begin the study of astronomy, he participated in the reunions of the first

IWA conference (standing committee and continental delegates), held in London from September 26-29. Marx was responsible for the conference programme, the purpose of which was to plan the international congress for 1866. *The Workman's Advocate* was recognised as the IWA's official organ and the following discussion topics, proposed by Marx and S. G. Fribourg of Paris, were adopted for the coming congress: co-operative labour; reduction of working hours; female and child labour; direct and indirect taxation; trade unions; standing armies; the problem of co-ordinating and combining national efforts in the struggle against capital; checking the Muscovite influence in Europe through national independence and the re-establishment of the Polish state. The French delegates also proposed the discussion of religious ideas and their socio-political effects. The first IWA congress was set for May 1866 in Geneva.

Despite his precarious financial situation Marx was unwilling to compromise himself or his work on the 'Economics': In October he received an offer from a close collaborator of Bismarck's, Lothar Bucher, to contribute monthly articles on economics to the Prussian state news organ, *Der Staatsanzeiger;* Three members of the Berlin working men's association solicited Marx to assume the leadership of the ADAV as a member of a three-man directorate (Nov. 13). Marx turned down both offers.

After all the delays he had had with his 'Economics', Marx now found the International weighing on him like an 'incubus' and he would have been glad to get rid of it, according to a letter to Engels on December 26. As a director of *The Workman's Advocate* he was charged with turning it into a 'respectable' paper. The Reform League was enjoying enormous success and had recently held the largest working men's meeting since Marx had been in London. The various meetings of these organisations cost him three evenings per week and much writing on the side, yet Marx realised that if he were to withdraw, 'the bourgeois element which is now watching us (foreign infidels) with displeasure from behind the scenes would win the upper hand' (letter to Engels, Dec. 26).

Towards the end of the year Marx studied agricultural chemistry in connection with his discussion of ground rent and found that Liebig and Schönbein, in particular, were 'more important for these matters than all economists put together' (to Engels, Feb. 13, 1866). He now completed what he thought was the definitive manuscript of *Capital* in draft. However, book II was in very rudimentary form and he was never to work on book III again to make it finally ready for publication. This last thick manuscript of book III (more than 850 printed pages) is of all his posthumous writings including the *Grundrisse* the smoothest and best written. In contrast to book I, written simultaneously, book III deals with the concrete side of the production of capital under real world conditions and is entitled 'The Total Process of the Production of Capital'. Some of the problems touched upon there, still topics of debate today include: the average profit rate; the transformation of commodity values; the law of the tendency of falling profit rates; the role of credit in capitalist production; the transformation of surplus profit into ground rent. Whereas book I treats the production of capital from a purely abstract standpoint, the method of book III is empirical and approaches the production process from the actual situation of a market economy determining prices, etc. Contrary to what is frequently maintained, these two books complement rather than contradict one another: the harmonious relation between them Marx demonstrated in his lectures on 'Wages, Price and Profit'.

1866 Marx began the year with a new spurt of energy. Determined to finish the final copy of his *Capital* manuscript as soon as possible, he edited and recopied the material written during the past two years, beginning with book I. In January he announced to Dr Kugelmann that he hoped to finish by March and then bring the text to Hamburg himself.

At the beginning of the year intrigues developed with the International which stemmed from the Proudhon-orientated members within the CC and in the Brussels IWA group. The 'opposition party' published 'smears' against the CC leadership and attacked various members, whom they accused of being Bonapartists. However, Marx saw that:

The real key to the dispute is the *Polish Question*. These fellows have attached everything to the Muscovitism of Proudhon-Herzen ... messieurs the Russians have found their latest allies in the Proudhonised section of the 'Jeune France' (letter to Engels, Jan. 5).

He suggested to Engels that he write an answer to the most recent anti-Poland publications of this group, especially since its members were opposed to any discussion of the Polish Question at the IWA Congress. On January 22 Marx took part in a commemorative meeting, organised by the members of the Polish emigration and the IWA together, on the anniversary of the Polish revolt of 1863-64. Marx spoke in the name of the IWA, expressing their solidarity with the emancipatory cause in Poland. The IWA, Marx informed Kugelmann, had now made such great strides that, to the three existing journals which represented it in England, Belgium and French Switzerland, a fourth was being added: *Der Vorbote*, organ of the German speaking section in Switzerland. Moreover, the Reform League had had a sensational effect in England with its recent labour meeting: *The Times* of London had devoted two successive leading articles to a discussion of this phenomenon.

By February excessive nightwork had undermined Marx's health; his furunculosis returned and obliged him to stay in bed. While convalescing he was too weak to tackle theoretical material, he wrote Engels, and added instead a historical section to the part on the work day which he had already written—an addition not planned in the original concept (*see* letter to Engels, Feb. 10). Most concerned about Marx's recurrent disease, Engels conferred with his own doctor and then advised Marx to take small daily doses of arsenic. 'This affair is truly getting too serious,' he warned, 'and if your head, as you say yourself, is not up to the mark for the theoretical things, then let it rest a bit from higher theory. Stop the night-work and lead a more regular life' (Feb. 10). He suggested that Marx give the publisher the first part of the manuscript, book I of the volume, for instance, to satisfy both public and publisher and not lose any time himself. Marx replied to Engels's proposals with a description of his latest furuncle and the doleful comment: 'If I had enough money, that is to say, enough >—O for my family and if my book were finished, I wouldn't care a bit, were I to land up tomorrow in the knacker's yard, alias kick the bucket. However, under the aforementioned circumstances this is not yet possible' (Feb. 13). He therefore agreed to follow the doctor's orders with arsenic and also to deliver Meissner the first volume of the 'Economics' as soon as it was completed without waiting to finish the rest. Although the manuscript was ready, in its present form it was enormous and 'cannot possibly be edited by anyone but me, not even you', he wrote Engels (*ibid.*).

During Marx's illness the differences within the IWA led to a great crisis: bourgeois elements took over the *Workingmen's Advocate*, turning it into the liberal *Commonwealth*. From his sick-bed Marx was able nevertheless to intervene to have Eccarius retained on the editorial staff. Liebknecht suggested that the IWA use the *Social-Demokrat* as its organ. But as Marx remarked to Engels, 'What we want is just exactly the disappearance of the *Social-Demokrat* and of all Lassalleanism' (Feb. 10). The commotion within the CC was intimately related to the rivalries and jealousies over the journal. The Frenchman Le Lubez used the opportunity to stir up animosity against the so-called 'German influence' within the Association. A pro-Mazzini faction led by Wolff tried to push through a resolution declaring the IWA's solidarity with the Italian leader. To counter these moves, Marx, who was provisional secretary for Belgium, assembled a group of the IWA's foreign secretaries at his home on March 10 to discuss a course of action. At the next meeting on March 13 they presented a united front in protest against the intrigues. As Marx later wrote to Engels, the English members saw clearly that 'the whole continental element is associated with me to a man and there is nothing in the way of *German* influence, as M. Le Lubez insinuated' hoping to prove that Marx as leader of the English faction kept down the continental members (March 24). Speaking in reference to the previous discussion of Mazzini and his merits as a working class leader, Marx pointed out that Mazzini's interests were not compatible with those of the IWA, that he was a supporter or 'centralist isolation' and understood working men's associations to be a sort of 'benefit society'. Marx subsequently explained the controversy to his cousin Nannette Philips in a letter written on March 18. Mazzini, jealous of the IWA's success, had been stirring up discontent with the opposition to Marx's leadership, although 'leadership' was not the object of his ambitions:

But having once fairly embarked in an enterprise which I consider of import, I certainly, 'anxious' man that I am, do not like to give way. Mazzini, a most decided hater of freethinking and socialism, watched the progress of our society with great jealousy.

In a countermove, staged by Marx, Orsini declared that Mazzini was utterly without significance in the Italian workers' movement, and was incapable of understanding the goals of the IWA:

'As it was, I carried a complete victory over this redoubtable adversary. I think that Mazzini has now had enough of me and will make bonne mine à mauvaise jeu' (letter written in Eng., quoted in IRSH I, 1956, pp. 108-111).

The day after this confrontation in the CC, Marx left London under doctor's orders for a stay by the sea in Margate. Lodged in a private boarding house fronting the sea, Marx was rid of all company; he even abandoned his books. 'I have become myself a sort of walking stick,' he wrote to Nannette, 'running up and down the whole day, and keeping my mind in that state of nothingness which Buddhaism considers the climax of human bliss.' 'In the evenings one is too tired to do anything but sleep,' he added to Engels (March 24). He still found time, however, to tend to some of his correspondence. Writing to Dr Kugelmann on April 6, he reported that he would soon be returning to London, where he hoped to get on with the neglected 'Capital' manuscript. As for current political affairs in Germany, Marx remarked that the situation looked 'rather discouraging': 'If our philistines would only realise that without a revolution which would do away with the Habsburgs and the Hohenzollerns ... there is finally going to be a new thirty-years' war and another division of Germany!'

Marx's prolonged absence and the passivity of the English leaders in the IWA had permitted a new round of plotting and intriguing in the meantime. Marx felt that under the circumstances it would be too soon to hold the IWA congress in May: 'Even if the congress should be a failure, the English wouldn't care a rap. But for us it would be *a European disgrace*! !' (April 6). However, after his return from Margate on April 10 Marx succeeded through letters and personal appeal in forcing through a resolution, in the teeth of French opposition, which fixed a new date for the congress in September (May 1).

Information reached Marx through Engels and others that a shipload of German tailors had been imported to Edinburgh as strike breakers in a local movement to attain higher wages and that two further shiploads were on their way. In early May Marx wrote 'A Warning' addressed to the German tailors, which was printed in several German newspapers and distributed as a hand-bill. In it Marx condemned the lack of solidarity between brothers in the struggle against capital and appealed to the honour of the Germans:

to prove to foreigners that they, together with their brothers in France, Belgium and Switzerland, know how to defend their common class interests and do not lend themselves to being *weak stooges* of capital in its fight against labour (*Documents* 1 : 335f.).

As Marx reported to Engels (April 23) and to Liebknecht (May 4), the *Commonwealth* was having trouble making ends meet although its circle of readers was growing steadily. Penny-paper as it was, it needed more capital behind it in order to become self-supporting. 'If in the meanwhile the paper is not worse than it is, this is the merit of Fox who is forced to carry on a continual struggle,' he explained to Engels. In March and May the *Commonwealth* published a series of three articles by Engels on 'What does the working class have to do with Poland?' These articles, inspired by Marx in January, caused quite a sensation among the paper's readership in suggesting that war against Russia was a precondition for the reconstruction of Poland. In the CC Fox criticised Engels for stating that the division of Poland was due to the corruption of the Polish aristocracy. Although the Poles expressed the desire to see Engels continue the series, the project was never realised.

On May 4 Marx informed Liebknecht that the IWA's move to aid the striking tailors and wireworkers by preventing the importation of strikebreakers from the Continent had succeeded. The IWA was an international force and 'This proof of its immediate practical importance has struck the practical English mind'. In answer to the IWA's challenge Mazzini now formed an 'International Republican Committee'. Despite his gesture, Marx reported to Engels, 'our Association is gaining ground every day. Only in Germany on account of that ass Liebknecht (good fellow as he is!) is there nothing to be done' (May 17).

Again ill, and plagued by heavy financial debts into the bargain, Marx was absent from the CC meetings in late May and early June when the group discussed the adjournment of the Congress, the admission of new English members and an appeal to the Paris students and the workers of all countries, which had been written by Paul Lafargue and published in *Le Courier français* on June 10.

In his June correspondence with Engels Marx gave a detailed account of the 'Jeune France' movement: It seemed that among the French students a kind of Proudhonism reigned; they were preaching peace, declared war out-dated and nationalities to be nonsense, and opposed both Bismarck and Garibaldi:

As polemics against chauvinism their doings are useful and comprehensible. But as Proudhon-worshippers (my good friends Lafargue and Longuet also belong to their number) who think that all Europe must and will sit on its ass and wait until the 'messieurs' in France abolish 'La misère et l'ignorance' ... they are grotesque (June 7).

Following a debate in the CC on the Austro-Prussian war, Marx recounted to Engels the essence of his remarks, in particular, on the 'Jeune France' and its 'Proudhonised Stirnerianism'.* Their notions of politics, Marx had told the group, were based on individualism and mutualism, whereby small groups or communes were to be organised into an association rather than a state: 'This is exactly what Fourier expected from his phalanstère modèle.'† The audience burst out laughing when Marx commented that Lafargue, who wanted to abolish nations and nationalities, had addressed them in French with the result that nine-tenths could not understand. 'I inferred later on,' Marx told Engels, 'that most unconsciously he seemed to understand by negation of nationalities their absorption into the French model nation' (June 20). After several sessions of debates and discussions the CC finally passed a resolution on the war, stating:

That the Central Council of the International Working Men's Association consider the present conflict on the Continent to be one between Governments and advise the working men to be neutral and to associate themselves with a view to acquire (sic) strength by unity and to use the strength so acquired in working out their social and political emancipation (Minutes, July 17).

On Marx's proposal two resolutions were adopted in the CC on July 24: that the Council take the necessary steps to encourage representation of the Italians at the forthcoming

---

* By this expression Marx was characterising the movement's orientation as fundamentally egoistic but qualified by Proudhon's ideas of social individualism to be realised through federal organisation.

† Fourier conceived of a project for co-operative socialist communities called 'phalansteries' (analogous to 'monasteries'), in which labour would be based on the principle of attraction as generated by human passions and competition would be abolished.

Congress; that the seat of the Council be retained at London. On July 31 he presented a list of eleven proposals for discussion at the Congress as decided the preceding September by the London Conference. He recommended at the same time that an enquiry on working class conditions be conducted using a schedule worked out by Marx and the sub-committee. The points of this enquiry, edited by Marx, and the other proposals of the sub-committee were adopted unanimously by the Council.

Marx was now hoping to finish the manuscript of the first volume of his 'Economics'—and he calculated the whole at three volumes—before October. If he was to meet this deadline without further damage to his health he saw the impossibility of attending the congress, although he was continually engaged in preparations for it. He explained to Dr Kugelmann: 'I consider that what I am doing through this book is more important for the working class than anything I could ever accomplish personally at any congress whatsoever' (August 23). In spare moments, when not occupied with the 'Economics' or the IWA, Marx studied the works of Auguste Comte 'because the English and the French make such a fuss about the fellow. What captivates them is the encyclopedic element, the synthesis. But it is miserable compared to Hegel!' (to Engels, July 7). He also read and excerpted from what he termed a 'very important work' by Pierre Trémaux, *Origine et transformations de l'homme et des autres bêtes* (1865). Trémaux had taken 'a very significant step beyond Darwin', Marx wrote to Engels, in his interpretation of the phenomenon of cross-breeding and of the geological formations of the earth as they affect man (Aug. 7). A discussion ensued on Trémaux after Engels had read the book, commenting that it 'is not worth anything, pure construction in contradiction to all the facts, and for every proof it gives it still has to give a further proof' (Oct. 2). Marx defended Trémaux's basic idea about the influence of geological elements, especially the soil, on human development (*see* letter of Oct. 3). The two friends also continued their discussion of the Austro-Prussian war by correspondence. Marx made the general remark that: 'Our theory of the determination of the *organisation* of labour *through the means of production*, where it is demonstrated any more brilliantly than in the man-slaughtering industry?' (July 7).

On August 6 Marx's 21-year-old daughter Laura became engaged to the young medical student Paul Lafargue, who had first been drawn to Marx in the IWA, 'but soon transferred the attraction from the old man to the daughter' (Marx to Engels, Aug. 7). Before the engagement became formal, however, Marx asked Lafargue for 'positive information on his economic circumstances' (Marx to Engels, Aug. 13), explaining the reason for his caution:

You know that I have sacrificed my whole fortune for the revolutionary struggle. I do not regret it. On the contrary. If I had my life to start over, I would do the same. Only I would not marry. As far as it is within my power to do so, I want to protect my daughter from the dangerous precipice where her mother's life was dashed to pieces (Aug. 13).

Jenny Marx pawned articles of clothing in order to pay for her daughter's engagement; several creditors were threatening legal action and the family was trying anxiously to hide the 'real state of affairs' from the young fiancé (*see* Marx to Engels, Nov. 8). The uncertainty of their situation disturbed Marx's work during the day; he began working at night and thus provoked a new attack of furunculosis. The idea of emigrating to America in order to find better means of employment became enticing, yet he eventually rejected this solution. As he wrote to Kugelmann, 'I consider it my calling to remain in Europe and finish this task to which I have devoted so many years' (Aug. 23).

The First International Congress of the IWA was held in Geneva from September 3-8. Discussion centred around the 'instructions for delegates' which Marx had prepared. At a session called to debate the active electoral rights of the individual members, delegate Cremer of London defended the interests of the members who were not working men: 'Among these members I shall mention only one to you, Citizen Marx, who has consecrated his entire life to the triumph of the working class' (Sept. 8; Freymond 1: p. 56). James Carter, also from London, added that men who were so wholly devoted to the cause were too rare to be shoved aside:

The bourgeoisie did not triumph until the day when, rich and powerful in number, it allied itself with science and it is the so-called bourgeois economic science which, in giving it prestige, continued to maintain the power of the bourgeoisie. May those men who have devoted their lives to the economic question and who have recognised the justness of our cause and the necessity of social reform, may these men come to the working men's congresses in order to destroy bourgeois economic science (*ibid.*, p. 56).

On the whole, Marx wrote to Kugelmann, the results of the Congress had surpassed his expectations. He had chosen the points of the discussion programme in accordance with his desire to promote immediate understanding and co-operation between the working men of various nations and to create a viable organisational form for working men as a class. All of his points were unanimously adopted by the Congress. The Parisians, Marx remarked, seemed to have been full of 'Proudhonist phrases': 'They chatter about science and don't know anything'; they were disdainful of the class struggle as a source of revolutionary force; what they defended under the rubric of anti-authoritarian individualism was nothing more than ordinary bourgeois economics 'only idealised in a Proudhonian manner'. Marx also reported that simultaneously a labour congress had taken place in Baltimore (late August) which had pleased him very much with its achievements: 'Organisation for the struggle against capital was their motto, and, remarkably enough, most of the demands I had proposed for Geneva were also presented there through the true instincts of the working men' (Oct. 9).

Following the Congress Marx was nominated president of the CC in a demonstration of force against the French members who had moved to exclude all but manual workers from the organisation and particularly from its leadership (Sept. 25). Marx declined the nomination, considering himself 'incapacitated because he was a head worker and not a hand worker' (Minutes). The Council reappointed him to the post of foreign secretary for Germany, however. By the end of the year Marx was able to report to Engels that two French revues, *Revue des deux mondes* and *Revue contemporaine*, had carried information on the Congress and the International in lengthy articles and had termed this movement 'one of the most important events of the century' (Dec. 17).

The job of editing *Capital* for the printer's was finally nearing its end. In November Marx announced to Engels that he would soon be sending Meissner the first pages of the manuscript for volume 1, which was to encompass books I and II of the following plan:

book I: the production process of capital

book II: the circulation process

book III: the various forms assumed by capital in the course of its development

book IV: on the history of the theory.

Books III and IV were to be published later in separate volumes (*see* letter to Engels, Oct. 13). The announcement that 'the first batch of the manuscript' was going off to the printer's (Nov. 10) brought a cry of joy from Engels, who promised to drink to his friend's health: 'This book has done a lot to break you and once it has been shaken off, you will become an entirely different fellow' (Nov. 11).

1867 As the new year began Marx was not making the expected progress with the last stage of his manuscript. Troubled by furuncles and insomnia, again in financial difficulty, he could not finish as quickly as he had planned and hoped. He was toying with the idea of going to the Continent in order to find some new arrangement for a future income, but the imperative desire to finish the first volume made him put off his plan until later. Of course Engels came to the family's aid with occasional banknotes and cases of wine.

When sending the first section of his manuscript to Meissner Marx had written that he would be presently delivering only volume 1. Although Meissner objected to this procedure, Marx replied that he would be unable to deliver all of the books I-IV without another long delay.

During the final months of work on the first volume, Marx continued to participate in the GC meetings. On January 22 he attended a meeting in commemoration of the 1863 Polish insurrection. Here he pronounced a fiery speech against Russia, the 'bastion of European reactionism', demanding the independence of Poland as precondition of European freedom. Had the serf emancipation wrought significant changes in Russia? he asked. Had Russia's threat to Europe diminished?:

No, only the blindness of the ruling classes in Europe has reached its peak. Above all, nothing has changed in Russia's politics ... Its methods, tactics, manoeuvres may change, but the guiding star of its politics—world rule—is unchangeable (MEW 16:202).

Peasant emancipation actually facilitated governmental centralisation in Russia, Marx noted, broke the feudal system of rule,
created a broad new source of military recruitment and
strengthened the peasants' adherence to the central power, i.e.
the Czar: 'It did not free them from Asiatic barbarism, for
civilisation is a process of centuries' (MEW 16:203). In face of
the Russian threat Europe had but one alternative: either to
let itself be invaded by the Muscovites or re-establish itself 'with
a wall of 20 million heroes in order to gain time to complete its
social transformation' (MEW 16:204).

On February 28 Marx also spoke at a gathering to celebrate
the 27th anniversary of the founding of the German Working
Men's Educational Association. He spoke on the slavery of
wage labour, which gives the individual the impression of having
freedom of action while forcing him in reality to sell his labour
power for sums sufficient only to procure him the basic necessities of life. Marx concluded with an expression of his conviction
that of all the European working men the Germans were the
most capable of carrying out a radical social revolution: (1)
They were of all the least handicapped by religious prejudices;
(2) they need not pass through a long phase of bourgeois social
development; and (3) they would, through their geographic
situation, be forced to declare war on Eastern barbarism, whence
all reaction against the West began (MEW 16:524).

Apart from his work on the manuscript and his activities in
the IWA, Marx read two works by Balzac, both 'full of wonderful irony' (letter to Engels, Feb. 25). One of them, Le Chef
d'oeuvre inconnu (1832), Marx recounted to Engels, was the
delightful story of a genial artist, so intent on producing on
canvas with the greatest exactness the image he had in his head,
that he reworked, retouched and corrected his painting until
finally nothing remained. During the early part of the year
Marx also helped the tailor Eccarius with a series of articles
entitled 'A Workingman's Refutation of J. S. Mill', which was
published in the IWA Journal Commonwealth.

On April 2 Marx reported to Engels that the manuscript of
the first volume of Capital was finished and he estimated its
bulk at about 25 printer's sheets. His plan was to take the work
himself to Meissner in Hamburg in order to have the opportunity
to speak with him about publishing the first volume alone.
However, he lacked the money for the trip and to redeem his

clothing and watch from the pawnbroker's. Engels, who burst out in an 'irrepressible' cry of 'hurrah', sent his friend £35 for the travel expenses.

Marx arrived in Hamburg on April 12 and immediately turned his precious cargo over to Meissner who promised that it would be sent to the printer Wigand in Leipzig within the week. The manuscript which Meissner received contained only six divisions, corresponding to the plan of the *Grundrisse* and the 1863 plan for books I and III, except for two chapters on productive and unproductive labour and the results of the production process, which were now lacking. Subheadings were later made at Engels's insistence for the first German edition, while the second German and first French editions were divided into 33 chapters. The plan for the rest of *Capital* was discussed and Meissner proposed that three volumes be made of the material instead of two. 'He is in fact against my concentrating the last book (*the historical part*) as I had planned. He said that, from a bookseller's point-of-view and for the "shallow" mass of readers, he is counting most on this part' (Marx to Engels, Apr. 13). While awaiting the first proof sheets from Wigand, Marx went on to Hanover, where he was the guest of the well-known gynaecologist Ludwig Kugelmann. Kugelmann, in Marx's words, was a 'fanatical adherent' of his and Engels's doctrines and of both of them as people. 'He annoys me at times with his enthusiasm,' Marx remarked, 'which is inconsistent with his coolness in medicine. But he *understands* and is a *thoroughly good man*; he makes no concessions, is capable of sacrifices and, what is more, he is *convinced*' (Apr. 24). In his library Kugelmann had an excellent collection of Marx's and Engels's works, 'better than both of us put together', and promised them copies of *The Holy Family*. Marx used the days in Hanover between April 17 and mid-May to attend to his neglected correspondence. On April 17 he wrote to J. P. Becker, editor of the *Vorbote* in Geneva, announcing the forthcoming publication of *Capital*, volume 1 (The Production Process of Capital), which he expected to appear in May. This volume would surely be, he remarked, 'the most terrible missile ever launched at the heads of the bourgeoisie (landed property owners included)'. Becker was encouraged to help publicise the book's appearance. In a letter of April 24 Marx reported to Engels about a visit on the preceding day from 'Bismarck's Satrap' Warnebold, who in the name of the Prussian minister had extended the offer to employ Marx and his 'great talent' in the service of the German people. Marx also wrote to Siegfried Meyer in New York, thanking for the letters which had been a 'true consolation' for him during the last long period of material and physical distress. His long silence had been occasioned by the concentrated work on *Capital* and his very poor health, which obliged him to centre his efforts on completing his manuscript:

I must laugh at the so-called 'practical' men and their wisdom. If one wanted to be a beast, one could naturally turn one's back on the sufferings of mankind and save one's own skin. But I would really have considered myself *impractical* if I had died without finishing my book at least in manuscript form (Apr. 30).

Marx then addressed a request to the renowned natural scientist, scholar and IWA member, Ludwig Büchner in Darmstadt, asking for assistance in finding a suitable translator for *Capital* into French. He explained to Büchner, whose own work on *Kraft und Stoff* had already been translated into French, that it was essential to free the French from the idealised petit-bourgeois thinking they had inherited from Proudhon (May 1).

Marx did not receive the first proofs of his book until May 5, his forty-fifth birthday. The type-setting errors were insignificant, he found, but there was no manuscript at hand for verification. He was thus persuaded to bring his visit with the Kugelmanns to an end and return to London to await the proofs there. On his return via Hamburg, Marx again saw Meissner and promised him the delivery of volume 3 of *Capital* (books II and III) in the autumn and volume 4 in winter (book IV). With this Marx hoped soon to have a solid financial basis under his feet and a secure future. 'Without you,' he confessed to Engels, 'I would never have been able to finish this work and I assure you that it has always haunted me like a nightmare to have let you ruin and waste your fine talents in commercial affairs on my account and to have obliged you to live through all my petites misères' (May 7). However, Marx justly foresaw that he would have a difficult year ahead before receiving payment for his book.

As the proof sheets arrived in London, Marx would correct and then send them on to Engels in Manchester. Engels reread the whole and returned them to Wigand. Following Kugelmann's suggestion that Marx append a 'supplementary, more didactic explanation of the form of, value in chapter 1, Engels read the text to provide Marx with critical aid. 'The philistine is not used to this kind of abstract thinking,' Engels remarked, 'and will certainly not torture himself with it for the sake of the *form of value*' (June 16). He proposed that sub-headings be added within the chapters to help the reader follow the argument. He found that 'the important second sheet suffers from the weight of the carbuncles. But nothing more can be done now and anyone who is capable of thinking dialectically will still understand it' (*ibid.*). Marx hoped that nonetheless Engels was satisfied with his work: 'Your satisfaction with it up to this point is more important to me than anything the rest of the world may say of it. In any case I hope that the bourgeoisie will remember my carbuncles their whole life long' (June 22). Marx solved the problem of a more didactic explanation of the form of value by adding an appendix to be read in place of the corresponding pages in the text. It was intended 'not only for philistines, but also for the young people, eager for knowledge' and explained in short that:

These gentlemen, the economists, have hitherto overlooked the very simplest matter, that the form: 20 *yards of linen*=1 *coat* is only the undeveloped basis of 20 *yards of linen*=£2, and that therefore the *simplest form of a commodity*, in which its value is not yet expressed in relation to all other commodities but only as something *differentiated* from its own natural form, contains the *whole secret of the money form* and therefore in germ *all the bourgeois forms of the product of labour* as well (to Engels, June 22).

Engels also brought up a question which he was sure would be one of the first that industrialists and bourgeois economists would find to reproach Marx's value theory. If the worker's wages represent only half his working time, then this value alone enters into the price of the commodity produced and therefore no surplus value can be created. Marx replied that such questions would be answered in book III (vol. 2) since they presupposed both the discussion of the transformation of the daily value of labour power into the price of this labour and the transformation of surplus value into profit—presupposing in turn the process of capital circulation. In the projected exposition in book III 'It will be shown whence the philistines' and ordinary economists' way of thinking originates: namely, from the fact that their brains perpetually reflect only the immediate form of the circumstances and not their inner relationship. If by the way the latter were the case, would a *science* then be necessary at all?' (June 26). Marx explained that he had no intention of anticipating all such questions in the first book, for that would disrupt the dialectical method. The present method of presentation set traps, moreover, for the less profound bourgeois economists and others.

In the Preface, written on July 25, he addressed this work to the reader who is 'willing to learn something new and therefore to think for himself' and declared his purpose in writing was to disclose the 'economic law of motion of modern society'. Through his analysis of social disintegration and change in England, Marx expressed the hope that other countries would learn and profit:

... their own most important interests dictate to the classes that are for the nonce the ruling ones the removal of all legally removable hindrances to the free development of the working class (*Capital*, v. 1, p. 9).

Having once discovered the 'natural laws of its movement', no country could, however, make spectacular progress for 'it can neither clear by bold leaps, nor remove by legal enactments, the obstacles offered by the successive phases of its normal development. But it can shorten and lessen the birth-pangs' (*ibid.*, p. 10).

On August 16 the last page of proofs had been corrected. 'Only thanks to you,' Marx wrote to Engels, 'has this been possible! Without your self-sacrifice for me I would never have been able to accomplish the enormous tasks of the three volumes. I embrace you, full of thanks!' (Aug. 16). The thousand copies of the first edition left the press about September 2. Presumably in order to avoid the censor, the chapter which forms the logical conclusion to the whole and ends with a quotation from *The Communist Manifesto*—chapter XXXII on the 'Historical Tendency of Capitalist Accumulation'—was placed before the chapter on 'The Modern Theory of Colonisation'.

While correcting the proofs for *Capital* Marx absented himself from the GC meetings until July 9. There, under pressure from Lafargue, Marx proposed that at the forthcoming congress a discussion be held 'on the practical means by which to enable (sic) the International Working Men's Association to fulfil its function of a common centre of action for the working classes, male and female, in their struggle tending to their complete emancipation from the domination of capital' (Minutes, July 9). Together with Lafargue Marx edited an address to members and affiliated societies inviting them to participate in the congress planned for September in Lausanne. Marx himself refused to be the GC delegate; he then brought up the matter of the Peace Congress which was to be held on September 5 in Geneva, pointing out that the IWA was 'in itself a peace congress, as the union of the working classes of the different countries must ultimately make international wars impossible ...' (Minutes, Aug. 13). Large standing armies are the natural result of the present social development and are used in general to suppress internal agitation. Those who wish 'peace-at-any-price', however,

would fain leave Russia alone in the possession of the means to make war upon the rest of Europe, while the very existence of such a power as Russia was enough for all the other countries to keep their armies intact (ibid.).

Writing later to Engels, Marx gave an account of the discussion at this August 13 meeting. Behind the Peace Congress were organisers such as Louis Blanc, Garibaldi and Victor Hugo who had been forced to recognise the IWA as a 'power'. Marx saw this as extremely important. The GC finally decided not to send an official delegate to the Peace Congress but left the members free to attend as individuals. Lessner and Eccarius attended the congress along with the IWA Congress in Lausanne on September 9 and kept Marx informed on proceedings at both. The favourable results of this year's Congress decided Marx to attending the coming year in order to fight personally against the Proudhonists. Until the publication of his book, and while the association was still taking root, Marx had tried to manage things from the side-lines. Now he felt the time had come for him to appear personally on the stage. He reported to Engels on the IWA's recent success: 'The lousy Star that had wanted to ignore us completely declared in yesterday's lead article that we are more important than the Peace Congress.' Despite all the intrigues against the leadership from within the organisa-

tion and despite the opposition from without, Marx had retained his influence on the IWA : '... when the next revolution
comes, perhaps sooner than it seems, *we* (i.e. you and I) will
have this powerful engine in *our hands*. Compare this with the
results of Mazzini's operations, etc., for the past thirty years!
And without any financial support!' (to Engels, Sept. 11).

Wilhelm Liebknecht, recently re-elected to the North German
Reichstag as representative of the Saxonian working men, corresponded frequently with Marx who provided him with directives
for action. Engels commented that Liebknecht had learned
enough from them to realise that 'the only good policy is *to
vote against everything without exception*' (to Marx, Oct. 13).

The *Vorbote* began publicising *Capital* in the October issue
with an unsigned letter to the editor from Jenny Marx which
explained the nature of Marx's work:

Marx naturally has no specific remedies at hand for the crying needs
of the bourgeois world, which now calls itself socialist as well, no
pills, no slaves, no lint to heal the gaping, bloody wounds of our
society. But it seems to me that he has drawn the most daring
conclusions from the practical results and applications of the historic
development of modern society (MEW 16:549).

The 'conspiration de silence' which met the appearance of
Capital made Marx 'fidgety' (cf. letter to Engels, Nov. 2). However, he did receive a letter from one interested reader, the
tanner Joseph Dietzgen from St Petersburg. Dietzgen, who was
of German origin, wrote Marx a long letter, full of admiration
for his inestimably valuable research 'on behalf of both the
working class and science'. He had read all of Marx's earlier
writings until he had mastered Marx's important thoughts,
Dietzgen added : 'The first pamphlet *Zur Kritik*, which appeared
in Berlin, I studied at the time with great diligence and I must
admit that no book, be it ever so voluminous, has ever brought
me so much new, positive knowledge and instruction as this
small booklet' (Oct. 24; MEW 31:674). He explained to Marx
his own theory of a materialist *Weltanschauung* and remarked
that 'science is not so much a matter of facts as it is of explanations for these facts'.

Marx's book continued to produce no echo in the German
press and he wrote to Kugelmann that 'If there were six men of
your calibre in Germany, the opposition of the mass of philis-

tines and the *conspiration de silence* on the part of the specialists and the journalist rabble would have been overcome at least to a degree which would permit serious discussion to begin. But we must wait! Contained in this word is the whole secret of *Russian politics'* (Dec. 7). Marx provided Kugelmann's wife with reading instructions for *Capital*: first the sections on the working-day, co-operation, division of labour and machinery, finally that on primitive accumulation (cf. letter to Kugelmann, Nov. 30). He corresponded with Victor Schily in Paris with regard to a French translation by Elie Reclus and reserved the right to make certain changes in the German text before translation. While awaiting the response to *Capital*—financial and otherwise—Marx again found himself deeply in debt and continued to suffer from furunculosis and insomnia, all of which troubles hindered him in his work for the second volume.

The Irish Question and the Fenians became a topic of some importance for Marx during the latter part of the year. Following the trial of the Fenians in Manchester, he reported to Engels on the efforts of the IWA and the Reform League to stir up sympathies for the Fenians within the working class. This affair had given him a new perspective on the Irish Question. 'I used to think that Ireland's separation from England would be impossible. Now I consider it to be inevitable, even if the separation should be followed by a federation' (to Engels, Nov. 2). On November 19 and 20 in the GC the issue of the condemned Fenians was the topic of a discussion in which it was maintained that the working class and the Fenians opposed the same enemy, 'the territorial aristocracy and the capitalist'. An address to the British government on the Fenians, written by Marx and adopted at the November 20 meeting, requested a commutation of the Fenians' sentence as 'an act not only of justice, but also of political wisdom' (*Documents* 2:180). Marx also prepared a speech on the Irish Question. However, after the execution of the Fenians on November 23, he deemed it more suitable to let one of the English members speak in his place to express their regret for the vengeful act of the British government. Had he spoken, Marx wrote Engels, he would have been unable to deliver the necessary objective analysis of the situation but would have let loose a 'revolutionary thunderstorm' (cf. letter of Nov. 30). It was the Englishman Fox who spoke on this occasion, Marx reported, touching on political and international aspects of the

Irish movement, but on the whole his speech was too superficial and full of banalities. Fox's resolution was referred back to committee. Marx pointed out to Engels that Ireland was in the midst of a great economic change, which the British ignored. Fenianism was in fact a 'lower orders movement' to resist the present system of the British for 'clearing the estate of Ireland', whereby they desired to turn Irish soil into grazing land for their stock-farming. He summed up Ireland's needs as:

1. Self-government and independence from England.
2. Agrarian revolution. The English cannot accomplish it for them even with the best will, but they can give them the legal means to accomplish it themselves.
3. Protective tariffs against England (Nov. 30).

Marx also lectured on the Irish Question to the German Working Men's Educational Association on December 16.

Engels wrote a number of book reviews of *Capital*, which were published in various German and English newspapers. For the *Beobachter* (Stuttgart, Dec. 12-13) he adopted directives provided by Marx in a letter on December 7, where the latter gave an ironic criticism of his own 'subjective tendential conclusions, and the positive scientific developments'. Marx referred to his new materialist method of treating economic relations as a 'fundamental enrichment of science'. As 'tendential' he saw the demonstration that present society carries within itself a new and higher form, in other words, the depiction from a social standpoint of the 'same gradual process of revolution which Darwin proved in natural history'. Finally, Marx emphasised that *Capital*'s subjective tendency, 'i.e. the manner in which he imagines or presents the end result of the present movement, the present social progress has nothing to do with his (theoretical) development of the economic relations proper'.

1868 This year brought, instead of the hoped-for financial independence and security, continued illness and dependency on Engels for all the family's financial needs. Marx, who suffered continually from severe headaches and carbuncles, went on with his studies for the third book of *Capital* until about May. He delved into ground rent and agronomy, reading Karl Nikolaus Fraas's *Klima und Pflanzenwelt in der Zeit* (1847), *Die Natur der Landwirtschaft* (1857) and *Die Geschichte der Landwirtschaft*

(1852); Johann Heinrich von Thünen's *Der isolierte Staat in Beziehung auf Landwirtschaft und Nationalökonomie* (1862-63) and John Chalmers Morton's *Encyclopaedia of Agriculture* (1855). He devoted particular care to the study of Georg Ludwig Maurer's book *Einleitung zur Geschichte der Mark Hof-, Dorf- und Stadtverfassung und der öffentlichen Gewalt* (1854), where he found new proof of his view that in the early days of European settlements Asian and Indian forms of property ownership were current (*see* letter to Engels, March 14). Maurer's 'extraordinarily interesting' work gave a new aspect to primitive times and to the subsequent development of independent *Reich* cities in Germany in the struggle between peasantry and serfdom :

In human history it is the same as in palaeontology. Things which are right in front of one's nose are, in principle, ignored even by the most important heads thanks to a certain judicial blindness. Later when time has ripened, one is amazed to find that the unseen has left its traces everywhere (March 25).

Marx also shared with Engels his findings on Fraas's book, *Klima und die Pflanzenwelt*, which showed that land cultivation 'when it proceeds naturally and not under *conscious control* ... leaves deserts behind, Persia, Mesopotamia, etc., Greece. Again therefore an unconscious socialist tendency !' (*ibid.*)

Because of his health Marx could not attend the GC meetings during the first part of the year; financial considerations made him think seriously of going to live in Geneva, where the lower cost of living would permit him to live on half the amount required in London. Two things kept him from taking this step: the IWA and the unfinished *Capital*, for which he needed to work at the British Museum Library. He also expected to profit financially from the English sales of *Capital*, once it had been translated. 'Aside from that,' he wrote Kugelmann, 'if I were to leave here at the present critical time, the whole working men's movement, which I influence from behind the scenes, would fall into very bad hands and undoubtedly be led astray' (March 17).

Numerous critiques of *Capital* finally appeared. One in particular, written by the economist Eugen Dühring in 1867, Engels characterised as full of 'embarrassment and fear. The good vulgar economist is thunderstruck and doesn't know what to say' (to

Marx, Jan. 7). Marx found Dühring's critique 'rather decent', although he had misunderstood various things. 'The most amusing, however, is that he classes me with Stein because I use dialectics and Stein thoughtlessly puts together the most trivial things in awkward trichotomies' (Jan. 8). By March Marx had come to understand Dühring's 'curiously embarrassed tone' in reviewing his book:

Ordinarily he is a most impertinent, insolent fellow who sets himself up as a revolutionary in political economy ... He knows very well that my method of development is *not* Hegel's, that I am a materialist and Hegel an idealist. Hegel's dialectics is the basic form of all dialectics, but only *after* it has been stripped of its mystical form and this is precisely what differentiates my method from his (Marx to Kugelmann, March 6).

Freiligrath wrote to thank Marx for a copy of *Capital*, remarking that 'many young businessmen and industrial entrepreneurs are enthused about the book'. Here, he added, would *Capital* fulfil its real purpose, apart from serving scholars as a reference work (April 3; *Chronik*, p. 267).

On April 2 Laura Marx and Paul Lafargue were married in London and went to Paris shortly thereafter for their honeymoon. Marx wrote to his daughter with the request that she enquire about the copies of *Capital* which he had sent for Paris friends and excused himself for this intrusion, saying:

You'll certainly fancy, my dear child, that I am very fond of books, because I trouble you with them at so unseasonable a time. But you would be quite mistaken. I am a machine condemned to devour them and then, throw them, in a changed form, on the dunghill of history (to Laura, April 11).

In late April Marx took up work on book III of *Capital*, intending to elaborate a better presentation of the relation between profit rate and surplus value rate. Writing to Engels on April 22, he explained the solution he had found to the question of rising profit rates, in times of inflation, corresponding to falling profit rates in deflationary periods. 'The difficulty lies in the confusion of the *rate of surplus value* with the *profit rate*.' With decreasing monetary value labour productivity is augmented, the value of machinery (constant capital) sinks, so that the profit rate rises although the actual rate of surplus value remains constant. On April 30 Marx presented Engels with the plan for book III, in which he intended to work out the 'transformation of surplus value into its various forms' (i.e. profit, interest and land rent) and its relation to the other two books. Whereas in book I the reader was simply given an abstract explanation of the conversion process of capital, in book III the actual market conditions would be examined, 'thus the social interlacing of the various capitals, elements of capital and revenue ($=m$) with one another'. Profit was in fact only a name for a kind of or category of surplus value, 'only the illusory form in which the latter appears', containing, however, in reality an element which differentiates it from surplus value. This element is the value 'c' or constant capital; surplus value contains, by contrast only the element of variable capital, i.e. labour. Thus the actual profit rate may differ in various ways from the surplus value rate—a phenomenon previously inexplicable for political economy. Marx also intended to explain the movement of capital as the difference between capitals employed in the various production sectors. Other topics for book III were the tendency for profit rates to fall with increasing industrial development; merchant capital as contrasted to productive capital; profit divided into the entrepreneur's earnings and into interest; the transformation of profit into land rent; and 'finally since those three [wage labour, land rent, profit (interest)] constitute the respective sources of income for the three classes of land owners, capitalists and wage labourers—we have in conclusion the *class* struggle to which the movement and break-up of the whole affair is reduced' (April 30).

In May Marx began working on book II, in particular on the problem of the turnover of capital and the amount of circulating capital advanced in an enterprise. He requested information from Engels, commenting that 'what is practically interesting and theoretically necessary in political economy are so highly divergent that one can't even find the essential material as in other sciences' (May 16). Already foreseeing the end of his 'Economics', Marx wrote to Joseph Dietzgen that he wanted to undertake a book on dialectics and declared that 'the true laws of dialectics are to be found already in Hegel, in a mystic form, however. The problem is to divest them of this form' (May 9).

Marx continued to provide Engels with directives for writing critiques of *Capital*. He explained the reasons for the C-M-C and M-C-M equations in illustrating the two different circulation processes of capital. Thereupon, Engels prepared a review for the journal *Fortnightly Review* (cf. Marx to Engels, May 23). Marx also sent the socialist journalist Wilhelm Eichhoff information for a forthcoming pamphlet on the IWA, at 'just the right moment to make propaganda for the International in Germany' (Marx to Engels, June 6). A lengthy correspondence ensued between Eichhoff and Marx as a result of this project and Marx presented him with an abundance of material—'whose actual contents exceeded my expectations', the latter wrote in thanks. 'In any case it will certainly impress others as it did me' (June 29, IISH). In this pamphlet Eichhoff intended to underline Marx's role as the 'veritable party head', around whom the working men were now grouping (July 18). He incorporated into it documents from the IWA and much material about the trials of the IWA French members in Paris the same year. About Marx Eichhoff wrote: 'Thus it was a German who gave the International Working Men's Association its definite direction and organisation' (Eichhoff, *The IWA*, p. 5).

Under debate in the GC was the matter of the next international Congress, scheduled for September in Belgium. Marx had proposed that the Congress be held elsewhere because of the Belgian government's new anti-foreigners' laws. However, since the Belgian members did not want to make concessions to the government, the resolution was rescinded on June 17. Meanwhile, the French branch of the Council was again concocting rumours about alleged ties between the GC and Bonaparte. One of these French troublemakers, Felix Pyat, spoke at a public meeting in London, demanding the assassination of Bonaparte. The Council thereupon decided to disavow Pyat's relations with the IWA and charge Marx with composing a resolution. Marx recounted the affair to Engels as an intrigue of the 'old parties, the Republican louts of 1848', who would now like to get rid of the IWA which represented 'a thorn in their flesh'. Marx warned the French branch that if their stupidities did not stop, they would be thrown out of the organisation. They could not permit fifty such imbeciles 'to endanger the International Association at a moment when it is beginning to become a serious power in view of the circumstances on the Continent' (Marx to Engels, July 7).

During a discussion in the Council on the influence of machinery in the hands of the capitalists, Marx noted that the first effects had not been as expected: working hours were first lengthened, and reduced only when the workers showed signs of deteriorating physically through the increased labour intensity; women and children were forced to labour in the factories. Here Marx commented that he believed 'every child above the age of nine ought to be employed at productive labour a portion of its time, but the way they are made to work under existing circumstances is abominable' (Minutes, July 28). Machinery had, moreover, completely changed the relations of farm labour and industrial labour—there was no longer any freedom of labour. On the other hand, machinery had also caused labour to organise while disintegrating all former social and family relations: these circumstances were to engender a positive development in favour of labour.

Prompted by Kugelmann's remarks on a critique of *Capital* which had appeared in the Leipzig *Centralblatt* (Jan. 1868), Marx gave his Hanover friend a lengthy explanation of the scientific significance of the value theory. Even if he had not included a separate chapter devoted to value, Marx reasoned, the analysis of real circumstances which was given would demonstrate adequately the actual value relationships in political economy. The necessity of distributing social labour is a natural law; only the form of this distribution can change. In a society based on private exchange of the products of individual labour its form is 'exchange value'. Science therefore has the task of investigating how the value law manifests itself in a particular society, for the relative exchange values of products are not directly equivalent to their respective values. It is science's task to discover the inner relationships between phenomena and not stop with the observing of outward appearances. This was therefore the great difference between Marx's political economy and traditional bourgeois economics, which held the explanation of value based on exchange relations to be an ultimate economic truth (Marx to Kugelmann, July 11).

On August 4 Marx informed Engels of the final break between the IWA and the so-called French branch, which had accused Marx and the others of being ambitious and deceitful. Marx now thought it would be a good plan to move that the Council be transferred from London to the Continent: 'This will show those asses in Paris etc., that we are not at all concerned about this agreeable dictatorship' (to Engels, Aug. 4). Engels counselled prudence: the sacrifice would be too great, if the GC were transferred into the hands of those who were incapable of directing such a movement, whatever their good intentions. 'The larger the dimensions of the affair, the more important it is that *you* have control over it' (August 6).

At this time Marx was practising an attitude of neutrality vis-à-vis the ADAV, whose congress he declined to attend on the pretext of preparing for the IWA's own congress in Brussels. He published a message in the *Social-Demokrat*, congratulating the ADAV for having adopted in their programme the fundamental principles of all working men's movements: agitation for political liberty, regulation of the working day and concerted action on an international level between the working men's groups (Aug. 28; MEW 16:316).

Among Marx's tasks for the Brussels Congress was the preparation of the Council's report. Delivered September 7 and adopted by a unanimous vote of the Council members, this report stressed the significance of the IWA not as a sectarian organisation or a theoretical construction but as

the spontaneous growth of the proletarian movement, which itself is the offspring of the natural and irrepressible tendencies of modern society. Profoundly convinced of the greatness of its mission, the IWA will allow itself neither to be intimidated nor misled. Its destiny, thenceforward, coalesces with the historical progress of the class that carry in their hands the regeneration of mankind (Sept. 1; *Documents* 2:329).

Marx sent Lessner and Eccarius, who attended the Congress as delegates of the GC, advice and recommendations for their participation in the debates, especially for those on war and mutual credit—in opposition to the Proudhonists on the latter question. As far as war was concerned Marx did not feel that the working class was as yet sufficiently organised 'to throw any substantial weight into the scales' and advocated that the Congress should pass a resolution to the effect that war between Germany and France would be equivalent to civil war. Marx also wished to see a statement added, saying that war could benefit only Russia (cf. Marx to Lessner and Eccarius, Sept. 10), but doubted that the resolution in this form would be approved by the French and the Belgians. In fact the following text was finally adopted:

All European wars, and notably that between France and Germany, must be considered today as civil wars, benefiting Russia at the most whose social status is not yet at the heights of modern civilisation (Freymond 1:403).

The German delegates at the Congress adopted a resolution recommending *Capital* to the working men of all countries and urging its translation. It stated further that 'Marx has the inestimable merit of being the first political economist who has scientifically analysed capital and dissolved it into its component parts' (*Documents* 1: Sept. 11). All in all, the Congress went passably well, Marx wrote to Engels, despite the superior number of French and Belgians, the former being 'very jealous of London' and anxious to have the seat of the GC transferred elsewhere (Sept. 12). There were also several good press reports on the IWA and its Congress in the London papers. The GC was, however, dissatisfied with the reporter-role assumed by Eccarius, who magnified his minor role at the Congress so as to make himself the 'leading man' and misrepresented the contents of resolutions and their originators. He received a sharp censure from the Council. Marx reported to Siegfried Meyer in New York about the reception of the Congress in the British press: 'It is the first time that *The Times* has abandoned its derisive tone when speaking of the working class and takes it "very" seriously' (Sept. 14).

The ADAV was disbanded by the Leipzig police on September 16; a group under the leadership of von Schweitzer reconstituted itself under the same name in Berlin three weeks later, while those who distanced themselves from Schweitzer's Lassalleanism grouped around Liebknecht and Bebel. The Liebknecht-Bebel faction was opposed in particular to Schweitzer's stand on the trade union question, since he evidently wished to monopolise and subject them to his personal influence. In a letter to Engels Marx commented on the German working class movement: it was time that these people learned to act independently of a higher authority:

A race which has been so bureaucratically schooled has to go through an entire course in 'self-help'. On the other hand, however, they definitely have the advantage of beginning the movement, historically speaking, under more highly developed conditions than the English and, as Germans, have heads on their shoulders which are capable of generalising (Sept. 26).

Although Marx instructed Liebknecht on tactics for the campaign against Schweitzer and the other Lassalleans, he refused to interfere himself or launch an action in the name of the IWA. When Schweitzer himself asked Marx to mediate in the dispute between himself and Liebknecht and Bebel, Marx replied that as secretary for Germany in the GC he had no choice but to observe the strictest neutrality. However, this did not exclude the possibility that he might one day criticise the Lassalle cult in his private capacity as a writer. Again Marx specified the points of difference between Lassalle and himself. From the outset Lassalle had believed that he had found a 'cure-all' for the problems of the masses and this attitude lent his agitation a sectarian, religious note. 'He committed Proudhon's mistake of not seeking the real basis for his agitation in the existing elements of the class movement but wanted to prescribe to the movement its course according to a certain doctrinaire formula' (Marx to J. B. v. Schweitzer, Oct. 13).

In September Marx was informed by the St Petersburg economist Nikolai Danielson that the first translation of *Capital* was being made into Russian. Reporting this unexpected news to Kugelmann, Marx said: 'It is an irony of fate that the Russians, whom I have fought constantly for the past twenty-five years, not only in German but also in French and English, have always been my "patrons".' All this interest of the Russians was not to be overestimated, however, for 'the same Russians who are educated in the West and yearn passionately for the most extreme radicalism offered in Europe, become scoundrels once they enter the civil service of their native country' (Oct. 12). On the request of the Russian publisher N. P. Poliakov as transmitted by Danielson, Marx furnished the latter with autobiographical material for an introduction to the new edition along with a bibliography of his works, most of which were long out of print (Oct. 7).

For his works on the 'Economics', Marx was now investigating Blue Books and other documents on Irish property relations and tenant rights, which he had found by accident in a small secondhand bookshop in London. These papers helped him enormously with his analysis of ground rent; he explained to Engels why:

Only by replacing conflicting dogmas with conflicting facts and the real antagonisms can political economy be changed into positive science (Oct. 10).

In October Dietzgen sent Marx the manuscript of his work, *Das Wesen der menschlichen Kopfarbeit* [The Essence of Human Brain Work] for critical appraisal. Marx commented that Dietzgen's writing 'turned in circles', lacked 'dialectic development' and ought to be greatly condensed (to Engels, Oct. 3). Engels found that it showed remarkable instinct and would be 'even brilliant if one could be *sure* he had discovered it *for himself*' (Nov. 6). Marx rejected Engels's suspicion that Dietzgen might have borrowed from other writers, adding that 'it is his misfortune that it was precisely Hegel whom he did *not* study ...' (Nov. 7). To Meyer and August Vogt in New York Marx remarked that, judging from his correspondence with Dietzgen, the latter was 'one of the most genial working men' he knew (Oct. 28). Dietzgen wrote a review of *Capital* for the *Demokratisches Wochenblatt* upon Marx's request (Aug.-Sept.). In December Marx wrote to Kugelmann about Dietzgen's manuscript, saying that it contained 'despite a certain confusion and excessive repetitiveness much excellent material and—as the independent effort of a working man—is even much to be admired' (Dec. 5).

In November Marx was invited to dine at the home of the English journalist Charles Collet, former collaborator on Urquhart's *Free Press* and now editor of the *Diplomatic Review*. Marx elaborated his views on the 1844 Bank Act, currently subject of debate between Urquhart and Collet. Marx subsequently formulated these views in a series of letters to Collet, one of which, published in the *Diplomatic Review* on December 2, argued that this Act was more than a boon for Russia on the British money market: 'this law *literally* delivers England, the richest country in the world, *to the mercy of the Muscovite government*, the most insolvent country in Europe' (MEW 16:335).

Late in November J. P. Becker of the IWA in Geneva wrote

to Marx, in the name of the *Alliance de la démocratie socialiste,* that this newly founded organisation desired admittance to the International. Shortly thereafter Michael Bakunin, who headed the *Alliance,* spoke at a meeting of the Peace and Freedom League in Berlin in favour of legislation to equalise the economic differences between classes and individuals. Marx was strongly critical of this standpoint, which, apart from being totally unrealistic, denied the necessity of revolutionising the property relations that lay at the source of this inequality. On December 15 Bakunin's request that the *Alliance* be admitted to the IWA was formally presented to the GC through Becker. Marx recounted the happenings to Engels on the same day: Becker had written that the society should accept the Russian group to make up for its 'failing "idealism" ', but the Council had decided to repudiate the interlopers publicly and Marx was charged with writing the decree. 'I regret this whole thing because of old Becker,' he confessed to Engels, 'Yet our society cannot commit suicide on account of old Becker' (Dec. 15). Engels agreed that the GC could not allow Bakunin's organisation to exist within the IWA: 'There would be two general councils and even two congresses; that's the state within the state and from the outset a conflict would break out between the practical council in London and the "idealist" and theoretical council in Geneva' (Dec. 18) Engels advised Marx not to attribute too much importance to this 'Russian intrigue': 'When dealing with a Russian one must never lose his temper' (*ibid.*). The *Alliance's* programme, he added was the most lamentable he had ever read: 'Siberia, a belly and the young Polish girl friend seem to have made of Bakunin a perfect ox' (Dec. 18).* On December 22 the GC passed Marx's resolution on the *Alliance,* which stated that the presence of a second international organisation within the IWA would lead to disorder and make the Association the 'play-thing for intriguers *of all race and nationality*' (*Documents* 3:388). This resolution was communicated confidentially to all the member groups of the IWA on the Continent in order to avoid an open dispute and to save Becker from attacks. Alerted

---

* For his revolutionary activities of 1848-49 Bakunin languished six years in a Russian prison, suffering from scurvy and malnutrition, until in 1857 the Czar Alexander II offered him the alternative of Siberian exile. There he married a young Polish woman and found a gainful employ as a merchant's agent. After four years thus spent he finally escaped down the Amur river and boarded a ship to America.

by a friend that Marx opposed his party programme, Bakunin at once wrote him an effusive assurance of his friendship and admiration:

I am doing now what you began to do twenty years ago. Since my solemn public adieus to the bourgeoisie at the Bern Congress I have known no other society, no other milieu than the world of the working man. My fatherland is now the International, and you were one of its principal founders. So you see, dear friend, I am your disciple and proud of it (Dec. 22).

Engels was now negotiating for a settlement with his partner in the company Ermen and Engels in order to retire from commerce altogether. He asked Marx for a complete statement of all his debts and proposed a yearly income of £350 for the Marx family, a sum which he would be able to guarantee out of the settlement for the coming 5-6 years. Marx was 'completely *knocked down*' by his friend's generosity. Their debts, he wrote, amounted to some £210 but he was certain that the sum mentioned for the yearly income would suffice for them, since Laura and Paul Lafargue were now living in Paris. His oldest daughter Jenny had recently, without her father's knowledge, accepted employment as tutor for a Scottish family living in London, in order to help with expenses and to have a change of surroundings. His wife Jenny, Marx added, had completely lost her good humour through the trials of the past years, 'explainable through the circumstances but not any pleasanter for all that—and torments the children to death with her complaints and irritability, although no children support everything in a more jolly way than they do. There are limits to everything' (Nov. 30).

Writing to Kugelmann about his prospect of good fortune, Marx inquired if his wife were active in the German women's emancipation campaign and declared: 'I think that the German women should begin by pushing their men to self-emancipation' (Dec. 5). In his next letter Marx again took up the question of women's emancipation, remarking that the Americans were making greater progress in this respect than the English, who were handicapped by their narrowmindedness, but less so than the so-called 'gallant' Frenchmen. In the spirit of Fourier he said:

Everyone who knows anything about history knows also that great historical revolutions are impossible without female ferment. Social progress can be measured precisely by the social position of the fair sex (the ugly ones included) [Dec. 12].

1869 On January 1 Marx received a very special New Year's gift: 'the dignity of grandfather' (to Engels, Jan. 1). However, illness kept him from enjoying his new role as grandfather of Charles-Etienne Lafargue and from working on his 'Economics' until mid-February.

Marx informed Engels of the decision taken in the Council against the admittance of Bakunin's *Alliance* and of the subsequent letters of solidarity from member groups in Brussels, Rouen, Lyon, and elsewhere. Not a single dissenting voice was heard. 'It is clear that this group did not proceed quite honestly from the fact that we were not informed about their founding and their doings until *after* they had tried to win over the Brussels group, etc.' (to Engels, Jan. 28). Liebknecht reported, moreover, that in Switzerland and Germany a break was in the offing and could be avoided only if Becker were to put an end to his relations with Bakunin and himself abandon his dictatorial manner. During Marx's illness Jenny Marx wrote to Becker, warning him gently that 'one can't quite trust the Russians' (Jan. 10).

After a long bout with flu and the London fog Marx resumed his correspondence with Kugelmann, whom he informed about the latest critiques of *Capital*:

A lecturer in political economy at a German university writes to me that I have fully convinced him, but that his position absolutely *forbids* him and other colleagues from *expressing* this conviction. The cowardliness of the academic mandarins, on the one hand, and the conspiracy of silence with the bourgeois and reactionary press, on the other, are doing me great harm (Feb. 11).

Marx also reported on a letter written by Arnold Ruge to a Manchester business man Steinthal. Ruge characterised *Capital* as an 'epoch-making work', which went over the heads of many, but he nevertheless expressed his assurance that the book would exert a powerful influence on its audience (cf. Ruge to Steinthal, Jan. 25).

Once again in attendance at the GC meetings, Marx proposed on February 16 that the question of landed property, credit and general education be placed on the agenda for the year's Congress. Under the pretext that the resolutions passed by the German section of the London GC in Geneva (1867) formed part of the platform adopted in Brussels (1868), the IWA now published these resolutions as a fly-sheet.

Despite recurrent hepatitis Marx returned to work on his 'Economics' in February, thinking that he could finish volume 2 by summer when he planned to return to the Continent to deliver it and pay another visit to Kugelmann. In March Marx read Hippolyte Castille's *Les Massacres de Juin* 1848 (1869) and Auguste Vermorel's *Les Hommes de* 1848 (1869) and was prompted to remark that 'the Parisians are formally rehearsing once more their recent revolutionary past in order to prepare themselves for the impending new revolutionary business' (to Kugelmann, March 3). As a 'Sunday amusement' he was also studying organic chemistry. Engels was requested to prepare a report for the GC on the regulations of the coal miner's guilds in Saxony. Adopted on February 23 in Council this report was translated by Marx into German and published in the *Social-Demokrat* and other German journals.

From Paris Lafargue, who was often in the company of the Blanquists, wrote to Marx that Blanqui himself had a copy of *Misère de la philosophie* which he often lent to friends and that the French leader 'has the greatest esteem for you ... He has found the best word I know for Proudhon, he calls him a hygrometer' (cf. Marx to Engels, March 1).

On March 4 Marx received a letter from the Alliance declaring that, in compliance with the GC's resolution of December 22, the statutes and programme of their organisation had been changed to permit the sections to be disbanded as sections of the *Alliance* and reconstituted as member groups of the IWA. Marx then drafted a letter to the Alliance, which was accepted by the Council on March 9 and permitted the sections to join the International as long as their statutes did not conflict with the principles of the IWA and its general trend towards 'the complete emancipation of the working classes'. The sections were asked to strike from their statutes phrases dealing with the 'social, political and economic equalisation of classes', which apart from being unrealistic contradicted the 'historically necessary, superceding "abolition of classes"', the true aim of the proletarian movement (*Documents* 3:311). With these reservations the Council declared itself prepared to accept Bakunin's *Alliance* sections into the IWA. In a private letter to Eccarius the *Alliance* indirectly answered the Council's critique of its programme, maintaining that it had done more with its 'revolutionary' programme for the working class movement in Spain and Italy and elsewhere, than the IWA had done in years. Were the IWA to repudiate the *Alliance's* programme, moreover:

we would cause a *split* between the countries with a '*revolutionary*' *working men's movement* [Italy, Spain, France and Switzerland] ... and the countries with a *more slowly developing* working class (viz. England, Germany, United States and Belgium). In other words a split between the vulcanic and plutonic working men's movements on the one hand and the aqueous on the other. What is really amusing is that the Swiss represent the revolutionary type (Marx to Engels, March 14).

For two reasons Marx was now interested in acquiring British nationality. As a British citizen he would be able to travel undisturbed to France where he wished to visit his daughter and her family negotiate for a French translation of the first volume of *Capital* (Marx to Engels, March 20).

After reading an article by the English socialist John Malcolm Ludlow on Lassalle, Marx was persuaded to send Ludlow a copy of *Capital* together with a letter pointing out certain errors in the article. It was not Marx who propagated Lassallean principles in England but Lassalle who borrowed Marx's theoretical precepts, applying them, however, in a manner totally different from Marx's. His practical nostrums, government aid to co-operative societies. Marx remarked, 'I call by courtesy *his*'. (April 10).

On May 4 the Council adopted an address, entitled 'The Belgian Massacres' and prepared by Marx, calling on the workmen of Europe and America to support the striking miners of Seraing who had been brutally victimised by the Belgian government playing the 'gendarme of capital'. In Belgium, 'model state of continental constitutionalism, the smug well-hedged little paradise of the landlord, the capitalist and the priest', crimes were being committed against the working class which hastened rather than delayed the inevitable catastrophic crisis of capital (*Documents* 3 : 312ff.). On May 12 Marx presented a second appeal, to the working men of America, cautioning them to avoid a war 'not hallowed by a sublime purpose and a great social necessity', such as that which threatened between England and America. On the working class devolved the task of proving that it was now conscious of its own social responsibility and 'able to command peace where their would-be masters shout war' (Documents 3:321). Both addresses were passed over in silence by the London press.

In preparation for the next international Congress, César De Paepe of Belgium asked Marx to elaborate his views on the question of landed property in order to counter the arguments of the French and Belgian Proudhonists (early July). In the Council on June 22 a five-point programme was adopted for the Congress:

1. Landed property.
2. The right to inheritance.
3. The utilisation of credit by the working class.
4. The question of general education.
5. The influence of trade unions on the working class emancipation.

On July 6 a discussion on landed property took place in the Council. Marx said that social necessity demanded that feudal property be transformed into the common property of the peasantry. 'In England the proprietor has ceased to be a necessity in agriculture.' He strongly criticised the notion of there being an 'abstract natural right' to property: 'everything, every possible form of oppression has been justified by abstract right; it was high time to abandon this mode of agitation', he concluded (Minutes, July 6).

During a brief visit to Manchester with his daughter Eleanor (May 25-June 14) Marx made the acquaintance of the English geologist John Dakyns and was impressed with the child-like naïvety and utter lack of arrogance that characterised this devoted man of science, who was so eager to share his discoveries with others. Marx wrote to his daughter Jenny that 'Dakyns is also an outspoken enemy of the Comtists or positivists. We agree that the only positive thing about them is their arrogance' (June 10).

After his return to London Marx wrote a Preface for the second edition of The Eighteenth Brumaire which was published by Meissner in Hamburg on July 20. Here Marx expressed the hope that this new edition would dispel some of the confusion which accompanied the current use of the term 'Caesarism' as a superficial historical analogy:

One forgets Sismondi's celebrated dictum: 'The Roman proletariat lived at society's expense, while modern society lives at the proletariat's expense'. Given such totally different material and economic conditions between the class struggles in antiquity and those of modern times, the resulting political forms can have no more in common than the Archbishop of Canterbury and the high priest Samuel (MEW 16:359).

On July 1 Engels announced that the 'doux [sweet] commerce' was now finished for him, that the details of his settlement with Ermen had been worked out and that he had celebrated his first day of freedom by taking a long walk in the fields with his young guest Eleanor.

Marx received a letter from Liebknecht in July, full of 'musts' which Marx had no intention of fulfilling. The Germans should first join the IWA and create their own strong party organisation, Marx explained to Engels, then he would be interested in eventually joining their activities. 'Moreover, it must be clearly understood that for us the new organisation must be neither a "people's party" nor a Lassallean church' (July 3). Were the IWA and Marx to intervene at the present time in the affairs of the German social democrats, the changes thus accomplished would have been made under pressure instead of being 'the free action of the working men themselves'. Marx turned down Liebknecht's invitation to attend the congress at Eisenach.

Unable to procure himself a legitimate passport, Marx travelled incognito to Paris for five days in July, where he spent his time exclusively within the family circle and took long walks through the streets on both sides of the Seine (cf. Marx to Engels, July 14). He noticed in particular the changes wrought by Haussmann in the *quartier* near the Louvre.

The question of inheritance rights was put to the IWA for discussion by the Bakuninists. Marx spoke on the matter in the July 20 session of the GC, remarking that it was uninteresting for the working class to debate this issue for it had nothing to inherit in any case. Instead, Marx emphasised, 'Our efforts must be directed to the end that no instruments of production should be private property . . . If we had such a state of things, the right to inheritance would be of no use' (Minutes, July 20). For the present the abolition of inheritance rights would cause only hardships and fear of the future. The working class's immediate goal should be to effect a progressive taxation of inheritances. Marx termed the Bakuninists' agitation on this question reactionary and false. He therefore prepared a four-point resolution on inheritance, which was based on his arguments from the June 20 debate and adopted by the Council on August 3. Here Marx stated that:

The disappearance of the right of inheritance will be the natural result of a social change superseding private property in the means of production; but the *abolition of the right of inheritance* can never be the *starting-point* of such a social transformation (*Documents* 3 : 323).

Faced with numerous problems within the IWA and unable to work effectively because of illness, Marx confided to Engels that: 'If I knew of people anywhere who would not compromise us with their stupidities, I would be very pleased to see the General Council removed from here. This business is getting tiresome' (Aug. 4). On August 10 the Council continued its debate on the points of the coming congress programme with point four, on general education. Marx declared himself in favour of compulsory public education at lower levels, while he thought that higher education should be paid for. 'A proper system of education was required to bring about a change of social circumstances,' Marx states, yet social change was needed to establish a proper educational system and 'therefore we must commence where we were' (Minutes, Aug. 10). The discussion was continued on August 17, when the Council members agreed to a resolution that mental education should be combined with bodily labour, gymnastics and technological training. Marx spoke against instruction in schools on subjects that 'admitted of party or class interpretation' (Minutes).

Becker in the meantime had drawn up a list of theses concerning the future organisation of a socialist party in Germany as a branch of the IWA. In a letter to Engels on July 30 Marx criticised Becker's project as artificial and arbitrary and said that it contained no elements of the real historical relations in the present labour struggle. He suspected that there was more to this project than met the eye:

It is most obvious that the fat Bakunin is behind all this. If that damned Russian really thinks that he is going to work his way up to the head of the worker's movement with intrigues, then it is time he was taught a good lesson and that we raised the question of whether a Panslavist has any right at all to be a member of an international working men's association (July 30).

In August the German journal *Die Zukunft* published Engels's first biographical sketch of Marx crediting him with the principal authorship of *The Communist Manifesto*. Of *Capital* Engels said: 'This work contains the results of a whole lifetime of study. It is the political economy of the working class reduced to its scientific expression' (MEW 16: 365).

Between August 7-9 at the congress in Eisenach the German Social-Democratic Working Men's Party was founded (SDAP). Members of the new party were encouraged to join the IWA as individuals. Marx was kept informed on the proceedings at the congress by Liebknecht whom he criticised for his lack of good political sense:

The idiot believes in the future '*state of democracy*'! As the case may be, this means either constitutional England, or the bourgeois United States or miserable Switzerland (letter to Engels, Aug. 10).

Marx composed this year's report of the Council to the Congress which was held in Basle, Switzerland from September 7-11. The report stressed the role of the Council in the economic struggles of the working class, especially its support of strikers in Switzerland and France, and recounted the harassments and persecution to which the various national groups were subjected. Marx, who again did not personally attend, received regular reports from Lessner. The resolution, proposed by the GC, on the right of inheritance was rejected. The Congress resolved instead that society had the right to abolish private property and convert it into communal property. An adminstrative resolution was passed, giving the Council the right to suspend a section from the organisation until the next congress. One of the sequels to the Basle Congress was the founding in London of a Land and Labour League, whose programme, drawn up by Eccarius with the help of Marx's suggestions, contained demands for financial and fiscal reforms, reforms of the educational system, nationalisation of land, reduction of working hours and the Chartist demands for universal suffrage and the abolition of standing armies. The League worked in co-operation with the IWA.

From early September until October 11 Marx travelled on the Continent, accompanied by his daughter Jenny. In Siegburg, Germany, they paid a visit to Joseph Dietzgen, who had recently emigrated from Russia. In Hanover, while a guest of the Kugelmann family, Marx was visited by a deputation from a local branch of the trade union led by J. B. von Schweitzer, refused their invitation to lecture to their organisation, but nevertheless expounded his view of trade unions as 'schools for socialism'. He told them that the working class trade unions have no need of political organisations for they already represent the true working men's party and as such present an imposing bulwark against capital (Sept. 30).

After his return from Germany Marx received from Danielson in St Petersburg a 500-page Russian manuscript, written by a certain N. Flerovsky and said to be the result of fifteen years' research. He then began learning Russian in order to read this work dealing with the situation of the working class and peasantry in Russia. At this time he was working on the section of book III which concerned land rent and differential rent. He did considerable reading on the Irish question as well as works by Arthur Young, Edward Gibbon Wakefield, Edward Davies, John Patrick Prendergast, speeches by John Philpot Curran and pamphlets of E. and A. O'Connor.

Following a demonstration for the imprisoned Fenians in London on October 24, Marx spoke to the Council pointing out the fact that 'at least a part of the English working class had lost their prejudice against the Irish' (Minutes, Oct. 26). On November 16 the Council debated the problem of the British Government's attitude towards the Irish. Marx denounced Gladstone's conduct as inspired by the traditional 'policy of conquest', and proposed a resolution which would express the Council's admiration for the 'spirited and high-souled manner in which the Irish people carry on their amnesty movement' (Minutes, Nov. 16). The debate was continued at the next 'fiery, heated, violent' session on November 30. Marx repeated his standpoint that 'political prisoners are not treated anywhere so badly as in England'; his resolution on the British Government in the Irish amnesty affair was finally adopted by a unanimous vote.

Writing to Kugelmann on November 29, Marx told of his anti-Gladstone campaign in the Fenian affair and stated categorically that England's working class would never accomplish anything important before separating itself from the government's politics on Ireland. The first condition of the English emancipation—namely the fall of the landed aristocracy—would never be achieved as long as the aristocracy maintained its 'heavily fortified outposts in Ireland' (Nov. 29). The present relation to Ireland handicapped not only England's internal social development, but also its foreign policy, notably its relationship with Russia and America. The treatment accorded the Fenians was symbolic of British rule in Ireland:

England has in fact never governed Ireland in any other way and *cannot* do so as long as the present relation continues—except through the most abhorrent reign of terror and the most despicable corruption (*ibid.*).

For the next debate on Ireland Marx now planned to speak on the three most important points in Ireland's movement:

1. Opposition to the lawyers and *trading politicians* and *blarney* (sic); 2. Opposition to the *dictates* of the clergymen, who ... are traitors; 3. Build-up of the *agricultural labouring class* against the farming class (letter to Engels, Dec. 10).

In contrast to his earlier views, expressed, for example, in the *Daily Tribune*, Marx now held that, apart from any humanist considerations, the Irish question was of the utmost importance for the social movement because 'the English working class can *never accomplish anything* before it has gotten rid of Ireland!' (*ibid.*).

The secretary of the Geneva IWA committee informed Marx in October that Bakunin was busy disorganising everything through his tyranny. Writing in a Swiss journal the latter had implied, moreover, that the German and English working men had no need of individuality and were therefore able to submit to the 'communisme autoritaire' of the General Council. 'Bakunin, in contrast, represents *le collectivisme anarchique*. Anarchy reigns in any case in his head, where there is room for only one clear idea—that Bakunin must play first fiddle' (Marx to Engels, Oct. 30). Marx made an issue of Bakunin's most recent manoeuvre at a GC session on December 14. There it was decided to address a message to the Federal Council of Romance Switzerland in reply to the scandalous attacks by Bakunin and his cohorts on the Council. Marx sketched out the intended reply in a letter to Engels on December 17, observing that: 'As soon as a Russian moves in, all hell breaks loose'. With all four organs of the IWA not at his disposal, Bakunin was trying to win status in Germany through an alliance with Schweitzer and in France by flatteries to the editors of the journal *Le Travail*. Marx interpreted this to mean that Bakunin 'thinks the moment has come to pick a public quarrel with us and assigns himself the role of guardian of true proletarianism' (Dec. 17).

1870 At the turn of the year the Lafargues made Marx a grandfather for the second time; this child, a daughter, died, however, about two months later. Marx's health continued to be poor and, unwilling as he was to restrict his many activities, he was finally too ill to leave the house after mid-January and missed the Council meetings for the next month.

At a special session of the GC on January 1 Marx presented the draft of the circular, which he had composed in reply to the attacks published in the Geneva IWA organ *Egalité*. Under Bakunin's influence the editors of *Egalité* had reproached the Council with neglecting its duties and criticised the combination of the General Council with the federal council for England. Marx explained the reasons for the latter:

Although revolutionary *initiative* will probably come from France, England alone can serve as the *lever* for a serious *economic* revolution ... It is the only country where the *capitalist form*, i.e. combined labour on a large scale under capitalist masters, embraces virtually the whole of production ... where the *great majority of the population consists of wages labourers* ... where the class struggle and organisation of the working class by the *Trades Unions* have acquired a certain degree of maturity and universality (*Documents* 3:401f.).

Since England thus had the 'material necessity of social revolution', the GC would invest it with the 'spirit of generalisation and revolutionary fervour'. It was consequently better placed there than elsewhere. Marx's circular also replied to an accusation of *Egalité* which necessitated a definition of the Council's stand on Ireland. He repeated the statement that precondition for English social emancipation was the transformation of Ireland's forced union with England into a confederation or into complete independence of the two countries (*Documents* 3 : 405).

While Marx was ill, Jenny wrote a letter to Engels describing her husband's recent activities—'he has begun studying Russian as if it were a matter of life and death'—and seeking their friend's aid in persuading Marx to change his habits. Jenny added in a wistful tone: 'How often I secretly wished you had been here during the past years, Herr Engels. Many things would have been otherwise' (Jan. 17). Engels thereupon wrote to Marx warning in a gentle manner that 'if only in the interest of your second volume, you need to change your way of living' (Jan. 19).

It was none other than Bakunin who had received the commission to translate *Capital* into Russian for the St Petersburg publisher. Writing to Alexander Herzen on January 4, Bakunin called the work 'Marx's economic metaphysics'. Following Marx's move against his intrigues within the Geneva organisation, Bakunin had moved to the Ticino in Switzerland and six of his adherents had left the staff of *Egalité*. Bakunin, Marx wrote to Engels (Feb. 10), 'imagines that we are "*too bourgeois*" and therefore incapable of understanding and appreciating his lofty conceptions about the "right of inheritance", equality and the suppression by the "International" of the state system as it has existed up till now'. According to a letter recently communicated to Marx (Henri Perret to Hermann Jung, Jan. 4) Bakunin and his friends had only nominally disbanded the *Alliance* and continued their plots to bring confusion into the IWA. Their method was to place *Alliance* members in the federal councils of each country they desired to infiltrate. Marx quoted Perret as saying that Bakunin and his men were 'authoritarian and tolerate no contradictions', that furthermore they took recourse to slander and deliberate lies to attain these ends (Marx to De Paepe, Jan. 24).

After practising his Russian on Herzen's book *Prison and Exile*, Marx began his study of Flerovsky's book in February. He reported to Engels that, judging from the first 150 pages that he had read with the aid of his dictionary, the work was original and rich in valuable observation, especially of the family life and customs of the Russian peasants. Even more, he found that Flerovsky was free from mysticism, socialist doctrine and nihilist excesses and a decided opponent of 'Russian optimism'. He compared the situation of the Russian peasantry with that of the rural population in France under Louis XIV—both bore a heavy burden of taxation. Marx concluded from his reading 'that the present conditions in Russia are no longer tenable, that the emancipation of the slaves has only accelerated the process of dissolution and that a terrible social revolution is imminent' (Marx to Engels, Feb. 12). Marx's critique of Flerovsky was not entirely positive, however, for he thought the author erred by believing in the *'perfectibilité perfectible'* of the Russian nation and in *'le principe providentiel'* of communal property in its Russian form (cf. letter to Paul and Laura Lafargue, March 5). Nevertheless, Russia's importance in Europe was not to be under-estimated: the two great nations of present-day Europe were, in Marx's opinion, England and Russia.

With her father's assistance Jenny Marx wrote a series of articles appealing for the amnesty of the imprisoned Fenians. The articles appeared under the pen-name J. Williams in the liberal Paris daily *La Marseillaise* in March and April. The purpose of Jenny's articles, as Marx explained to Engels, was:

to show *how* the English press suppresses *facts* which appear in the Irish papers and finally publishes them only when on an exceptional occasion they come from Paris. The English press is soon going to realise that the idyllic days of systematic lying and suppression of the facts are over (March 10).

On a motion by Marx the GC resolved to admit to the International a Paris organisation called the *Société des prolétaires positivistes*, whose programme professed orthodox Comtism. Although its members were all working men, the society was fundamentally philosophical rather than proletarian and opposed 'every religion but Comte's' (Minutes, March 15). The society was admitted under the condition that it drop 'positivism' from its official programme, since this conflicted with the statutes of the IWA. 'As for the rest,' Marx told Engels, 'it is their affair how they harmonise their private philosophic views with the views in our statutes' (March 19).

Bakunin meanwhile continued the attacks against Marx using the various IWA journals as his media. When Liebknecht's journal, the *Volksstaat*, published a reply by Bakunin to another article written by Marx's friend Borkheim, Marx protested to Liebknecht for aiding this intriguer and reproached him also for the traces of Lassalleanism in his paper (cf. Marx to Engels, March 16).

Sometime at the beginning of the year Marx began working on the problem of landed property for the second book of *Capital* (on the circulation process of capital). On January 24 he wrote De Paepe for detailed information on the Belgian system of property in land and asked for a list of the most important books on land and agriculture in Belgium.

As far as his health allowed, Marx devoted his time chiefly to the activities of the IWA. On March 22 he accepted an offer to represent the newly founded anti-Bakuninist Russian section in the General Council. The group based their request to Marx on the similarity in the 'practical character of the movement' in Russia and Germany and stated that they were anxious to check Panslavism in Russia by promoting the International. In his message of acceptance Marx praised their express desire to work for the emancipation of Poland. In so doing, he wrote, 'Russian socialists take on themselves the lofty task of destroying the military regime; that is essential for the overall emancipation of the European proletariat' (*Documents* 3 : 410).

Kugelmann transmitted for Marx a confidential communiqué to the SDAP in Germany, which included the January 1 circular and a detailed letter exposing Bakunin's European activities since his meeting with Marx in November 1864. Marx depicted Bakunin as deceitful, treacherous, ambitious to make of the International his own personal tool and 'one of the most ignorant men in the field of social theory'. Announcing the foundation of the new Russian section in Geneva, 'La Jeune Russie', he expressed the optimistic conviction that 'at least on the terrain of the *International* this highly dangerous game of intrigues will thus soon be over' (March 28; MEW 16 : 420).

During April both Bakunin and the Irish question continued to absorb Marx's attention. Reporting to Meyer and Vogt in New York, Marx said that his lengthy study of Irish conditions and their relation to England had led him to conclude that: 'The decisive blow against the ruling classes in England (and this blow is decisive for the working men's movement all over the world) is to be struck *not in England* but *only in Ireland*' (Apr. 9). He called on the Americans to co-operate with the Irish working men, a step which would be the 'greatest deed' they could presently accomplish.

Henri Verlet, a member of the staff of the journal *La Libre Pensée* in Paris, wrote to ask Marx's advice about founding a new Paris branch of the IWA. Through Lafargue Marx sent Verlet a letter of recommendation and warned against giving the new section any sort of sectarian label, which would be contrary to the nature of the proletarian movement.

The general aspirations and tendencies of the working class emanate from the real conditions in which it finds itself placed. They are therefore common to the whole class although the movement reflects itself in their heads in the most diversified forms, more or less phantastical, more or less adequate. Those to interpret best the hidden sense of the class struggle going on before our eyes—the Communists are the last to commit the blunder of affecting or fostering Sectarianism (to Lafargue, Apr. 18).

The following day Marx sent Lafargue a letter intended to prepare the latter for his post as special correspondent from the GC to the Paris Federal Council. Outlining Bakunin's conspiratorial activities within the IWA, Marx commented that under the pretext of making 'la propagande théorique' Bakunin had created his own organisation in the International which was 'by and by to be converted into an instrument du Russe Bakounine'. The programme of this *Alliance* contained three points, abolition of inheritance, equality between classes and abstention of the working class from politics, demonstrating clearly Bakunin's failure to see that 'every class movement *as* a class movement is necessarily and was always a *political* movement. This then is the whole theoretical baggage of Mahomet-Bakounine, a Mahomet without a Koran', Marx concluded (Apr. 19, *Annali*, 1, p. 173f.).

In the GC on April 26 Marx moved that the IWA dissolve all ties with the London journal *Bee-Hive* which now 'preached harmony with the capitalists', whereas the Association's principles declared open war against capitalist rule. The motion was passed and Marx was charged with editing a declaration to this effect.

From Geneva Marx received on April 29 copies of the first Russian edition of *The Communist Manifesto*, published late in 1869. Its translator, presumed to be Bakunin, was not named. At the end of the month Marx was called to the deathbed of his friend and IWA comrade-in-arms Karl Schapper, who expressed to Marx his last wish: 'Tell all our people that I remained true to our principles. During the reactionary period I had much to do to raise my family. I have lived as a hard-working labourer and die as a proletarian' (Marx to Engels, April 28).

On May 3 Marx reported to the Council on police reprisals in Paris against members of the International. He proposed that they issue a statement which emphasised that the IWA was on no account a secret society plotting against the French emperor. Rather,

if the working classes, who form the great bulk of all nations, who produce all their wealth, and in the name of whom even the usurping powers always pretend to rule, conspire, they conspire publicly, as the sun conspires against the darkness, in the full consciousness that without their pale there exists no legitimate power (Minutes, May 3).

Despite arrests in numerous French cities, protest committees were being formed with increased participation of the working men—striking evidence that the IWA was proletarian and open. Marx attributed great importance to these incidents, saying in a letter to Engels that 'the French government has finally done what we have wanted for such a long time—to change the political question, empire or republic, into a question of life and death for the working class' (May 18).

In his absence from the Council meeting on June 21 Marx was entrusted with the task of writing an address on the lock-out of the building trades in Geneva. He presented this appeal to the working class, on behalf of the Swiss strikers, at the meeting on July 5. In order to avoid a possible conflict over the retention of the General Council in London Marx proposed that they suggest at the next congress to transfer the seat to Brussels (June 28).

On July 3 Marx was visited for the first time by the Russian emigrant Hermann Lopatin, who informed him of the relations between Bakunin and the terrorist Sergei Nechayev, of Chernyshevsky's banishment to Siberia and Flerovsky's to a village somewhere in the Russian Northwest.

The Council established an agenda for the coming Congress in Mainz, including questions on the abolition of public debts; relations between political action and the proletarian social movement; the practical means of converting land into communal property; the conditions for co-operative production on a national scale; and the means of suppressing war. Drawn up by Marx and approved in council on July 12, this agenda was published as a handbill in London and reprinted in translation in several European newspapers. An expanded version was sent by Marx to Jung, corresponding secretary for Switzerland, who transmitted it for publication in Swiss and Belgian newspapers.

On July 19 the Council appointed Marx to draw up an address on the Franco-Prussian war. Marx's standpoint on the war was that, for the future of European democracy, it would be more advantageous for the French to suffer defeat. He explained his views in a letter to Engels:

If the Prussians are victorious, this will also be a victory for the centralisation of state power, which benefits the centralisation of the working class. German predominance, moreover, will shift the centre of gravity of the West-European working men's movement from France to Germany, and you need only compare the movement since 1866 in both countries to see that the German working class is both in theory and in organisation ahead of the French. Its ascendancy in the world theatre over the French would at the same time mean the ascendancy of our theory over Proudhon's (July 20).

After receiving a request from the *Pall Mall Gazette* in London to be its war correspondent in Prussia, Marx, who turned down the offer, suggested to Engels that he furnish this paper with military articles on the war. He reasoned that although the *Gazette* was a conservative daily its foreign policy was anti-Russian and it enjoyed a wide readership in military circles as the only 'non-venal' paper in London (*see* letter to Engels, Aug. 3). Between July 1870 and February 1871 Engels published a series of 59 articles in the *Gazette* under the heading 'Notes on the War'.

Marx's address on the war was approved by the GC on July 23 and published as a fly-sheet in London that same month, and later in French, German and Russian translations. It began with a reference to the IWA principles as set down in the Inaugural Address, whereby the working class desired to see the simple laws of justice and morality govern the relations between nations, and appealed to the German people to prevent the present war from degenerating into a war against their French brothers. It warned Germany to beware of the 'dark figure of Russia', which was willing to offer Prussia its aid. 'Let them remember that, after their war of independence against the first Napoleon, Germany lay for generations prostrate at the feet of the Czar' (*Documents* 4 : 327). The war was being conducted for reasons of defence and ought not to be turned into a war of aggression. In the name of the English working class the Council declared in this address its fellowship towards both peoples and its conviction that 'whatever turn the impending horrid war may take, the alliance of the working classes of all countries will ultimately kill war' (*Documents* 4 : 328).

On July 28 Marx wrote to both Lafargue and Engels on the subject of the war, expressing the same views incorporated into the Address. 'In point of fact,' he added to Lafargue, 'the war of classes in both countries [France and Germany] is too far developed to allow any political war whatever to roll back for long time [sic] the wheel of history ... For my own part, I should like that both, Prussians and French, trashed each other alternately, and that—as I believe will be the case—the Germans got *ultimately* the better of it. I wish this, because the definite defeat of Bonaparte is likely to provoke Revolution in France, while the definite defeat of the Germans would only protract the present state of things for 20 years' (*Annali* 1, p. 178f.). Somewhat later, writing again to Engels, Marx criticised the Disraeli-Gladstone plan for an alliance between Britain and Russia and said he wished to see the English council members take an open and energetic stand against it (Aug. 3). He passed on news of the publicity given to their Address on the war by J. S. Mill, who had expressed his high esteem for it: 'There was not one word in it that ought not be there; it could not have been done with fewer words' (quoted in *La Première Internationale*. ed. C. Abramsky, Paris, 1968, p. 81). Richard Cobden's Peace Society had also declared its solidarity with their views and promised financial aid for the publication of the Address (Aug. 8).

Marx learned that Prussian militarists and the arch-patriotic bourgeoisie had proposed the annexation of Alsace and Lorraine. Seeing in this proposal the first move towards inevitable war between Germany and Russia allied with France, Marx thereupon addressed a letter to the central office of the SDAP, stating that the only outcome of such a situation would be perpetual war in Europe and the ruin of both France and Germany through mutual self-destruction. Only an honourable peace with France:

will rid Europe of the Muscovite dictatorship, integrate Prussia into the German nation and permit the Western Continent a peaceable development, and finally aid the genesis of the Russian social revolution, whose elements only need such a push from without for their development—and thus will also benefit the Russian people (*Documents* 4:332).

The *SDAP* printed this letter as part of its manifesto on the war, issued on September 5, and also published it in their newspaper *Der Volksstaat* on September 11.

Using military arguments furnished by Engels, Marx wrote in early September a second Address on the Franco-Prussian war, which was published as a leaflet in English on September 11-13. This Address opposed the anachronistic method of determining national boundaries on the basis of military considerations and warned that: 'History will measure its retribution, not by the extent of the square miles conquered from France, but by the intensity of the crime of reviving, in the second half of the 19th century, *the policy of conquest!*' (*Documents* 4:337). After attacking the perennial system of standing armies and Russia's traditional domination over Germany, Marx hailed the advent of the French Republic, despite certain misgivings about its middle-class republican composition. He admonished the French to forget the past and the Revolution of 1793, insisting that: 'They have not to recapitulate the past, but to build up the future. Let them calmly and resolutely improve the opportunities of Republican liberties, for the work of their own class organisation' (*Documents* 4:341).

In a letter to F. A. Sorge on September 1 Marx maintained that the war would lead to an unavoidable conflict between Germany and Russia. A second war of this kind, he added prophetically, 'will act as the midwife to the inevitable revolution in Russia'. At this time Marx began actively agitating for the recognition of the new French Republic by England. In a provocative letter to the British historian and positivist Edward Beesly Marx demanded: 'Are you going to permit your queen and your oligarchy to abuse upon the dictate of Bismarck England's immense influence?' (Sept. 12) Beesly, who characterised Marx as the most influential man in the IWA and Europe's greatest authority on the working class movement, published an article in the *Fortnightly Review* on the International and its two war addresses, denouncing the conspiracy of silence in the so-called 'free' English press against the French Republic (Nov. 1).

About mid-September Engels moved to London with Lizzie Burns and set up their household not far from the Marxes in Maitland Park. From this date the two friends saw each other almost daily. On October 4 Engels was elected to membership in the General Council of the IWA. Marx reported to the Council on October 11 that a *coup* attempted by Bakunin in Lyon, where he proclaimed the abolition of all official powers and institutions, had ended in failure.

In a letter to Beesly on October 19 Marx reported that the Paris groups had been the first in the country to proclaim the Republic and that their move had been echoed in Toulouse and Marseille, where the IWA also had strong sections. Other information which he had received, however, left little reason for rejoicing for it showed that 'the bourgeoisie as a whole prefers Prussian conquest to the victory of the republic with socialist tendencies'.

In December Marx was addressed by Friedrich Bolte, secretary of the New York Labour League, who wrote in the interests of working men's groups in Chicago and New York to gain their admittance to the IWA. Bolte wrote that sufficient interest in the International existed in the USA to warrant the creation of a central committee there to administrate affiliation, propaganda activities and contributions. Between December and February 1871 Marx several times met the Russian revolutionary Elise Tomanovsky, sent to London by the Russian section in Geneva to discuss with him questions pertaining to the IWA and to the specific problems of rural communes in Russia.

On December 13 Marx sent Kugelmann the most recent publications of the IWA and commented on the present course of political events. The Germans seemed to him to be 'drunk with conquest', pleased to be able to exercise power over their 'subjects' after a long period of subjection to the authoritarian dictates of the monarchic system. In England public opinion, which had been pro-Prussian at the outset, had been completely reversed now that signs of the Russo-Prussian alliance had become evident and after the people had learned of the barbaric excesses of the victorious troops. Marx conjectured about the unpleasant consequences if it should be possible to besiege and then starve out Paris. 'However the war may end,' he concluded, 'it will have given the French proletariat practice in the use of arms, and that is the best guarantee for the future' (Dec. 13).

1871 This year was marked by Marx's active participation in the cause of the French Republic, first with practical directives to the Commune leaders, later with material support for the refugees from Paris.

Marx took a strong stand against the Bismarck regime in Prussia and its subservience to the Czar. In a letter to the editor of the London *Daily News*, he exposed the tactics of the Prussian system which had brought about the arrest of Liebknecht and Bebel on charges of high treason. Published on January 19 under the heading 'The Freedom of the Press and Debate in Germany', Marx's letter closed with the words: 'France—its cause fortunately far from desperate—is at this moment fighting not only for its own independence but also for the liberty of Germany and of Europe' (MEW 17:285).

Information on the difficulties of the Prussian occupational forces in France, which Marx received from Johannes Miquel, was passed on through Lafargue to the Government of National Defence. Marx, still agitating for the recognition of France's new government by England, reported in detail to Meyer on January 21 concerning the present stand of the IWA in Europe and the hostility of Gladstone's government towards France. 'Unfortunately,' he observed, 'the present French government thinks it can conduct a revolutionary war without a revolution'. Discussions in the GC centred around the reception of the new French government as well. On January 31 Engels opened a debate on the attitudes of the English working class towards France and spoke out against the Comtists who 'advocate a compromise to make wage-labour tolerable in order to perpetuate it; they belong to a political sect who believe that France ought to rule the world ... they demanded that France be restored to the position it occupied before the war' (Minutes). He underlined the importance of restraining England from diplomatic sanctions against France and Russia from military interference, adding that only England was powerful enough to oppose Russia. Had war been declared against Russia, France would have been saved and Poland restored. Now, however, 'Russia will enter on a war of conquest, perhaps before a year is over, and Europe will have to fight minus France'. Marx seconded Engels's remarks.

Both Bismarck and Bonaparte were 'mediocre scoundrels',

Marx wrote to Kugelmann while following the day-to-day course of the war and predicted: should France use the period of the cease-fire to reorganise her armies and give the war a 'truly revolutionary character', Prussia might still take an unexpected beating (Feb. 4). Moreover, if she continued to hold out, foreign governments would certainly be induced to support her cause. To Lafargue Marx remarked on a change in popular sentiment in England where the Gladstone ministry seemed to be poised for a fall. 'It may be kicked out. The public opinion here is now again *warlike* to the highest degree. This change has been worked by Prussia's demands ... John Bull sees in this a menace against England and a Russian intrigue 'and these demands have indeed been suggested to Prussia by the St Petersburg cabinet' (Feb. 4).

Engels reported to the Council on the International's progress in Europe and America. The trade unions in Birmingham and Manchester were now directly affiliated with the IWA; fifty of their German members were under arrest. He underlined the necessity of forming a proletarian party in each country, everywhere with individual political programmes. 'Universal suffrage gives us an excellent means of action and parliament and excellent basis for propaganda making', he stated (Feb. 13; MEW 17:288). Marx in turn reported on the police persecutions in Germany and Austria and on the activities of the Council member Auguste Serraillier in Paris. Marx said that recognition of the French Republic was the precondition of social change in France. 'If that did not succeed all the rest must fail. France was internationally paralysed and at home, too, while Prussia had Russia at her back' (Minutes, Feb. 14).

On March 7 Marx communicated to the Council a letter received from the New York Committee which repeated its desire to function as the central committee for the North American sections. After lengthy debate it was decided to recognise this committee as representatives of only those groups who actually had delegates in it. Marx was charged with composing a letter which would encourage the Americans to do their utmost to promote the IWA activities.

From March 21 onwards the Council discussed the recent proclamation of the Paris Commune. Engels gave a report describing conditions in Paris. The Council appointed a delegation to attend a republican meeting in London in support of the communards. The *Paris-Journal*, organ of the French police, published a forged letter which purported to show that Marx as 'le Grand Chef de l'Internationale' was dissatisfied with the actions of the French IWA members in the Commune and that they dealt excessively with political questions while neglecting the social. On March 23 Marx answered these calumnies with declarations published in the *Volksstaat* and other German and French journals. It is only natural, he wrote, for the responsible figures in the old society to feel threatened by the movement of the working class and to see the International, inasmuch as it was the instrument of the working class, as their common enemy. In their minds, therefore, 'every means used to destroy this enemy is good' (*Documents* 4:352). In a letter published on April 4 in the London *Times*, Marx replied to accusations that the Commune had been organised from London. Serraillier wrote to the Council that the reactionary opposition had been spreading the rumour of Marx's leadership in the Commune. '*Le mot d'ordre* of the reactionaries is that Marx commands the French members of the IWA, causes them to strike in order to increase wages and make German competition easier. It's stupid but nevertheless the Council ought to reply to it' (March 30). Leo Fränkel also wrote on March 30 to announce his election to the Commune's Labour and Exchange Commission and asked for Marx's advice which 'would be very valuable for the committee'. In contrast to the rumours being spread by the French police, the Prussian agents in France made it known that Marx was an agent of Bismarck (*see* Marx to Liebknecht, April 4). Lafargue wrote from Paris that although the Commune enjoyed much popular interest and enthusiasm it lacked leaders: 'Couldn't Engels come here to put his talents at the disposal of the revolution?' he asked (Apr. 8).

In a letter to Kugelmann Marx evaluated the Commune's goals and the behaviour of its participants, whose heroism, historical initiative, selflessness he found admirable, their chief fault being 'good-naturedness'. Their original error, Marx thought, was to delay in declaring war on the Versailles government: 'Held back by scruples, they missed the right moment'; then they prematurely abandoned the central committee to make way for the Commune, 'again because of such "high-principled" conscientiousness! Be that as it may, the present uprising in Paris ... is the most glorious deed of our party since the June insurrection.' In short, the Commune demonstrated for Marx that the precondition of a genuinely popular revolution in Europe was not the transfer of state power from one hand to another but the destruction of the entire military-bureaucratic apparatus (Apr. 12). In a second letter to Kugelmann on the Commune he discussed the role of contingency in revolution. 'World history would indeed be an easy affair if the fight were taken up only under the condition of infallibly favourable chances.' As part of the contingency which makes or breaks each revolutionary attempt Marx noted the individual character of the leaders. Should chance favour the Commune or not, this fight had nevertheless brought the class struggle to a new phase of development: 'No matter how the affair may immediately turn out, a historically significant new starting point has been won' (Apr. 17).

Serraillier announced to the Council in April that he had been elected to the Commune (second *arrondissement*); Fränkel reported that he had been chosen to the executive commission in his capacity as delegate of the Department of Labour and Exchange. Fränkel again asked Marx for his advice, and then remarked:

The few lines of your last letter attest to your willingness to aid all peoples, all working men and especially the Germans in understanding that the Paris Commune has nothing in common with the renowned German rural commune. In so doing you will have performed a great service for our cause (Apr. 25).

During a period of ill health in April and May Marx was unable to attend the Council meetings but he prepared instead an address on the Commune which he had promised for the end of May. Meanwhile in Council, Engels reported on the military situation of the Paris government, which he described as 'good', adding that their defence was strengthening. The celebration of Robert Owen's centenary caused Engels to remark on Owen's merits as a socialist thinker and activist that 'there were things to be found in his writings that had yet not been superseded'. He had been the first of his class to put a stop to the shameful system of female and child labour in the factories (Minutes, May 9).

On May 23, in announcing that he would present his address at the coming Council session, Marx told the members he anticipated the end of the Commune. However, momentary defeat did not exclude ultimate victory. 'The principles of the Commune were eternal and could not be crushed; they would assert themselves again and again until the working classes were emancipated' (Minutes, May 23). Marx's address on *The Civil War in France* was read to the Council and adopted unanimously without discussion on May 30.

In this animated piece of writing Marx told the story of the events which turned Thiers's 'government of national defence' into a 'government of national defection', fighting not the Prussian invaders but the working people of Paris. He attacked with particular vehemence the figure of Louis-Adolphe Thiers, a 'monstrous gnome' who had 'charmed the French bourgeoisie for almost half a century, because he is the most consummate intellectual expression of their own class corruption' (*Documents* 4:360). By capitulating to the Prussians Thiers incited a civil war against Paris and the Republic. To his counter-revolution— 'a slaveholders' rebellion' as Marx termed it—there was but one major obstacle: armed Paris whose brave inhabitants resisted both the German assault and the new tyranny of the National Defence Government. When on March 18 the Thiers government had been driven from the capital and the Commune proclaimed, the new government represented not a simple take-over of the established state machinery for its particular purposes, but rather:

The cry of 'social republic', with which the Revolution of February was ushered in by the Paris proletariat, did but express a vague aspiration after a republic that was not only to supersede the monarchical form of class-rule, but class-rule itself. The Commune was the positive form of that republic (*Documents* 4:381).

The first act of the new government had been to suppress the standing army and substitute for it the armed population: 'the Commune was to be a working, not a parliamentary, body, executive and legislative at the same time' (*Documents* 4:382). Moreover, it was to be the form representative of political organisation in the great industrial centres; it restored the legitimate function of government to society's responsible agents —the people. On this basis, 'universal suffrage was to serve the people, constituted in Communes, as individual suffrage serves every other employer in the search for the workmen and managers in his business' (*Documents* 4 : 384). A viable, flexible, working class political form, the Commune of Paris was in no sense a reproduction of medieval communal organisations and its purpose was to accomplish the necessary changes in production relations to make co-operation and free association in labour possible. This form was in time to be extended to 'even the smallest country hamlet', Marx added (*Documents* 4 : 384).

In the first draft of his address Marx formulated the Commune's standpoint as regards state power even more explicitly, using a phrase later omitted in the published text. The revolution of the communards, he wrote, was directed not against the *form* of state power but 'against the *State* itself, this supernationalist abortion of society' and was 'a resumption by the people for the people of its own social life' (Karl Marx, *The Civil War in France*, Peking, 1966, p. 166). Nowhere in his writings is the nature of the Commune defined as clearly as it is here, although other statements presuppose such a conception of the Paris events, such as the following comment taken from the final manuscript : 'The very existence of the Commune involved, as a matter of course, local municipal liberty, but no longer as a check upon the, now superseded, State power' (*Documents* 4 : 385).

Finally, although the nature of the Commune was recognised to represent a certain progress beyond state organisation, the working men of Paris were not so blinded by the thought of realising a communist society as to ignore the immediate struggles and the long historical development which lay ahead of them. Their task was not to create ' "utopia" but to set free the elements of the new society with which the old collapsing bourgeois society itself was pregnant' (*Documents* 4 : 387). This then had been the 'historic mission' of Paris' communards. Their untimely defeat did not signal the 'final repression of new society upheaving, but the crumbling into dust of bourgeois society' (*Documents* 4 : 490f.).

Following the fall of the Commune and the bloody executions and trials of the communards, Marx continued to collect materials and documents relating to the events there. Apart from this he devoted himself with great intensity to the welfare of the Commune refugees in London. On June 13 in the London *Times* a notice appeared, which had been prepared by Marx and Engels and exposed the plans of Jules Favre, Thiers's foreign minister, to have the members of the IWA hunted down by all the governments of Europe. Favre's plans, made public in a circular on June 6, contained statements concerning the IWA which only repeated indefensible fabrications of the police prosecutors under the Empire. There was an immediate uproar in the bourgeois press against the IWA as soon as the address on *The Civil War* appeared (June 13). Marx announced to Kugelmann that the address 'is making a hell of a noise and I have the honour of being, *at this moment, the best calumniated and the most menaced man in London*' (June 18). In a letter to the *Daily News* on June 23 he openly acknowledged authorship of the address and assumed the sole responsibility for the accusations against 'Jules Favre and Co'.

Absorbed in these practical and political activities, Marx was unable to pursue at great length his theoretical work on *Capital*. Thanking Danielson for material on property relations in Russia, he informed him that he wished to rewrite chapter 1 of the first volume, which Danielson was in the process of translating. He had also found it necessary to undertake a thorough revision of the material for the subsequent volumes; finally, certain pertinent documentation, in particular on American property relations, had not yet reached him, and this had also delayed his work.

On July 3 he granted an interview to the London correspondent of the New York newspaper *The World*, which was published on July 18. Marx spoke about the Paris Commune and the relation of the IWA to this insurrection 'made by the workmen of Paris'. The International, he explained, was neither a secret conspiratorial organisation nor a centralised proletarian government but an organisational form 'which gives the greatest play to local energy and independence. In fact the International is not properly a government for the working class at all. It is a bond rather than a controlling force.' Speaking of the IWA's goals—'the economic emancipation of the working class by the conquest of political power'—and the means to achieve them, Marx stated that legal means lay open to English workers: 'Insurrection would be madness where peaceful agitation would more swiftly and surely do the work.' However, where repressive laws and police interference prevent the wage-earners from organising and assembling, 'the violent solution of social war' is inevitable. Strikes he interpreted as expressions of the emancipation movement in face of the 'moral' opposition of the authorities. The calumnies of and falsifications about the IWA were expressions of the resistance to the new social force. This latter statement was most ironically confirmed by the reporting of a second interview Marx granted on July 20 to the *New York Herald's* London correspondent. The published account of their conversation (Aug. 8) prompted Marx to deny immediately 'all and every responsibility for the statements attributed to me in that report ... Of what I am reported to have said, one part I said differently, and another I never said at all' (Aug. 17). These falsifications of Marx's thoughts on the IWA, the class struggle and the Commune were reprinted in part in the Paris newspaper *Le Gaulois* on August 22.

During the days of the actual Commune the American ambassador in Paris, Elihu B. Washburne, had played 'politics' with the leaders of the new government, assuring them of his sympathy and favour, while declaring to the bourgeois press that they were 'rebels who well deserved their fate'. Marx exposed Washburne's treacherous behaviour in letters to the editors of various IWA organs (July). He commented on this phenomenon of lies produced by the modern press in a letter to Kugelmann on July 27 :

Up till now it was thought that the Christian myths during the Roman Empire had been possible only because the printing press had yet to be invented. The daily press and the telegraph which spread their fabrications over the entire surface of the earth in an instant, create more myths ... in a day than could be produced earlier in a century (July 27).

There was no end to the scandalous lies. On July 30 the Berlin *Nationalzeitung*, organ of the Prussian government, published a statement to the effect that 'socialist agitators', Marx among them, were enriching themselves at the expense of the unsuspecting working class. Marx's rejoinder appeared on August 26 in the London *Public Opinion*, one of several journals which had taken up these lies in their columns. He underlined the fact that all the members of the General Council except the general secretary worked entirely without remuneration (cf. MEW 17 : 398).

In a precarious state of health due to overwork and excitement, Marx spent a fortnight by the sea in Brighton before the IWA Conference scheduled for September 17 in London. On September 9 the Council adopted an agenda for this Conference to which only a limited number of sections had been invited. Marx was delegated to prepare the Council's report, but circumstances prevented him from doing so in writing and he delivered it orally at the close of the meeting. Topics before the conference members included the organisation of the IWA in countries where it was prohibited; manifestos against government persecutions; the power of the delegates of the General Council; new translations of the statutes.

At the first session on September 17 Marx emphasised the private nature of their gathering and gave three reasons for its being closed: first of all, the Association must take steps to reorganise in view of the measures being taken against it in several European countries; secondly, it must reply to the provocations of these governments; lastly, the Swiss conflict must be resolved. At the third session Marx took the floor on a proposition which would create new sections of the IWA, reserved exclusively for female members. He said that it was very important for women to be able to form such sections as they wished, since they preferred to discuss among themselves. 'Women play a very great role in life,' he added, 'they work in the factories, they participate in the strikes, in the Commune, etc. They are more zealous than men' (Freymond 2:168). This proposition for all-female sections was adopted without objection.

A discussion was held on Edouard Vaillant's proposition that political abstention is contrary to letter and spirit of the IWA. Marx seconded Vaillant, saying that 'faulty abstention' had contributed to the defeat of the Commune by permitting a majority of Bonapartists and intriguers to establish a dictatorial committee in Paris. 'The movement in France failed because it had not been sufficiently prepared' (Sept. 20; Freymond 2:195). The discussion on political activism continued into the next session on September 22. Marx spoke at length on the history of abstentionism as propagated by utopianists and sectarian thinkers. He stressed that the IWA should actively defy all governments which attacked and persecuted them:

We must say to them: we know you represent force armed against the proletarians. We will have recourse to peaceful means to oppose you where possible. And to arms when that be necessary (Freymond 2:202).

At the same session the conference was addressed by the commission charged with investigating the Swiss conflict. Speaking for the commission, Marx said that the *Alliance's* statutes were contrary to the principles of the IWA and seconded the statement of delegate Utin, condemning both secret societies and Bakunin's activities in Russia. For the rest, Marx said that he had great confidence in the Russian social movement: 'secret societies are useless in Russia', where the IWA is accessible to the working class and where 'associative spirit is high, solidarity great and the people enjoy ample individual liberty' (Freymond 2:222). At the final session on September 23 Marx declared that he was opposed to the formation of secret societies, even in countries where working men's organisation was prohibited. Mystical and authoritative, secret societies were a danger to the spirit in which the association was founded and 'in complete contradiction to the proletarian movement' (Freymond 2:225). A last word was spoken at this session on the conspiratorial activities of Bakunin and his relations with Nechayev. Marx proposed that he be given an opportunity to justify his actions and that extracts from the records of the Nechayev trial be published.

At the conclusion of the Conference a banquet was held to commemorate the IWA's seventh anniversary. Marx spoke to those in attendance on the nature of the movement which had led to the creation of an international working class society. Its uniqueness lay in its popular character and in the maturity of the present conditions found in Western industrial countries. 'The organised persecutions by the governments against the International are comparable to those persecutions in ancient Rome whose victims were the first Christians,' he added. The task of the International would continue, therefore, to be the organisation and co-ordination of the working forces for the future combat (Sept. 25).

The Jura Federation in Switzerland, which was under Bakunin's influence, did not let the event of the closed London Conference pass without comment. It immediately convoked a congress at Sonvillier on November 12, following which a circular was issued to the federations of the IWA in all countries. This circular accused the GC of wanting to impose its 'personal doctrines' on the IWA, and repudiated the resolutions of the conference, which tended to transform the International into a 'hierarchic' and authoritarian regime of disciplined sections. It demanded moreover that a full plenary IWA congress be called immediately. The Federation declared itself opposed to all directive authority, 'even if this authority is elected by and has the consent of the working men' (Freymond 2 : 265).

In a letter to Bolte, secretary of the American Federal IWA Council, Marx observed that the fight against sectarianism within the International was not yet finished. After replying to the Proudhonists and Lassalleanists, Marx was now exposed to attacks of 'Bismarckianism' and 'Pan-Germanism' from the Bakuninists, whereby 'the crime consists in the fact that the English and French elements are dominated (!) *in matter of theory* by the German element and find this domination, i.e. German science, very useful and even dispensable' (Nov. 23). In a postscript to this letter Marx differentiated between 'isolated economic movements', e.g. the movement for a shorter working day in a single factory, and the 'political movement of the working class', e.g. the fight for an eight-hour labour law.

Marx's daughter Jenny provided the Kugelmann family with a long and detailed account of their political activities in London at the end of the year. She described the misery of the Commune refugees and their difficulties in finding work, lodging, etc.: 'They are literally dying in the streets of this great city,' she told her friends, 'this city which has developed to its highest perfection the principle *chacun pour soi*' (Dec. 21-22). After five months of aid to the banished communards, the funds of the IWA were now exhausted. Jenny was herself out of work since the Monroes, whose children she tutored, had discovered her relation to the *chef petroleur* [head troublemaker] who defended the 'insane Commune movement'.

1872 In January Marx finished revising the text for the second German edition of *Capital*, volume 1, and sent the manuscript to the publisher Meissner. The new edition was not brought out until 1873. In the meanwhile he had succeeded through Longuet and the Lafargues in finding a French publisher for a translation of the first volume. Maurice Lachâtre was to publish *Capital* in a series of separate booklets with the author carrying the costs of printing and materials, while Joseph Roy was contracted to do the translation. In need of financial support for this new venture Marx turned to his cousin August Philips in Amsterdam, but received a categorical refusal, couched in the words: 'If it's necessary, I am prepared to help you, my friend and relative, even with money; but for your political or revolutionary purposes I shall not do the same' (Jan. 26, IRSH I, 1956, part 1, p. 111).

For the last time Marx devoted considerable effort and attention to IWA activities. Engels, too, since his move from Manchester, was fully absorbed in the International and served as foreign secretary for Spain and Italy. Since the two men were in close, daily contact, the work of the one often reflected the thought or the inspiration of the other.

In answer to the reproach of 'authoritarianism', directed at the Council by the Bakuninist Carlo Terzaghi of Turin, Engels rejected the attempt to equate 'authority' with 'evil' in a letter to Terzaghi himself:

I know nothing more authoritarian than a revolution, and when you impose your will on others with bombs and bullets, then it seems to me that authority is being exercised ... Do what you want with authority, etc., after the victory, but for the battle itself we have to collect all our forces and concentrate them on a single point of attack (Jan. 14-15).

After a number of calumnies against Marx had appeared in the London weekly *The National Reformer*, Council member John Hales answered their author Charles Bradlaugh's portrayal of Marx as the 'grand chef du conseil' with a letter to the editor of the *Eastern Post*. In fact, the Council had no hierarchy of officers; Marx had no more important a position than the others and 'he would be the first to protest if one assumed that he occupied a higher position' (Feb. 3). Marx also replied later in 1871-72 to Bradlaugh with three letters to the editor of the *Eastern Post*.

The internal struggles of the IWA finally induced Marx and Engels to compose a 'private manifesto', which was quietly distributed to the Council's supporters among the sections. Entitled *Fictitious Splits in the International*, this circular reviewed the history of the *Alliance*, Bakunin's career as a Panslavist and racist, his manoeuvres to bring the IWA under his 'personal dictatorship', and the demands made by the anarchists in the Sonvillier circular of November 1871. The authors replied at length to the anarchists' accusations of 'authoritarianism' and 'centralisation' in the organisation of the IWA and depicted the *Alliance* as a sectarian group, useful and logical only 'at a time when the proletariat has not yet developed sufficiently to act as a class' (*Documents* 5 : 388). Constructive at the outset of the movement, such sects constrict the more mature working class. Behind Bakunin's 'sectarianism', however, was nothing more than anarchism and he proclaimed that anarchism within the ranks of the IWA was 'the most infallible means of breaking the powerful concentration of social and political forces in the hands of the exploiters'. The ruling powers themselves could never have imagined anything more suitable for assuring the continuance of the existing order (*Documents* 5 : 407). This paper, written in French, was adopted by the Council on March 5 and published in June in Geneva.

The Council engaged in a lengthy debate on the American sections during March, when it was decided that the existence of two federal councils there conflicted with the IWA statutes. Moreover, in future all new American sections must be composed of at least two-thirds wage-earners. This was because :

The social conditions of the United States, though in many other respects most favourable to the success of the working class movement, peculiarly facilitate the intrusion into the *International* of bogus reformers, middle-class quacks and trading politicians (*Documents* 5 : 412).

Late in March a 3000-copy first Russian edition of volume 1 of *Capital* appeared in St Petersburg. Within six weeks about 1000 copies had been sold. The Czar's censure committee passed it without alteration because of the text's abstruseness and its strict scientific argumentation (cf. Marx to Sorge, June 21).

Marx was appointed by the Council to a committee whose task was to write a protest address against the police terrorism menacing the IWA sections in Ireland. The address was read in Marx's absence by J. P. MacDonnell on April 9. The spread of the International to Ireland, it explained, threatened to end antagonisms between Irish and English working men, an advance which the British government opposed by resorting to police chicaneries. The so-called liberal British governed Ireland 'in a truly Prussian way, under what is called the Free British Constitution' (*Documents* 5 : 149).

During May Marx was in the process of correcting the proofs for the second edition of *Capital*, volume 1, along with Roy's French translation of the same work. He had been obliged to rewrite much of *Capital* to make it comprehensible to a French audience. He also received the proofs of *The Civil War in France*, which came out in June in a first edition of 9000 copies. To Danielson, who had sent a copy of the Russian edition of *Capital*, Marx praised the translation as 'masterful'. By contrast Roy's work had been much too literal and Marx had much to do to correct it:

I am so overworked, and in fact so many things interfere with my theoretical studies, that after September I shall *withdraw* from the *commercial concern* [IWA], which at this moment weighs on my shoulders principally and has, as you know, ramifications all over the world. *Mais, est modus in rebus*, and I can no longer afford— for some time at least—to combine two sorts of business of so very different character (May 28).

Marx also requested from Danielson any information on Bakunin's influence in Russia and on his role in the Nechayev affair.

Once again Marx found himself the object of slanderous attacks in the press. An anonymous article appeared in the Berlin newspaper *Concordia* on March 7 under the heading 'How Karl Marx Quotes'. This article was in actuality written by a German economist Lujo Brentano in an attempt to discredit Marx's scientific and scholarly reputation and 'proved' that Marx had falsified material used in the IWA Inaugural Address. Marx repudiated these statements in a letter published in Liebknecht's journal *Der Volksstaat* on June 1. Brentano's attack continued with a second article on July 4, to which Marx again replied in *Der Volksstaat* on August 7. After Marx's death Brentano, in 1890, began his slanders afresh and Engels wrote a refutation which appeared between December 1890 and February 1891 and was entitled 'On the Brentano Affair against Marx for Alleged Falsification of Quotations. A Historical Account with Documentation'.

Marx was eagerly anticipating the next congress of the International, which—as he wrote to César De Paepe on May 28— would 'mark the end of my slavery. After that I am going to become a free man again and shall accept no further administrative function, neither in the General Council nor in the British Federal Council'. The congress was proposed for the first Monday in September. The principal subject of discussion was to be the

IWA's organisation and was divided into two parts: (1) the rights and duties of the federal councils; (2) those of the General Council. On June 11 in Council Marx stated that he would support a motion to abolish the General Council altogether 'but under no circumstances would he accept the proposition of Bakunin to retain the GC and make it a nullity' (Minutes, June 11). On June 10 the Jura Federation published a bulletin in answer to the *Fictitious Splits* which consisted of attacks by Bakunin and several of his followers on Marx and Lafargue. In face of 'Marxian calumny', 'Marxian law' and 'Marxian politics' Bakunin demanded the right to defend himself at the next congress. The authors of this bulletin repeated their argument that the General Council was of no use to the working class movement, underlined the Council's authoritarian nature and wrote off Marx as a 'metaphysician or abstractor of the quintessence', who had 'habits of mind which seem to have remained with him from the Hegelian school' (Freymond 2 : 315).

A letter from Marx to Sorge on June 21 seems to have presaged the importance of the Hague Congress, for Marx wrote emphatically: 'The next congress will be a matter of life and death for the International. You and at least one other person, if not two, must come.'

On June 24 Marx and Engels composed a short preface to the second edition of *The Communist Manifesto*, published this year in Leipzig. Referring to the experiences of the Commune, the first attempt by the proletariat to hold political power, the authors declared that recent events made the *Manifesto* at least in part out-of-date:

One thing especially was proved by the Commune, *viz.*, that 'the working class cannot simply lay hold of the ready-made state machinery and wield it for its own purposes' (SW 1 : 22).

Vaillant proposed to the Council on July 23 that the resolution of the London Conference on the necessity of political action be incorporated into the statutes. Marx and Engels seconded this proposal. Then, Marx moved that the statutes be amended to require that each section contain three-quarters wage-earners in order to prevent the infiltration of bourgeois elements. Both proposals were carried.

Jenny Marx repeated her father's desire to retire from the IWA after the next congress when writing to Ludwig Kugelmann on June 27. 'But, until then, he is still going to have an enormous lot of work both within the Council and without to prepare for the great battle which will be fought out at the next congress in Holland.' Marx wrote himself to Kugelmann on July 29 to urge his friend's attendance and remarked that before he left the International he wanted 'at least to protect it from the destructive elements'. While compiling his material against Bakunin, Marx asked Danielson to obtain for him a reputedly menacing letter written by Bakunin or under his directives to the Swiss representative of the St Petersburg editor, who had advanced him a large sum of money on his translation of *Capital* (Aug. 15).

Late in August six delegates for the Hague Congress were selected by the Council and Marx, who was among them, was also charged with writing the Council's annual report. From Utin Marx received information on the Nechayev trial, from Lyubavin the desired threatening letter written on Bakunin's behalf. With this material Marx put together a new report for the Congress on the *Alliance* and Bakunin.

Accompanied by his wife and daughter Eleanor, Marx arrived in The Hague on September 1 for a consultation on matters of procedure for the actual congress sessions. He was elected to a committee in charge of verifying the delegates' credentials, which met from September 2-4. On September 3 Marx moved that a special commission be appointed to examine the affair of the *Alliance*. The matter was placed on the agenda following the examination of the mandates. Marx kept up a steady attack against the *Alliance* during these preliminary sessions.

At the first public session of the official Congress on September 5 Marx's report was read in five languages. Here particular attention was paid to the influence of the IWA in creating an attitude of internationalism among the French and German workers and mentioned the many conflicts in which the IWA was involved: defensive wars against the European governments; the Franco-Prussian war and the Civil War in France. Thanks to the International the working class had at once recognised the significance for its movement of the Paris Commune.

On September 6 discussion was opened on the question of the powers of the General Council. Marx spoke in favour of extending the Council's powers by permitting it to suspend federal councils as well as individual sections. He added that he would prefer seeing the Council abolished than turned into a 'letter-box' as Bakunin proposed. 'The General Council has neither an army nor a budget, nor has it any moral authority and will always be impotent if not based on the consensus of the whole Association' (Freymond 2 : 355). The same day Engels proposed in the name of ten other Council members that the GC be transferred from London to New York, where 'the party is more truly international than anywhere else'. His motion was passed by 26 votes to 23. Shortly thereafter a closed session of the committee charged with the *Alliance* question was convened. Engels read the report which Marx had prepared and the latter took the floor to argue that the *Alliance* had never ceased to exist as a secret society within the IWA and that Bakunin was involved with dubious persons, witness his letter to Lyubavin and his relations with Nechayev. The committee concluded there-upon that, although the *Alliance* evidently existed as a secret group within the International, the actual proof furnished was insufficient; that Bakunin had used fraudulent means to obtain the goods of others and that therefore his expulsion was justified; that Bakunin's associates in the Jura Federation should be expelled for belonging to a secret society, the *Alliance*.

The resolution of the London conference on the political action of the proletariat was adopted into the statutes of the IWA on September 7. The new General Council in New York was chosen by the Congress delegates and then finally at the very close of the Congress the commission's proposals to exclude Bakunin and five others were passed by a majority of the forty-two members present.

On the 8th the Amsterdam section of the IWA held a meeting which was attended by many of the Hague delegates. Speaking partly in Dutch, partly in French, Marx summed up the results of the Congress and emphasised the importance of the political along with the social fight carried on by the working class. In order to establish a new organisation of labour it must seize political power by methods which would differ from country to country. In some, notably America and England, it was possible that the proletariat would achieve its goals by peaceful means; in others 'it is violence that must be the ferment of our revolutions; at a certain moment we shall have to call upon violence in order to establish the reign of labour' (MEW 18 : 160). Marx also defended the authority of the General Council, which, since all its decisions were subject to the agreement of the federations, carried only moral weight. He closed with an appeal to the IWA's fundamental principle: solidarity of the working class. Only when this life-saving principle of the proletarian organisation had been secured among all the workers of the world would they be able to achieve their goal. As for himself, 'the rest of my life will be dedicated as all my past effort has been, to the triumph of the social ideas which some day—and let us hold this one conviction—will bring about the universal rule of the proletariat' (MEW 18:161).

Although now freed of his responsibility in the General Council, Marx remained for some time the object of attacks and slanders in the press and the English federal council of the IWA. In a letter to Danielson on December 12 Marx said that he feared an act of revenge from Bakunin and his friends and warned Danielson that 'these fellows are capable of every dirty trick'. The *Alliance* had begun a war of defamation against Marx and his supporters, hoping to split the IWA into two camps. 'Yet their final defeat is certain,' Marx wrote, 'and will help us at the very least to clear the Association of the undesirable or imbecilic elements which have managed to force their way in here and there.' In the same letter Marx requested biographical material on Chernyshevsky, whose writings he wished to propagate in the West. Lopatin recalled in his autobiography (1922) that Marx had had great respect for Chernyshevsky, whom he held to be the only contemporary economist with original ideas (cf. *Reminiscences of Marx and Engels*, p. 202). Marx also disclosed to Danielson that he intended to deal with the Russian form of landed property in volume 2 of *Capital*. In the meanwhile, he was extremely busy correcting proofs and the French translation of volume 1. He was assisted in the latter task by Charles Longuet, who had married Marx's daughter Jenny on October 10.

VI
1873-1883

1873   After a brief economic upswing, business begins to fear overproduction; the panic develops into a general economic crisis in Europe. As before, Europe's recession is preceded by a commercial slump in America.

—   The Prussian parliament passes the so-called May Laws, requiring candidates for the priesthood to submit to state examinations and follow a prescribed course of study. Further, these laws, which form part of the *Kulturkampf* (*see* above, p. 192), also make it easier for a person to leave the Church and ease ecclesiastical punishment.

—   The three emperors who met the preceding year in Berlin now conclude an alliance, the *Dreikaiserbund*, in which they agree to isolate France from the European diplomatic consortium and to diminish rivalries between themselves for the sake of hegemony in the Balkan region.

—   In face of widespread political dissension, the Spanish king abdicates and the Republic is proclaimed. However, the prevailing chaos makes it impossible to constitute a government; civil war ensues. Dictatorial powers are usurped by Emilio Castelar, while uprisings are instigated by the Carlists, supporters of the pretender Don Carlos and by the Alfonsists, partisans of his brother.

1874   The *World Postal Union* is established at an international conference held in Switzerland.

—   At the *Reichstag* elections in Germany 6 members of the *SPAD* (Eisenach Party) win seats in the parliament along with 3 members of the Lassallean *ADAV*.

—   Gladstone's liberal ministry is defeated at the polls in England and Disraeli becomes the new Prime Minister. This same year he passes a measure of social legislation which limits the length of the working-day.

—   In Spain Castelar resigns and is succeeded by Marshall Serrano, whose government proclaims Alfonso king. The country is not freed from Carlist harassment until 1876, when Don Carlos himself is expelled from the country.

1875   Disraeli passes a Public Health Act and an Artisans' Dwelling Act and repeals the 1871 Criminal Law Amendment which prohibited certain strike actions (i.e. picketing).

—   At a congress in Gotha, Germany, the two rival working class parties, the *SDAP* and the *ADAV*, unite to found the *Sozialdemokratische Arbeiterpartei Deutschlands* (Social-Democratic Workers' Party of Germany). Their platform, the Gotha Programme, calls for government aid for projected production co-operatives and for free general education. It demands, further, that the working class be granted the right to form coalitions and that social and factory laws be passed.

—   Russia signs a convention with Japan by which it acquires the island of Sachalin and Japan the Kurile Islands.

1876   The first French labour congress is held in Paris. Present are representatives of the labour unions, co-operatives and mutual aid societies.

—   Plekhanov and others in St Petersburg who support a revolutionary transformation of Russian society form a secret society which is first known as the 'narodniki' or 'troglodytes' but later assumes the designation 'Land and Liberty' (*Zemliia i voliia*).

—   Bulgarian Christians in Herzegovina and Bosnia rebel against the treatment to which they are subjected by the Moslems and by the Porte. Serbia and Montenegro aid the insurgents, whereupon the Serbo-Turkish War is declared. England and Russia attempt to mediate and to effect reforms in the Turkish rule. The Great 1877 Powers sign the London Protocol against the protest of Turkey who refuses to comply with the reforms it specifies. Russia declares war on Turkey and occupies Rumania. Victories at Plevna, Schipka Pass and Sophia strengthen Russia's foothold in Turkey and the Czar's troops gradually approach Constantinople.

— A religious issue provokes a government crisis in France under Prime Minister MacMahon. The dissident parliament is dissolved and new elections held. Although the republican, anti-clerical factions win a clear victory, MacMahon is unwilling to constitute a republican cabinet and re-establishes the old monarchist one. Parliament refuses to acknowledge government

— legislation until MacMahon submits to their pressure. Sweeping changes are made in the administration, a striking success for the republicans' key man, Léon Gambetta.

— The British Parliament proclaims Queen Victoria Empress of India.

— At the *Reichstag* elections the Social-Democratic Party wins 9% of the votes cast and 12 seats in parliament.

— At Birmingham, England, Joseph Chamberlain organises a new National Liberal Federation, based on the principle of democratic local organisations.

1878 With Constantinople endangered, Turkey decides to negotiate. At San Stefano Russia thus lays down the following conditions for peace: (1) Montenegro, Serbia and Rumania are to become independent; (2) Bulgaria is to remain under the sovereignty of the Porte but be granted a Christian prince; (3) Turkey is to institute religious reforms and pay an indemnity in money and land to Russia. However, these conditions arouse the displeasure of Austria and Britain, who feel threatened by the prospect of increased Russian power in the Balkans. Threatening the Czar with war, Disraeli brings about his participation at a congress in Berlin, the objective of which is to modify the provisions of the San Stefano Peace. The territorial divisions of the latter are reduced, thereby restoring the European part of Turkey. Austria is given the protectorate over Herzegovina and Bosnia; Montenegro, Serbia and Rumania gain their independence; and political equality is proclaimed in all territories separated from Turkey as well as in Turkey itself.

1878   After two unsuccessful attempts on the life of the Prussian king a law is passed forbidding both socialist organisations and newspapers and giving the government the authority to expel persons who represent a danger to the state. Despite the Anti-Socialist Law, which is to be valid until the end of the 1870s, the social-democrats win 9% of the *Reichstag* votes and 9 mandates.

—   The student Bogoljubov, who had been arrested for demonstrating with the *Zemliia i voliia*, refuses to salute the city prefect Trepov as the latter visits the St Petersburg prison in July 1877. Bogoljubov is beaten and removed to a foul and humid dungeon, where he spends several weeks. In January 1878, to avenge this act, the young Vera Zasulich—at 27 she has already had ten years of revolutionary experience—shoots and seriously wounds Trepov, letting herself be arrested immediately thereafter. At the trial, held in April, she is acquitted by a sympathetic jury and flees the country to live in Geneva.

1879   Germany and Austria-Hungary sign a Vienna Alliance, agreeing to support one another with all their military power in case of an attack by Russia. They also pledge benevolent neutrality in case of attack by any other state unless Russia should support the aggressor.

—   The resignation of MacMahon and his replacement by Jules Grévy marks the transition to a republican presidency in France.

—   The French labour party holds a second congress at Marseilles. Under the influence of Jules Guesde the delegates approve a programme based on the principles of collectivist socialism.

—   In Ireland a Land League is founded to defend the economic interests of the Irish peasantry. Banned by the government in 1881, it continues to operate secretly until the late 1880s.

— The St Petersburg 'Land and Liberty' movement is succeeded by a group called *Narodnaia Voliia* (The Will of the People). This secret society, too, tries to assassinate the Czar, but the attempt misfires.

1880 *Narodnaia Voliia* makes another attempt on the life of Alexander II, but the bomb which explodes in the dining room of the Winter Palace in St Petersburg leaves him unscathed.

— The Anti-Socialist Law in Germany is renewed for another ten years.

— Gladstone is returned as Prime Minister of Britain, pledged to extend the county franchise.

— A new French ministry under Charles de Freycinet passes a series of anti-clerical measures directed in particular against the Jesuits, who are expelled from the country. Public education is secularised and the participants in the 1871 Commune are finally granted political amnesty.

1881 Henry Hyndman establishes the Democratic Federation in England. Two years later, in 1883, he will be joined by William Morris in re-constituting the organisation as the Social Democratic Federation.

— Again, despite the Anti-Socialist Law, the German social-democrats with 6.1% of the votes and 12 seats in the *Reichstag*.

— France extends her colonial possessions with the occupation of Tunis. The Treaty of Bardo secures her protectorate over this territory, which has long been the object of rivalry with Italy because of the latter's commercial interests there.

— Russian emigrants in Switzerland, among them Vera Zasulich, Plekhanov and Akselrod, form an organis-ation of revolutionary propaganda. They are known under the name of their journal *Cherny Peredel* (The Black Redistribution).

— In St Petersburg, meanwhile, the terrorist group *Narodnaia Voliia* assassinates Alexander II. Under the reign of his successor, his son Alexander III, the group is finally liquidated. In the East the territorial expansion of Russia continues with the subjugation of Tekke-Turkmenen.

1881   With the participation of the new Czar, the *Dreikaiserbund* of 1873 is renewed in order to prevent France from establishing close diplomatic relations with Russia and thus threatening German and Austro-Hungarian security.

1882   A third partner, Italy, joins the 1879 Alliance and is promised military aid if attacked by France. Italy fears disruption of her North African trade relations as a result of the Treaty of Bardo.

—   Rumania joins the Triple Alliance with Germany, Austria and Italy.

—   The Fabian Society is founded in England with a programme of municipal socialism and state control over labour conditions.

—   The German parliament passes the first national laws for a system of general health insurance.

—   The Russian emigrants in Geneva found the first Marxist party *Osvobozhdeniia truda* (Liberation of Labour).

THE AMERICAS

1874-76 After the death of the Mexican president Benito Juarez, a prolonged struggle for the succession ensues. Ultimately Porfirio Diaz is elected president and restores order to the country until his death in 1911.

1877   Railroad workers organise a strike in the United States.

1882   The American Congress passes the first laws restricting immigration.

1883   North American telegraph operators and glass blowers conduct successful strikes.

ASIA AND AFRICA

1877   Britain quells the resistance of South African colonialists and annexes the territory of the Transvaal Boers.

1878-80 A third uprising of the Afghans against British occupation begins. Royal forces put down the revolt and set up an ameer (Mohammedan chieftain) who is favourably disposed towards the Crown as against Russia. British troops are then withdrawn from the country.

1880 The Boers repudiate the British annexation of their land and war erupts in South Africa. British troops suffer an early reversal.

1881 France continues to extend its colonial empire by capturing the city of Hanoi in Tonkin. In 1884 war is declared between France and China.

— Gladstone negotiates peace with the Boer settlers, granting them independence within the British empire but reserving to parliament the right to veto treaties which they conclude.

1882 At Alexandria an Egyptian uprising against the presence of British, Greek and Italian consuls occurs. The movement is answered by a British bombardment of the port and occupation of Suez. France is at the time preoccupied by incidents elsewhere and thus, by default, Egypt becomes a British protectorate.

— Under the pretext of suffering from prejudicial trade laws passed by the government of Madagascar, France attempts to negotiate a new trade agreement. Failing
1883 to obtain the desired results, the French send troops to occupy the country.

SCIENTIFIC AND TECHNOLOGICAL PROGRESS

1876 Alexander Graham Bell completes his work on the invention of the telephone.

1877 Nikolaus August Otto introduces a silent, internal combustion gas engine, the first four-stroke engine to use compression.

— The first refrigerated transport vehicles are put into use in the United States.

— Thomas Edison constructs the first phonograph.

1878 Edison creates the first incandescent electric lamp.

1880   Louis Pasteur isolates the germ of chicken cholera and prepares the first vaccination for fowls.

—   The St Gothard tunnel between Switzerland and Italy is completed.

1882   Marcel Deprez realises the first long-distance conduction of electrical energy.

IMPORTANT BOOKS PUBLISHED

1873   François Guizot: *Histoire de la France.*
1873-77 Leo Tolstoy: *Anna Karenina.*
1874   Léon Walras: *Eléments d'économie politique pure.*
—   Albert F. E. Schäffle: *Die Quintessenz des Socialismus.**
1875   Sir Henry Sumner Maine: *Lectures on the Early History of Institutions.**
1876   Peter Lavrov: *Gosudarstvennyi element v budushchem obshchestve* (The State Element in Future Society).*
—   L. T. Townsend: *The Chinese Problem.**
1877   L. H. Morgan: *Ancient Societies or Researches in the Lines of Human Progress.**
—   John Richard Green: *History of the English People.*
1879   Henry George: *Progress and Poverty.**
—   Heinrich von Treitschke: *Geschichte Deutschlands im 19. Jahrhundert.*
—   John Stuart-Glennie: *Europe and Asia.*
—   Jules Guesde: *Collectivisme et Révolution.**
—   Maxime Kovalevsky: *Obchtchinnoiie zemlevadienniie* (Rural Property).*
1882   V. V. Vorontsov: *Sud'by kapitalizma v Rossii* (The Fate of Capitalism in Russia).*
1883-85 Friedrich Nietzsche: *Also sprach Zarathustra.*

KARL MARX
1873-1883

1873 It is perhaps extreme to term the last decade of Marx's life
'a slow death', as his biographer Franz Mehring and others
after him have done; yet this long period of illness was certainly
one of agony and decline as well. There was scarcely a day when
he did not suffer from fierce headaches, chronic hepatitis, bronchial or pulmonary infections or furunculosis. High cerebral
blood tension, and the resulting danger of apoplexy, forced him to
reduce his work day to a minimum; he made frequent trips to
the seaside and to mineral springs, hoping to restore his health.
He seemed, however, to be unaware of his deteriorating physical
state, expected improvement to come and read with a passion
that betrayed his invincible belief in a future period of renewed
creativity, when he would accomplish all his unfinished projects.
He filled about fifty notebooks with excerpts from his readings—
nearly 30,000 pages covered with his minuscule handwriting.
The tons of material which he consumed and collected amazed
Engels, who continued to be Marx's greatest ally in the proletarian struggle and his most intrepid defender against the
calumnious attacks from the jealous and threatened bourgeoisie.
Marx resumed time and again the work on volume 2 of *Capital*
without ever finishing the manuscript as planned. Apart from
circulars, speeches and other short compositions, Marx's writing
was restricted to his correspondence.

In January he composed a number of brief writings: On the
3rd the London *Times* published his refutation of an article
in the same paper, which had insinuated that he was the
'autocrat' of the proletarian movement; for the Italian
Almanacco Repubblicano per l'anno 1874 he wrote an article

on 'Political Indifference', which was published at the end of the year. This article consisted of a critique on the Proudhonian and Bakuninist doctrine according to which the working class should abstain from political action. The result of these principles—proclaimed as 'freedom, autonomy and anarchy'—would be simply the social liquidation of the worker. Marx underlined the necessity of a two-fold fight by the working class: first, through economic movements, such as coalitions and strikes, and secondly political means, i.e. the struggle for political ascendancy, the replacement of the bourgeois dictatorship with the revolutionary dictatorship of the proletariat, accomplished when necessary by means of force and violence (MEW 18: 299f.). Further, he composed an 'Afterword' for the second edition of *Capital*, volume 1, which was published in May by Meissner, and used this opportunity to thank Kugelmann for his valuable suggestions on a more lucid presentation of the value theory. Marx quoted at length from the Russian economist I. I. Kaufman and subscribed to his definition of the dialectic method used in *Capital*, emphasising that this method is the direct opposite of Hegel's, for whom the thought process was the demiurge of reality. 'For me,' Marx wrote, 'the world of thought is nothing more than the material world transposed and translated in the human mind' (*Capital*, vol. 1 : 27). It is the function of rational dialectics to comprehend and affirm the existing state of things while recognising at the same time the negation of that state and its inevitable break-up.

... it regards every historically developed social form as in fluid movement, and therefore takes into account its transient nature not less than its momentary existence; ... it lets nothing impose upon it, and is in its essence critical and revolutionary (*Capital*, vol. 1 : 28).

In the name of the British Federal Council Marx wrote a circular in answer to the attacks from the Hales faction, which was attempting to split the Council and itself assume leadership (*International Herald*, Jan. 11). Later, in February, Marx informed Bolte in New York about the congress which these English secessionists had held and at the same time criticised the decision of the NY General Council to expel the entire Jura Federation from the IWA. While the Council might use its power to suspend groups, if secessionists seriously desired to break away from the International there was no need to expel them: the GC had only to affirm the fact of their separation from the IWA! This was illustrated by the Hague Congress, whose great achievement, Marx wrote, 'was to drive the rotten elements to the point where *they excluded themselves*, that is, they withdrew. The procedure of the General Council threatens to ruin this effect' (Feb. 12).

Marx corresponded regularly with Danielson in St Petersburg and received a number of works in Russian from his economist friend, which permitted him to undertake a study of Nikolaus Ziber on Ricardo's theory of value and capital, Alexei Golovachev and Alexander Skrebitsky on the peasant question during the reign of Alexander II. While studying the history of communal property, Marx came to the question of its genesis and development as debated in the 1850s by the historian Ivan Beliayev and Boris Chicherin, a philosopher with liberal tendencies (March). Danielson sent Marx an extensive, critical review of the literature on this problem, in particular on the Russian agricultural community, the *obshchina* (May 22).

Suffering continually from severe headaches and insomnia, Marx decided to go to Manchester in May to consult Engels's friend and personal physician Dr Eduard Gumpert. He was advised to limit his working hours to four a day. During his stay in Manchester he received a letter from Engels in which the latter disclosed his recent reflections on the dialectics of natural science. Bodies are inseparable from their movements and can be observed and studied only in their dynamic relations to one another: 'Knowledge of the different forms of movement is the knowledge of bodies. The investigation of these different forms of motion is therefore the chief task of natural science' (May 30). On the margins of this letter were notes written by Engels's friend Carl Schorlemmer, a chemist and Manchester professor, who recorded his agreement with the points made on the relation of motion to the various branches of natural science. Marx reserved comment until he had an opportunity to discuss the matter with Schorlemmer and Samuel Moore. In the meanwhile he and Moore (in Manchester) discussed the possibility of determining mathematically the laws of crisis in capitalist production on the basis of tables for the development of prices, discount rates and other criteria (Marx to Engels, May 31).

Since Marx's health had made him incapable of pursuing all

his old activities with the same intensity, Engels had taken on a great part of their correspondence dealing with the working class movement. Writing in both their names to August Bebel on June 20, Engels advised the SDAP on its strategy in dealing with the ADAV and the Lassalleans. The SDAP must keep in mind its long-term goal, i.e. to work effectively within the working class, in view of which goal the splinter groups or sects such as the Lassalleans were not only unimportant but could also be detrimental to the real movement, should they be incorporated into it. 'We must not let ourselves be fooled by the cry for "unity". Those who use this word the most are the greatest troublemakers, such as the Swiss Jura-Bakuninists just at the moment, the instigators of all dissention, who cry for nothing more loudly than for unity.' Engels remarked that Hegel was the first who said that 'a party proves itself victorious by being able to tolerate divisions'. The proletarian movement would pass through various stages of development, leaving various groups and individuals behind it: 'this alone explains why the "solidarity of the proletariat" manifests itself in actuality through different party groupings everywhere, which fight one another to the death just as the Christian sects did during the worst persecutions of the Roman Empire'.

Between July and October Marx continued his studies of agricultural property relations in Russia and read works sent by Danielson and written by such historians and publicists as Beliayev (*Krestiane na Rusi*—The Peasants in Russia), Vasily I. Sergeevich, V. Skaldin. He continued correcting the Roy translation of *Capital* and, with Engels, composed the concluding remarks for a pamphlet on the *Alliance*, prepared in French by Engels and Lafargue. The Engels-Lafargue publication appeared in London and Hamburg at the beginning of September and reported on both Bakunin's activities in Europe and the *Alliance* conspiracies in Spain, France, Italy and Switzerland. It contained the text of the infamous 'revolutionary catechism', found in the papers of Nechayev and attributed to Bakunin. In the conclusion Marx and Engels compared the achievements of the two organisations, the IWA and the *Alliance*. The latter's 'high-sounding phrases on autonomy and free federation and all their war cries against the General Council were nothing more than a mask for their true purpose: the disorganisation of the International and thus its subjection to the secret, hierarchic and autocratic control of the *Alliance'* (MEW 18:440). Also included in this pamphlet, entitled simply *The Alliance de la démocratie socialiste and the International Working Men's Association*, was Bakunin's 'Appeal to the Officers of the Russian Army' (1870). Here Bakunin went as far as to praise the virtues of secret organisation 'which finds its strength in the discipline, passionate devotion and self-abnegation of its members and in their obedience to a *unique* omniscient *committee*, known to no one' (MEW 18:433).

Marx and Engels decided not to attend the IWA Congress held in Geneva in September and predicted that it would be a fiasco, albeit an 'inevitable' one: America and England could send no delegates, the latter for financial reasons; the Italians, French, Spanish and Germans had also refused the invitation and it therefore became clear that the Congress would assume a purely local character. In view of the present conditions in Europe and this weak demonstration of solidarity Marx concluded that it was time to let the formal organisation of the International more or less dissolve while maintaining the Council to prevent its falling into the hands of 'idiots' or 'adventurers'. However:

Events and the unavoidable development and complication of things will spontaneously assure the rebirth of the International in an improved form. Meanwhile it will suffice to keep the ties with the most useful elements in the different countries from slipping out of one's hands, but otherwise not to care a whit about Geneva's local decisions and simply ignore them (Marx to Sorge, Sept. 27).

On September 2 Jenny Marx-Longuet's first child was born. Since the two Lafargue children had died in 1872, little Charles Longuet became Marx's sole living grandchild. The same month Marx sent copies of the new edition of *Capital* to Herbert Spencer and Charles Darwin. Darwin acknowledged the receipt of this volume with a note to the effect that he understood little of the subject, yet he surmised: 'Though our studies have been so different, I believe that we both earnestly desire the extension of knowledge, and that this in the long run is sure to add to the happiness of Mankind' (Oct. 1, IRSH, IX, 1964, part 3, p. 465).

Marx and his daughter Eleanor travelled to Harrogate on November 24, where they spent 3 weeks drinking the waters. Marx, who was suffering from chronic cephalitis, was examined by Dr Gumpert in Manchester and warned that he risked an apoplectic attack. Gumpert forbade him to work and recommended long and vigorous walks at the seaside. Despite these efforts at treatment, Marx's bout of furunculosis continued after his return to London.

Kugelmann wrote to Marx on December 28, reporting that *Capital* had recently been reviewed in the journal *Im neuen Reich* and that through Miquel he had learned that there would probably be no danger of police persecution if Marx returned to Germany to live, provided he refrained from political demonstrations.

1874   Marx resumed his studies for *Capital* and the readings in Russian. He was particularly absorbed in the problems of the agricultural sector, for book III, including plant physiology and the theory of chemical fertilizers. He also examined in detail the official publications of the English government (blue books) on recent economic problems and theory.

In March he received a visit from Lopatin, who passed on to him a series of articles by Ziber on 'Marx's Economic Theory'. During this month Marx read Bakunin's *Gossudarstvennost i anarkhia* [Statehood and Anarchy] published in 1873 in Geneva, and excerpted from it, while making extensive commentaries on selected passages. He was especially interested in Bakunin's views on the 'anarchist' Slav peoples as opposed to the Germans, whom he termed '*étatists*'. Bakunin wrote that 'the Germans seek their life and freedom within the state; for the Slavs the state is a grave. They seek their emancipation outside the state not only by fighting against the German state, but by an all-embracing popular revolt against every state through social revolution' (MEW 18:609). He attributed to Marx the notion of a 'people's state', i.e. a hierarchical government controlled by a small intellectual élite which imposed its will on the masses. Bakunin also dealt with the 'national' German hatred of Russia, with panslavism, the Polish Question and the Russo-German alliance. He made a vicious personal attack against Marx and the 'Marxists', calling Marx a 'Hebrew' who 'unites in himself, one might say, all the virtues and all the defects of this talented race, ... extraordinarily ambitious and vain, quarrelsome, intolerant and as absolute as Jehovah ... vengeful to the point of madness' (MEW 18:626) and capable of the basest intrigues to augment his own power, influence or position. Marx remarked that Bakunin:

> would like the European social revolution, whose economic basis is capitalist production, to take place at the level of the Russian or Slavic agrarian peoples and pastoral tribes and not surpass this level... Not the economic conditions but the *will* is the basis of his social revolution (MEW 18:633f.).

Marx wrote in his notes that radical social revolution is possible 'only where the industrial proletariat under capitalist production has assumed a significant position in the masses'. To be victorious a social revolution must be able to accomplish as much for the modern peasantry as the French Revolution did for the peasants in its time. Marx countered Bakunin's attack on the label 'scientific socialism' as applied to Marx's writings, saying that he had never used this term 'except in contrast to utopic socialism', such as that of Bakunin and Proudhon, which put unrealistic fantasies into people's heads 'instead of limiting itself to the science which recognises the self-produced social movement of the people' (MEW 18:636).

In April and May Marx again spent three weeks at the seaside in Ramsgate. Dr Gumpert, whom Marx visited in Manchester, advised him to take the waters at Karlsbad. After returning to London on May 5 he went back to work on the French translation of *Capital* and finished all but the last three instalments before leaving again for a short stay at Ryde on the Isle of Wight with his wife Jenny.

In June and July news came from Germany that sympathy for Eugen Dühring was steadily increasing within the ranks of the social democrats. Disturbed by this news, Marx and Engels wrote to Liebknecht, Blos and Hepner to warn of the dangers inherent in this tendency, distancing themselves from Dühring's views as expressed his *Kritische Geschichte der Nationalökonomie und des Sozialismus* (1871).

Towards the end of their stay at Ryde the Marxes were informed of the sudden death of little Charles Longuet, a blow which shook them both profoundly. Marx confided in Kugelmann that:

> In this respect I am not as stoic as in others, and family suffering always hit me very hard. The more one is cut off from the external

world, as I am, the more one is emotionally involved in one's own most intimate circle (Aug. 4).

In letters to both Kugelmann and Sorge, Marx reported on the present standing of the proletarian movement in Europe and America. In particular Marx told Sorge that the American movement, despite political and economic handicaps, seemed to be progressing. Its greatest obstacle, he noted, was 'the professional politician who immediately falsifies every new movement and seeks to transform it into a new 'commercial enterprise' (May 18). In England the International was practically dead, Marx wrote to Sorge, and the only action going on was among the agricultural workers, while the industrial proletariat was trying to rid itself of its leaders! He regretted that they had not been elected to Parliament, which would have been the 'surest way to get rid of the pack'. Europe seemed heading for a general war, he added: 'We must pass through that before thinking about any decisive external effectiveness of the European working class' (Aug. 4).

Having now decided to take the trip to Karlsbad, Marx applied once again for British citizenship, which would facilitate his passage into Austrian territory without danger of arrest (Aug. 1). His demand was turned down on August 29 for a reason not communicated to the applicant, viz that 'This man was not loyal to his king'. Shortly before his own departure Marx accompanied his daughter Jenny to Eastbourne, where she joined Engels and his wife for a stay at the seaside and a tour of the island of Jersey. A letter which Marx wrote to his daughter to Eastbourne reveals how much he was touched by the loss of his grandchild:

The house is dead now, since the little angel no longer fills it with life. I miss him at every step. It hurts me so to think of him and yet how can one banish from one's mind the thought of such a sweet, fine little fellow. But I do hope, my child, that to please your old father, you are keeping up your courage (Aug. 14).

Accompanied by Eleanor, who had recently suffered a nervous breakdown, Marx left for Karlsbad on August 19. There, father and daughter diligently followed their doctors' orders taking the waters at this famous mineral spa. Eleanor reported to her sister Jenny on September 5:

Still I think Papa is better, and the waters are sure to have a good effect. We are very exact indeed in all our duties. Fancy Papa being ready dressed and at the 'brunnen' [spring] by six o'clock, frequently still earlier! We take long walks, and altogether get on very well here (quoted in Tsuzuki, *The Life of Eleanor Marx*, p. 37).

They were in the company of the Kugelmanns and a number of the latter's friends, mostly doctors of medicine like Kugelmann. Marx grew irritable from the effects of the strenuous treatment and was soon unable to tolerate the philistine milieu in which he found himself, even less the pedantic ways of his constant companion Dr Kugelmann. Their friendship suddenly grew very distant, as Marx took issue with Kugelmann's attitude towards his wife. To Engels he wrote that:

This arch-pedantic, bourgeois, narrow-minded philistine deludes himself, namely in imagining that his wife is unable to understand, to comprehend his Faust-like nature, full of higher *Weltanschauung*, and he torments the little lady in a most abominable fashion, although actually she is superior to him in every way (Sept. 18).

However he reported spending pleasant hours in the company of Frau Kugelmann's brother Max Oppenheim of Prague, who invited Marx to visit him at his home on the return trip.

While Marx was in Karlsbad the 7th annual International Congress of the IWA was held in Brussels (Sept. 7-13). There was an open confrontation between the anarchist 'anti-authoritarian' delegates from Belgium, Spain and the Jura and, standing alone as partisans of political engagement, Eccarius and the two German delegates. Sorge, who did not attend the congress and had submitted his resignation as secretary general of the Council, vainly attempted to have the GC adjourned indefinitely. Replying to Sorge's report in Marx's absence, Engels supported Sorge's step and added that it marked the end of the old International:

And this is good. It belonged to the period of the Second Empire, when the oppression everywhere in Europe proscribed unity and abstention from all internal polemics to the newly reawakening workers' movement (Sept. 12 & 17).

For ten years the IWA had served the development of the European working class; its old form had now grown obsolete, for the movement had intensified both in depth and in breadth. Engels concluded: 'I think the next International—after Marx's writings have been at work for some years—will be directly communist and will openly proclaim our principles' (*ibid.*).

Eleanor and her father left Karlsbad on September 21, travelling via Dresden and Leipzig, where they met Liebknecht, Blos and other representatives of the SDAP. Liebknecht proposed to Marx to reprint his *Revelations on the Communist Trial in Cologne* in the SDAP organ *Volksstaat* (Oct.-Jan. 1875). He was also interested in bringing out new editions of the *Misère* and *The Holy Family*. Passing then to Berlin, they visited Jenny Marx's brother Edgar von Westphalen and thereafter to Hamburg where Marx spoke with Meissner and with other members of the SDAP.

On November 8 an outsider, August Glib, informed Marx and Engels of a pending *rapprochement* between the SDAP and the Lassallean ADAV. A conference had been convened, at which it was planned to adopt the basic elements of the IWA programme into their statutes and strike out the 'immediate demands', formulated in the Eisenach programme.

At the close of the year Marx returned to his Russian studies, reading N. G. Chernyshevsky's works *Cavaignac* and *Pisma bez adresa* [Letters without Addresses].

1875 For the republication of the *Revelations* in the *Volksstaat* Marx wrote an 'Afterword', dated January 8, in which he reviewed the events of 1851-52 in light of two decades of experience with the working class movement. Now he saw them as part of the general atmosphere of frustration, which followed in the wake of the 1848 defeats. In part, both the comportment of Willich and Schapper and the bitterness of Marx's own attack on these 'involuntary accomplices of our common enemy' could be explained by their thwarted revolutionary energies. The principles for which they had all fought in those days had in the meanwhile been triumphant in the statutes of the IWA. The Cologne trial had thus become for Marx a symbol of the state's utter impotence to check or restrain the development of the working class movement. 'Society,' he concluded, 'will not reach its equilibrium until it revolves around the sun of labour' (MEW 18:570).

With Engels, Marx participated on January 23 in a meeting held in commemoration of the Polish uprisings of 1863-64. Marx addressed the audience on the relations of the working class to Poland and explained the proletarian interest in and sympathy for the Polish cause as having three sources: their natural sympathy for oppressed peoples; Poland's specific geographic, military and historic position as buffer between the great powers of Russia, Prussia and Austria; and most importantly, the fact that 'Poland is not only the sole Slavic race, but also the only European people which has fought and is still fighting as a *cosmopolitan soldier of the revolution*' (MEW 18: 574). Poland, who shed its blood in the American war of independence, the French Revolution and all other European revolts including the recent Commune, had therefore but one true ally in Europe: the party of the working class.

In January Marx finished the last corrections and revisions for the French edition of *Capital*. On April 28 he wrote an 'Epilogue' which followed the last instalment in mid-May. Marx explained that certain changes had been made—in the form of the argumentation and addition of material—in order to make it more intelligible to the French reader. Therefore, he observed, 'whatever the literary defects of this French edition may be, it possesses a scientific value independent of the original and should be consulted even by readers familiar with German' (*Capital*, vol. 1: 22).

At the beginning of the year Marx passed on to Engels a publication by Peter Tkachev entitled *An Open Letter to Mr. F. Engels, Author of the Articles on Emigrant Literature*, remarking that Engels should 'lash into it in a light-hearted manner'. In reply to Tkachev Engels then included in his series on 'Emigrant Literature' which appeared in *Der Volksstaat* a number of articles subtitled 'Social Problems in Russia' (Apr. 16-21). This material was later reprinted as a pamphlet and accompanied by introductory remarks. Engels refuted Tkachev's contention that Russia would more easily and more quickly produce a social revolution than the West European countries. In order to have a proletarian victory, Engels argued, there must be not only a proletariat but also a bourgeoisie which has developed the productive forces to an extent that will permit class differences to be eliminated henceforth. Therefore, for Tkachev to say that this revolution would be more easily accomplished in Russia 'only proves that he still has to learn the ABCs of socialism' (MEW 18: 557).

The proposed union of the Eisenach socialists and the Lassallean party became imminent; a programme was drafted and sent to Marx and Engels for their comments. Engels wrote in both their names to Bebel and sharply criticised this 'weak and insipid' text. Should it be accepted, Engels remarked, they would be unable to support the party and, moreover, would be forced to consider seriously taking a public stand against it. In addition to the faulty constructions it placed upon the phrasing in the IWA statutes, the programme lacked any mention of the real proletarian organisation in trade unions and failed to include the 'first condition of all freedom: that all functionaries be responsible for all their official actions to every citizen before the ordinary courts and according to normal law' (March 18-28). Engels felt that on the whole this programme was a step backwards from the Eisenach platform since it incorporated Lassallean 'socialist' measures and would certainly lead to a rift in the party within a year.

On May 5 Marx wrote his own critique of the programme in a letter addressed to Wilhelm Bracke, a leading member of the SDAP and Reichstag deputy. Point for point, he analysed the new programme, known as the Gotha Programme, and within the framework of his critique developed several important aspects of his views on the future communist social organisation. He stressed, for example, the international scope of the economic struggle carried on by the working class, its goal not a more 'equitable' distribution of the products of labour, but a fundamental change in the production relations themselves. From this point, Marx proceeded to a brief discussion of the problem of distribution in an emergent communist society, i.e., in one which has introduced common ownership of the means of production but not yet developed the full potential of the system. What the individual producer gives society in one form he receives from it in another. 'Right' is here equality according to an equal standard, labour, yet it is inequality in respect of the actual contents of what the individual receives, since human productive capacity varies greatly. Marx concludes that:

Right by its very nature can only consist in the application of an equal standard; but unequal individuals (and they would not be different individuals if they were not unequal) are only measureable by an equal standard in so far as they are brought under an equal point of view, are taken from one *definite* side only ... (MEW 19:21).

Right should therefore be unequal instead of equal. This difficulty of the first phase of communist social development would, however, be overcome after the division of labour and antithesis between intellectual and manual labour had disappeared—after labour had been transformed from a means of life to the 'prime necessity of life'. Only when the individual is finally permitted an 'all-round development' of his capacities, increasing society's productive force in correspondence with his own development, 'only then can the narrow horizon of bourgeois right be completely superseded and may society inscribe on its banner: From each according to his ability, to each according to his needs' (MEW 19:21).

In his critique of the Gotha conception of a 'free state', Marx pointed out that the state is rooted in bourgeois society and production relations. The transformation of society into communist society will also affect the state and, during the transitional period, the political form will necessitate 'the revolutionary dictatorship of the proletariat' (MEW 19:28). The class struggle leading to this dictatorship would be fought in the arena of the democratic republic, the last form of the state under bourgeois production relations. Quite in contrast to Marx's picture of the future society, the programme of the SDAP was 'tainted through and through by the servile belief in the state of Lassalle's sect, or, what is no better, by democratic miraclefaith ... both equally remote from socialism' (MEW 19:31).

In the last half of the year Marx frequently met Lavrov and exchanged views on books and on world events. In a postscript to one of their conversations on Traube's experiments in creating artificial cells, Marx wrote to Lavrov that that was a great and most appropriately timed step. Helmholtz and others were propagating the doctrine whereby the nuclei of terrestrial life were said to have been created by meteors. 'I detest such explanations that solve a problem by banishing it into another sphere', Marx concluded (June 18).

Again, from August 15 to September 11, Marx was in Karlsbad to take the waters. He returned via Prague, where he paid a short visit to Max Oppenheim. The stay seemed to have done him much good, for, as Engels wrote to Bracke on October 11, he returned 'completely changed, full of energy, fresh, alert and healthy and can now soon return seriously to work'. The Gotha Programme, Engels remarked in the same letter, was enjoying a much better fate than it deserved:

Working men and bourgeois and petit-bourgeois alike read into it what should be there but isn't and no one from either side has come to the idea of publicly examining one of those wonderful sentences as to its real contents. This situation has enabled us to keep silent about it (Oct. 11).

Both before and after his sojourn in Karlsbad Marx spent most of his reading and study time on works connected with Russia, her economic and agricultural situation. He read Alexander Engelhardt on agricultural problems and agrochemistry, Juri Samarin and Theodore Dmitriev on revolutionary conservatism, Kavelin and Alexander Koshelev, and began a study of statistics and documents on the fiscal problems in Russia, after having received ten volumes of reports from the Russian fiscal commission (1872) through Danielson.

Invited by Lavrov to attend the December 4 meeting on Poland organised by Valeri Vrublevsky, Marx was forced to refuse because of his health. However, he wrote Lavrov that his participation would not have added anything new to the views he had already expressed on Poland's situation, 'namely that Poland's emancipation is one of the preconditions for the emancipation of the working class in Europe. The new conspiracies of the Holy Alliance are a renewed proof of this' (Dec. 3).

Sometime in the course of this year Marx had worked out a detailed mathematical scheme for the relation of surplus value to profit, as presented in the third book of *Capital*. In mid-December he wrote to Dietzgen that once he had finished with the 'Economics' he intended to write on the subject of dialectics.

1876   For the most part Marx's readings in this year, and they were considerable, centred around the questions of agriculture, primitive communal property relations and Russian economic relations. In March he read and excerpted from works on physiology by Johannes Ranke and M. J. Schleiden; in May G. L. Maurer on the history of the *Mark* and socage farms (cf. readings for 1868 as well). He made a thorough study of Russian relations of landownership and the money market, of Haxthausen's book on the rural constitution in Russia, took up monographs on Russian history and finally extended his research on primitive communal property relations to Spain and the Slav peoples (Hanssen, Demelich, Utieshenovich and Cardenas). Examining the related field of legal relations, Marx read works on common law, comparative French and Hindu Law. In April he read from two English authors, Carlyle (*Oliver Cromwell's Letters and Speeches*) and Yates (*The Natural History of the Raw Material of Commerce*). For *Capital* he wrote sections dealing with differential rent and rent as the simple interest on capital incorporated into land (book III).

He was invited to speak at a celebration on February 7, honouring the founding of the London Working Men's Educational Society. The roots of this movement which the Society represented began with the League of the Just and the Communist League, Marx informed his audience, and its newest offshoot was the German Social-Democratic party.

In order to extend his study of agricultural relations, property relations in general and credit to further countries, Marx requested Sorge to send him a recent catalogue of books published since 1873 on these topics so that he might procure himself the relevant American literature. He also requested Fränkel in Budapest to send him literature. The latter reported to Marx that he had been arrested in Vienna for participation in the Paris Commune and was soon to stand trial. In the statement he had given to the examining judge Fränkel had insisted that for his actions during the Commune he was responsible only to history and not to a court of law; moreover, the Commune government had been a legitimate one, elected by popular mandate (March 28).

On May 10 Marx became the grandfather of a little boy, Jean Longuet, son of his daughter Jenny and the first of his grandchildren who would live to reach maturity.

While Engels was spending a few days at Ramsgate, he corresponded with Marx on the problem of Eugen Dühring's growing influence among the German social-democrats. Marx suggested that Dühring's work be submitted to a rigorous critical examination. Engels agreed to take on this task and began collecting material on Dühring, whose writing he termed 'high-sounding banalities—nothing more, in between complete nonsense, but everything arranged with a certain talent for his public' (July 25).

Bakunin's death on July 1 occasioned numerous memorials in European papers, one of which, Marx commented in a letter to Engels (July 26), portrayed Bakunin as the ' "giant" of the revolution'. The *Alliance* used this tragic event as the occasion for a reconciliation with the *SDAP*. Liebknecht declared himself favourably disposed to such a development.

On August 15 Marx again arrived in Karlsbad in the company of his daughter Eleanor. Their journey by train via Cologne and Nuremberg had been all but uneventful for the hotels were crowded with music-lovers and Wagner fans headed for the Bayreuth festival and so the two travellers found lodging in neither Nuremberg nor Weiden, where they were finally obliged to spend the night on the benches of the railway station. Marx wrote his daughter Jenny about the phenomenal attraction of Wagner for the German public:

Everywhere you are pestered with the question: What do you think of Wagner? Very characteristic of the Neo-German Prussian Reich's musician: he and his spouse (the one who is separated from Bülow), the cuckold Bülow and their common father-in-law Liszt are living together, all four, in perfect harmony; they embrace, kiss and adore one another and thoroughly enjoy themselves. If, apart from that, you keep in mind that Liszt is a Roman monk and Mme Wagner ... is the 'natural' daughter of Mme d'Agoult (Daniel Stern), then you could not imagine a better *libretto* for Offenbach than this family group with its patriarchal relations (End of Aug./Sept.).

While in Karlsbad Marx received from Lavrov his recent work on *The State Element in Future Society*, which he promised to read at a later date, since his treatment at the waters, long walks in the environs of the city and conversations with new friends consumed his day from morning to evening. He became acquainted with the Jewish historian Heinrich Grätz, with whom he discussed the defects of Russian Czarism. On their return home Marx and his daughter stopped over in Prague for a visit with Oppenheim and then in Kreuznach, where Marx recounted to Eleanor stories from the early days of his marriage.

After returning to London on September 23 Marx concerned himself with finding a publisher for a German edition of Prosper Lissagaray's work, 'the first *authentic* history of the Commune'. presently being brought out by a Brussels publisher. Marx suggested to Wilhelm Bracke in a letter of September 23 that the German translation be started as soon as possible and offered to review and correct the translation himself. The book was important, he assured Bracke, not only for the party but for the German reading public in general.

During Marx's absence the *Revue des deux mondes* had published a critique of *Capital* which for Marx was exemplary proof of the 'idiocy of our bourgeois "thinkers"'. The author, Emile de Laveleye, was 'naïve enough to admit that once one recognised the doctrines of Adam Smith or Ricardo or even—*horrible dictu*—those of Carey and Bastiat, there is no way of avoiding the revolutionary conclusions of "*Capital*"' (to Lavrov, Oct. 7).

With the SDAP now considering the offer of brotherhood tendered by the Geneva anarchists. Marx wrote to warn Liebknecht that these 'incorrigible intrigants', who had systematically worked towards the dissolution of the IWA, would imagine that they could work their way back into the movement in order to continue their destructive role. Apart from party affairs, Marx commented on European politics and emphasised that the SDAP should take a critical stand against Bismarck's foreign policy. The only active European country seemed to be Russia and the source of this stagnation was 'Bismarck's official coquetry with Russia', which paralysed the whole Continent, disarmed Germany and 'damned the latter to the ignominous role it is presently playing, a role which is truly "Europe's disgrace"' (Oct. 7). In England, Marx reported, a new political constellation was in ascendancy: Gladstone and Russell were in retreat and the enlightened working class elements had called a protest meeting against the pro-Panslavic trends within their own ranks. Liebknecht was called upon to treat these themes in his articles for the *Volksstaat*, to expose the 'wretchedness of the traditional bourgeois press in Germany, which although allegedly anti-Russian never dared criticise the foreign policy of Bismarck'. Liebknecht responded to these suggestions with a series of polemical articles on European politics and Russia. Marx also furnished the Urquhartist Charles D. Collet with information on Gladstone's pro-Russian politics, which Collet used in preparing a series for the *Diplomatic Review* (early Nov.).

1877 At the beginning of the year Marx studied the Eastern Question and Gladstone's role in the current Russo-Turkish conflict. In January he read various official documents and examined statistics pertinent to Britain's relations with the East. He also made excerpts from Sir Adolf Slade's book *Turkey and the Crimean War* and finally prepared several articles attacking

Gladstone's pro-Russian foreign policy. Through the mediation of Maltman Barry, journalist for a conservative British paper and former member of the IWA General Council. Marx published these articles anonymously in widely read, conservative London news organs. 'Mr Gladstone and the Russian Intrigue' appeared on February 3 in the *Whitehall Review* and was later reprinted in the *Morning News* and other government journals. The second article, 'Mr Gladstone', was published on March 3 in *Vanity Fair*; on March 10 in the same paper 'The Agitator Unmasked' appeared. Marx exposed, among other things, Gladstone's relations with the 'unofficial agent' of the Russian diplomatic mission in London, Mme Novikov.

Jenny Marx reported to Sorge on January 20 that her husband was very absorbed in these studies and writings and 'highly elated about the firm, honourable stand taken by Mahomet's sons against all the Christian humbugs and hypocritical atrocity mongers. He was convinced that, whatever the outcome of the actual conflict, revolution would break out in Russia itself (cf. Marx to Dr Freund, Jan. 21). Marx was also pleased about the recent electoral victory of the German social-democrats, which 'not only gave our highly esteemed German philistines a rather brutal shock, but the ruling classes in England and France as well' (to F. Fleckles, Jan. 21).

Marx received a letter from his Karlsbad acquaintance Grätz, who thanked him for the copies of his works and said that he especially enjoyed the *Civil War in France*: 'Paris all truth, Versailles all lies. When a man like you pronounces these words of damnation, it is as if the verdict had been delivered at history's Last Judgment' (Feb. 1; IISH). From his own writings Grätz suggested that Marx would be interested in reading about Solomon, a 'hard realist' who preferred this world to the hereafter and 'preached the rehabilitation of the flesh'.

Marx was approached by a young Irish parliamentarian, Keyes O'Clery, who wished to collect information on police and legal persecutions in contemporary Russia. O'Clery wished to present a resolution whereby Russia would be required to make certain reforms in its own system before demanding that they be introduced in Turkey. Marx communicated this request to Lavrov who provided an article with the pertinent information (Marx to Lavrov, March 16).

Shortly before the actual declaration of war between Turkey

and Russia, Marx conjectured in a letter to Bracke that Russia and Prussia entertained a secret agreement which permitted the former to advance its troops through Rumania without inciting the opposition of the Western powers. He noted that 'the working class pays much too little attention to the Eastern Question and forgets that the ministerial policies wantonly play with the life and the money of the people' (Apr. 21). By contrast, sufficient public opposition could put a stop to the Prussian machinations, which most probably planned for another division of Poland or even a war on the side of the Czar.

For health reasons Marx refused an offer to collaborate on a new journal to be edited by Franz Wiede in Switzerland. He explained to Engels that he would very much like to see a 'truly scientific socialist journal' started up to provide a forum for critique and rebuttal, for theoretical discussion and to 'expose the absolute ignorance of the professors and lecturers and at the same time help enlighten the minds of the general readers, working men and bourgeois alike' (July 18). However, he seriously doubted whether Wiede's publication would permit and encourage rigorous theoretical discussion and the 'ruthlessness', which he held to be the first condition of all critique. More probably, it would turn out to be 'bogus-scientific'.

Commenting on the news of a strike movement in America, Marx wrote to Engels that this rebellion, although it would be eventually defeated, might nevertheless promote the constitution of a 'serious working men's party' there (July 25).

The SDAP published a number of articles in its journal Vorwärts (formerly Volksstaat) which depreciated the parliamentary struggle in France for a democratic order. Marx and Engels were roused to oppose this stand on the question of monarchy vs. bourgeois democracy energetically. Writing to Liebknecht on July 2, Engels pointed out that essential to France's development was the establishment of the working men's movement under a bourgeois republican regime and not a monarchy. He argued that, moreover, the 'meaningless dispute about the form of the state' should cease and the republican state exposed as what it really is: 'the classic form of bourgeois rule and simultaneously the source of its own dissolution'.

Engels was now occupied with his articles against Dühring, which were sent to Liebknecht for publication in Vorwärts (1877-78). At the beginning of August Marx finished writing a chapter for Engels dealing with Dühring's views on political economics. Then, for the chapter on socialism, he began investigating various writings by Robert Owen, including *The Revolution in the Mind and Practice of the Human Race*, which in Marx's words contained a resumé of Owen's entire doctrine. He sent Engels Quesnay's *Tabelle économique*, 'in view of the date of its publication one of the most genial generalisations produced by political economy' (to Engels, Aug. 8), and advised him to use it primarily for his own orientation and, for texual clarity, to explain the simple general movements of capital in his own words.

Marx interrupted his studies in August and September for a lengthy stay in the Ahr valley in Germany with his wife and Eleanor. There, all three took the waters and enjoyed the tranquillity of a 'fortunate' region, which had not yet been infected by modern means of transport (Marx to Engels, Aug. 17). Following this treatment, they spent two weeks in the Black Forest and returned to London on September 27.

Marx now recommenced his study of Owen's writings: *The Crisis* (1832-34), *A New View of Society* (1813-14), *Proposed Arrangements for the Distressed Working Classes* (1819). He also continued with his Russian studies, reading and excerpting from works by the Russian economist and statistician I. I. Kaufman. His health permitting, he was investigating Russian conditions on the basis of official and unofficial sources and was convinced, he wrote to Sorge, that revolution was pending in Russia:

All levels of Russian society are now caught in a process of complete economic, moral and intellectual decomposition. This time the revolution is going to start in the East, hitherto the unassailed bulwark of the counter-revolution and its reserve army (Sept. 27).

After various delays in finding a translator for the German edition of Lissagaray's *Histoire de la Commune de 1871*, Marx rejected an unsatisfactory translation prepared by Isolde Kurz and suggested to Bracke that he turn the text over to Wilhelm Blos (one of the *Vorwärts* editors) for completion and revision. In the same letter he criticised the unsatisfactory journalism of the German socialists, especially since the SDAP's reconciliation with the Lassalleans and the followers of Dühring, and referred to the articles in *Vorwärts* as 'juvenile school-book exercises' (Oct. 23).

Beginning sometime in November Marx rewrote the first chapter of book II of *Capital*, for which he had drafted two chapters (XIX and XX, about 70 pages) sometime in the spring. He requested new material from Sorge—a 'blue book' on the Pennsylvania miners (letter to Sorge, Oct. 19)—and from Sigmund Schott (Nov. 3). To Schott he explained the procedure which had been followed in writing *Capital*:

Confidentially speaking, I in fact began 'Capital' in just the reverse (starting with the 3rd, the historic part) of the order in which it is presented to the public, except that the first volume, the one begun last, was immediately prepared for publication while the two others remained in that primitive state characteristic of all research at the outset (Nov. 3).

Marx corresponded with Blos on the translation of Lissagaray's book. In a letter of November 10 he remarked that both he and Engels were utterly indifferent to popularity. During the International he had avoided all attempts to push him into the public eye. As for the so frequently heard accusation of 'authoritarianism', Marx said that he had not joined the Communist League until the passages favourable to the 'cult of authority' had been removed from the statutes.

Sometime in November he prepared a letter to the editor of a Russian journal, *Otetshestvennia Sapisky*, refuting the views presented there by N. K. Michailovsky. Marx disputed Michailovsky's assertion that his theory of capital was a 'universal philosophical theory of the general course of development imposed on all peoples, whatever their historic circumstances' (*Oeuvres* 2:1555). In other words, he made no claim to have developed a philosophical theory of general social development whose chief virtue was supra-historicity. According to Michailovsky Marx also propagated the theory that Russia, in order to attain socialism, must abolish the system of rural communal property and develop along the lines of West European capitalism. In his unpublished reply Marx wrote that his broad studies on Russia had led him to conclude the contrary: if Russia continued the present course of capitalist development, embarked upon in 1861, it would lose 'the best chance history has ever offered to people' to avoid the disastrous vicissitudes of capitalist society (*Oeuvres* 2:1553). This new trend of Russian economic progress was destined to transform its peasantry into proletariat and 'then, once dragged into the turmoil of capitalist economy, it will have to endure the inexorable laws of this system, in the same way as the other profane peoples' (*Oeuvres* 2:1554f.).

November marked the founding in France of Jules Guesde's newspaper of 'scientific socialism', *Egalité*, which declared its support for the republican parliamentary movement and its belief that 'the natural and scientific evolution of humanity is inevitably leading it to the collective appropriation of the land and of the instruments of labour' (Nov. 18).

1878 In this year Marx again consumed a considerable amount of reading material. The focal point of his interest was material pertinent to the third book of *Capital*. On money and banking he read John P. Gassiot's *Monetary Panics and Their Remedies* (1869), Charles Mann's *Paper Money, the Root of All Evil* (1872), A. Walker's *The National Currency and the Money Problem* (1876), along with Pietro Rota and I. I. Kaufman; he also delved into works on the Russian peasant communes, agronomy and geology (James F. W. Johnston, Johann Gottlieb Koppe and Joseph Beete Jukes for the latter two subjects) and read two books sent him personally by their authors: John R. Dakyns's *The Antiquity of Man* (1877) and John K. Ingram's *The Present Position and Prospect of Political Economy* (1878). Mathematics was reintroduced into Marx's study programme sometime this year; he continued his efforts in algebra and higher mathematics until shortly before his death and filled numerous notebooks with remarks and outlines of mathematical theory. Towards the end of this year he read works by Leibniz and Descartes on natural science and mathematics.

With the Eastern Question again a central issue in European politics, Marx was afforded a chance to comment on Russia's role in the East. Requested by Liebknecht to provide information for articles on the Russo-Turkish conflict, Marx produced two lengthy letters on the reasons for this crisis and for its outcome, explaining, moreover, his own standpoint, as follows: (1) After considerable study he was convinced that in Turkey the peasantry, and therefore the mass of the population, was 'the most able and morally the most representative of the European peasantry'; (2) a Russian defeat would have accelerated social revolution in that country and brought change to all Europe.

That the Turks were not triumphant was due both to England's and Austria's betrayal and to the Turks' own failure to produce a revolution at Constantinople. 'A people which does not know how to strike a revolutionary blow at such moments of the most acute crisis is lost.' Russia and Prussia had been in league in this war; with Prussian aid in checking Austria, Russia was able to manoeuvre and only thanks to Russian support was the Bismarck regime maintained in power: 'Russia's defeat, revolution in Russia—that would sound the death knell for Prussia,' Marx concluded. However, seen in a wider perspective, Austria's and Turkey's collapse meant that the old order of post-Napoleonic Europe was crumbling. The break-down would continue to manifest itself in local and then in continental wars which 'will accelerate the *social* crisis—and with it the *defeat* of all these phoney, sword-brandishing powers' (Feb. 4). In his second letter—both were later published as an appendix to Liebknecht's pamphlet *Zur orientalischen Frage oder Soll Europa kosakisch werden?* [On the Eastern Question, or Should Europe Turn Cossack?; March]—Marx commented on the positive results of the Russian victory, i.e. it caused a split in the ranks of England's liberal party. Through the corruption of the trade-union leaders and professional agitators the working class had gradually been assimilated in this party. Now, a Russian victory exposed the true leanings of the liberal leaders and ended the paralysis of the proletariat in England (Feb. 11).

After an attempt on the life of the Prussian Emperor Wilhelm I in May, reprisals were taken against the social-democrats, although the SDAP was in no way involved in the act. One of Bismarck's agents in this anti-socialist campaign was Lothar Bucher, a former member of the IWA. Marx challenged Bucher, in a letter to the *Daily News* on June 12, to avow publicly that the goals and teachings of the working class movement had nothing to do with such acts of political vengeance. The panic created around this incident and the measures against the SDAP, he added, served the sole purpose of facilitating Bismarck's course.

Marx's attention was caught by an article entitled 'The History of the International Working Men's Association', which a former General Council member George Howell had written for the London journal *The XIX Century*. Howell claimed to be telling the story of the rise and fall of the IWA and Marx's role in it and maintained, for example, that Marx had sown seeds of dissention by introducing from the outset 'religious ideas' into the International. In an article which appeared on August 4 in *The Secular Chronicle* Marx replied to Howell with his own view of the International's merits and achievements: 'not with a well-filled treasury but with its intellectual force and selfless energy' had the IWA won a world-wide reputation and historical distinction (MEW 19:147). Although formally disbanded, the working class movement continued to make headway in all of Europe and was entering a higher phase of development, its goals in part achieved. In future, however, 'the working men's international must still undergo many changes before the last chapter of its history is written'.

In October Marx prepared an exposé of Howell's IWA history and Franz Mehring's *Die deutsche Sozialdemokratie* for a book by the English clergyman Moritz Kaufmann on *Utopias; or Schemes of Social Improvement from Sir Thomas More to Karl Marx*. He also provided Maltman Barry with information on German socialism which Barry used in preparing various lectures and articles (Aug.). Finally, he corresponded with another English journalist, John Stuart-Glennie, who was planning a new news organ and wanted material on socialism as one of the political powers of the future (July-Aug.).

The first edition of Engels's *Anti-Dühring* appeared in Leipzig about July 8. Broadly conceived, this work gave a critique of Dühring's philosophical thought, his political economy and socialism from what Engels held to be the Marxian standpoint. He defined this standpoint in the Introduction saying that its two great pillars were Marx's 'discoveries' which 'transformed socialism into science': first, the 'materialist conception of history' and, secondly, 'the revelation of the secret of capitalist production through surplus value' (MEW 20:26). As he explained further in the chapter devoted to capital and surplus value, Marx's 'discovery' of the function of surplus value 'laid bare the mechanism of present-day capitalist modes of production ... exposed the nucleus around which the entire modern social order has crystallised' (MEW 20:190). Engels gave a similar presentation of Marxian theory in a biographical article which he wrote on Marx for the Braunschweig *Volks-Kalender* of 1878.

Marx's daughter Jenny was again delivered of a son on July 4. Like four other Marx grandchildren before him, little Henri

Longuet was not to outlive childhood and died in 1883 at the age of 4. During this summer Marx's wife Jenny was particularly ailing, her symptoms those of the cancer which would ultimately cause her death. Engels's wife Lizzie also became gravely ill and died on September 12. Jenny Marx spent the summer in Worcester, where Marx joined her from September 4-14.

After the second attempt on the life of Emperor Wilhelm, a bill was proposed to the *Reichstag* which would prohibit all socialist organisations and press organs on the grounds that the social-democracy was a threat to the general welfare. Marx was half-decided to prepare for the London *Daily News* a report on the *Reichstag* debates that ensued on September 16-17 concerning the proposed 'socialist law'. On the basis of the official steno-graphic reports he began working out a selection of the parlia-mentary statements and speeches and accompanied the lengthy quotations with his own commentary. After only a few pages he interrupted his work and left the manuscript unfinished and unpublished. It is, nevertheless, relevant to note how Marx would have defended the social-democracy against the attacks of the Prussian government. Refuting the pretended relation between social-democracy and violence, Marx argued that the goal of this movement was simply the emancipation of the working class and the social reversal essential to this end. When the powers-that-be place no obstacles in the path of this historical development, the change may be achieved peacefully. For example:

if in England or in the United States the working class wins the majority in Parliament or Congress, it could then use legal means to abolish the laws and institutions obstructing its development—and this, of course, only to the extent demanded by this social develop-ment. Yet, nevertheless, the 'peaceful' movement might change into a 'violent' one if those interested in retaining the old conditions resist ... (MEW 34:448).

When putting down the legally incontestable movement of the working class majority, the government uses whatever 'legal' means are still in its power and brands the workers as 'rebels'.

Marx had prepared only seven pages for book II of *Capital* during the summer and then interrupted his writing until November, when he informed Danielson that volume 2 would probably be finished in a year's time. Another Russian, the historian Maxim Kovalevsky, met Marx in London shortly after his return from Moscow, where he had taught at the university. He reported on the present commotion in the Russian press, caused by a debate on *Capital* and on the hostile and brutal treatment afforded the Montenegrin students by their Russian hosts (cf. Marx to Engels, Sept. 17 and Marx to Danielson, Nov. 15).

Towards the end of the year Marx made a number of comments on the status and future of the working class movement in America. He predicted that the Americans would try in vain 'to destroy the power of the monopolies and the fatal—as far as the *immediate welfare* of the masses is concerned—influence of the large companies, which since the outbreak of the Civil War has been usurped with ever-increasing speed by industry, landed property, the railways and finance' (letter to Danielson, mid-Nov.). In an interview granted to a correspondent of the *Chicago Tribune* on December 18 (published Jan. 5, 1879), Marx said that America needed an independent working class party, separate from trade union influence:

They can no longer trust politicians. Rings and cliques have seized upon the Legislature and politics has been made a trade. But America is not alone in this, only its people are more decisive than in Europe. Things come to the surface quicker. There is less cant and hypocrisy than there is on this side of the ocean.

Asked about the effectiveness of socialism in guiding the international action of the working class, he remarked that proletarian action was a spontaneous movement whose purpose was unclear at the outset. The socialists indeed participate in the movement but are not its initiators; they 'merely tell the workmen what its character and its ends will be'.

1879 Marx's own steadily worsening state of health and the illness of his wife prevented him from continuing the composition of *Capital*, volume 2, although he covered an enormous amount of literature relevant to it. He read Kovalevsky's work on Russian rural communal property, studied Russian fiscal questions, using material sent by Danielson, and put together an extensive bibliography on matriarchal law (Johann Jakob Bachofen, Lewis Henry Morgan). He also took up the history of ancient Rome and Greece (Johann Friedrich Reitemeier's

Geschichte und Zustand der Sklaverei und Leibeigenschaft in Griechenland [1879]; Rudolf von Ihring, Ludwig Lange, Ludwig Friedländer and Karl Bücher on various aspects of ancient Roman institutions). On England and its colonial affairs Marx studied Alexander Redgrave's *The Factory and Workshop Act* (1878) and his book on *The Textile Factories* (1879), Francis W. Rowsell's *The Domesday Book of Bengal* (1879) and William Carleton's *Traits and Stories of the Irish Peasantry* (1830). Sometime this year he investigated the ideas of Jules Guesde as presented in the book *Collectivisme et Révolution* (1879).

At the beginning of the year Marx received a visit from the distinguished English diplomat, Sir Mountstuart E. Grant-Duff, who conversed with Marx about the proletarian social movement. Sir Grant-Duff addressed a letter to the Empress Frederick of Germany shortly after his visit on January 31, candidly revealing his opinion of the Marxian views:

It was all very *positif*, slightly cynical—without any appearance of enthusiasm—interesting and often, as I thought, showing very correct ideas when he was conversing of the past and the present, but vague and unsatisfactory when he turned to the future. [...]

But supposing I said the rulers of Europe came to an understanding amongst themselves for a reduction of armaments which might greatly relieve the burden on the people, what would become of the Revolution which you expect it one day to bring about?

'Ah was his answer they can't do that. All sorts of fears and jealousies will make that impossible. The burden will grow worse and worse as science advances for the improvements in the Art of Destruction will keep pace with its advance and every year more and more will have to be devoted to costly engines of war. It is a vicious circle—there is no escape from it'. [...]

The above will give Your Imperial Highness a fair idea of the kind of ideas about the near future of Europe which are working in his mind.

They are too dreamy to be dangerous, except just in so far as the situation with its mad expenditure on armaments is obviously and undoubtedly dangerous.

If however within the next decade the rulers of Europe have not found means of dealing with this evil without any warning from attempted revolution I for one shall despair of the future of humanity at least on this continent. ('A Meeting with Karl Marx'. *The Times Literary Supplement*, July 15, 1949).

After several months of silence in his correspondence, Marx

resumed writing to Danielson in April and explained this long interruption as due to ill health. He now returned to discuss an earlier letter of Danielson's and took issue with the latter's comparison of America with Russia. It was impossible, he said, to find real analogies between the two countries: 'In the former the expenses of the government diminish daily and its public debt is quickly and yearly reduced; in the latter bankruptcy is a goal more and more appearing to become unavoidable. The former has freed itself ... of its paper money, the latter has no more flourishing fabric than that of paper money ... the latter reminds you rather of the times of Louis XIV and Louis XV ...' America was exceeding even England's tempo of industrial development and its masses were quicker and endowed with greater political means to achieve their goals. In response to this critique Danielson furnished Marx with detailed information on agricultural productivity in Russia, as taken from the *Zemstvo* statistics (July 26).

Carlo Cafiero, one-time anarchist and outspoken enemy of the General Council in the IWA, had now become a populariser of Marx's *Capital*. He sent Marx a recently published pamphlet containing his choice of excerpts from Marx's theoretical work and a preface. Marx thanked Cafiero on July 29 and commended the selection and composition of the pamphlet, whose merits were far superior to the previous efforts to make *Capital* accessible to a wider audience. However, the preface, Marx noted, lacked 'proof that the *material conditions* necessary for the emancipation of the proletariat are spontaneously produced with the advance of capitalist production'. At a later date, he added, Cafiero might produce an enlarged edition which would place more emphasis on the 'materialist basis of "Capital"'.

Now that the Socialist Law had made socialist action legally impossible Marx and Engels seriously considered collaborating on an illegal socialist news organ that Liebknecht and others wished to found. When assuring the SDAP of their participation, however, they emphasised that only Carl Hirsch was capable of editing such a journal which would not make compromises with petit-bourgeois elements in the party nor concessions to the government. After the new editors were announced to be Karl Höchberg and Eduard Bernstein, Marx and Engels withdrew their support, basing their action on the likely prospect that Höchberg, 'theoretically a very muddled head', would turn the paper into an organ of 'social-philanthropy' and deny it the 'proletarian-revolutionary' character essential to the working class political movement (Engels to Bebel, Aug. 4).

Marx spent nearly all of August and September at the seaside, first in Jersey and then in Ramsgate after receiving news that Jenny Longuet, who was residing in Ramsgate, had given birth to a son Edgar on August 17. Marx remained with his daughter until late in September and reported to Engels that the sea air had a very favourable effect on his health. While in Ramsgate Marx received from the labour offices in the American states of Ohio, Massachusetts and Pennsylvania a number of official publications and bulletins, which Sorge had requested on his behalf. Engels also sent Marx a recent publication by Höchberg, the *Jahrbuch für Sozialwissenschaft und Sozialpolitik*, and asked for his opinion on how to proceed against Höchberg's activity within the German proletarian movement. Höchberg claimed that Social-Democracy had brought the 'Socialist Law' upon itself by transforming the socialist movement into a working class movement, a step which had served only to provoke the bourgeoisie. Marx replied that an immediate, blunt and merciless stand must be taken against Höchberg and proposed that they first write in protest to the SDAP leaders before openly disavowing their relations with the German party. In both their names Engels composed a 'circular letter' on September 17-18, while Marx was still in Ramsgate, and sent it to the party leadership in Leipzig.

In this letter Engels exposed the fallacy of those elements which had infiltrated the party in the belief that the working class was incapable of emancipating itself but needed 'the leadership of "educated and propertied" bourgeois' who would instruct the proletariat about its own interests. These 'educated' Germans also thought that the bourgeoisie was not to be fought against but won over by propaganda. In short, they denied the class struggle as an unpleasant, 'coarse' phenomenon, leaving only humanism and 'empty phraseology about "justice"' as the basis for socialism. While the movement needed people who would add 'educative elements' to it, Höchberg and his clique were not such people. Moreover, Engels emphasized, those from other classes who wished to join the proletarian movement had better drop their class prejudices and 'wholeheartedly adopt the proletarian viewpoint'. Finally, Engels summed up the standpoint which he and Marx had defended for the past forty years—the class struggle as the driving force in history:

The emancipation of the working classes must be accomplished by the working classes themselves. Therefore, we cannot cooperate with people who openly state that the workers are too uneducated to emancipate themselves and must be freed from above by philanthropic grand- and petit-bourgeois (Sept. 17-18).

Although Höchberg was nominally removed from the editorial staff of the *Sozialdemokrat* thereafter, the paper continued to give space to the 'petit-bourgeois-socialist' views of the Höchberg group. Marx and Engels consequently wrote to Bebel on November 16, declaring that they could not lend their support to a party which permitted such viewpoints to have access to its official paper.

1880 Marx worked irregularly on the manuscripts for books II and III of *Capital*, while doing much reading on problems of land and soil and the fiscal problems pertaining to the development of predominately agricultural countries (on ground rent: the Italian economist Achille Loria; on geology G. Allen; as well as works on the Irish land question, Australian commercial development and American and Indian agriculture). He read a work entitled *La Sociologie d'après l'Ethnographie* (1880) by the Frenchman Charles Letourneau and studied the statistical books published by the Czarist government in Moscow for the years 1877-79. Late in the year he took 98 pages of notes on Morgan's work *Ancient Society* (1877) and subsequently began extensive studies on ancient times (in English, Maine, Sir John Budd Phear and Sir William Boyd Dawkins; in German, Rudolf Sohm).

In mid-March Marx received a letter from the French socialist Jules Guesde, who professed to share Marx's views on the proletarian movement. He declared himself in favour of violence as a necessary means to achieve the party's goals, affirmed that a party must be founded as a 'conscious army' before going into action and added that for some time impulse and direction in the party would have to originate from 'above', i.e. from those who were more knowledgeable. 'Under these conditions,' Guesde wrote, 'I have devoted myself since my return to forming an "independent and militant working men's party", which you quite rightly declare to be "of the greatest importance" in view of the events now in the making' (end of March, MEW 34 : 505).

For Guesde and the French socialist party Marx drew up an 'enquête ouvrière', a questionnaire which would enable them to compose a statistical picture of the living and working conditions of the proletariat, their mental and physical states of being, their relations to others within their class and to their employers. The list of 101 questions delved, moreover, into the matter of safety precautions in the factories or workshops, unemployment in times of crisis, the use of leisure time, strikes and their effects, trade-unions and co-operative organisations within the given industrial sector (Oeuvres 1 : 1529-1536).

Marx's Misère de la philosophie was republished in instalments in Guesde's Egalité beginning in April. In May both Guesde and Paul Lafargue came to London to discuss with Marx and Engels the programme of the French socialist working men's party, which the two Frenchmen and others were in the process of forming out of the existing party of French socialists. Guesde wrote in French, at Marx's dictation, a theoretical introduction to the programme, beginning with a list of 'considérants' based on the Marxian view of proletarian emancipation. 'Considering that the working class, without distinction as to race and sex'— the programme began—'can be free only when it is in collective possession of the means of production, the emancipatory endeavour must be undertaken through the action of an independent political party of the working masses, using all means at their disposal.' This introduction was followed by a 'minimal programme'—a 'means of organisation and struggle' on the electoral front (Oeuvres 1 : 1538). In a letter to Sorge later in the year (Nov. 5) Marx recounted his meeting with Guesde and termed the programme they had drawn up as 'a tremendous step forward' which brought the French down to earth from their 'cloud of phraseology'. The subsequent adoption of this programme by nearly all political working men's groups proved in Marx's eyes 'that this is the first real labour movement in France'.

A French translation by Paul Lafargue of the most interesting theoretical sections from Engels's Anti-Dühring now appeared in the French monthly La Revue socialiste under the title 'Socialisme utopique et socialisme scientifique' (March-May). These same excerpts were later brought out in book form with a preface by Marx who remarked that Engels's writing represented 'in a certain sense an *introduction to scientific socialism*' (MEW 19:185).

In June Marx's doctors forbade him to work—he was suffering from nervous exhaustion—but the progressively worsening state of his wife's health prohibited him from going to the Continent for treatment. The whole family, including the two sons-in-law, spent the month from mid-August to mid-September in Ramsgate. As Marx wrote to Danielson, he had been sent to the sea 'to do nothing and to cure my nerves by *far niente*' (Sept. 12). Because of his state of health he was unable to furnish Danielson with the requested article on Russian economics, but advised his friend himself to publish the statistical evaluations he had made on agricultural reforms in Russia and authorised him to use any material from his letters which might be of value for his writing.

After his return to London Marx met Liebknecht who had come to discuss the problems within the party ranks caused by the infiltration of opportunistic elements. Marx and Engels declared their intention of refraining from interference in internal party difficulties and intrigues on the staff of their 'miserable' newspaper, the *Sozialdemokrat*. Liebknecht promised to begin a renewal and improvement of the party organisation. On behalf of the victims of the 'Socialist Law' Marx solicited material aid from the journalist John Swinton in New York (Nov. 4).

In September he studied the programme of the Russian terrorist organisation *Narodnaia Voliia* (The People's Will), whose headquarters were in St Petersburg. He was in close contact to one of their exiled members, Lev Hartmann, presently living in London. This group stood in opposition to the anarchist propaganda organisation which was named after its periodical *Cerny Peredel* or Black Repartition. The former group, Marx wrote to Sorge (Nov. 5), along with the intellectuals at the Russian universities showed great interest in his writings.

Anticipating the publication of volume 2 of *Capital*, Marx asked Charles Darwin's permission to dedicate the work to him. Darwin replied on October 13 that consent would imply approval and since he knew nothing of the subject in question, he could not consent. Darwin wished, moreover, to avoid injuring the religious feelings of his family and feared that Marx's book contained 'direct arguments against Christianity and theism' (IRSH, 1964, part 3, p. 465f.).

In connection with the work on *Capital*, Marx now requested from Sorge material on industrial development in California, noting that 'California is very important for me because nowhere else has the upheaval caused by capitalist centralisation been accomplished in such a shameless way—at such a rapid tempo' (Nov. 5). In the following months he examined statistical material on the American economic situation and read 'The Kearney Agitation in California' (1880) by Henry George.

An international meeting was held in Geneva to celebrate the 50th anniversary of the 1830 Polish Revolution (Nov.). Marx, Engels, Lafargue and Lessner addressed an open letter to the assembly. As former members of the General Council of the IWA they called attention to the intimate relationship between the Polish emancipatory movement and the overthrow of the existing military and political structure in Europe. The Polish insurrection of 1863 had, in particular, 'by occasioning the common protest of English and French working men against the international intrigues of their government formed the point of departure for the International', which was founded in 1864 (MEW 19:239f.).

The English social reformer Henry Mayers Hyndman, who was entertaining plans to found an English working class party, met Marx frequently during this year. Hyndman's decided opposition to violent revolution as a means of emancipating the working class provoked Marx to a letter, written December 8, which qualified the circumstances under which he held violence to be necessary. In England, Marx said, revolution did not appear to be necessary, yet it remained a possibility. The working class gains peaceful concessions from the government only through pressure from without. When the proletariat fails to use its legal freedoms and powers efficiently, this pressure breaks down. 'If the inevitable evolution turns into a revolution, it would be the fault not only of the ruling classes but of the working class as well.' He cited Germany as an example of how the proletarian movement, while keeping within the bounds of legality, nevertheless comes into conflict with the government. In the case of the SDAP 'their crimes were not *deeds*, but *opinions*, which displeased their sovereigns' (Dec. 8).

Sometime between late 1879 and the end of 1880 Marx began a critique and refutation of passages in Adolf Wagner's *Lehrbuch der politischen Oekonomie* [Textbook of Political Economy (2nd ed. 1879)] which attributed to Marx a 'socialist system' and falsely construed his value theory. Marx made some twenty-odd pages of notes and commentary, but left the work unfinished. Wagner failed, for example, to differentiate between the theories of Marx and Ricardo, the latter having dealt with labour 'only as a *measure of value*' and therefore established no connection between value theory and the 'essence of money', as had Marx. Ricardo had, moreover, confounded value and production costs, whereas Marx had emphasised, as early as the 1859 *Zur Kritik*, that '*values* and *production* prices (which express simply the costs of production in money terms) *do not* coincide' (MEW 19:359). Stating that commodities as values have a 'double nature', Marx rejected the argument that certain goods have a social use value for the commodity as a whole: 'Where the state itself is a capitalist producer, as in the exploitation of mines, woodland, etc., its product is a "commodity" and has therefore the specific nature of every other commodity (MEW 19:370). 'Value', according to Marx, represents only the 'social character of labour' and is produced through the 'expenditure of "social" labour power' (MEW 19:375). Wagner also attributed to Marx the view that surplus value created by the worker was 'unjustly' appropriated by the capitalist. On the contrary, Marx replied, '... at a certain point the production of commodities necessarily becomes "capitalist" commodity production and, according to the law of value which governs this production system, the "surplus value" is due not to the working man but to the capitalist' (MEW 19:375).

1881   Marx's interest in Russia continued: during the course of this year he studied the development of Russian economy since the emancipation of the serfs (Skrebitsky, Golovatchev, Skaldin, Danielson, Janson, Chernyshevsky). America, on the other hand, provided the field for his investigation of big business and in this connection he read articles from *The Atlantic Monthly*: Lloyd's 'The Story of a Great Monopoly' (1881; about the Standard Oil Company), House's 'The Martyrdom of an Empire' (1881); also Grohmann on 'Cattle Ranches in the Far West' (1880) and Cliffe-Leslie's article on 'Political Economy in the United States' (1879) from the *Fortnightly Review*. He promised the *Narodnaia Voliia* an article on the Russian rural commune. His contact with Danielson continued and, when two Russian economists Ziber and Kablukov visited London in January, Marx was afforded a further opportunity to become acquainted with contemporary economic thought in their country.

After reading Danielson's *Outline of Russian Political Economy Since the Reform* he wrote the author a lengthy appraisal in a letter of February 19. Danielson's work was 'in the best sense of the word "original"' and Marx now encouraged him to investigate the problem of the 'wonderfully increasing indebtedness of the landlords, the upper class representatives of agriculture'. He explained to Danielson as well the reason for Russia's cycle of good and bad harvests. Finally, he spoke of the system employed by the British railways of incurring new debts to pay off the old, in essence the same method used for European public debts, and remarked that 'this pleasant method must one day or another terminate in an ugly catastrophe' (Feb. 19).

On February 18 Marx received a letter from the revolutionary Vera Zasulich, a member of the Geneva group 'Black Repartition' who had won a certain notoriety through her attempted assassination of the Prefect Trepov in 1878 (cf. p. 282). She posed Marx the question of Russia's future economic and social development: would her country have to be transformed on the basis of capitalist industry or could the rural commune be used to found a new collective order? She alluded to certain Russian 'Marxists' who held the first opinion and condemned the revolutionary *Narodniki*, the populists who supported the rural commune, to the role of passive spectators in this economic transformation. Her letter inspired Marx, despite his illness and his other obligations, to undertake a thorough investigation of Russia's socio-economic structure. Considering the peculiarities of that country's historical development, he was unwilling to apply, without reflection, to its situation the conclusions he had drawn from the study of West European countries.

Marx now made three long drafts in French for a reply to Vera Zasulich's questions before composing the final letter in a very succinct and sketchy form. Russia, he began in the first draft, could gradually develop the rural commune to an element of collective production on a national scale. Since it was contemporary with capitalist production, the commune had more-over the advantage of being able to appropriate capitalism's positive achievements without suffering its same instability and crises. Capitalism now found itself in a period of serious crisis, 'in opposition to science, to the popular masses and to the productive forces to which it gives rise—in short, in a crisis will end only with its own abolition, with the return of modern societies to the "archaic" type of property and collective pro-duction' (*Oeuvres* 2:1568). To the third draft Marx added that the rural commune, which still existed in many Asian countries, was in fact 'the most recent type', the 'last word' in archaic social forms and that the same could be said of the German rural community (*Oeuvres* 2:1562). The Russian rural commune was unique in that it existed both on a national scale and in a modern 'historic milieu', which made it the contem-porary of a higher culture and connected to a world market in which capitalist production predominated (*Oeuvres* 2:1566). However, for the rural commune to remain viable as an insti-tution under threat from within through the spread of private property and from without by technological progress, 'a Russian revolution is necessary to save the Russian commune':

If the revolution should take place at the right moment, if it concentrates all its forces to ensure that the commune may develop freely, the commune will soon become an element of social regener-ation in Russia and of superiority over the countries enslaved by the capitalist regime (*Oeuvres* 2:1573).

In the letter which Marx actually sent to Vera Zasulich, dated March 8, he said that, to clear her mind of doubts about his 'so-called theory', *Capital* contained no arguments for or against the peasant commune. Apart from *Capital*, however, his research on Russia had convinced him that the commune would be the mainspring of its social regeneration but that to make certain it would also function as such 'one would first have to eliminate the deleterious influences which assail it from every direction and then secure it the normal conditions for natural develop-ment' (*Oeuvres* 2:1558).

Not long after receiving Vera Zasulich's questions he was asked another by F. Domela Nieuwenhuis regarding the measures that a socialist government should take after 'victory'. Marx replied to his Dutch comrade that it was impossible to answer such a question at present, that 'we cannot solve any equation which does not have the elements of its solution within the given data'. It was certain that no socialist government would ever be installed in a country which failed to provide those conditions that would enable it 'to intimidate the bourgeois mass and thus gain time—the first desiratum—for lasting action' (Feb. 22). The Paris Commune, Marx explained, could not be taken as an example of or model for a socialist government, since only a minority of its members had been socialist while the uprising itself had not extended beyond the capital under exceptional circumstances of war. Such conjecture about the future programme of action, Marx found, only diverted attention from the immediate struggle. Scientific insight into the change presently in progress should be 'sufficient guarantee that at the moment when a really proletarian revolution breaks out, the conditions of its immediate, direct (albeit certainly not idyllic) *modus operandi* will be given as well'.

Unable to attend a Slav meeting presided over by Lev Hartmann on March 21 in London, Marx and Engels sent a message in which they welcomed the recent events in St Petersburg—the attempted assassination of the Czar—ten years after the defeat of the Paris Commune as a harbinger of the Russian commune to come (March 21). At this time Marx was in contact with the Russian revolutionary Chaikovsky, who informed him about the attack on the Czar and the persons involved, members of the St Petersburg terrorist group, *Narodnaia Voliia*. In a letter to his daughter Jenny, Marx described these people as 'thoroughly capable ... simple, objective, heroic'. Their aim was not to preach 'tyrannicide as "theory" and "panacea"' but to teach Europe that their way was 'specifically Russian, a historically inevitable mode of action' and that all moralising about it was utterly meaningless. He attacked sharply, by contrast, the Geneva *Cherny Peredel* Russians, 'doctrinaire, confused anarcho-socialists', who lacked any influence whatsoever on the present course of events in their home country (Apr. 11). In mid-April Marx received from the St Petersburg group a message praising his work and soliciting his assistance in awakening Europe's sympathy and support for the Russian revolutionary movement.

On April 29 Marx wrote a letter to Jenny, congratulating her on the birth of her fourth son Marcel. Children born today, he predicted, have before them 'the most revolutionary period which human beings have ever had to live through. It is not good to be so old that one is capable only of foreseeing and not of seeing' (Apr. 29).

Early in June Marx broke off relations with Hyndman, whom he had often advised in recent months on the *rapprochement* between British trade union leaders, represented by Hyndman, and members of Parliament who were interested in forming a new working men's party. Hyndman had provoked this rupture by quoting long passages from *Capital* without giving the source, reasoning that Marx's name was anathema among the British (Marx to Sorge, Dec. 15). He did, however, acknowledge in the preface his indebtedness 'to the work of a great and original writer'.

When writing to Sorge in New York on June 20, Marx commented on a book by an American author which he read during the first half of the year. Henry George proposed in *Progress and Poverty* that the solution to the problem of economic disparity would be the public appropriation of land rent. This proposal was not new, Marx remarked: it originated with the bourgeois economists of the 18th century and was mentioned in *The Communist Manifesto* as one of the transitional measures leading to communist society. Both George and the bourgeois economists had overlooked surplus value and thus left wage labour and capitalist production fundamentally unchanged: 'The whole thing is simply an attempt, trimmed with socialism, to save *capitalist rule* and indeed to *re-establish* it on *an even wider basis* than its present one.' Marx reproached George as an American economist, moreover, for having failed to investigate the fact that even in his country where land was accessible to the broad masses 'capitalist economy and the corresponding enslavement of the working class have developed more rapidly and more shamelessly than in any other country!' (June 20).

Despite the steadily declining state of his wife's health Marx acquiesced in Jenny's desire that he and Helene Demuth accompany her to Argenteuil, near Paris, for a visit with her daughter and grandchildren. They stayed in France from July 26 until the middle of August when, alerted that Eleanor in London had suffered a nervous collapse, Marx returned home immediately. His wife returned several days later with Helene and from this time on, until her death some four months later, remained bed-ridden. In October Marx contracted pleurisy, which was complicated with bronchitis and the beginnings of pneumonia. For several days his life was in serious danger and, as he recounted to Danielson: 'for three of the last six weeks of her life I was unable to see my wife, although we lay in two adjoining rooms' (Dec. 13).

Marx was 'rather disagreeably affected' by a letter he received from Meissner at the end of October, notifying him that a third edition of *Capital*, volume 1, was now necessary, for he wished to devote himself entirely to finishing the second volume. On November 30 he was sent a copy of E. Belfort Bax's article, number 12 in the series 'Leaders of Modern Thought', which portrayed Marx as one of the great modern socialist thinkers and economists. This praise and recognition of her husband's work lightened the last days of Jenny Marx's life, for she succumbed to her long illness on December 2. Marx, still suffering from his bronchitis, was advised by the doctors not to leave the house. Remembering his wife's words shortly before her death—'We are no such *external* people.' (Marx to Jenny Longuet, Dec. 7)—Marx stayed away from his wife's funeral. Engels spoke at the graveside, paying tribute to this woman with the sharp, critical mind, so much tact and energy, who never sought public acclaim or attention for herself:

What she achieved only those who have lived with her know. Yet I am sure that we shall often miss her spirited and clever counsels, spirited without ostentation, clever without betraying anything of honour ... If there was ever a woman who found her greatest happiness in making others happy, then it was this woman (MEW 19:295).

1882 Marx spent the greater part of this year on the Isle of Wight and the other side of the Channel in search of warmer, drier climate than in England. Despite illness and the distractions of travel he found time to read a number of works on Egypt, then a book by the English naturalist John Lubbock entitled *The Origin of Civilization and the Primitive Condition of Man* (1870) and to continue his studies on Russia, especially its agricultural situation (Gerhard Mineiko, Alexander Engelhardt, Vasily Semevsky, Alexander Skrebitsky). He read in the original

Russian Vorontsov's *Sud'by Kapitalizma v Rossii* [The Fate of Capitalism in Russia, 1882].

The doctors advised Marx and Eleanor to a stay in Ventnor on the Isle of Wight during January. Eleanor, Marx wrote to Laura, 'is very laconic, and seems indeed to endure the sojourn with me only out of the sense of duty as a self-sacrificing martyr' (Jan. 4; *Annali* I: 208). His youngest was under mental pressure that was destroying her health and Marx did not want 'for anything in the world that this child should imagine herself being sacrificed on the family altar in the role of 'nurse' to an old man' (Marx to Engels, Jan. 12). On January 16 they returned to London; Marx's condition was much improved, but he was advised to escape the damp London fog as soon as possible and seek the warmth of the Mediterranean in Algiers.

Marx also corresponded with Engels from Ventnor on matters other than his and Eleanor's health. On January 5 he reported receiving a letter from Dietzgen concerning the latter's recent studies in 'dialectic cognition' and the works of Hegel. To this Marx commented sarcastically that 'the poor fellow has gone forward "backwards" and "arrived" at the Phenomenology. I consider the case incurable.' In a letter written on the 12th he criticised the reform proposals of the Swiss economist Karl Bürkli, which he learned about in the journal *Arbeiterstimme*. Bürkli's system of 'interest-bearing mortgage bank notes' originated with the Pole August Cieszkowski, Marx remarked, and the same ideas of credit money had been discussed as early as the founding of the Bank of England.

Before Marx left for the Continent on February 9, he and Engels prepared a preface to the new second Russian edition of *The Communist Manifesto*. Recalling that the first edition of the *Manifesto* in 1847 ignored completely the position of the proletarian movements in America and Russia, the authors now offered a brief description of the progress registered in those two great countries and characterised Russia as the 'vanguard of revolutionary action in Europe'. Here as well Vera Zasulich's question about the future of the Russian *obshchina*, put to Marx a year earlier, resounded and the reply was:

The only possible answer to this today is: should the Russian revolution become the signal for a proletarian revolution in the West. so that the two complement one another, the present system of communal land ownership in Russia may serve as the departure point for communist development (MEW 4 : 576).

On his way to Algiers Marx spent several days with Jenny and her family and had occasion to speak with the socialist leaders Guesde, Gabriel Deville and José Mesa in Paris. By the time he arrived in Africa he was again suffering from pleurisy and found the weather there disappointingly cold and damp. On March 1 he wrote Engels a detailed account of his state of health since his arrival. Apart from his pleurisy and bronchitis, the loss of his wife caused Marx much suffering, and he wrote Engels that he was frequently overcome by waves of 'profunda melancholia'. The letters Marx composed during this year were written in a peculiar mixture of English, German and French, more so than was his usual habit, and contained an abundance of errors in construction and grammar. He noticed this fact himself, but, he told Engels, the realisation always came 'post festum. Shows you that as regards the *sana mens in sano corpore* there's still something to be done' (March 28-31).

He visited a friend of Charles Longuet's in Algiers, the civil judge Albert Fermé who told Marx about the Arab customs for regulating land ownership and described the system of colonial oppression. Judges who did not comply with the colonialists' demands to sentence innocent Arabs to prison were in grave danger of losing their own lives in that country. According to Fermé, however, 'the British and the Dutch surpass the French with their shameless arrogance, pretentiousness and cruel Moloch-like passion for vengeance on the "lower races"' (Marx to Engels, Apr. 8).

The adverse weather gave Marx no respite from his chronic bronchitis and he finally decided to return to the French coast, where the weather was reported to have been exceptionally dry during the past months. He spent a month, from May 7-June 7, in Monte Carlo where he was pursued, however, by inclement weather. The region impressed him with its great natural beauty 'enhanced by art—I am referring to the gardens which have been extended as if by magic up the barren cliffs and descend from precipitous heights often right down to the edge of the delightful blue sea—like terraced hanging Babylonian gardens', he wrote Eleanor (May 28). However he confessed having little desire to visit Monaco's chief attraction and enterprise—the casinos. In gambling 'there can be no question of intelligence, calculation, etc.; based on some sort of evaluation of probabilities, you can only reckon with 'chance' favouring you, provided you have a sufficient sum to wager ... And with all that,' he exclaimed, 'what child's play the casino is compared to the stock-market!' The excellent medical treatment which he received enabled him to banish the last traces of pleurisy although his lungs were permanently weakened from the long series of infections. In June he travelled to Argenteuil and went from there to Enghien each day to drink the waters at the mineral springs. Although much of his day was taken up with the trip to Enghien and with his grandchildren, Marx still found time to read two new pamphlets by the Italian economist Achille Loria and reached the same negative conclusion about their contents as did Engels. They decided that henceforth their attitude towards Loria could only be 'ironically defensive' (to Engels, August 3).

After several weeks in Switzerland—Vevey, Lausanne and Geneva—accompanied by his daughter Laura, Marx returned briefly to Paris, where he observed the goings-on of the two wings of the French socialist party (*Parti des travailleurs socialistes*) at their respective congresses in Roanne and St Etienne. 'Marxists' and 'anti-Marxists', he wrote Engels, '*both types* have done their best to spoil my stay in France' (Sept. 30).

Marx spent but three weeks in London before returning to Ventnor on November 3, where a new bronchial infection restricted his activities and forced him to stay indoors. He read about the recent experiments of the French physicist Marcel Deprez, who had demonstrated the long-distance transmission of electrical impulses at the Munich Electrical Exposition. In connection with his study of Deprez's work Marx also read Edouard Hospitalier on *La Physique moderne, Les Principales Applications de l'électricité* (1880) and, inspired by remarks by Samuel Moore passed on to him by Engels, studied differential calculus. After looking through Lafargue's recent articles in *Egalité*, he wrote to Engels that it was high time Lafargue put an end to his 'childish boasting about future revolutionary atrocities' and abandon his role as the 'patented oracle of scientific socialism' (Nov. 11). For Marx, Lafargue was 'the last disciple of Bakunin who seriously believes in him' and his other son-in-law was 'the last of the Proudhonists. Que le diable les importe!' he exclaimed to Engels. On November 2-3 Engels reported to Bernstein that Lafargue and the other 'self-styled "Marxists"' had often provoked Marx to say: 'one thing is certain, that I am no Marxist'. This remark can, of course, also be taken as a protest against any kind of name-worship as fetishistic and contrary to the principle of self-emancipation on which the working class movement is based. Marx also wrote to Laura, referring indirectly to her husband, that anarchists 'are in fact pillars of the existing order and do not derange anything. In spite of themselves it is their own heads which are innately *le chaos*'. Further on in this same letter he reported on his growing popularity in Russia, where his success delighted him more than in any other country, for he felt he was damaging a power which together with England formed the true bulwark of the old society (Dec. 14).

Marx reported on December 18 from Ventnor that he found Engels's recent article on 'The *Mark*' very good and that the Channel weather was cool and damp.

1883 On January 11 Jenny Longuet died in Paris of a serious pulmonary disease, presumed to have been tuberculosis. Eleanor went immediately to Ventnor to fetch her father, who was suffering from another attack of bronchitis. In London he developed an ulcer on one lung which ultimately caused his death on March 14. Eleanor later recounted how 'he went out of his bedroom to his study in Maitland Park, sat down in his armchair and calmly passed away' (quoted by Liebknecht in *Reminiscences*, p. 129).

To Engels fell the task of informing his comrades-in-arms about their great loss. He began on the day of Marx's death with letters to Liebknecht and Bernstein. To the latter:

Only one who was constantly with him can imagine what this man was worth to us as a theorist and at all decisive moments in practical matters as well. His genial views are going to disappear with him from the scene for long years to come. Those are things which are still beyond the capacities of the rest of us. The movement will take its course, but it will miss the calm, timely and considered intervention which has saved it hitherto from many a wrong and wearisome path.

And to Liebknecht:

What we all are, we are through him; and what the movement is today, it is thanks to his theoretical and practical activity. Without him we should still be stuck in the mire of confusion.

On the following day, March 15, Engels wrote the news to Sorge:

'Death is not a misfortune for him who dies but for him who survives', he used to say, quoting Epicurus. And to see this mighty genius lingering on as a physical wreck for the greater glory of medicine and as an object of ridicule for the philistines ... —no, it is a thousand times better as it is, a thousand times better that we bear him, the day after tomorrow, to the grave where his wife lies at rest (March 15).

The burial took place on March 17 at Highgate Cemetery in the north of London. Engels again, for the second time in fifteen months, spoke at this graveside. He addressed the participants in English:

Just as Darwin discovered the law of development of organic nature, so Marx discovered the law of development of human history: the simple fact, hitherto concealed by an overgrowth of ideology, that mankind must first of all eat, drink, have shelter and clothing, before it can pursue politics, science, art, religion, etc.; that therefore the production of the immediate material means of subsistence and consequently the degree of economic development attained by a given epoch form the foundation upon which the state institutions, the legal conceptions, art, and even the ideas of religion, of the people concerned have been evolved, and in the light of which they must, therefore, be explained, instead of vice-versa, as had hitherto been the case.

But that is not all. Marx also discovered the special law of motion governing the present-day capitalist mode of production and the bourgeois society that this mode of production has created. The discovery of surplus value suddenly threw light on the problem, in trying to solve which all previous investigations, of both bourgeois economists and socialist critics, had been groping in the dark....

Such was the man of science. But this was not even half the man. Science was for Marx a historically dynamic, revolutionary force. ... For Marx was before all else a revolutionist. His real mission in life was to contribute, in one way or another, to the overthrow of capitalist society and of the state institutions which it brought into being, to contribute to the liberation of the modern proletariat, which *he* was the first to make conscious of its own position and its needs, conscious of the conditions of its emancipation (Quoted in *Reminiscences*, p. 348f.).

Marx's son-in-law Longuet next read an address sent by Lavrov in the name of the Russian socialists:

The Russian socialists bow before the grave of the man who sympathised with their strivings in all the vicissitudes of their terrible struggle, a struggle which they shall continue until the principles of the social revolution have finally been triumphant. The Russian language was the first to have a translation of *Capital*, this gospel of contemporary socialism. The students of the Russian universities were the first whose fortune it was to hear a favourable presentation of the theories of this powerful thinker whom we have now lost ... (MEW 19:337).

Telegraphic messages were read from the French Workers' Party in Paris and the Spanish Workers' Party in Madrid, and finally Liebknecht spoke in the name of the German social-democrats, confirming the words that had already been uttered about his 'unforgettable teacher and faithful friend'.

Engels's second task was, together with Eleanor, to prepare for publication the many manuscripts Marx had left. He immediately investigated the drafts for *Capital* and found that Marx had accumulated more than a thousand pages for the second and third books, which he now expected to publish in one volume. It was not until 1885, however, that Engels managed to finish recopying, editing and constructing the second book, which he then published as a separate volume, while the third book did not follow until 1894.

Apart from his role as literary executor, Engels suddenly found himself defending his friendship with Marx, a relationship which many believed to have been detrimental to one or the other:

The refrain of the bad Engels who had seduced the good Marx has been sung countless times since 1844, alternating with the other refrain about Ahriman-Marx who lead Ormuzd-Engels astray of the virtuous path (Engels to Bernstein, Apr. 23).

1883-1985 In the years which intervened before his death in 1895 from a cancer of the digestive tract, Engels prepared the following editions and re-editions of works by Marx or by them both: In 1883 he wrote a Preface for the third German edition of *The Communist Manifesto*. Here he declared that the idea of proletarian revolution as the key to the emancipation of all society from capitalist oppression, exploitation and from class struggle, 'this fundamental idea belongs solely and exclusively to Marx' (MEW 4:577). A fourth German edition was brought out in 1890; an English edition in 1888 translated by their friend Samuel Moore; in 1892 a Polish edition and 1893 an Italian. In 1885 Engels prepared a new edition of the *Revelations on the Communist Trial in Cologne*, prefacing it with a 'History of the Communist League'; also a third edition of *The Eighteenth Brumaire*; and a German edition, translated by Kautsky, of the *Poverty of Philosophy*. In 1886 he published Marx's 'Theses on Feuerbach' in an appendix to his own writing entitled *Ludwig Feuerbach and the End of Classical German Philosophy*. The *Critique of the Gotha Programme* appeared as a pamphlet for the first time in 1891 and in the same year a re-edition of the *Civil War in France* and a Spanish translation of the *Poverty of Philosophy*, whose second German edition came out in 1892. In 1884 Engels republished Marx's *Wage Labour and Capital*, which had first appeared in the NRhZ in 1849. An English edition of this text was brought out in 1885 along with Marx's speeches before the Cologne jury in the trials of the NRhZ. Included in his publication of 1894, *On the Matter of Brentano versus Marx for Alleged Falsification of Documents*, were Marx's articles from 1872. On the basis of Marx's excerpt notes and critical remarks on Lewis H. Morgan's *Ancient Society* Engels composed *The Origin of the Family, Private Property and the State*, published in 1884. Finally in 1895, shortly before his death Engels finished a re-edition of the *NRhZ-Revue* articles on the class struggles in France.

SELECTED BIBLIOGRAPHY OF MARX'S WRITINGS

(P) indicates a manuscript that was first published posthumously.

I. 1835-1843

ORIGINAL TITLES	ENGLISH TITLES
(P) Abiturientenaufsätze (1835; MEGA 1,2 : 164-182).	Seven *Abitur* compositions
(P) Gedichte und andere literarische Versuche (1836-37; MEGA 1,2 : 3-89).	Poems and other literary efforts.
Wilde Lieder (1841; EB1 : 604-605).	*Wild Songs.*
(P) Schriften über die Philosophie Epikurs : 1. Vorarbeiten (1839; EB 1 : 16-255). 2. Doktordissertation : (*Differenz der demokritischen und epikureischen Naturphilosophie* (1840-41; EB 1 : 259-373).	Writings on Epicurean Philosophy : 1. Preliminary work 2. Doctoral Thesis : *The Difference between the Philosophies of Nature in Democritus and Epicurus.*
Artikel aus *Anekdota* und *RhZ* (1842-42; MEW 1 : 3-200).	Articles published in *Anekdota* and the *RhZ.*
(P) *Kritik des Hegelischen Staatsrechts* [§§ 261-313] (1843; MEW 1 : 203-333).	*Critique of Hegel's Philosophy of the State* [§§261-313].

II. 1844-1849

Briefe aus den *Deutsch-Französischen Jahrbüchern* (1844; MEW 1 : 337-346).	A Correspondence of 1843, published in the *Deutsch-Französische Jahrbücher.*

ORIGINAL TITLES	ENGLISH TITLES
Zur Judenfrage (1844, *Deutsch-Französische Jahrbücher;* MEW 1 : 337-346).	On the Jewish Question.
Zur Kritik der Hegelschen Rechtsphilosophie. Einleitung (1844, *Deutsch-Französische Jahrbücher;* MEW 1 : 378-391).	Contribution to a Critique of the Hegelian Philosophy of Right. Introduction.
(P) Ökonomisch-philosophische Manuskripte [Pariser Manuskripte] (1844; EB 1 : 467-588).	Material for a critique of political economy, with a final chapter on the Hegelian Philosophy [Paris Manuscripts].
Kritische Randglossen zum Artikel 'Der König von Preussen und die Sozialreform' (1844, *Vorwarts!;* MEW 1 : 392-409).	Critical Remarks on the Article 'The King of Prussia and Social Reform'.
Die heilige Familie oder Kritik der kritischen Kritik. Gegen Bruno Bauer und Konsorten (1845; MEW 2 : 3-223).	*The Holy Family or Critique of the Critical Critique. Against Bruno Bauer and Consorts* (with Engels).
Eine Kritik des Buches *Das Nationale System der Politischen Ökonomie von F. List* (1845; *Beiträge zur Geschichte der Arbeiter Bewegung.* Heft 3, 14, Jahrgang 1972, pp. 423-46). Abbrev. BZG.	A critique of F. List's book *Das National System* ...
(P) Thesen über Feuerbach (1845; MEW 3 : 5-7).	Theses on Feuerbach.
(P) *Die deutsche Ideologie.* Kritik der neuesten deutschen Philosophie in ihren Repräsentanten Feuerbach, B. Bauer und Stirner, und des deutschen Sozialismus in seinen verschiedenen Propheten (1845-46; MEW 3 : 13-530).	*The German Ideology.* Critique of the Most Recent German Philosophy ... (with Engels).
Misère de la Philosophie. Réponse à 'la Philosophie de la misère' de M. Proudhon (1847; *Oeuvres* 1 : 7-156).	*The Poverty of Philosophy. A Reply to 'The Philosophy of Poverty' by M. Proudhon.*

ORIGINAL TITLES	ENGLISH TITLES
Karl Grün : Die soziale Bewegung in Frankreich und Belgien oder die Geschichtsschreibung des wahren Sozialismus (1847, *Das Westphälische Dampfboot*; MEW 3 : 473-520).	Karl Grün : The Social Movement in France and Belgium or the Historiography of True Socialism.
Der Kommunismus des *Rheinischen Beobachters* (1847, DBrZ; MEW 4 : 191-203).	The Communism of the *Rheinischer Beobachter*.
(P) Arbeitslohn (1847; MEW 6 : 535-556).	Wages.
Die moralisierende Kritik und die kritisierende Moral/Beitrag zur deutschen Kulturgeschichte/Gegen Karl Heinzen (1847, DBrZ; MEW 4 : 331-359).	The Moralising Critique and the Criticising Morality. A Contribution to German Cultural History. Against Karl Heinzen
Discours sur la question du libre échange (1848; MEGA 6 : 435-447).	*Free Trade. A Speech Delivered before the Brussels Democratic Club.*
Manifest der kommunistischen Partei (1848; MEW 4 : 459-493).	*Manifesto of the Communist Party* (with Engels).
Forderungen der kommunistischen Partei in Deutschland (1848, NRhZ; MEW 5 : 3-5).	Postulates of the Communist Party in Germany.
Lohnarbeit und Kapital (1849, NRhZ; MEW 6 : 397-423).	Wage Labour and Capital.
Ca. 100 Artikeln in der NRhZ (MEW 5 & 6).	Approx. 100 articles in the NRhZ.

III. *1850-1856*

Die Klassenkämpfe in Frankreich. 1848 bis 1850 (1850, NRhZ-*Revue*; MEW 7 : 11-107).	The Class Struggles in France. 1848-1850.
Ansprachen der Zentralbehörde an den Bund (1851, *Kölnische Zeitung*; MEW 7 : 244-254 & 306-312).	Addresses of the Central Committee to the Communist League.

ORIGINAL TITLES   ENGLISH TITLES

Der achzehnte Brumaire des Louis   The Eighteenth Brumaire
Bonaparte (1852, *Die Revolution;*   of Louis Bonaparte.
MEW 8:114-207).

(P) Die grossen Männer des Exils   The Great Men of Exile.
(1852; MEW 233-335).

Enthüllungen über den Kommunis-   *Revelations on the*
ten-Prozess zu Köln (1853; MEW   *Communist Trial in Cologne.*
8:405-470).

8 articles on Lord Palmerston (1853,
Free Press and NYDT; re-ed. in
The Story of the Life of Lord
Palmerston. London, 1969, pp. 116-
233).

Der Ritter vom edelmütigen   *The Knight of the Noble*
Bewußtsein (1853; MEW 9:489-   *Consciousness.*
519).

Revelations on the Diplomatic
History of the Eighteenth Century
(1856, *Free Press*; re-ed. *Secret*
Diplomatic History of the Eighteenth
Century. London, 1969, pp. 49-136).

Ca. 100 Artikel aus der NOZ (1855;   Approx. 100 articles in the
MEW 10 & 11).   NOZ.

Approx. 160 correspondent's reports
in the NYDT (1852-1856).

6 articles in *The People's Paper*
(1856).

IV. *1857-1863*

(P) Grundrisse der Kritik der   Outlines for a Critique of
politischen Ökonomie. Rohentwurf   Political Economy. Draft.
(1857-58; Berlin, 1953, pp. 35-980).

Zur Kritik der politischen   *A Contribution to the*
Ökonomie. Erstes Heft (1859; MEW   *Critique of Political*
13:7-160).   *Economy. Part One.*

ORIGINAL TITLES	ENGLISH TITLES
Herr Vogt (1860; MEW 14 : 385-686).	Herr Vogt.
(P) Theorien über den Mehrwert (1861-63; MEW 26.1, 26.2, & 26.3).	Theories of Surplus Value.
Approx. 176 correspondents' reports in the NYDT (1857-62).	
10 Artikel aus dem Volk (1859; MEW 13).	10 Articles in Das Volk.
Verschiedene Artikel aus der Reform [Hamburg] und der Allgemeinen Zeitung [Augsburg] (1859; MEW 14).	Various articles in the Hamburg Reform and the Augsburg Allgemeine Zeitung.
9 articles for The New American Cyclopædia (1857-60) + 7 in collaboration with Engels.	
Ca. 175 Artikel aus der Wiener Presse (1861-62; MEW 15).	Approx. 175 articles in the Vienna Presse.

V. 1864-1872

Inaugural Address and Provisional Rules of the IWA (1864; Documents 1 : 277-291).	
Über P.-J. Proudhon (1865, Der Social-Demokrat; MEW 16 : 25-32).	On P.-J. Proudhon.
(P) Das Kapital. Kritik der politischen Ökonomie. Drittes Buch : Der Gesamtprozeß der kapitalistischen Produktion (1865; MEW 25).	Capital. A Critique of Political Economy. Book III : The Process of Capitalist Production as a Whole.
(P) Value, Price and Profit (1865; SW 1 : 361-405).	
Das Kapital. Kritik der politischen Ökonomie. Erstes Buch: Der Produktionsprozeß des Kapitals (1867; MEW 23 : 49-802).	Capital. A Critique of Political Economy. Book I : The Production Process of Capital.

ORIGINAL TITLES | ENGLISH TITLES

Communication privée et communication confidentielle du Conseil général contre Bakounine (1870; Freymond 2:133-144).

Two documents, a confidential circular and a private letter, against Bakunin.

Le Gouvernment anglais et les prisonniers Fénians. I & II (1870, L'Internationale).

The English Government and the Imprisoned Fenians.

Two Addresses of the General Council of the IWA on the Franco-Prussian War (1870; *Documents* 4:323-342).

Address on the *Civil War in France* (1871; *Documents* 4:356-416).

General Rules and Administrative Regulations of the IWA. Official Edition (1871; *Documents* 4:451-469).

Les Prétendues Scissions dans l'Internationale (1872; Freymond 2:266-296).

Fictitious Splits in the International (with Engels).

VI. *1873-1883*

L'Indifferenzia in materia politica (1873, *Almanacco Repubblicano per l'anno* 1874; Marx, Engels, *Scritti italiani*, Milano, Roma, 1955, pp. 98-104).

Indifference in Political Affairs.

Conclusion de la brochure *L'Alliance de la démocratie socialiste et l'Association internationale des travailleurs* (1873; Freymond 2:383-478).

Conclusion of the pamphlet *The Alliance of Socialist Democracy and the International Working Men's Association* (with Engels and Lafargue).

(P) Konspekt von Bakunins Buch *Gossudarstvenno i Anarkhiia* (1874; MEW 18:599-642).

Notes and Commentary on Bakunin's book *Statehood and Anarchy*.

ORIGINAL TITLES	ENGLISH TITLES
(P) Randglossen zum Programm der deutschen Arbeiterpartei (1875; MEW 19 : 13-32).	Critique of the Gotha Programme.
Mr G. Howell's History of the International Working Men's Association (1878, *The Secular Chronicle*).	
(P) Zirkularbrief an Bebel, Liebknecht, Bracke, u.a. (1879; MEW 19 : 150-166).	Circular letter to the leaders of the German Social-Democracy.
(P) Das Kapital. Kritik der politischen Ökonomie. Zweites Buch : Der Zirkulationsprozeß des Kapitals (1869-79; MEW 24).	Capital. A Critique of Political Economy. Book II : The Process of the Circulation of Capital.
Questionnaire pour une enquête ouvrière (1880; Oeuvres 1: 1529-1536).	*Questionnaire for Working Men.*
Considérants du Programme du Parti Ouvrier Français (1880; Oeuvres 1 : 1538).	Introduction to the programme of the *Parti Ouvrier Français*.
(P) Randglossen zu Adolf Wagners *Lehrbuch der politischen Ökonomie* (1880; MEW 19 : 355-383).	Marginal Notes on Adolf Wagner's *Lehrbuch der politischen Ökonomie*.
(P) Réponse et trois brouillons de la réponse à Vera Zassoulitch (1881; Oeuvres 2 : 1557-1573).	Drafts and final letter written in reply to Vera Zasulich.

Summary of Important Dates in the Composition of Capital

1845 Contract concluded with the publisher Leske (Darmstadt) for a two-volume work to be entitled 'Critique of Politics and Political Economy'.

1847 Contract with Leske annulled.

1851-52 Readings on economics (the problem of money) and cultural history.

1857-58 Elaboration of the manuscript known as the *Grundrisse* (ca. 700 printed pages) in two chapters, on money and on capital.

1859 Publication of the first booklet of A *Contribution to the Critique of Political Economy*.

1861 (Aug.) 1863 (June) 23 unedited notebooks of writing, including the first draft of *Capital* book I along with the theories on surplus value and topics developed in the later manuscript of book III.

1864-65 Production of *Capital* book III in manuscript form.

1865 (March) Contract signed with Meissner in Hamburg for publication of *Capital* in two volumes (900 pages), manuscript to be delivered in May.

1866-67 Editing of the final manuscript for *Capital* book I, instalment sent to editor mid-November 1866.

1868 Intermittent work on the manuscript of book II.

1870 Partially completed elaboration of the first chapters of book II.

1872 Publication of the Russian translation of *Capital* book I.

1872-75 Publication of the French translation of *Capital* book I by Lachâtre (Paris) as a series of consecutive booklets.

1873 Second German edition of *Capital* book I.

1875 Writing of (unedited) notebook entitled 'The Relation of the Rate of Surplus Value to the Rate of Profit' (book III).

1875-78 Further attempts to finish the manuscript of book II.

GENERAL BIBLIOGRAPHY

[N.B.: The reader will find listed below the materials used in preparing this chronology with the exception of the works already given in the Note on Abbreviations.]

I. BIBLIOGRAPHICAL GUIDES

Marx, Engels Verzeichnis. Werke, Schriften, Artikel. Dietz Verlag, Berlin, 1966. Includes index of titles for articles published in foreign languages.

Rubel, Maximilien, *Bibliographie des oeuvres de Karl Marx* avec en appendice un répertoire des oeuvres de Friedrich Engels. Rivière, Paris, 1956. *Supplément à la bibliographie des oeuvres de Karl Marx.* Rivière, Paris, 1960.

II. ENGLISH TRANSLATIONS OF MARX'S MOST IMPORTANT WRITINGS

K. Marx, F. Engels, *Basic Writings on Politics and Philosophy.* ed. L. Feuer, Garden City, N.Y. 1959.

K. Marx, *Capital. A Critical Analysis of Capitalist Production.* Volume I. ed. F. Engels, Moscow, 1959.

— *Capital. Critique of Political Economy.* Volume II. Book II: The Process of Circulation of Capital. ed. F. Engels, Moscow, 1957.

— *Capital. A Critique of Political Economy.* Volume III. Book III: The Process of Capitalist Production as a Whole. ed. F. Engels, Moscow, 1962.

K. Marx, F. Engels, *The Civil War in the United States.* New York, 1937. Chiefly reports from the Vienna *Presse,* but also a few NYDT articles from 1861-62.

K. Marx, *Critique of the Gotha Programme.* Moscow, n.d.

— *Critique of Hegel's 'Philosophy of Right'.* ed. J. O'Malley. Cambridge Univ. Press, 1972. 1st ed. 1970. Includes Marx's 'Contribu-

tion to a Critique of Hegel's Philosophy of the State. Introduction'
as well.
— *Early Texts*. ed. D. McLellan. Oxford, 1971.
— *Early Writings*. ed. T. B. Bottomore. London, 1963.
— *The Economic & Philosophic Manuscripts of 1844*. ed. D. Struik,
New York, 1964.
— *The Grundrisse*. ed. D. McLellan. London, 1971. Contains 136
pages of excerpts from the most important sections of this 1000-
page manuscript.
— F. Engels, *The Holy Family or Critique of Critical Critique*.
Moscow, 1956.
K. Marx, F. Engels, *Letters to Americans*. New York, 1953. Includes
several English originals as well, e.g. addresses to the American
Presidents from the IWA.
— *Selected Correspondence*. Moscow, n.d.
K. Marx, *Selected Writings in Sociology and Social Philosophy*. Lon-
don, 1956. ed. T. B. Bottomore and M. Rubel.
— *Writings of the Young Marx on Philosophy and Society*. ed. L.
Easton and K. Guddat. Excerpts from writings up to *The Poverty
of Philosophy* (1847).

III. MARX'S WRITINGS IN ENGLISH

K. Marx, F. Engels, *The American Journal of Marx and Engels*. ed.
H. Christman. New York, 1966. A Selection of NYDT articles with
an appendix of Marx/Engels articles prepared by Louis Lazarus.
— *Briefe über 'Das Kapital'*. Berlin, 1954. Letters are reproduced
here in the original language of their composition, e.g., English
letters written to Danielson and Ludlow.
— *Ausgewählte Briefe*. Berlin, 1953. Again a selection of letters in
the original language of their composition.
K. Marx, *On China*. 1853-1860. Articles from the NYDT. ed. D.
Torr. London, 1951.
— *Annali I*. Milano, 1958. A selection of Marx family letters in
English.
K. Marx, F. Engels, *On Britain*. Moscow, 1953. Apart from the
English articles from the NYDT, this volume contains translations
from German newspaper articles, letters on Britain and Engels's
Condition of the Working Class in England.
K. Marx, *The Civil War in France*. Peking, 1966. Includes the texts
of Marx's two drafts to this address as well.
K. Marx, F. Engels, *On Colonialism*. Moscow, n.d. Articles written
1850-1888, dealing especially with China and India.
K. Marx, *On Colonialism and Modernization*. ed. S. Avineri. Garden

City, N.Y., 1968. Correspondent's reports from the NYDT on China, India, Mexico, etc.

K. Marx, F. Engels, *Revolution in Spain*. New York, 1939. NYDT articles and 1 Marx article from the *New American Cyclopedia*.

— *The Russian Menace to Europe*. ed. P. Blackstock and B. Hoselitz. Glencoe, Illinois, 1952. Articles by Marx from the NYDT and the NOZ.

K. Marx, *Secret Diplomatic History of the Eighteenth Century & The Story of the Life of Lord Palmerston*. ed. L. Hutchinson. London, 1969.

— *The Ethnological Notebooks of Karl Marx (Studies of Morgan, Phear, Maine, Lubbock)*. ed. Lawrence Krader, Assen, 1972.

— *Manuskripte über die polnische Frage* (1863-1864). ed. with an introduction by Werner Conze and Dieter Hertz-Eichenrode, S'-Gravenhage, 1961. Contains unpublished English and German drafts on Prussia, Poland and Russia.

— *Notes on Indian History* (1664-1858). 2nd imp. Moscow, n.d. [1947].

IV. BIOGRAPHICAL SOURCES. DOCUMENTATION

Blumenberg, Werner, *Karl Marx in Selbstzeugnissen und Bilddokumenten*. Reinbeck bei Hamburg, 1962.

Eichhoff, Wilhelm, *Die Internationale Arbeiterassociation. Ihre Gründung, Organisation, politisch-sociale Thätigkeit und Ausbreitung*. Berlin, 1868. Photomech. reprod. Zürich, 1964.

Grünberg, Karl, *Die Londoner kommunistische Zeitschrift und andere Urkunden aus den Jahren 1847-1848*. Leipzig, 1921.

Gründungsdokumente des Bundes der Kommunisten. Juni bis September 1847. Hrsg. von Bert Andréas. Hamburg, 1969.

Marx-Engels-Lenin-Institut Moskau, *Karl Marx. Chronik seines Lebens in Einzeldaten*. Zürich, 1934. Abbrev. *Chronik*.

K. Marx, F. Engels, *Die russische Kommune*. Kritik eines Mythos. Herausgegeben von Maximilien Rubel. München, 1972. Articles, letters, notes and conversations revealing Marx's and Engels's standpoint on Russia.

— *Tagebuch der Pariser Kommune*. Berlin. 1971. Includes letters from Frankel, De Paepe, Kugelmann, etc. to Marx.

McLellan, David, *Karl Marx, His Life and Thought*. New York, London, Evanston, San Francisco, 1973.

Monz, Heinz, *Karl Marx. Grundlagen der Entwicklung zu Leben und Werk*. Trier, 1973. Study of the family background of the Marxes and the Westphalens.

Reminiscences of Marx and Engels. Moscow, n.d.

Rubel, Maximilien, *Karl Marx. Essai de biographie intellectuelle.* Nouv. éd. Paris, 1971, 1st ed. 1957.

— *Marx Chronik/Daten zu Leben und Werk.* München, 1968.

Schiel, Hubert, *Die Umwelt des jungen Karl Marx & Ein unbekanutes Auswanderungsgesuch von Karl Marx.* Trier, 1954.

Tsuzuki, Chushichi, *The Life of Eleanor Marx 1855-1898. A Socialist Tragedy.* Oxford, 1967.

IV. SECONDARY LITERATURE IN ENGLISH ON MARX'S THOUGHT

Avineri, Schlomo, *The Social and Political Thought of Karl Marx.* Cambridge University Press, Cambridge, 1968.

Hook, Sidney, *From Hegel to Marx.* New ed. Ann Arbor, 1962.

Kamenka, Eugene, *The Ethical Foundations of Marxism.* London, 1962.

McLellan, David, *The Young Hegelians and Karl Marx.* London, 1969.

— *Marx before Marxism.* Penguin Books, 1972.

Mattick, Paul, *Marx and Keynes.* Porter Sargent Publisher, Boston, 1969.

Nicolaievsky, Boris and Otto Maenchen-Helfen, *Karl Marx, Man and Fighter.* J. B. Lippincott Co., London and Philadelphia, 1936.

Ollman, Bertell, *Alienation. Marx's Conception of Man in Capitalist Society.* Cambridge University Press, Cambridge, 1971.

Roll, Eric, *A History of Economic Thought.* Faber and Faber, London, 1961. Chapter VI: 'Marx.'

Zeitlin, Irving, *Marxism: A Re-Examination.* D. Van Nostrand Co., Inc., Princeton, 1967.

— *Ideology and the Development of Sociological Theory.* Prentice Hall, Englewood Cliffs, New Jersey, 1968.

BIOGRAPHICAL GLOSSARY

Annenkov, Pavel Vasil'evich (1812-1887), Russian landowner, liberal critic and publicist. He made frequent visits to Central Europe and became acquainted with Marx in Brussels in 1846. In his *Memoires* (published in 1880) he depicted Marx at the time of the conflict with Weitling in the Communist Correspondence Committee (March 1846).

Bakunin, Michael Aleksandrovich (1814-1876), anarchist, proponent of anti-political collectivism and federalism. Born of an aristocratic Russian family at Torjok and educated at the St Petersburg military academy, he served as an officer in the Imperial Guard until 1834. In 1840 he began studying philosophy at the University of Berlin but soon abandoned his academic plans and emigrated first to Paris and then Switzerland. Animated by encounters with Proudhon, Weitling and other radicals, he became interested in modes of practical revolutionary activity. In 1851 he was sentenced to exile in Siberia for his participation in the 1849 Dresden uprising but escaped in 1861 and returned to Europe. He spent the rest of his life in Italy and Switzerland, where he founded the International Brotherhood and the *Alliance internationale de la démocratie socialiste*. In 1869-70 he became involved with the fanatic nihilist Sergei Nechayev and the two men collaborated in writing several revolutionary pamphlets. After the conflict with Marx and his expulsion from the IWA in 1872, Bakunin retired to Lugano.

Bangya, János (1817-1868), Hungarian colonel. He participated in the 1848-49 uprisings in his country and then went into exile in Europe, where he was active in the expatriated revolutionary circles and became a close collaborator of Kossuth (1850-53). He served simultaneously as a secret agent of the Austrian, Prussian and French police; he later entered the service of the Turkish military in the same capacity.

Barry, Maltman (1842-1909), cobbler by trade and British journalist. He was a member of the IWA and reported on the proceedings of The Hague Congress for the London press. He later turned away from socialism and joined the Conservative Party.

Bauer, Bruno (1809-1882), Young-Hegelian and prominent member of the Berlin *Doktorklub*. He taught protestant theology at the Universities of Berlin (1834-38) and Bonn (1839) but lost his post due to his radical Bible critique. Thereafter he began a career as a journalist with national-liberal leanings; he later collaborated on a conservative newspaper, the *Kreuzzeitung*.

Bauer, Edgar (1820-1886), Young-Hegelian, brother of Bruno Bauer. He emigrated to England in 1849 after participating in the German Revolution and then returned to Prussia in 1861 when granted political amnesty. He subsequently entered the Prussian civil service.

Bax, Ernest Belfort (1854-1926), British socialist and editor. He was a founding member of Hyndman's Social Democratic Federation and edited the socialist journals *Justice* and *Today*.

Bebel, Ferdinand August von (1840-1913), Leipzig turner, Social-Democratic Party leader. He was elected to the German *Reichstag* for the first time in 1867 and founded, together with Liebknecht, the 'Eisenach Party' in 1869. His political views and activities brought him a total of 54 months of imprisonment. Apart from his parliamentary duties on behalf of the socialist movement, he also contributed numerous writings—the most significant of which was the successful book on *Die Frau und der Sozialismus* (1879; Woman and Socialism), an attack on the religious and other prejudices hindering women's emancipation. He was the first in the German parliament to demand female suffrage.

Becker, Hermann (1820-1885), German publicist and member of the Cologne Communist League (1850-51). As a defendant in the Cologne communist trial he received a prison sentence in 1852. He later became a member of the *Fortschrittspartei* (1862), then joined the national liberals (1886) and finally reached the peak of his political career as Lord Mayor of Cologne.

Becker, Johann Philipp (1809-1886), brushmaker by trade, leader of the Geneva IWA and editor of the German language IWA journal *Der Vorbote* (Geneva, 1866-71). After participating in the 1832 Hambach Festival of students and intellectuals he emigrated to Switzerland. During the 1848 Revolution he returned to Germany and organised civil militias there. When the insurgency was suppressed, he again fled to Switzerland.

Bernays, Ferdinand Cölestin (1815-1889), German publicist. He emigrated to the USA in 1840, then returned to Paris, where he joined the staff of the German-language journal *Vorwärts!*. In 1844, as editor-in-chief, he was condemned to two months' prison for the paper's anti-Prussian attacks. Along with Marx, Ruge and Heinrich Börnstein he was ordered to leave France in January 1845, while serving this sentence. Later, he emigrated to Austria.

Bernstein, Eduard (1850-1932), bank clerk by profession, initiator of the revisionist movement within the German social-democracy. Forced into exile because of the anti-socialist laws in Germany, he edited the party's organ *Der Sozialdemokrat* from 1881-90, first in Switzerland, later in England, where he remained until 1901.

Blanqui, Louis-Auguste (1805-1881), radical French socialist. He participated in all uprisings in France from 1830-1870 as well as in the Paris Commune, organised secret societies of revolutionary proletarians and spent a total of 36 years in prison or exile for his political doings.

Blind, Karl (1826-1907), South German politician and journalist. He took part in the 1849 Baden uprising and belonged to the short-lived provisional government there. After the victory of the conservative forces he fled first to Paris and then London. He belonged to the London German Workers' Educational Association and became involved in the Vogt affair as author of the anonymous pamphlet *Zur Warnung*. Later on, he returned to the Continent and wrote for a Vienna newspaper.

Blos, Wilhelm (1842-1880), German social-democrat, journalist. Forced to abandon his studies in philology, he first worked in a customs office, then took to writing for various organs of the social-democracy in Constance, Braunschweig, Leipzig. At 28 he was elected to the German *Reichstag* and continued his political career through World War I to become President of the free state of Württemberg at its close.

Bracke, Wilhelm (1842-1880), German social-democrat, merchant in Braunschweig. At 23 he founded and played an active part in the Braunschweig section of the ADAV. During Marx's visit to Kugelmann in 1869 he made the acquaintance of the former and immediately began studying *Capital*. In the same year he broke with the Lassalleans and assisted at the founding of the Eisenach Party. During the period of the 'Socialist Law' he was active in communal politics and in 1877 was elected to the *Reichstag*.

Bradlaugh, Charles (1833-1891), British lawyer and militant atheist. He edited the London weekly *National Reformer* (1872) and presided over the League of Free Thinkers. His popular Sunday Lectures were attended by the Marxes during the late 1850s.

Bucher, Lothar (1817-1892), Prussian politician and journalist. He was a member of the Prussian constituent assembly in 1848, then a member of the revolutionary parliament. After a decade of exile in London he returned to Germany to engage again in politics and became a close collaborator of Bismarck's from 1864 to 1886.

Bürkli, Karl (1823-1901), Swiss tanner, socialist and advocate of Fourierist principles. He was active in the Zürich section of the International.

Claessen, Heinrich Josef (1813-1883), M.D., Rhenish liberal. He was editor of the *Rheinische Monatsschrift für praktische Ärtze* and a principle supporter of the Cologne *Rheinische Zeitung*.

Cluss, Adolphe (1820-1891?), Rhenish democrat, member of the Communist League. After the 1848 Revolution he emigrated to the USA and worked in Washington, D.C., as a Naval Yard engineer.

Collet, Charles Dobson, British journalist, Urquhartite. He was a member of the editorial staff of the London *Free Press* between 1855-64.

Dakyns, John R. (d. 1910), British geologist, member of the IWA.

Dana, Charles Anderson (1819-1897), American journalist, Fourierist. He was editor-in-chief of the *New-York Daily Tribune* and the *New American Cyclopaedia*.

Danielson, Nikolai Francevich (1844-1918), Russian economist and populist who used the pseudonym 'Nikolai-on'. He translated the first book of *Capital* with Lopatin, and books II and III on his own.

Demuth, Helene (1823-1890), close friend and family aid of the Marxes. She joined them for the first time in Paris in 1849 and shared their fate in exile in Brussels and London. After the death of Marx and his wife, she joined Engels's household.

Demuth, Henry Frederick (1851-1929), London workman, son of Helene Demuth and reportedly of Karl Marx.

De Paepe, César (1842-1890), Belgian socialist, compositor by trade. In 1871 he received the degree of Doctor of Medicine. He was active in the Belgian section of the IWA and later helped found the Belgian Workers' Party (1885).

Dietzgen, Joseph (1828-1888), German tanner, self-taught material-ist philosopher. He developed a novel theory of knowledge based on monism, thus anticipating a society in which intellectual and manual labour would no longer be separated. After emigrating to Russia following the 1848-49 Revolution, he returned to Siegburg (Ger-many) in 1869 and founded a section of the IWA there. He was later active in the SDAP. When the anti-socialist laws were passed, he emigrated to the USA and worked as editor in the German language press in New York and Chicago.

Domela Nieuwenhuis, Ferdinand (1846-1919), Dutch social-demo-crat, initiator of the socialist movement in his country.

Dronke, Ernst (1822-1891), radical German publicist, member of the Communist League and staff member of the NRhZ. In 1849 he emigrated to Switzerland and then London, where he retired from political life and devoted himself entirely to commercial affairs.

Dühring, Eugen Karl (1833-1921), German economist and socialist. He taught at the University of Berlin from 1863-77 and was the author of a so-called 'system of all sciences'.

Duncker, Franz Gustav (1822-1888), German journalist and pub-lisher. He joined the *Fortschrittspartei* in the 1860s and helped establish reformist trade unions.

Ebner Hermann (1805-1856), German journalist, teacher and contri-butor to the Augsburg *Allgemeine Zeitung*. Beginning ca. in 1840 he acted as a secret agent to the Austrian government.

Eccarius, Johann Georg (1818-1889), Thuringian tailor. He emigrated to England in the 1830s, joined the League of the Just, later the Communist League, and participated in the founding of the German Workers' Educational Association. He also played an important role in the IWA from the beginning and fulfilled various functions in the General Council, serving at the same time as secretary of the Land and Labour League. In the 1870s he became associated with the British trade union movement.

Eichhoff, Wilhelm (1833-1895), German socialist journalist. He participated actively in the working class movement in Berlin, joined the IWA and the SDAP. With Marx's aid he wrote a history of the IWA (1868).

Elsner, Moritz (1809-1894), Silesian publicist, democrat. He was a delegate to the Prussian national assembly in 1848 and edited the *Neue Oder-Zeitung*.

Engels, Friedrich (1820-1895), eldest son of a well-to-do Barmen industrialist. He was educated along strict pietistic lines and in view of entering his father's cotton-spinning enterprise. After a brief commercial apprenticeship he served one year as a volunteer artillerist in Berlin, attending lectures on Hegel at the University in his free time. He was soon known as a decided spokesman of the Young Hegelians. In 1843 his father sent him to Manchester to continue his apprenticeship in the English branch of the firm Ermen and Engels. There he made the acquaintance of the young Mary Burns, a factory worker who first brought him into contact with the English workers' movement and who became his life-long companion until her death in 1863. His contact with the German working class movement and with communist ideas Engels thanked to his encounter with Moses Hess upon his return to Germany in 1845. It was not until late this same year that he and Marx first embarked upon the intimate collaboration which was to last nearly 40 years.

Feuerbach, Ludwig (1804-1872), German philosopher and Hegel student who departed from his teacher's 'rational mystics' to undertake a psychological critique of religion and anthropology and to stress sensualism as a means of comprehending human existence. His critique strongly influenced the Young-Hegelians.

Fox-André, Peter (d. 1869), British journalist and positivist. Active in the London working class movement, he served the IWA as press correspondent (1865-69) and was also a member of the executive committee of the Reform League.

Fränkel, Leo (1844-1896), Hungarian-born goldsmith. He emigrated to Germany in the early 1860s and to France in 1867 and was active as an organiser of the French IWA. He played an important part in the Paris Commune, where he served as chairman of the labour commission. After the fall of the Commune, he emigrated to England but eventually returned to his native Hungary and there helped found a workers' party.

Freiligrath, Ferdinand (1810-1876), German poet, on the staff of the *Neue Rheinische Zeitung* from 1848-49. He belonged to the Communist League and gained a certain repute as a poet of the 1848-49 Revolution. In 1851 he emigrated to England, where he worked in a bank and was one of the intimates of the Marx family. He finally returned to Germany in 1868.

Gans, Eduard (1798-1839), law professor at the University of Berlin and student of G.F.W. Hegel. He edited the posthumous writings of his teacher and opposed the 'historic school of law', distinguishing himself for the reception of the writings of Saint-Simon and his critique of the class conditions in capitalism.

Graetz, Heinrich (1817-1891), author of an important history of Judaism.

Grün, Karl (1817-1887), pseudonym of Ernst von der Haide, a German writer and translator of P.-J. Proudhon. He began a career as journalist for the *Mannheimer Abendzeitung* in 1842 but was expelled from the *Land* of Baden for his constitutionalist-liberal views. Under the influence of Moses Hess he became a 'true socialist' and went to Paris where he sought contact with Proudhon. He was forced to leave France in 1847 and took up residence in Trier, working there on the staff of the *Trierische Zeitung*. In 1848 he was elected to represent Trier in the Prussian national assembly, 1849 in the Chamber of Deputies.

Guesde, Jules (1845-1922), pseudonym of Mathias Basile, socialist and journalist. To escape the repercussions of the fall of the Commune, he fled France for Switzerland in 1871 and there became part of the federal or collectivist movement led by Bakunin. In 1877 he returned to France to found *Egalité*, the first French newspaper devoted to the propagation of 'scientific socialism'. The Marseilles congress of the French national trade unions approved in 1879 his proposal to create a new proletarian political party. The following year the party adopted a 'minimum programme', drafted by Marx with Guesde's assistance.

Gumpert, Eduard (d. 1893), German M.D. in Manchester and friend of Engels.

Hales, John, London worker, member of the General Council of the IWA. He served as general secretary of the Council in 1871 and as secretary of the British federal council. In the late 1870s he continued his activity as a representative of labour in the London Commonwealth Club.

Harney, George Julien (1817-1897), British labour leader, Chartist, journalist. He was the publisher of the *Northern Star* and other liberal newspapers and belonged to the Communist League. In 1863 he emigrated to the USA and served as assistant secretary of state in Massachusetts before returning to England in 1888.

Hartmann, Lev (1850-1913), Russian revolutionary, member of *Narodnaia voliia*. After making an unsuccessful attempt on the life of Czar Alexander II, he fled to England.

Hatzfeldt, Sophie Countess von (1805-1881), close friend and benefactor of Ferdinand Lassalle. He helped her win a seven-year-long divorce suit against her husband.

Heine, Heinrich (1797-1856), German poet and writer. After a brief career in commericial affairs, he studied law, received his degree in 1825 and began work as a journalist in Munich. He abandoned this career as well in favour of travel on the Continent and in England, and finally settled in Paris in 1831 after the July Revolution. Beginning in 1836 he received a pension from the French government which enabled him to spend the rest of his life in financial security in France.

Heinzen, Karl (1809-1880), publicist from Prussia. He served in both the Dutch and Prussian armies, emigrated in 1844 to Switzerland and then returned to Baden to fight in the 1849 uprising. After a stay in England he ultimately settled down in the USA and worked as a journalist (1850).

Herwegh, Georg (1817-1875), German poet. He met Marx in Berlin while studying theology, but soon abandoned his academic plans and took refuge in Switzerland. After the 1848 Revolution he assumed Swiss nationality and stood close to the Lassallean movement.

Hess, Moses (1812-1875), self-taught socialist writer and publicist, the 'father' of German communism. He advocated a 'philosophy of action' and as early as 1842 actively defended the socialist cause in his writings. He was the chief representative of 'true socialism'. Together with Engels he founded the *Gesellschaftsspiegel* in 1846. In 1849 he was condemned to death for his role in the South German Revolution but escaped from Germany to live as an emigrant, primarily in Paris. During the 1860s he collaborated in the developing German workers' movement.

Hyndman, Henry Mayers (1842-1921), British lawyer and labour union leader. In 1881 he founded the Democratic Federation, which became the Social Democratic Federation in 1904, and later played a leading role in the British Socialist Party.

Jones, Ernest Charles (1819-1869), British lawyer and Chartist. He edited the *Northern Star* and other liberal publications. In 1847, when he first made Marx's acquaintance, Jones was permanent chairman of the Polish Committee, active member of the Fraternal Democrats and of the German Workers' Educational Association and a vigorous Chartist propagandist. He was sentenced to two years' prison for 'seditious speech' in 1848 along with five other prominent London Chartists.

Jung, Georg Gottlob (1814-1886), publicist in Cologne, district court lawyer. As a young man he belonged to the Young Hegelians and helped found the *Rheinische Zeitung*. In 1848 he was a delegate to the Prussian constituent assembly. After 1866 he adhered to the cause of the national liberals.

Kinkel, Gottfried (1815-1882), German art historian. Appointed professor in Bonn in 1845, he participated in the 1848-49 uprisings at the risk of his academic career, then fled to London. He did not return to the Continent until 1866, when he assumed a post as archaeology professor in Zürich.

Köppen, Carl Friedrich (1808-1863), teacher and historian in Berlin. His close, life-long friendship with Marx began while they were members of the *Doktorklub*.

Kossuth, Lajos (1802-1894), Hungarian lawyer and politician. In 1847 he served as finance minister in his country's government and the following year promulgated the Hungarian declaration of independence. Failure of the revolutionary movement forced him to emigrate to England. He received an amnesty in 1867 but declined to return to Hungary.

Kriege, Hermann (1820-1850), German writer and journalist, 'true' socialist. He emigrated to New York in 1845 and edited there the weekly journal *Volks-Tribun* (1846). He participated in the Frankfurt Parliament after his return to Germany in 1848.

Kugelmann, Ludwig (1828-1902), M.D., gynaecologist in Hanover. He had participated in the 1848-49 Revolution and entered into correspondence with Marx in 1862 through his interest in the latter's publications. He joined the IWA and was a delegate to the congresses of Lausanne and The Hague.

Lachâtre, Maurice (1814-1900), French socialist and publisher of the first French edition of *Capital* book I.

Lafargue, Laura, née Marx (1846-1911), daughter of Karl Marx and Jenny von Westphalen. She married Paul Lafargue in 1868 and bore him three children, none of whom survived early childhood. She and her husband committed suicide together in 1911.

Lafargue, Paul (1842-1911), Marx's son-in-law, French socialist and pamphleteer. Born of French parents in Santiago de Cuba, he studied medicine in Paris and London but abandoned this discipline for a political career. He helped found a French section of the IWA and, following the general amnesty of the defeated communards in 1880, returned to Paris, where he worked closely with Jules Guesde in the French Workers' Party.

Lassalle, Ferdinand (1825-1864), leading German socialist politician, founder of the ADAV (1863). He authored a voluminous work on *Heraklit der Dunkle* (1858). The keystones of his political programme were demands for universal male suffrage and production co-operatives to be realised through an alliance with Bismarck under the hegemony of the Prussian state.

Lavrov, Petr Lavrovich (1823-1900), Russian sociologist, publicist. He was involved in the Narodniki movement both in Russia and in exile. He edited the populist journal *Vpered!* (1873-76), first in Zürich and then in London. Lavrov also participated in the Paris Commune and was a member of the IWA.

Le Lubez, Victor P. (1834-?), French émigré in London. He was one of the founding members of the IWA and corresponding secretary for France until his expulsion in 1866 for calumny and intriguing.

Lessner, Friedrich (1825-1910), German tailor from Thuringia. He became friends with Marx and Engels during the days of the Communist League and was one of the defendants in the Cologne trial. He emigrated to London in 1856, where he became active in the IWA and was a member of the General Council (1864-72).

Liebknecht, Wilhelm (1826-1900), German socialist leader and journalist. He abandoned his university studies to participate in the 1848 Revolution and then went into exile in Switzerland. A year later he emigrated to London and did not return to Germany until 1862. In 1867 he was elected for the first time to the German *Reichstag*; he founded the German social-democratic party (SDAP), together with Bebel, and edited the party's news' organs.

Lissagaray, Hippolyte Prosper Olivier (1839-1901), French republican and journalist. He participated in the 1871 Commune and wrote a noteworthy history of its events. He later edited the Paris journal *La Bataille.*

Longuet, Charles (1833-1903), son-in-law of Karl Marx, journalist. He studied law in Paris and participated in the Paris Commune as editor of the *Journal officiel.* He remained in exile after the fall of the Commune until 1880. He married Jenny Marx, the Marxes' eldest daughter, in 1872, and taught at King's College, Oxford. In Paris once again he engaged in politics and worked on the staff of *Egalité.*

Longuet, Jenny née *Marx* (1844-1883), eldest daughter of Karl and Jenny Marx, wife of Charles Longuet. Shortly after the birth of her sixth child and first daughter she succumbed to the severe asthma from which she had been suffering for many years. Four of her children survived her to reach adulthood.

Ludlow, John Malcolm Forbes (1821-1911), British Christian socialist.

Marx-Aveling, Eleanor (1856-1898), Marx's youngest daughter and, together with Engels, co-executor of his literary testament. After abandoning plans for a dramatic career, she devoted her energies to the British socialist movement. She was the common-law wife of the dramatist Edward Aveling, whom she both nursed during long periods of illness and supported financially. She was also very attached to Freddy Demuth, her half-brother. Unable to support the psychological strains of her existence, she committed suicide by taking poison.

Mazzini, Guiseppe (1805-1872), Italian national patriot. He spent the 1850s and 1860s in exile in England; in the early part of this period he sought support within Bonapartist milieus. He finally returned to Italy in 1870.

Meyer, Siegfried (1840-1872), German mining engineer. He was a member of the Berlin section of the Lassallean ADAV, then helped found the Berlin IWA section. In 1866 he emigrated to America, joined the New York German communist club and organised various IWA sections in that country.

Miquel, Johannes (1828-1901), German liberal democrat. After participating in the Communist League, he began a career as lawyer in Göttingen (1852), in 1859 helped found the National Association —first expression of liberal opposition to the policies of Bismarck— and then held various responsible positions on both local and national levels. From 1890-1901 he was Minister of Finance and in 1897 received the title of nobility.

Moll, Karl Joseph (1813-1849), Cologne watchmaker. He was one of the most active members of the London League of the Just and of its successor, the Communist League. He was killed in action during the Baden uprising in 1849.

Moore, Samuel (1830-1912), Manchester judge, close friend of Marx and Engels. He translated the first book of *Capital* into English. After 1889 he exercised his profession as judge in Asaba, Africa.

Nechayev, Sergei Gennadiyevich (1847-1882), Russian terrorist, 1869-71 a close associate of Bakunin. He organised anarchist student unions in St Petersburg and was responsible for the brutal death of one of the students. He escaped to Switzerland in 1869 but was extradited three years later. He died in prison in St Petersburg.

Owen, Robert (1771-1858), British social reformer, industrialist. His factory at New Lanark became, under his direction, a humanist's model of production. As early as 1816 he elaborated his first plan for a system of co-operative manufacturing and consumption. Between 1825-29 he tried to establish such a community at New Harmony (USA); however, this attempt ended in failure. He returned to England and formed the Grand National Consolidated Trades' Union (1833), whose goal was to construct a new national labour commonwealth, but this project too collapsed after scarcely a year.

Philips, Lion (d. 1866), Karl Marx's uncle, banker in Zalt-Bommel, Holland. He was charged by Henriette Marx with the administration of her estate.

Philips, Nannette (1846-1885), daughter of Lion Philips, Marx's cousin. In 1871 she married the Protestant clergyman Roodhuizen.

Proudhon, Pierre-Joseph (1809-1865), French socialist and writer, printer by trade. A self-educated man born of peasant stock in Besançon, he became the well-known advocate of 'social individualism' and authored the political catchword 'property is theft' as well as a scheme for establishing 'people's banks'. In 1848 he was a *député* to the national assembly; a year later he was sentenced to three years' prison on charges of sedition.

Ruge, Arnold (1802-1880), German radical, publicist. A member of the Young-Hegelian movement, he was sentenced to five years' confinement in the fortress of Koburg. In 1837, together with E. T. Echtermeyer, he founded the *Hallesche Jahrbücher für deutsche Kunst und Wissenschaft* which continued as the *Deutsche Jahrbücher* until its suppression by the Saxonian government in 1843. As a delegate to the 1848 Frankfurt Parliament he organised the radical left. A year later he took refuge in London, where he collaborated with Ledru-Rollin and Mazzini. He returned to Germany in 1866.

Schapper, Carl (1813-1870), German socialist. After studying forestry in Germany, he emigrated to London in 1840 and played a central role in the League of the Just and the Communist League. He returned to Cologne and Wiesbaden to participate in the revolutionary events of 1848-49. After 1850 he was again in London where he led the 'anti-Marx' faction of the disbanded League. In 1865 he joined the General Council of the IWA.

Schorlemmer, Carl (1834-1892), German chemist. He fought in the Baden uprising of 1849 and then emigrated to England, where he became professor of chemistry in Manchester and a fellow of the Royal Society.

Schweitzer, Johann Baptist von (1833-1875), Frankfurt lawyer. He took over the leadership of the ADAV in 1867 after Lassalle's death and held this post until 1872 when he resigned to devote himself to literary projects.

Serraillier, Auguste (1840-ca.1873), French shoemaker, communard. He belonged to the General Council between 1869-72 and was sent in September 1870 to Paris, where he joined the government of the Commune in the second *arrondissement*. He returned to London after the Commune was routed.

Sorge, Friedrich Adolf (1827-1906), German music teacher. He participated in the Baden 1849 uprising, fled to Switzerland and then, via Belgium, landed in New York in 1852. There he was active in socialist circles and established the American Federal Council of the IWA.

Stirner, Max (1806-1856), pseudonym of Johann Caspar Schmidt, nihilist philosopher. Beginning in 1835 he taught at a girls' boarding school in Berlin; he later worked as a newspaper correspondent. In his writings he opposed the views of the liberal Young-Hegelians with a postulate of 'absolute egoism'.

Szemere, Bartholomäus (1812-1869), Hungarian lawyer and politician. In 1848 he occupied the post of Minister of the Interior and was named Prime Minister the following year. After the government's fall he fled to Paris, then London, and was the spokesman of the left-wing emigration.

Tkachev, Petr (1844-1885), Russian revolutionary, Jacobin. In Switzerland since the early 1870s he collaborated on the journal V*pered!* (Forward!) with Lavrov; a quarrel concerning the role to be played by an elitist dictatorship in the social revolution led to a rupture between them. In his *Tasks of Revolutionary Propaganda*, directed against Lavrov, he supported the view that one must 'make' the revolution.

Urquhart, David (1805-1877), British diplomat and Tory politician. He served in the foreign service in Turkey during the 1830s and was elected to Parliament in 1847. He founded and edited the *Free Press* (1855), later renamed the *Diplomatic Review* (1866-77).

Utin, Nikolai Issakovitch (1845-1883), son of a well-to-do Russian wine dealer. He joined the populist movement *Zemliia i Voliia* while a student in St Petersburg and in 1863 emigrated to Switzerland. He was active in the Geneva section of the IWA, edited the journals *Egalité* (1870-72) and *Narodnoe Delo* (1868-70). The latter later became the organ of the Russian internationalists in Geneva.

Vaillant, Marie-Edouard (1840-1915), French civil engineer and physicist, socialist, communard. He belonged to the Commune government as director of educational affairs. After its fall he escaped to England and joined the General Council of the IWA.

Vogt, Karl (1817-1895), German nationalist, professor at the University of Giessen. He belonged to the provisional government of 1849 and to the *Reich* regency in Stuttgart (Baden). After suppression of the liberal movement, he fled to Switzerland and finally received a professorship there.

Weitling, Wilhelm (1808-1871), German journeyman tailor, militant communist and propagator of the social revolution. He headed the League of the Just from 1839-42; in 1841 he emigrated to Switzerland, where he engaged in journalistic and propagandistic activities until his expulsion in 1846. Via Belgium, where he first met Marx and Engels, he emigrated to New York. At the outbreak of the 1848 uprisings he returned to Berlin and Hamburg but fled anew to the USA in 1849. There he founded the Liberty League and as its news organ the *Republik der Arbeiter* (1851-54). The League sponsored a communist community called 'Kommunia'. Shortly before his death he participated in a IWA reunion.

Weston, John, British Owenite worker, inventor of the cylindrical sewing machine. He was one of the founding members of the General Council of the International and treasurer of the Land and Labour League.

Westphalen, Edgar von (1819-1890), brother of Jenny Marx. He belonged to the Brussels Correspondence Committee in 1846, emigrated subsequently to the USA but returned after many years to take up residence in Berlin.

Westphalen, Ferdinand Otto Wilhelm Freiherr von (1799-1876), step-brother of Jenny Marx, Prussian civil servant. He served as Minister of the Interior from 1850-58.

Weydemeyer, Joseph (1818-1866), Prussian officer, socialist. He abandoned his military career and worked as a field engineer for the Cologne-Mindener railway, during which time he also belonged to the Communist League. He emigrated to the USA in 1851 and founded in New York the journal *Die Revolution* (1852), later in Cincinatti *Die Stimme des Volkes* (1860). After serving in the Union army as a brigadier general, he edited *Die Neue Zeit* in St Louis.

Willich, August (1810-1878), Prussian officer. He resigned his commission in 1847 to become a carpenter in Cologne. He commanded a volunteer corps in the 1849 Baden uprising, then emigrated to London where he played a central role in the Communist League activities. Finally in 1853 he emigrated to America and worked there as a journalist. In the Civil War he served the North as an officer and attained the rank of brevet major general. After the war he was elected to a government post as auditor and later engaged in politics in support of the People's Party, founded in 1873.

Wolff, Wilhelm (1809-1864), teacher and journalist from Breslau (Silesia, Germany). In 1845 he was indicted for infractions of the press laws and fled to Brussels where he first became acquainted with Marx and Engels. He belonged to the Brussels Correspondence Committee, the Central Committee of the Communist League and the editorial staff of the *Neue Rheinische Zeitung*. He served in the Frankfurt National Assembly as a deputy from Breslau and after its dissolution emigrated to England (1851). He passed the rest of his life as a schoolteacher in Manchester. Marx dedicated the first volume of *Capital* to him.

Zasulich, Vera Ivanova (1851-1919), Russian revolutionary, member of the *Narodnia voliia*. She fled to Switzerland after acquittal for her attack on the St Petersburg prefect (1878) and was, together with Akselrod and Plekhanov, one of the first Russian 'Marxists'.

Zerffi, Gustav (1820-1868), pseudonym for Gustav Hirsch, Hungarian journalist. He participated in the Hungarian Revolution of 1848-49, then emigrated to London. For a time he served the Austrian government as a secret agent but later became an art historian in London and secretary of the National Art Union.

INDEX